Underwater Lives

Underwater Lives

Humans, Species, Ocean

Clare Brant

BLOOMSBURY ACADEMIC
LONDON • NEW YORK • OXFORD • NEW DELHI • SYDNEY

BLOOMSBURY ACADEMIC
Bloomsbury Publishing Plc, 50 Bedford Square, London, WC1B 3DP, UK
Bloomsbury Publishing Inc, 1359 Broadway, New York, NY 10018, USA
Bloomsbury Publishing Ireland, 29 Earlsfort Terrace, Dublin 2, D02 AY28, Ireland

BLOOMSBURY, BLOOMSBURY ACADEMIC and the Diana logo are trademarks of
Bloomsbury Publishing Plc

First published in Great Britain 2026

Cover photo © Diver with manta ray, by Amanda Cotton,
courtesy of the Ocean Image Bank

A catalogue record for this book is available from the British Library.

A catalog record for this book is available from the Library of Congress.

ISBN: HB: 978-1-350-28047-2
         PB: 978-1-350-28051-9
         ePDF: 978-1-350-28048-9
         eBook: 978-1-350-28049-6

Typeset by Integra Software Services Pvt. Ltd.
Printed and bound in Great Britain

For product safety related questions contact productsafety@bloomsbury.com.

To find out more about our authors and books visit www.bloomsbury.com
and sign up for our newsletters.

*to everyone who cares for the ocean
and the marine beings who live in it*

Contents

Figures

Acknowledgements

Many people have helped me kit up to write this book. I am grateful to everyone who has made diving on paper so pleasurable – authors, critics, listeners, everyone who gave me ideas, invited me to talk and asked questions. The Leverhulme Foundation gave me a Major Research Fellowship which provided time to write, a luxury rarely available in academia: profound thanks to them, and for their civilized dealings, also a luxury rarely available in academia.

Thanks to everyone who helped me dive. At the Oxford Dive Centre, Kim Beaumont and Jessica Cox were inspiring models and excellent teachers. Seasearch provided challenges; my thanks to Bryony Chapman in Kent. I was lucky to have Michael Donnelly as a diving buddy. He proved how precious trust and dependability are; my usefulness in translating Scots was small but entertaining recompense. My thanks to Eileen Donnelly for her support too. My starting point was being given a copy of Diolé's *The Undersea Adventure*: when it dawned on me where it might lead, the idea for this book began. To the person who gave it to me, this is really your book: heartfelt thanks.

I owe a special thank you to Tim O'Hare, who set up seasearching near Mombasa where I learnt a great deal about marine beings especially on reef flats. For wonderful hospitality, diving and adventures, thank you Tim: the sunsets, sea caves, gin, cowries and nudibranchs, along with Disco Doris, were splendid.

Special thanks too to Dr Paul Cragg, from whom I learnt much marine biology, how wide the gap between arts and sciences can feel, and how to start crossing it. Magdalena Cragg provided generous hospitality, topped off by finest Akita, snoring gently under the table with her head on my feet.

In the life writing world I am really grateful to Julia Watson for her kind and astute support, and to Margaretta Jolly for upholding a mutual wavelength. Craig Howes and Julie Rak have kept IABA flourishing: my thanks to them and all those who tend that community. Thanks to Eike-Christian Heine for hosting and seeding an undersea group, its special issue in print and his introduction, which expands diving history in valuable ways. The editors of the *Journal of Environmental Humanities* kindly allowed me to re-use material for Chapter 3. Christopher Scharpf of Etyfish graciously answered my questions. I am grateful to the photographers who kindly allowed me to use their images, especially Alex Mustard, Christian Vizl and Amanda Cotton.

Refinements of all sorts came thanks to Max Saunders and Timothy Ashplant who generously commented on chunks despite immersion in their own projects. I owe the idea of unearthly to James Metcalf, who read samples with exceptional literary sensitivity and informed eco-theory. I am indebted to Claire Cox for inspirations, kindest encouragement and for being a splendid reader. Lydia Martens, my Leverhulme buddy, shared other and beautiful ways of seeing the sea. Andrew Kupfer made smart suggestions. Neil Bauldauf-Clark did literal heavy lifting by delivering weighty books with impeccable care. I am very grateful to John Lucas at Shoestring Press and Ruth O'Callaghan for supporting *Underwater Postcards* and my other poetry.

With Sarah Murphy, Adrian Arbib gave invaluable help with some illustrations, and James Waterfield nobly designed the map. Thank you to those at Bloomsbury who made the book: Lucy Strong, Aanchal Vij, Karen Weller, and Martin Tribe for patient copyediting. Colleagues at King's gave appreciated input: thanks to Geoff Browell, Chris Manias, Rowan Boyson, Clare Pettitt.

The hermitry required for writing was intense and many friends rescued me from ill effects by diversions, sociability and sometimes complete indifference to fish. Katherine Armstrong has given her steadfast support most generously. For all sorts of pleasures and cheering on, I am grateful to Bridget Lubbock, Sarah Spiller and Alex Thomson, Veronica and John-Dominic West-Harling, Jacqui Mansfield and Jim Noble, Nicola Watson and Michael Dobson, Teresa Bruś, Lucy Hannah, Charles Lock, Eric Larson, James Woodall, Jules Fletcher, Amy Thakurdas, Roger Perkins, Kay Sentance, Josephine Willmott, Katy and Hermione Waterfield, Andy and Gog Webb, Chris Hogg, Margaret and John Ellis, Yun Lee Too and George Rogers, Gordon Milne and Jo Denton, Henrietta Leyser, Matilda Leyser, Jane Wildgoose, Ruth Richardson and Brian Hurwitz, David W. Johnson, Elspeth Graham and Ruth Garner. Sadly Shirley Andrews, Miriam Fuchs, Niall McKillop, Jo Croft, Vital Peeters and Gooding are not able to read the book to whose spirit they nonetheless contributed. Thank you to Leo Kinlen for fish books, and Margaret-Alice Stewart-Liberty for delightful enthusiasm.

Thanks likewise to my Carter family, my Gooding family, and to Katie Gordon, Frankie Gordon and Tosh. Special thanks to Helena Webb for lively and wise input, and Luke Harmon and Olive Harmon-Webb for enjoying the sea. My Brant family's love and support are precious: deep thanks to Julia, Chris, Sarah, Katharine and Rory. My mother played a crucial role in keeping a watchful eye on me from numerous beaches while I explored the sea; from small child delights to adult enthusiasms, she has listened with inimitable love. To Richard Gordon I am most grateful for all kinds of special care, and to Minnow for sharing her deerhound universe.

Map Map of the world ocean and its oceans, showing some of the places visited by *Underwater Lives*. Designed by James Waterfield.

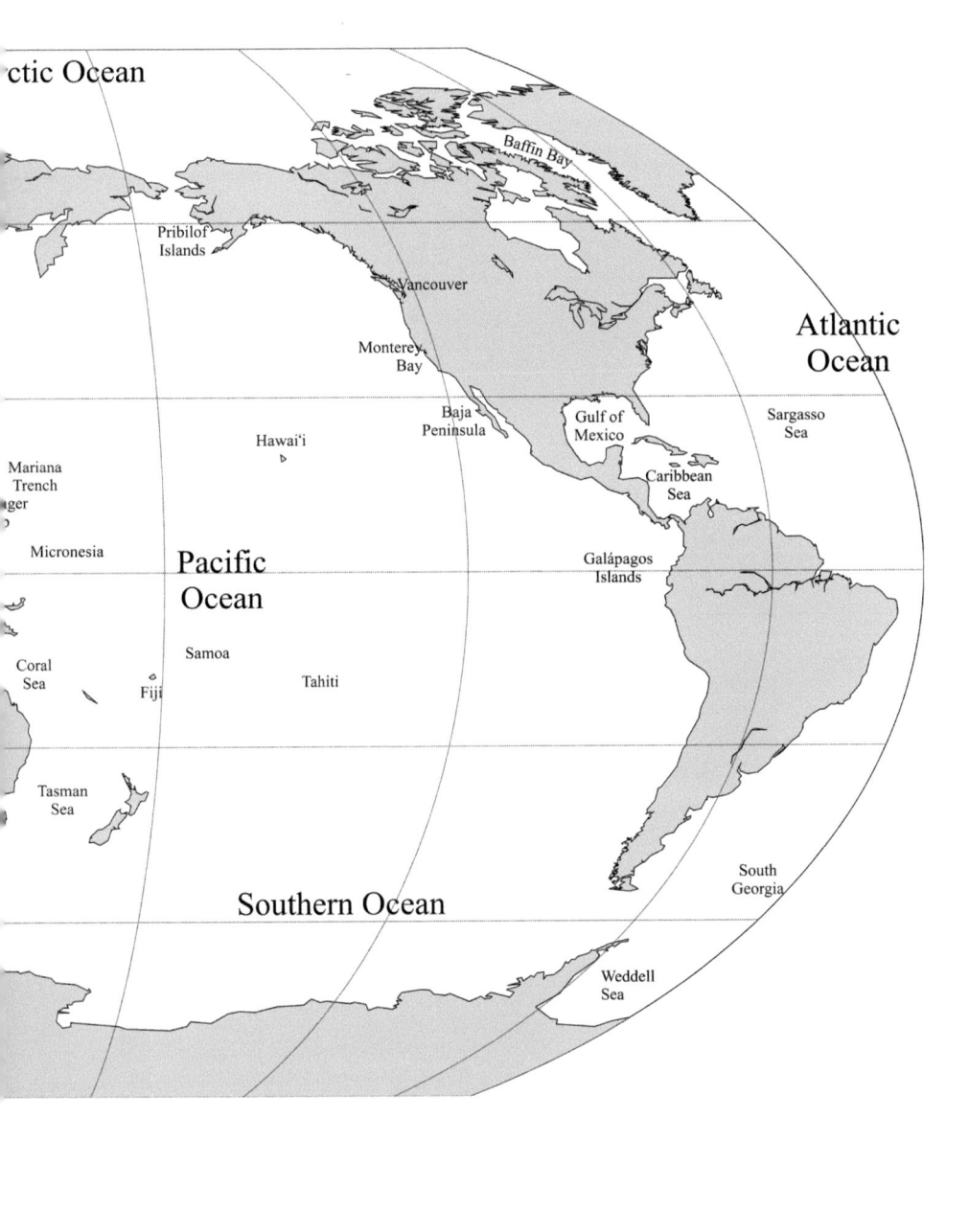

ctic Ocean

Baffin Bay

Pribilof
Islands

Vancouver

Monterey
Bay

Atlantic
Ocean

Baja
Peninsula

Gulf of
Mexico

Sargasso
Sea

Hawai'i

Mariana
Trench
iger

Caribbean
Sea

Micronesia

Pacific
Ocean

Galápagos
Islands

Samoa

Coral
Sea

Fiji

Tahiti

Tasman
Sea

Southern Ocean

South
Georgia

Weddell
Sea

Introduction

SIPHONOPHORE or, How Long Is a Piece of String?

In 2020 a siphonophore was discovered on an expedition to the deep water Ningaloo Canyons off western Australia, one of thirty new species reported. This was the headline one, styled as the 'longest ever' creature, at *c*.46 metres (150 feet). The superlative is important: it secured media attention. It's also symptomatic of descriptive tendencies in the Anthropocene, in how it picks up questions of scale: 'longest ever' connects space and time. The siphonophore was compared to a bus, a giant noodle, an eleven-storey building, and a blue whale (which it exceeds, being nearly twice as long as a female blue whale). It was also described as 'alien': in the words of one of the expedition scientists, 'it looked like an incredible UFO' (Lockwood 2020).

So this siphonophore is like things we know, and also like things we don't know. One science journalist headlined her report 'What The Heck Is This Long, Hypnotic Stringy Thing Floating in The Ocean?' (Koumoundouros 2020). The genus of *Apolemia* to which this siphonophore belongs is actually not new. *Apolemia uvaria*, this siphonophore's species, has been listed in the scientific literature since 1815. It even has a catchy vernacular name: in New Zealand, it's known as the 'long stringy stingy thingy' (Gordon 2016). Why the amazement? One reason is simply enormity: nobody knew siphonophores could be this big. Giant siphonophores, like giant squids, make gigantism potentially scary and certainly stretchy. 'The massive specimen is blowing scientists' minds', said one news website (Kooser 2020). One scientist still lucid enough to comment provided a context: 'What's fascinating about this particular part of the world is that it has not been explored … Any time people go down into the deep sea, it's so vast and yet so unexplored that it's very easy to make new discoveries and to see something we've never seen before. It is like being on a new planet' (Lockwood 2020).

Analogies between underwater and outer space have been commonplace since at least the 1950s – and yet, many decades on, that exploration trope still has traction. Note the epistemological stress on 'seeing' – 'see something we've never seen before'. Visual technology, able to show us things we can't see, and things that human eyes can't process – for instance in slow motion or time lapse – has developed considerably since the 1950s, so we can keep seeing the planet anew. This visuality helps to agglomerate humans as a species: we define the ocean not as an ancient habitat but as a new-to-us ecosystem which we can see with evolving prosthetic eyes.

Siphonophores are not usually poster species: they are not 'charismatic megafauna' like whales. But this became one. The press recognized its aesthetic beauty, comparing it to a galactic spiral. The spiral is functional; it extends the animal's hunting range. It is also beautiful. In September 2021, a Danish arts collective and the Woods Hole Oceanographic Institute (WHOI) partnered to project an image of a siphonophore onto the UN Secretariat Building in New York. The projection, titled 'Vertical Migration', was given considerable ideological freight. WHOI said in their press release that it was 'a symbol of the many working as one' because the organism is actually a collection of zooids, identical parts with variable functions like digestion and reproduction (WHOI 2021). The usual scientific term for this is or was colonial; you can see why they steered clear of that. The artists' collective added more symbolism in their press release. 'Because of sea-level rise, humans will also be migrating vertically in the coming centuries, to higher elevations and raised buildings. The siphonophore's story is our story' (SUPERFLEX 2021).

Is the siphonophore's story our story? It seems a metaphor-straining claim, erasing the differences between nightly vertical migration to the sea's surface and return to the deep and humans having to scramble upwards with no way down as sea levels rise. As narrative, metaphor and symbol, the siphonophore carries our cargo of aesthetics (it's stringy); visuality (surveillance of the deeps); emotions (empathy), and Anthropogenic responsibility (rising sea levels). It is a handy image for a frontier of language – what the heck is this thing – and how a name in itself can't settle relations with otherness. The skyscraper projection manifests a theme of expediency as the siphonophore's admirers celebrated its ability to remove carbon. One estimate said that 'siphonophores sequester between two to six billion tons of carbon each year into the twilight zone. This is several times the amount of carbon emitted by all the world's cars' (Duong 2021). The siphonophore is incorporated into an economy of useful-to-us, able to mitigate environmental damage by humans. The WHOI director, Peter de Menocal, said of siphonophores, 'These organisms make the earth habitable' (Duong 2021). What he means is they make it habitable for us. 'If we want to avoid the destruction of ocean ecosystems and the unknown consequences of ecosystem changes, we need to shine a light in the deep and learn the value of what's there. Science and art together shine this light in an especially important way' (WHOI 2021). A metaphor for Enlightenment science (shining a light) is retuned to the figurative work of video, a visual technology shared by art and science.

I start with this siphonophore because it neatly symbolizes many of the ways in which ocean creatures are currently represented: strange; stretching categories of imagination; useful to humans. It demonstrates how existing knowledges do not always join up, and how they can be forgotten, even in a digital age of far-reaching information retrieval. It is also an instance of art and science partnering in a story that links evolutionary deep time and the present. Linda Williams suggests that deep time 'is not only permanently beyond human control or management, but has an ontological status that cannot even be fully conceived by the human mind' (Williams 2019: 176). Hence we burden a siphonophore with our limited conceptions, and reach for outer space analogies.

The representation of this siphonophore is an example of entanglement, now a standard critical term in the eco-lexicon (Probyn 2016; Sheldrake 2020; Tsing 2015). We talk of en-tangle rather than tangle because the particle *en-* gestures to relationality;

entangle means we know we're bound up with other species but we don't always know how (Brant 2021: 126). Life writing can help show the relations between who and how. The siphonophore event is an instance of life writing diffracted through text (press), speech (interviews) and media (visual, digital and social). One underwater life form, the siphonophore, becomes a 'story' for humans, with a freight of symbolism.

The trope of entanglement has become something of a stopping place. Might we disentangle a bit, without losing that consciousness of complexity to which entanglement gestures? *Underwater Lives* uses three ideas as guide ropes. First, I propose to read underwater texts as life writing, a term that takes in a wide spectrum of personal writing, here featuring an autobiographical subject (a human) and a biographical subject (ocean and the lives therein). Second, underwater life writing – defined broadly – interleaves with arts and sciences, and other media besides text. This interleaving leads to accretions, not dilutions, for life writing, which can retain its own critical dynamics while contributing to blue humanities. Third, in putting life writing and marine biology together, I recalibrate relations between humans and the ocean so as to recognize better the importance of ocean inhabitants. To further this, I propose the term 'marine beings', lexically and philosophically equal to human beings. These three ideas run through all chapters. They provide theoretical scaffolding for the book's three connected sections – humans, species, ocean. These are headings that give different emphasis to materials and their critical discussion. They intertwine, but provide useful groupings. I discuss those concepts first – humans, species, ocean, with marine beings making a new link between species and ocean thinking. Then I take up disciplinary contexts – life writing, science and blue humanities – to outline their relevance to *Underwater Lives*.

HUMANS

The Anthropocene is unequivocally human-caused, though not all humans have contributed equally to it. Joan Lubin explains how recent humanities approaches to thinking the Anthropocene have addressed issues of human agency (2017: 145). She sees 'a new uncertainty about the stature of man, at once puny with respect to a newly expansive world and grotesquely bloated with newly staggering power over the world' (146). This contradiction has been seen before. The productions of Jacques-Yves Cousteau expressed both mastery and vulnerabilities. Cousteau resolved that into confidence: man will build cities in the sea. Fabien Cousteau, his grandson, updates Cousteau's *Conshelf* experiments (1962–65) with new ambitions for undersea living (Dunn 2024). Projects of populating underwater (Kelly 2022) continue to extend visions of human agency and collectivity.

I group the first four chapters of *Underwater Lives* under the heading of Human to flag up issues of agency, mastery, masculinity and reparative interventions. William Beebe provides a literary starting point: a key popularizer in the 1920s, he is also a reference point for later writers. Chapter 1 covers his underwater interests, from roughly 1900–40, his cosmic and microcosmic scales, and his unique imaginarium composed from fairy tales, global travels and supernatural tales. Helmet diving such as Beebe's gave way to 'goggling', then scuba and a generation represented by Jacques-

Yves Cousteau, in whose huge shadow are his fellow diver-writers Frédéric Dumas, Philippe Tailliez, Philippe Diolé and his rival Hans Hass. They produced a literature of adventure, circulating alongside film, which promoted the ocean as a place of thrill, audacity and fear but which also described marine lives in educative ways. Diolé was especially thoughtful. This generation is the focus of Chapter 2, on adventurous aquanauts. Memoirs by women in this era – Eugenie Clark, 'the Shark Lady'; Lotte Hass, 'the Girl on the Ocean Floor' – contest underwater masculinities: juggling research stations, children and sharks, they use life writing to help open up underwater to female divers and marine biologists like Sylvia Earle, known as 'Her Deepness'. Chapters 3 (showcasing sharks) and 4 (on corals) show how the position of humans in the ocean is readable from their encounters with other species. The dissolution of corals puts human responsibilities for damage and repair into sharp focus. Accounts of coral Edens provide context for the trauma of coral collapse; they remind us how recently pristine was possible and how quickly it has vanished. These chapters show underwater life writing dynamically changing its focus on what humans can do and should do in the ocean. 'What a confusing species we are, by turns murderous and merciful, negligent and attentive, angels of both death and salvation.' Carl Safina (2007: 240) is one of many writers who respond to the sea as an element that prompts reflections on humanity.

SPECIES

Species is an idea under pressure in the sciences. There are multiple critiques and some defences. One survey of how species' concepts are used by biologists found common ground and differences. The researchers noted that 'Although the idea of species may seem intuitive, a debate about the best way to define them has raged even before Darwin. So much energy has been devoted to the so-called "species problem" that no amount of discourse will ever likely solve it' (Stankowski and Ravinet 2021: 428). Nevertheless, schools still teach that a species is a group of individuals who breed together and produce offspring. Thus *Homo sapiens* is distinguished from *Homo neanderthalensis*. Except there is evidence to show these supposedly distinct species interbred, so now 'there is a tentative consensus that the genus *Homo* contains seven species: one extant, and the others extinct' (Rees and Sleigh 2020: 52). The authors of the volume *Human* in Reaktion's animal-themed series suggest humanity cannot be defined 'and perhaps should not even be thought of as species-bound' (Rees and Sleigh 2020: 22).

Homo sapiens is a multispecies organism. Every human contains bacteria, fungi, protists and other companions, as Donna Haraway reminds us (2008: 3-4). Stefan Helmreich makes this into *Homo microbis* (2016: 62-72), a figure through which to read the cultural constructedness of biology. Using embodiment to explore meshing of biological subjects, Astrida Neimanis salutes the core work of ecofeminist thinking:

> For four decades, ecofeminism in particular (e.g. Gaard 1993; Kheel 1993; Warren 1997) has been encouraging us to recognize the connections between the derogation of certain kinds of human bodies, and a mistreatment of environmental bodies, including other animals; queer feminisms (e.g. Ahmed 2006; Chen 2012;

Gaard 1997; Sandilands 2001; Seymour 2013) have asked us to pay attention to those bodies – both human and more-than-human – which challenge teleological norms and straight stories of proliferation and fecundity; anticolonial feminisms have asked us to resist human exceptionalism in our valuations of worlds that sustain us.

(Neimanis 2017: 8)

Multispecies thinking challenges the separability of humans whether as embodied individuals or collectively as a species. Yet for all its flaws, species is still a concept in use, and with reason. It survives – and thrives – in natural history, where it can counter the impersonality of big data science through acts of noticing. Anna Tsing and co-authors propose a field guide model for engaging (Tsing, Deger, Saxena and Zhou 2024) with what the authors call 'the patchy Anthropocene'. They support identification, including recognition of species, as a practice consonant with attention and care.

Robin Wall Kimmerer observes that 'In English, you are either a human or a thing. Our grammar boxes us in by the choice of reducing a nonhuman being to an *it*, or it must be gendered, inappropriately, as a *he* or a *she*' (2021:17). But species' names complicate that binary. When a thing carries a name conferred by humans and alluding to humans, it becomes a form of life writing, I argue in Chapter 5. The Linnaean naming system involves genealogies, networks, auto/biographies and authorities; it is governed by official rules and human affect. In comparison, Indigenous names in Micronesia pay more attention to habits and resemblances: what a creature is turns on what a creature looks like or does. In the Arctic, the Indigenous knowledge of the Inuit-Yu'pik peoples connects places, animal movements, aptitudes and preferences that confirm synergies between humans, ice and animals. Identification can be done in different ways.

It is becoming easier to match Linnaean species names with equally precise alternatives. Dual naming practices are emerging. In Hawai'i, a committee of Indigenous stakeholders and scientists promote 'a multidisciplinary and multisensory naming process that includes building and maintaining *pilina* (relationship) to species, to researchers, and to place.' It combines traditional knowledge and scientific knowledge, a collaboration that 'adds to our collective understanding and relationship, especially when connecting to these species through the *Kānaka* (Native Hawai'ian) sensibilities of sight, touch, smell, taste, hearing, and *na'au* (feeling).' Thus a giant sea pen newly spotted in the Pacific has a species name, *Solumbellula monocephalus*, and a Hawai'ian name, *Ihikūhola*, combining three words, for majesty, to stand or anchor, and springy or resilient (Ocean Exploration Trust 2025). Managing this dual naming is expansive – also a form of social justice, as Indigenous knowledge partners science. Expansiveness is a skill we can surely learn, just as we have learned to manage the contractions of organizations' names into acronyms.

Where Chapter 5 explores Western specificities of naming conventions, conversely, Chapter 6 enters underwater through the category of fish, a generalization at odds with specific identity. Sometimes this plurality can serve intersubjective imagination. As underwater photographer David Doubilet puts it (2003: 1), 'For humans, fish appear as alien creatures living in a weightless twilight world. For fish, human divers appear to be not just aliens but true monsters with giant blank, masked eyes and Medusa-like pipes sprouting from their heads, making violent bubbling noises.' More often plurality serves indistinguishability, a lack of individuality that limits recognition of fish sentience and society. Fish lit, including life writing for fishes, establishes fish as feeling subjects. Besides the life stories I discuss, there are many accounts of fish individuality in underwater life writing, tuned to species-specifics.

Chapter 7 takes up animalographies via the worlds of eels and salmon. In this fishography, a more precise term, writers use biography and biofiction to construct imaginative life cycle stories and present fish feelings with empathy. Life narratives distinguish between species, in particularities of place, attachment, migration, mating and death. Separability of species has implications for fish in aquaculture. Most farmed salmon are Atlantic, *Salmo salar*. They have a very different life narrative from their wild relatives. Escapees breed with other salmon species. '"27,000 farmed salmon on the run is a disaster for wild salmon," said Pål Mugaas, a spokesperson for Norske Lakseelver (Norwegian Salmon Rivers). "Science has proved that interbreeding between wild stocks and farmed salmon produce offspring that in the long term has low survival rate in nature"' (Bryant 2025). Human practices muddle species further.

I use the term 'Species', aware of its speciousness, for the middle four chapters which discuss life writing on fish – in singular and plural forms – and marine animals. Recent work in animal studies extends awareness of animal sensoriums, language and culture. It also breaks down human-other distinctions by insisting on the animality of humans. Melanie Challenger argues that humans choose to forget they are animals. 'The world is now dominated by an animal that doesn't think it's an animal. And the future is being imagined by an animal that doesn't want to be an animal. This matters' (2022: 1). Ed Yong investigates animal sensoriums that are beyond human reach, and hence hard to comprehend: 'a scientist's data are influenced by the questions she asks, which are steered by her imagination, which is delimited by her senses. The boundaries of our own Umwelt corral our ability to understand the Umwelten of others' (Yong 2023: 319). Writing beautifully of sea otters, Yong stretches those Umwelt boundaries. 'To some of the most sensitive paws in the world, the ocean is bright with textures to be felt, grasped, pressed, prodded, squeezed, stroked, and manhandled – or perhaps otterhandled' (2023: 159).

Since touch is a sense understood by humans, it provides ways to connect directly with other species. Chapter 8 looks at how the haptic is handled by writers of underwater lives. The eight-armed octopus is naturally an alluring life model here, but less fashionable beings also provide moments of contact that advance interspecies relations. Unexpected interspecies friendships challenge human assumptions about otherness. Different kinds of motherhood stretch imagination too. Chapter 8 ends with a section that thinks about data-gathering for species, quantification which is the opposite of intimate encounter. Assigning tags, numbers and digital doubles to marine animals contributes to a surveillance culture, officially for nature. Addressing gaps in life narratives – for instance, where do juvenile turtles go? – life writing builds on quantification to extend personalization in surprising ways, like giving individual sharks their own Twitter (now X) accounts (Brant 2023).

The interrelations between different kinds of humans and between humans and other life forms need careful distinction. 'If the Anthropocene arises from a kind of human exceptionalist approach to life, how can we address this with a term that puts humans right back in the centre'? asks Neimanis (2017: 11). As she says, 'much more needs to be made of the fact that "we" is probably the most fraught word in the English language' (2017: 14). The complications are demonstrated by her own use of 'we' in that challenge – how can we address this? – and she concedes 'I' is not the answer. In *Underwater Lives* I use 'we' to engage a welcome community of readers, aware that its generalizing carries troubling assumptions for societies beyond.

MARINE BEINGS

'One of our responsibilities as human people is to find ways to enter into reciprocity with the more-than-human world' (Kimmerer 2021: 54). Finding those ways has generated a substantial vocabulary. Like the inescapability of 'we', 'human' proves adhesive.

> 'The expressions "non-humans", "other-than-humans" or "more than humans" (Abram 1996) have the important advantage of containing in their plurality a multiplicity of forms, which are not limited to the "living", nor even the "visible" (or the "physical"). But they also have the great disadvantage of designating what is not, or not only, human. These terms remain thus somehow anthropocentric.'
>
> (Chamel and Dansac 2022: 2)

So too are posthumanism, transhumanism, inhumanism and many-more-than-human, even though they pull usefully away from human (Rees and Sleigh 2020; Grosz 2011; Price and Chao 2023; Kay Syrad, in conversation 2025).

The *Oxford English Dictionary* (*OED*) reports that *human being* is one of the 5,000 most common terms in modern written English. Its first use is 1694, in the writing of deist Matthew Tindal, who compares '*Posture* in human Beings' to modes of describing the Christian Trinity. Tindal was unhappy about theological fuzziness around the term 'person' (mostly he uses 'Man') – ironically, because 'person' now seems extendable to other life forms. 'Every non-human "this", like every human is merely the first instance of a linguistic ground to which attributes and properties can be conceptually attributed, and, whether attached to humans or non-humans, it is equally suitable to enable the emergence of a "person"' (Campagna 2018: 141). Personhood has been taken up as a legal identity for environmental entities such as rivers. Deep green ecologists advocate for the term 'being': thus in 1986 John Seed and Joanna Macy devised the Council of All Beings, in which humans take on the perspective of non-human beings through respectful ritual. In 2024 Friends of the River Exe in the UK staged an Assembly of River Beings to voice the concerns of all species in the river. In these activities, humans become other through acts of imagination and empathy. Yet human performativity is central to such ritualizing. How to escape the human?

I favour 'marine beings', analogous and equal to 'human beings'. It could be objected that humans and other land-based beings came from the sea; that some earth creatures returned to it; that some beings – marine iguanas, for instance, or fiddler crabs – are semi-terrestrial and semi-aquatic, and some live edgily in the splash zone and intertidal zone. At a stretch it could be said that humans underwater are temporarily human marine beings. Nonetheless, the term 'marine beings' encompasses marine mammals and reptiles, fishes, crustacea, molluscs, cnidaria, echinoderms, plankton, algae, seagrasses … any categorizing complications should not derail its usefulness as a rhetorically equal category to human beings. 'Marine being' avoids the American cultural associations of Haraway's term 'critters' (2008); it comprehends all scales. That diatoms (mostly marine) and dinoflagellates (ditto) appear in soil and freshwater too need not hamper usage. It may be objected that *marine* beings applies only to saltwater lives; to include fresh, one might say aqueous beings. Science uses 'marine' and 'freshwater' to differentiate, with 'brackish' (as in estuaries) describing mixed salinity. Although I use a range of terms – fish, invertebrates, pinnipeds – from the overlap where possible between vernaculars and scientific identities, I think it useful for blue humanities to have 'marine beings' as a sea-specific category. It is also a category with no inherent hierarchy: a feather star is as much a marine being as a whale. Any and every life form in the ocean is a marine being.

OCEAN

I use Ocean to frame the last four chapters of *Underwater Lives*, which discuss themes that are central to how the ocean is perceived. They show metaphysics, aesthetics, visual technologies and arts helping out language under pressure underwater. Should that be Ocean singular or Oceans plural? Atlantic, Pacific, Indian, Arctic and Southern (formerly Antarctic) Oceans are familiar terms. Richard Carrington's *A Biography of the Sea* (1960) uses 'The Story of the World Ocean', singular, in its subtitle. Its section titles use oceans, plural. What are the tensions now around plurality? The United Nations Decade of Ocean Science for Sustainable Development (2021–30) promotes ocean singular, with a vision locked on to humans: '*The science we need for the ocean we want*' (UN 2021). The UN's first principle of ocean literacy is 'The Earth has one big ocean with many features' (UNESCO 2018: 18). TBA-21 Academy, an art-science ocean group, favour oceans plural. Their fine essay collection *Oceans Rising* asks: 'What are the oceans' own "waves of knowing"? What ideas and memories do the oceans hold in their depth … ?' (Zyman 2021: blurb). From 2008 the United Nations promoted 8 June as World Oceans Day; from 2014, it wobbles between plural and singular (United Nations n.d.).

Choice of singular or plural may seem grammatically minor, but linguistic theory recognizes it carries issues of scale (Tiu et al. 2020). Ocean Census estimates that between one and two million species live in the ocean, of whom approximately only 240,000 have names. About 2,000 are newly identified each year, a rate little changed since the 1800s (Ocean Census 2023). The incompleteness of scientific knowledge of the ocean coexists with a contradictory view, that the enormity of that scientific knowledge makes it beyond comprehension. 'One thing I am trying to say here is that the data we now have on oceanography and marine biology are so vast that it is beyond the capacity of one person to know them all thoroughly', wrote zoologist Maurice Burton in *Under the Sea* (1960: 7), a generalist book respected enough to warrant a reprint in 2013. Vastness is also invoked in blue humanities. 'The singularity behind these currents of history and thought is Ocean as object, vast, moving, vibrant, imagined, and ungraspable collective' (Mentz 2020: 8). The ocean as hyperfact or the ocean drowning us in facts? Johan Normark proposes that water is a hyperfact, which he differentiates from the ungraspable enormity of Timothy Morton's hyperobject (2013). The hyperfact 'is vastly distributed, it can dissolve into most of its parts without affecting its "essence", and it can be in several physical states at the same time. Water is a typical hyperfact, existing on multiple scales, from molecules to the hydrological cycle' (Normark 2023: 231). A concept of the hyperfact is useful for evoking the spatial complexity of water, essential to oceanic thought, but it thinks abstractly about water as a medium regardless of the life forms in it.

Writing on undersea environmental aesthetics, Margaret Cohen and Killian Quigley argue for topographical specificity: 'Radical differences in underwater environments transfer themselves to radical differences in feeling, description, and definition' (2019: 4). Underwater life writing bears this out. Diving the same place at a different time can be a profoundly different experience. Changes in light, current, visibility and marine beings' movements create surprising alterities. In Chapter 11, I discuss affects that gloom attracts; it is one of a number of underwater conditions that produce differences in feeling, description and definition. Tsing and co-authors promote the patch as a model that combines field study, manageable scale and fine-grained attention (2024: 4). Underwater life writing gives much attention to patches: a dive site may be a patch or part of a patch.

My Ocean section starts with deep thinking via the deepest parts of the ocean. Life writings from descents to the abyss engage with effects of extreme depth on humans, psychological experiences unique to the deeps. They have much to report about phenomena like black smokers and hydrothermal vents, and their startling life forms that changed understandings of planetary life. Tropes of 'alien' and 'weird' protect against radical otherness by importing paradigms from terrestrial culture, a reflex against which the term 'unearthly' pushes back. Life writers use 'unearthly' to describe the deep ocean's environment; Chapter 9 explores the term's significance and durability. Intense blackness is evocative of pre-creation, bewildering and isolating to human observers. 'Unearthly' opens up a strange new sublime in which humans are cast back through time to aeons before. Compared to commonplace analogies between the deeps and outer space, 'unearthly' provides metaphysical profundity.

Chapter 10 thinks about visualities – what photographer David Doubilet calls 'a visual voice' (1999: n.p.). Illustrated texts draw our attention to ways of seeing, sometimes in black and white, a tonality preferred by wood-engraver Robert Gibbings (1946, 1949) and photographer Christian Vizl (2019). Then I examine how life writing and image making overlap and differ in memoirs by makers of natural history programmes. Televisual spectacle is sometimes a driver of narrative in these texts, sometimes at odds with the life writers' practices of intimacy, attention and states of affect. Image-makers' memoirs show very embodied humans representing sense experiences not transmitted on film, including relations with ocean. I take *The Blue Planet* and *Blue Planet II*, international successes in multimedia and print, as case studies.

Chapter 11 discusses aesthetics in relation to a triad of increasing depth: bubbles, gloom and bioluminescence. Their effects make air, opaque light and chemically produced light into phenomena of interest to both art and science. The aesthetics of bubbles are multispecies in their reach; dolphins play with them too. Bioluminescence is a visual language in the ocean; it is as yet barely readable by humans, who nonetheless bestow on it a fascinated aesthetic. Species' specificity reappears through the colours, duration, intensity and occasions of bioluminescent acts. The relations between science and magic that appear in reading bioluminescence are surprisingly not all tensions; they share big questions about the means and purposes of reading the ocean.

The arts are widely hailed for inspiring people to care about the ocean. 'Ocean art opens the empathy door' says British painter, photographer and diver Francesca Page (*Oceanographic Magazine* 2021). Arts-science collaborations 'extend ocean imaginaries beyond current understandings, and reconceptualize the ways oceanic space is understood and experienced' (Whittaker: 2023, n.p.). Bronwyn Bailey-Charteris argues that curators even more than artists demonstrate model practices of care, *cura*, for water worlds. In Chapter 12, I explore a selection of arts and contemporary artists to think about what different media and practices do with oceanic subjects. Common themes thread through them: touch, memory and oceanic love. Many make overlaps between ecofacts and artefacts; some involve marine being collaborators. 'Art forms have proved good to think with about "living with" in a multispeciesworld', say Kirksey and Helmreich (2010: 556). In the installation 'Zoodram 5' (2014) by Pierre Huyghe, for instance, a hermit crab trundles about with a Brâncusi mask affixed to its shell; categories of art and nature waver, exchange and combine. Glass, water and plastic have affinities of transparency and opacity, malleability and tonality; many glass artists use sea life subjects to express ideas about purity and pollution, vulnerability and timelessness. Plastic waste becomes art freighted with questions about use and value; in the case of ghost nets recycled into water beings, ancient cosmogonies are revivified in present-day materiality. The sculptures of Jason deCaires Taylor have interested critics (Loirot; Quigley; DeLoughrey) who see in them paradigms of mourning, metamorphosis and ecological accretion. Similarly popular is the *Crochet Coral Reef*, 'an ever-evolving nature-culture hybrid created by Christine Wertheim and Margaret Wertheim, that resides at the nexus of art, craft, science, mathematics, climate change, & feminist community practice' (https://crochetcoralreef.org). It demonstrates entanglement can show discipline (the skill of crochet) and glorious disorder. Remixing is everywhere, possible and desirable.

Yet the arts can bring simplicity too. Photography and dance share the import of floatiness and weight, through hair, fabrics and bodies. Getting the drift, swirl and sink of meanings, viewers and audiences can see embodiment and, more importantly, see what embodiment can do. The final section of Chapter 12 addresses music through life writing. Questions around sounds, music and language bring back some of the filters between humans and other species that used to validate human exceptionalism. The global circulation of whale song and the musicality of other cetaceans coexists with the reality of marine sound pollution from human activities such as drilling, mining, shipping, fishing and wind farming (Thyssen-Bornemisza 2021). We do not make music out of these sounds. Instead we turn to whales, who, like the siphonophore with whom I started, carry enormous symbolism for us, through their uniquely resonant music.

Underwater Lives joins up life writing and marine sciences; I outline some context and concepts to situate them next.

LIFE WRITING

Life writing is a way to describe personal writing such as memoirs, autobiographies, letters, diaries and accounts of lives by others, as in biography, history and the novel. Life writing is both a field of criticism and creative practice. Critics have used the term 'auto/biography' to indicate the close relations between autobiography and biography; 'life narrative' recasts those relations so as to engage with overlapping but differently facing questions (Smith and Watson 2010). As Craig Howes explains (2020b), life writing has evolved into a very capacious field:

> Initially adopted as a critical intervention informed by post-structuralist, postmodernist, postcolonial, and especially feminist theory of the 1970s and 1980s, the term also refers to the study of life representation beyond the traditional literary and historical focus on verbal texts, encompassing not only other media – film, graphic narratives, online technologies, performance – but also research in other disciplines – psychology, anthropology, ethnic and Indigenous studies, political science, sociology, education, medicine, and any other field that records, observes, or evaluates lives.

Howes summarizes its significance: 'there is no question that life representation, primarily through narrative, is an important consideration for scholars engaged in virtually any field dealing with the nature and actions of human beings, or anything that lives.' Reading texts and images together, and sometimes against each other, I use life writing to frame the changing relations between humans, other species and the ocean. *Underwater Lives* investigates how life writing conventions operate underwater; how writers pursue philosophical and ethical questions; how particular visual conventions shape what we see; how writing partners with other arts to convey ocean life, and what underwater life writings have to say about human relations with ocean lives, past, present and future.

In their compendium *Reading Autobiography*, Sidonie Smith and Julia Watson point out that 'the narrating "I" of an autobiographical text is often polyvocal, an ensemble of voices' and that 'much autobiographical narrative is relational, that it is often "the other's story"' (Smith and Watson 2010: 80, 216). For underwater life writing, relations are two-fold: the 'other' of marine beings who live underwater, and the 'otherness' of underwater itself. Since marine beings can be encountered in aquariums on land where some life writing engages with them (Love 2001; Montgomery 2015), it is useful to distinguish life writing set in the ocean.

'The ocean is a kind of anti-environment to the desk', proposes Melanie Jue, who sees the medium of underwater enabling 'a form of amphibious scholarship that remains attentive to the milieu specificities of ocean environments (be they shallow, pelagic, or deep) – and the critic's own norms – keeping track of surprising contexts for the use of concepts, or where they acquire new valences' (2020: 5). Jue limits diving to scuba; I include helmet diving, free diving and some submersible diving. But helpfully she offers synergies with life writing. 'I make the case for scuba diving as a humanities methodology that not only figures as a form of witnessing but also constitutes a meaningful interpretative practice that trains the diver from below' (Jue 2020: 32). This covers the diver, or the diver-critic. But what about the diver-writer and diver-reader? Or non-diver-reader? Life writing provides auto/biographical witnessing to create, share and convey meaningful interpretations between these constituencies.

Underwater Lives is not only about autobiographical acts: biographical acts happen simultaneously. There are explicit precedents, like Neville Peat's *The Tasman: Biography of an Ocean* (2010), advertised as telling an ocean's 'remarkable life story'. Using evolution as an equivalent to biography's conventional beginnings in infancy and childhood, Richard Carrington's *A Biography of the Sea* (1960) proceeds through geological time and how it shapes the world ocean, to the lives of sea organisms, ending with 'Man and the Sea' – a division using concepts of ocean, species and humans. These concepts interlace. I use them for convenience and to suggest different emphases, not rigid distinction.

Underwater life writing relates closely to travel writing, since writers are venturing to marine places. Encounters with others and experiences of difference are central to life writing and travel writing and they share literary forms like the memoir, letter and journal. In such genres, writing produces action. 'For so many adventures, the action is in the interpretation – the discovery is textual, overflowing with meaning' (Schaberg 2023: 7). Travel writing criticism and theory have similarly seen 'the broadening of the canon, the widening of social justice concerns, the questioning of the conditions of knowledge', as John Culbert puts it (2018: 345). Like travel writing, underwater life writing has an uncomfortable relation to petrocultures. Diving nearly always has a carbon footprint, and a place of privilege as a liberal expansion of horizons (downwards) which depends on the same fossil fuels that destroy ocean life. Underwater life writing contributed, ironically. In 1953 the geological manager of British Petroleum (BP) wrote to Jacques-Yves Cousteau, 'It appeared to us when reading your fascinating book, *The Silent World*, that the diving technique which you have so successfully developed and so admirably described, may have some geological applications' (Morton 2015: 9). The next year Cousteau conducted a survey from his ship *Calypso* for BP in the Arabian Gulf, gathering seabed rock samples that eventually led to drilling in the area. In the 1950s it could be cast as progress: 'never one to hide his lamp under a bushel, Cousteau later claimed that they had found the oil that turned Abu Dhabi from a little village to a modern city' (Morton 2015: 23). In the twenty-first century, the promotion of ecotourism binds diving and fossil fuels into further ethical complications.

Yet divers have contributed substantially to conservation mindsets, especially since the 1990s. As one who became a patron of *The Shark Trust* puts it, 'Diving can no longer be considered as just another seaside activity on a par with windsurfing, sunbathing and water-skiing. It is rather an opportunity to gain a first-hand insight into the fact that what exists beneath the waves must continue to do so' (Stafford-

Deitsch 1991: 59). Underwater life writing is important for its accounts of what used to be underwater. Some of what divers 'discovered' has now disappeared. Life writers report deteriorations and articulate the emotional confusions of environmental loss. They also maintain positive engagement through wonder and practices of care.

Memoirs of underwater are not exclusively about underwater. Many authors write about the workings of diving expeditions and shipboard life, especially its strains, fatigues and dangers. Forays underwater appear at intervals, episodes in between possibly more familiar nautical, social and scientific storytelling. This counterpoint rhythm makes the dives into narratives which are also roomy, open to including what is not narrative. They may have a stated scientific purpose or a general aim of discovery, but what can be discovered isn't known till you get there, or indeed till you emerge. The word foray is suggestive here: it relates etymologically to forage, finding food. What divers find includes food for thought.

The life inherent in life writing is usually assumed to be human. But it does not have to be: life writing can voice the lives of other beings. It can bring diver autobiography into dialogue with ecobiography (White 2020): underwater, that eco includes the ocean itself and the lives therein. Smith and Watson suggest five concepts, inseparable constituents, that life writing engages variously: memory, experience, identity, spatial location, embodiment and agency (2010: 63). These concepts all apply to underwater life writing – and to marine beings. 'If we take life to consist of experiences, the key questions concern the relationship between experience and narrative. If we are interested in life as a whole, questions of selfhood and identity become salient. Overall, the debate on the relationship between life and narrative is long and multifaceted', says Hanna Meretoja (2022: 273). She champions the idea of narrative identity: 'In this notion of narrative identity, "narrative" should be understood less as a noun than as an activity: as the temporal, interactional process of narrative reinterpretation that is constitutive of identity' (2022: 274, 283). It is a relational process, involving others. Constructing narrative identity for themselves, underwater life writers also construct narrative identity for other life forms. 'Life and narrative are not the same, but neither are they completely separate. They are interwoven in one another in endless, messy entanglements', says Meretoja. Life writing offers energizing alternatives to intractably knotty thinking. As Eva Haifa Giraud asks, 'What Comes After Entanglement?' (2019) Scientist memoirs about sea turtles are full of entanglements, literal and figurative; many double as campaigning literature, arguing for better practices of multispecies living. We can learn new relations from life writing. We can unlearn unkind practices. We can compare relations historically, and understand how and why attitudes change. 'My colleagues and I have transformed from adventurers in pristine places to conservationists in service to preserving the waters in which life can thrive and evolve', as Drew Harvell puts it (2025: ix-xx).

There is one form of life writing specific to underwater: the dive log. Partnering scuba certification cards from the 1970s on, official log books typically offered a small page per dive for recording information like time, depth and air consumption – data now uploadable to apps from the small but essential computers worn by recreational divers (S. Miller 2020). These logbooks could be customized – I came round to making my own, with much more space for writing about what I saw and experienced. Paper versions, traditionally signed by a buddy, were frequently customized with inked stamps featuring marine creatures. Your choice of animal was considered personally expressive. This diary genre has gone digital, though longhand versions survive. It awaits critical investigation.

SCIENCE: MYSTERIES AND SECRETS

How might blue humanities think about ocean sciences? In *The Mysterious Science of the Sea, 1775–1943*, Natascha Adamowsky argues that natural science in the long nineteenth century plays with mysteries: 'discoveries do not lose their aura of mystery, even for the discoverers' (2015: 38). What she calls 'the poetics of not knowing' continue to infuse underwater representation. *The Cousteau Mystery: A Novel* (2017) by Giovanni Lorecchio is a best-selling biofiction whose plot combines Cousteau and underwater secrets. This language of secrets and mysteries has a long and layered history, rooted in eighteenth-century ideas of Nature as 'veiled'. It is turbocharged by a mid-twentieth-century emphasis on adventure, especially from Cousteau, and enhanced by travel to previously hidden depths. No less useful than tracing origins is thinking through its appeal. Secrets and mysteries offer a reader – or viewer – initiation, confederacy and powerful knowledges. What's not to like? There are troubling aspects. One is that they require guides or interpreters, who take on some of the aura around what they divulge. Another is that secrets and mysteries are often described in terms of penetration, with all the phallocratic baggage that follows that term around. A third is a more theosophical problem: once you have unlocked secrets or penetrated mysteries, what next? There is no duty of care attached; knowledge is power in itself, whether benign or malignly used.

Underwater life writing draws much from science – indeed a significant proportion of it is written by people with science degrees or science-related jobs. Anthropologist Veronica Strang argues that science has disenchanted water bodies and hydrological flows, whereas animism, in the form of water serpent beings, restores holistic relations, via the message 'that all living kinds, including humans, inhabit and co-create a single indivisible world' (Strang 2023: 194, 229). The tension between science and magic is one I discuss further in Chapter 11; here I examine some frictions around science, because the authority accorded to science in underwater life writing raises important questions about how you read it.

John David Zuern helpfully identifies a parallel between science and life writing. 'Both scientific reports and autobiographical texts involve a pact between author and reader, based in part on the verifiability of factual claims, but also on the author's ethos as a credible witness' (Zuern 2024: 7). Witnessing in science, however, is subject to strict protocols governing credibility. In a passionate essay on Western scientific culture over his working life, Giovanni Bearzi asks, 'What does it take to bridge the gap between conservative scientific disciplines and the global conservation imperatives of our time?' (Bearzi 2020: 4). He researches Mediterranean dolphins, and reflects that when he began in the 1980s, 'incorporating passion and affection for nature into one's writing and presentations was generally deemed to be bad scientific practice, and those who were overt or explicit about their love for the planet or passionate about saving the ocean, the manatees or anything else could end up ostracized' (2020: 2). Bearzi thinks science could change more, ironically by using life writing. 'Our care for the living world should not only be made explicit but also become the core of compelling narratives we use to engage human society. We must aim to tell heartfelt, captivating stories centred on our own experience, bringing to life a capacity to think outside the box and dream big' (Bearzi 2020: 5). Heartfelt science reaches the parts that data cannot, via the storying of life writing. Or can it? Life writing scholarship proves that personal witnessing is no guarantee of being believed, even in situations of trauma (Gilmore 2017). Coral scientists' storying, discussed in Chapter 4, sadly proves it too.

Despite higher education's adoption (globally, in the 2000s) of public engagement as an essential activity in all disciplines, some critics regard science with hostility. 'The more we, Europeans or North Americans of the early twenty-first century, *know about* nature, thanks to the most advanced tools and methodologies of modern Western science, the less we are able to *relate with* nature' (Chamel and Danzac 2022: 1). Bruno Latour sensibly points out that not all scientists are the same. 'Scientists from various disciplines cannot be marshalled as if they all belonged to one and the same continuum. To employ a rather arcane term, the connections between them are not hierarchical, but heterarchical' (Latour 2017: 94). Some scientists, like Bearzi, can be most humane. And science can moult its own orthodoxies. Beliefs change. As Joan Lubin puts it, 'science has itself now become something of a humanism, charged with re-educating a public under the sway of an outmoded scientism – an absolute faith in technological deliverance' (2017: 162). Yet what counts as outmoded is contested, hence the continued faith in technological deliverance from climate crisis (Kolbert 2021). If science is unsure about emotions, variable and humanist, how should we read it?

In *Underwater Lives*, I try to recognize Western science in literary ways as a shifting discourse. The life sciences, those that study living things, involve life writing. Science is biographical when it relates the morphology and life history of a marine being; popular science is often autobiographical. Humanities scholars recognize popular science as a genre with a long history and wide genealogy (Muñoz Morcillo and Robertson-von Trotha 2020). '(N)ineteenth-century popular science texts, whether written by men or by women, constantly look at science from a literary point of view' (Talairach-Vielmas 2011: 5–6). The ideological mix was different then: 'wonder and religion were not only compatible with science but essential to the scientific method' (Talairach-Vielmas 2011: 13). Wonder is still an important constituent in underwater life writing. In *Reading for Wonder*, Glenn Willmott favours 'immersion' as a suitable word for the process of encountering wonder. It is suggestive of underwater. Seeing a powerful ethics in wonder through its capacity to create empathy, Willmott argues 'the humanities need to … reclaim the training of an extravagant, embodied imagination – alongside knowledge production – as a unique disciplinary value' (2018: 158). Imagination has long been explicitly endorsed by humane scientists; thus Rachel Carson's *The Sense of Wonder* (1965) ends with wonder flowing beyond science to include everybody. 'The lasting pleasures of contact with the natural world are not reserved for scientists but are available to anyone who will place himself under the influence of earth, sea, and sky and their amazing life' (Carson 1965: 89). Under such influence, wonder informs my readings of science in *Underwater Lives*.

At certain points in this book the critical arguments of life writing take a back seat while science is explained, contexts are sketched and framing concepts are laid out. The mix brings ideas together in ways characteristic of the disciplinary dissolves accompanying blue humanities. I turn to them next.

BLUE HUMANITIES

Attempting the first dive on scuba to fifty fathoms (*c*.100 metres), Cousteau reported 'I tried to fix my brain on reality, to attempt to name the colour of the sea about me. A contest took place between navy blue, aquamarine, and Prussian blue. The debate would not resolve' (Cousteau with Dumas 1953: 81). It's a nice metaphor for distinctions in critical thinking. Over the last decade, theorists have created many shades of blue (Oppermann 2023: 1). As different disciplines converge, critical terms invite scrutiny. How does *Underwater Lives* fit into blue humanities?

Discussing blue ecocriticism, Sidney L. Dobrin proposes literature is suspect because 'the very history of literature is inherently exclusive'. There are grounds to dispute that, and Dobrin himself draws on 'the textual ecologies that contribute to ocean formation in cultural imaginaries' (2021: 25, 14). Steve Mentz argues back for literature as 'a bridge-discourse to make water-infused ideas accessible for thinkers in many modes' (Mentz 2024: xv). Similarly, Killian Quigley provides an arc for ocean cultural imaginaries that is based in textuality and history: 'In confronting the unavoidable truth that anthropocenic oceans are sites of and for reading and writing, we can better comprehend the rich, strange weave of image, mode, and genre that inflect even our most resolutely future-oriented research projects with complex, and sometimes surprising, inheritances' (Quigley 2022: n.p.). *Underwater Lives* takes up that rich, strange weave, with life writing and marine biology providing the strongest threads. I use life writing as my main descriptor, one that certainly overlaps with literature but has more inclusivity. Craig Santos Perez says of scholars in blue humanities that 'They map a "Critical Ocean Studies" that flows across disciplines; dives into submarine depths and submersions; swims into multispecies entanglements; intersects with feminist, indigenous and diasporic epistemologies; recognizes the agency of a warming, rising ocean; and transforms our critical inquiries and reading practices' (Perez 2020: 2). Through a focalizer of life writing, *Underwater Lives* takes this agenda underwater.

Most oceanic critics want some kind of interdisciplinarity (Dobrin 2021: 12). A metaphor of ocean current mixing, a key part of the hydrological cycle, suits transdisciplinary interest in cultural imaginaries. Poetics – a familiar term in literary criticism – provides another meeting-place. Mentz proclaims, 'As the seas rise, oceanic scholarship spills its bounds. These intellectual currents can be conceptualized under the rubric of a "poetics" of planetary water' (2024: 1). He defines a generous reach for it: 'a poetics of planetary water aims to clarify the relationships between humans and water in all its forms and phases' (2024: 2). This includes environmental crisis. 'As the seas rise, heed the swimmers. And the surfers' (Mentz 2024: 51). I add divers, who prove to have at least as much literature as swimmers or surfers, probably more, and who uniquely witness and interpret underwater.

'The uncanniness of marine life increases with ocean depth', argues Richard Hamblyn (2021: 95). Stefan Helmreich (2009) and Melanie Jue (2020) read that uncanniness very productively as a cognate of science fiction; Helmreich makes 'alien' a cumulative descriptor of ocean itself. Aaron van Neste, however, sees a new turn in science fiction which makes us, not the ocean, the object of salvation:

> The water is coming for us, rising with the seas, and the aliens of this literature are its native inhabitants – they are nonhuman animals, humans who ally themselves with the nonhuman, extraterrestrials who take their form. In a critical shift characteristic of the Anthropocene, the sea may be able to save us *because* it is vast, unknown, and holds secrets. Perhaps disturbingly, salvation *must* be alien and external.
>
> (Van Neste 2022: abstract)

Tropes of 'alien' are abundant underwater. As Stacy Alaimo argues, they create convenient distance: 'Articulating marine depths with distant planets frames them as places to encounter pure, untouched otherness, without any of that nagging guilt, anxiety or responsibility that may accompany the contemplation of places clearly marked by histories of colonialism, climate injustice, or environmental devastation' (2013: 194). Although scientists and life writers are ready users of alien tropes, they also work to make underwater life intelligible in other ways and for which we have other language.

Most iterations of blue humanities stress the cross-disciplinary currents of environmental humanities as central to its growth:

> The environmental humanities, rather, seek out a diversity of ways to speak on a human scale about our times of rapid environmental change to audiences within and beyond the academy. They use the skills and tools of a range of disciplines – history, anthropology, literature, geography, philosophy – and then they must *throw away the disciplinary scaffolding* to reach beyond ivory tower readers and listeners.
>
> (Warde, Robin, Sörlin 2018: 178-9; authors' italics)

Warde, Robin and Sörlin value environmental humanities because they 'foreground the issue of *who* is telling the story, *from where* and *about whom*?' (2018: 178-9). That attentiveness to the cultural underpinnings of stories is well established in life writing scholarship, where it is considered a necessity. One can add other disciplines to their list – archaeology is a vital contributor to underwater thinking (Rich 2021) and an instance of how some terms retain discipline-specific appeal. Thus object-orientated ontology, or OOO, is of particular interest to archaeologists whose underwater studies invite thinking about the circulation of things (Rich and Campbell 2023). Playing on

Figure 1 Alien underwater. Artwork by Wally Wood for *Galaxy* science fiction magazine, No. 75, n.d. [1956]. Private collection. Note the symmetry of bubbles: the amphibian-looking alien, like the human, needs breathing equipment.

Foucault, Helmreich advocates for an underwater archaeology of knowledge, a mode that 'sometimes produces ghosts, illusions, phantoms' (2016: xv). Underwater life writing adds an underwater archaeology of imagination, a sort of subject-orientated ontology featuring divers as circulating entities.

Along with environmental humanities, a considerable body of water-related scholarship has appeared. It owes much to *Thinking with Water* (Chen, MacLeod and Neimanis 2013) and Astrida Neimanis's *Bodies of Water* (2017), which make a persuasive case for water as a medium circulating through humans and the world. Such hydrologic also informs the Hydrocene, Bailey-Charteris's alternative term for the Anthropocene. '*The Hydrocene as conceptual epoch recognises water as the central material and figure of the current times*' (Bailey-Charteris 2024: 8; her italics). Drawing attention away from the terrestrial logic and metaphors of the Anthropocene, the Hydrocene unites salt and fresh waters into a single system in which ocean – and air – make life on earth dependent on a Blue planet. That makes it a hyperobject, Timothy Morton's name for phenomena too vast for us to grasp (Morton 2013a). *Underwater*

Lives focuses on underwater, geographically vast but graspable; I present it through a kaleidoscope of subjects, places and topics in no way comprehensive, but indicative.

In joining blue humanities, my category of underwater life writing brings together materials from diver and scientist memoirs, natural history, popular science, visual culture and arts. It focuses on narrative, relationships and modes of perception; it attends to poetics and cultural imaginaries. It has a binding theme of patterns of relation, in a double sense: what these life writings relate, and what they say about relationships with underwater life. Close reading is an essential method here (Feder 2021): it is a version of that close listening which informs Indigenous knowledges, and it shows how poetics work. How you read a text is an argument in itself.

Texts about underwater show different attitudes that do not resolve into neat camps. 'Even for a single time period, then, it is possible to chronicle different cultural histories' of people and places underwater (Rozwadowski 2013: 16). As Helen Rozwadowski observes, physical and technical factors are important in the history of diving, 'but it equally demands consideration of culture and imagination. The desires of early divers … exerted at least as much influence on their perceptions and encounters as the technical capacities enabled by their equipment' (Rozwadowski, 2013: 1-2). Underwater literature in the 1950s and 1960s shows a surge of desires among divers, not all the same, nor quite the same as the desires they manifested through photography and film. Margaret Cohen's *The Underwater Eye* (2022) expertly analyses underwater film over much the same time period as *Underwater Lives*, and with an overlap of interest in *Blue Planet I* and *II*. She sees underwater books as tangential; I treat them as a wide circle. Through life writing, the inner lives of aquanauts appear. Words and images do not simply compete: they collaborate too. Hence *Underwater Lives* addresses some of the photography, video, film and digital texts that accompany underwater language-making acts.

Books created and extended popular interest in underwater. They situated diving in a wider cultural nexus than film alone. Books helped to disseminate visual text through illustrations and their captions, which direct readers' attention to particular things. Those explanations construct stories about photography and its capacities, provide identifications of species and behaviours, and display human interactions with species. They may follow or radically diverge from passages in the text which they ostensibly illustrate (Brant 2024b). Cousteau's *The Silent World* (1953) is now the best known of these texts, though it is important to note it was co-authored with Frédéric Dumas, and Cousteau frequently co-wrote in other books. His close associates were active writers, producing numerous autobiographical accounts of their particular interests. Underwater writing supplied extra and alternative material for those interested in the films, linked by the inclusion of still images in the books. The literature of underwater is important for how it represents the process of filming, including experiences often represented differently on the page from how they were shown on film. Margaret Cohen argues that 'After 1956, underwater documentation for a general public occurred increasingly in filmic media and dwindled in print, a trend that has continued to the present' (Cohen, 2014: 122). Underwater life writing does not decline, I think: it shifts registers and goes to different places.

Helen Rozwadowski argues the humanities remind us we know the ocean as much through imagination as through the sciences: 'The time to write ocean history is now … While present issues may seem to call for scientific and technological solutions, there remains a central and critical role for the humanities' (Rozwadowski 2018: 11-12). Other historians have tracked the intersections of underwater science and military interests – thus Antony Adler's *Neptune's Laboratory* (2019). Naomi Oreskes establishes how military funding was both enabling and constricting for twentieth-century American oceanography and marine geophysics (2021: 8). This is not only a historical matter. Elizabeth DeLoughrey argues that 'Perhaps because it does not lend itself to an easy poetics, the militarization of the seas is underrepresented in scholarship and literature emerging from the blue or oceanic humanities' (2021: 113). Seabed warfare is entering a dangerous era as superpowers use the ocean to protect and disrupt assets like pipelines and cables. Bigger, stealthier submarines revive the seabed as a theatre of war (Meyer 2023). As the Arctic melts, strategic interests conflict with ocean protection. Deep-sea mining and marine bioprospecting, or the hunt for genetic and biochemical material from marine organisms (Zhivkoplias et al. 2024) also challenge blue humanities to think beyond exploitative and exclusively human interests.

Disciplinary dissolutions may enable better recognition and more inclusion of Indigenous knowledges. Traditional ecological knowledge, TEK, brings different cosmologies, beliefs and practices, particularly around care and attention. Craig Santos Perez points out that Pacific ocean knowledges predate blue humanities (2020: 2) and run deep. Indigenous knowledges in the Global North suffer exclusions too, which some blue humanities scholars have addressed. Thus Oppermann restores the Fisherman of Halicarnassus, Cevat Şakir Kabaağaçlı, to view, and Dalla Costa and Chilese join up Global North and South through fisher peoples in *Our Mother Ocean* (2014). Although *Underwater Lives* foregrounds Anglophone and Eurocentric materials, Indigenous knowledges from the Arctic and Palau inform Chapter 5, and Chapter 7 draws on Nimiipuu (Nez Perce) and British indigenous knowledge concerning salmon and eels, to restore other and more holistic views.

CODA: MY UNDERWATER LIFE

Besides benefitting from a large bibliography, *Underwater Lives* draws on personal experience. For twenty years I went diving – initially as an antidote to academia, then as a joyous form of learning in itself. I studied marine biology to the equivalent of undergraduate level, took courses in description and identification through Seasearch (https://www.seasearch.org.uk) and contributed to its surveys. I loved being underwater. Before carbon footprints were so pressing an issue, I dived worldwide. I was lucky to meet people from whom I could learn, and very lucky to find a buddy who was completely trustable and fun. A guiding spirit gave me some oceanic books which eventually inspired *Underwater Lives*. A terrible fire destroyed my dive logs and associated notebooks, otherwise I might have written more autobiographically.

Although the future may well not care how many books we write compared to how we act, books can help spread ideas and activism. *Underwater Lives* has a partner, *Underwater Postcards* (Shoestring Press 2025), downloadable from https://kclpure.kcl.ac.uk/portal/en/publications/underwater-postcards/, a collection of poems in which I try out different and more political voicings on behalf of underwater subjects.

Let's go diving …

Part One

Humans

1

Helmeteering in Fairyland

When Rachel Carson dedicated *The Sea Around Us* (1951) to William Beebe (1877–1962), she evoked not just a personal friendship but a whole way of looking at the natural world. Now recognized as a pioneer of ecology, Beebe understood nature as much more than identifying organisms, though classification was important to him. In a long career as a naturalist, explorer, collector and writer, he promoted particular processes of attention. Patient watching in habitats, imaginative looking around and focused observation down microscopes were all ways to understand in greater detail a wide range of creatures, their lives and their interrelationships. Drawn first to birds – he authored a four-volume definitive work on pheasants – his lifetime interests expanded to jungles, insects, mammals, fish, marine life of all kinds including abyssal creatures, which he brought up in trawls and observed from a pioneering bathysphere in deep dives off Bermuda in the 1930s. What he called 'my passion for the study of a limited field, a sharply demarcated zone, such as a square yard of jungle or an isolated desert island' (Beebe 1924: 31) extended, through helmet diving, to underwater.

'The wise diver will refrain from written descriptions of his experiences' (Beebe 1934: 70). Yet Beebe's oeuvre is big – over eight hundred articles and twenty-one books, much of it for a general readership. His expeditions were usually in the service of the New York Zoological Society who employed him as Director, and through whom he published scientific papers as well as contributing live creatures to their zoo. Often in the happy position of having millionaire adventurers supply him with a vessel and funds, he set up research stations on land to enable researchers to be familiar with their subjects on a daily basis. He was innovative underwater too, using helmet diving to enter into undersea life as a witness of life forms in their own element. Yet his helmet was chivalric kit rather than shiny new tech: 'It suddenly occurs to me how knight-like I am as far as the metal casque goes, and then in spite of the strange world all about, my mind goes back to the long-ago Christmases when a new-published Henty book was an invariable and almost the best gift' (Beebe 1926: 71). He might have been thinking of *Those Other Animals* (1891) or *A Knight of the White Cross* (1896), typical of G. A. Henty's historical romance and quirky natural history. 'Physical activity features prominently in the stereotypical view of the Henty hero. This view leaves out the equally strong interests the fictional hero has in reading and the observation of natural phenomena as chosen activities', says Rachel Johnson (2006: 2).

The public success of Beebe's writings and their association with adventure ironically clouded his scientific reputation in some quarters. Certainly some of his articles are

light on science and laden with thrills, as befitted his bathysphere celebrity. But his
books are engaging memoirs of expeditions, explaining – and illustrating – life forms
encountered despite the hazards, challenges and dramas of weather and equipment.
'It is like rubbing the Aladdin's lamp of science!' exclaimed Henry Fairfield Osborn,
President of the New York Zoological Society, in his preface to *Galápagos: World's
End* (1924), Beebe's account of an expedition to the Galápagos Islands between March
and May 1923 on the *Noma*. In 1926, Beebe published *Arcturus Adventure*, about the
Sargasso Sea, Cocos Islands and Galápagos revisited; in 1932, *Nonsuch: Land of Water*
about Bermuda; in 1934, *Half Mile Down* about Bermuda and abyssal deeps; in 1937,
Beneath Tropic Seas, about Haiti; in 1938, *Zaca Venture*, about the Gulf of California; in
1942, *Book of Bays*, about the Pacific Coast from Mexico to Columbia. They were well
received. One reviewer acclaimed the mix of 'high romance, exact science, fascinating
history, wild adventure' as 'glorious' (1926: blurb). Another pronounced Beebe to be
'the greatest master of prismatic English now' (1926: blurb). Beebe spread identities
prismatically, between himself and colleagues, himself and readers. 'I have intentionally
used some unfamiliar words', he wrote, wanting to convey 'the mental viewpoint
of ourselves – my staff and myself; to let the layman realize how our knowledge is
bounded by ignorance' and 'with the desire that the reader should join us scientists
for a short space of time in a spirit of humbleness and wonderment in the presence
of the living results of this earthly evolution' (1938: 208). This appeal was not a naïve
belief. On a rare off day, Beebe wondered cynically about nature writing: 'what can we
do with the birds about us that every Isn't-nature-wonderful person is not doing?' and
answers his own question with refreshed faith in the infinity of discovery. 'One way to
alchemize this effect is to preface the fact with the short but often embarrassing adverb,
Why?' (1928: 187-8).

Beebe's alertness to representation shortens any distance between scientist and lay
reader: underwater is a world that tests everyone's ideas.

> In the course of time I have learned to tramp about coral reefs, twenty to thirty feet
> under water, so unconcernedly that I can pay attention to particular definite things.
> But after all my silly fears have been allayed, even now, with eyes overflowing with
> surfeit of color, I am still almost inarticulate. We need a whole new vocabulary,
> new adjectives, adequately to describe the designs and colors of under sea.
>
>   (Beebe 1928: 36)

Popular science is often cast as dilution of seriousness rather than its diffusion but in his
books, Beebe uses life writing to combine first-person feelings, on-the-spot narrative
and philosophical reflection – and to add them to science. Tita Chico has proposed
that from the seventeenth century on, literary imagination was an accepted part of
scientific knowledge. So the Royal Society's advocacy of a plain style in the 1660s was
not meant to exclude literary devices like plot and imagery. 'Selecting a metaphor bears
an uncanny resemblance to identifying an observed particular. Both must be well
chosen' (Chico 2018: 33). Beebe's interest in imaginative worlds for comparisons and
particulars makes him a vivid and original writer about oceanic life. Beebe was also
one of few writers of his era to don a diving helmet to see underwater life for himself.
(Robert Gibbings was another – discussed in Chapter 10).

Beebe's first book, *The Log of the Sun* (1906), uses a calendar structure to organize observations of the natural world, including explorations of tide pools in the Bay of Fundy, New Brunswick. His equipment was simple and home-made. Photographs of comb jellies, delicate balls of spun glass, were obtained by 'fastening the lens of a discarded bicycle lantern in a cone of paper blackened on the inside with shoe-blacking' (1906: 148). He dived, shivering, on a lungful of air and weighted by a stone. Though most of his attention in this book was on tide pools rather than the open ocean, he attends carefully to small lives like this ascidian: '*Boltenia*, the scientists call them, tall, queer-shaped things; a stalk six to eight inches in length, with a knob or oblong bulb-like body at the summit, looking exactly like the flower of a lady-slipper orchid' (1906: 160). *Boltenia* prompt him to set aside ideas of human superiority: 'If we soften the hard scientific facts which tell us of these dumb, blind creatures, with the humane mellowing thought of the oneness of all life, we will find much that is pathetic and affecting in their humble biographies from our point of view' (1906: 161). Scientifically, such creatures are perfectly adapted for their evolutionary niche, and most have an impressively long existence. In life writing terms, they have biographies worth reading. In spite of a Dickensian note of pathos, or perhaps because of it, humans become more humane by attending to other lives.

This double perspective underpinned Beebe's lifelong sympathy for small lives and makes his attentive looking into a compound of time frames. In the Galápagos Islands surrounded by black marine iguanas, *Amblyrhynchus*, he felt present in an age of reptiles, 'not gradual immersion in far distant evolutions, with impersonal interests in primitive nature, but make-and-break flashes of past and ultra present, action and reaction of primitive and sophisticative' (Beebe 1924: 54). Again and again struck by the longevity of other life forms, he places humans as latecomers, a humbling thought.

> As I casually unearthed some jewel of a leg-joint, well worthy of a setting in platinum, a slender rod splashed with mauve and crimson, with a galaxy of blue stars wound in a spiral about it, I realized more than ever what a casual thing is man upon the earth. For untold ages since thorny lobsters first crawled about in the waters of the upper chalk, perhaps sixty million years ago, beautiful detritus such as this has littered the tropical sands. Only by the merest accident had I stumbled upon it, and its shape become beautiful in my brain, its pigment colour in my eye. … Once we were taught that the earth was the centre of the universe; then that man was the raison d'être of earthly evolution. Now I was thankful to realize that I was here at all, and that I had the great honour of being one with all about me, and in however small a way to have at least an understanding part.
>
> (1924: 65–6)

Ditching here that reliance on 'we' which was common practice in nature writing, Beebe's first person responds feelingly to other life forms. One can argue he turns science into popular science by adding emotion, but it is life writing that humanizes science and decentres humans by pausing to celebrate a thorny lobster's leg-joint.

Beebe worked hard on these expeditions to encounter other lives. In the Galápagos Islands, for instance, 'From a landscape which superficially seemed utterly barren of life, we had extracted the greatest possible profit to be gained from photographing, both still and moving pictures, paintings in water colours and oils, specimens of all kinds, plants, flowers, minerals, insects, fish, lizards, birds' nests and eggs, and notes scrawled on every imaginable scrap of paper' (1924: 178). Beebe's activities could be described as insatiable, even rapacious – his colleague Ruth Rose uses burglary as a metaphor for their snatch-and-grab on one island. They take hundreds of creatures to kill for dissection or for display in a city zoo thousands of miles away, a life of wretchedly wrenched-away captivity. And yet Beebe does care about the biographies of creatures, wanting to understand their relationship to habitat, feeding, mating, nurturing habits, to each other – and to simply being alive, as in an account of ten minutes in the life of four sea lion pups playing at his feet while he writes, which gives juvenile pinnipeds their modernist moment (1924: 108). Despite snuffing out the very lives he admires, he reacts to their beauty and wants to share, by writing, deep appreciation of places and their biodiversity. As I read his accounts, I was able to look up organisms online, see pictures, read further information: a privilege enabled by technology, but also the patient and persistent work of people who take photographs, sort identities, post, collate and check information in databases. Most of this labour is too easy to take for granted: it still requires the devotion of naturalists. It was often physically difficult work for Beebe. On islands of lava the terrain is hot, steep and spiny; it has ferocious mosquitoes and sandflies, jagged rocks and coast-pounding surf. After one five-mile slog inland, he squats – the lava is too hot to sit on – for a rare complaint: 'My tongue seemed three times its usual size, and I watched the blood slowly drip from the big gouges in my legs resulting from frequent falls' (1924: 290). Back on board the *Noma*, he has a short time to recover before an evening shift: 'I went down into the glare of laboratory lights, and did many and various things, mostly ineffectively, with microscope and vials and forceps, paper and ink and words' (1924: 293).

This sort of narrative is diary-like in its sequencing – Beebe kept a journal – and it gives a quotidian texture to the books. Working rockpools, he encountered organisms also present in the open ocean, and learnt to recognize fish species confusingly coloured differently in different phases. He took on-the-spot notes and specimens before sorting impressions into narrative. Where his articles tend towards breezy highlights, his books thread activities more autobiographically, all in a day's work of looking, diving and thinking. Despite having motion picture cameras at work alongside him, he says little about that form of image-making. Instead he brings reef life alive by description which is like depiction in its emphasis on form, pattern, movement and colour. He refers self-consciously to poetical passages, keeping the reader in view, and he tends to end chapters on big cosmic notes. I discuss next his writings on microscopic life, as oceanic as reef diving. I exclude his engaging writing on birds, animals, insects and plants, the surface of the sea and tidal life (he is especially vivid on flying fish, insects and crabs) though it counterpoints and complements his underwater life writing.

MICROSCOPE LIFE

What Beebe looked at closely in the ship's lab were organisms too small for humans to see unaided. Yet they amplified knowledge of underwater life. Plankton and tiny crustaceans form a big part of ocean biomass, an agglomeration Beebe breaks down into species and individuals who have watchable life narratives. These narratives bring out characteristics so as to smooth the conceptual lurch from species to individual. Occasionally they are portraits, like 'Joey', a baby filefish, or 'My Word', a *Pterphryne* or Sargasso fish (1924: 12-13; 1926: 20). By reading the general and particular together, watching behaviours closely, Beebe saw anatomy in action, purposefully: 'We know the facts of these strange little lives: the *why* ever eludes us.' (1924: 28).

Beebe's trawls brought up bulging nets, day and night, whose treasures had to be quickly sorted, recorded and examined. Inspection of seawater under a microscope showed huge amounts of unknown, unnamed life. Sampling 1/150th of a quart jar, he calculated 271,080 organisms were in his fraction, meaning more than forty million were in the whole. This scale of vast and tiny could only be stabilized via a microscope. 'I took a three-inch frond of weed into the laboratory and watched it under my binocular microscope. I pretended the common little inhabitants were rare and began to observe instead of merely to see them' (1926: 18-19). A characteristic vision refresh introduces hydroids first, colonial animals that often look like small ferns or mosses. Beebe saw:

> the palms, the threes and the spiked clubs, all superlatively dainty and elegant, foresting these diminutive roof gardens of the sea. Here and there were more formal plantings, row upon row of beautiful ivory or alabaster chalices, from which sprang severe fountains of tentacles, – minute bryozoans or moss animals, – all arranged just so, like the alabaster vases of Italian gardens. The bryozoan beds were still exquisite when their occupants were dead and gone. The sere and autumn of the moss animals' year left a mosaic of thousands of flattened hexagons as perfect as honeycombs, as translucent as age-old moonstone.

Garden metaphors establish nature as art; distinctions between design and ornament disappear into legacies that reconnect art and nature in the mosaic, the honeycomb and the moonstone. Imagery organizes the otherwise overwhelming. Of another sample, he says 'I cannot recall having ever seen so many living creatures in so limited an area in all my life.' One of them is *Porpita porpita*, the blue button 'jellyfish' (it is not a jelly but a hydroid).

> At a distance they look like either quarters or silver dollars, according to age, but when I sit down in front of one floating in a glass dish, descriptions and similes pall. On my laboratory table is a beauty with a disk two inches across. I have seen unbelievably minute crystals of some rare mineral, or a thousand beams of sunlight radiating over still water which reminded me of this, but the delicacy of color and pattern are beyond all verbal or written appreciation. The center is yellowish gold, and from here to the periphery, about one hundred lines radiate and undulate. It is crenulated and waved, and the pale blue and dull yellow are inextricably mingled. The broad margin is deep, deep blue, and outside there are three to five ranks of delicate tentacles. Their long stems are beryl blue, while the rounded beads which double-line the tips are of the darkest ultramarine. Such is a hint of the beauty of one mote among the trillions on every side.

(1926: 60)

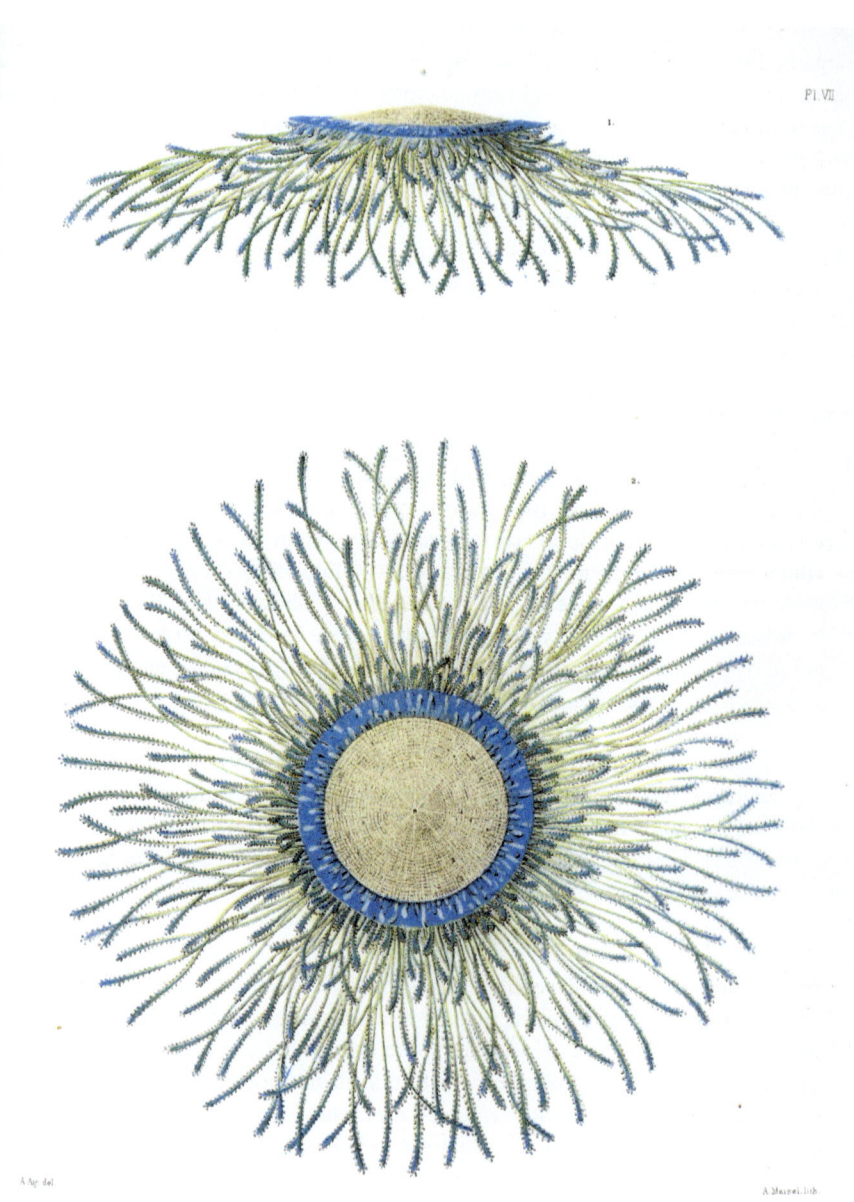

Figure 2 Blue button … *Porpita porpita* (1883), in profile and from above. Image courtesy of The Royal Society.

Beebe was sensitive to aesthetics and to individuality. A seemingly inert mass could be separated into pulsing lives. Taking multi-coloured jelly hauled up in *Arcturus's* net,

> I poured water upon it, and with the dilution came disintegration of the plankton. As the tens of thousands of atoms of jewelled jelly fell apart, each assumed the shape and character of a complete individual, and at once began to kick or breathe or swim or throb after its kind. Visible blood started to circulate, hearts were distinctly seen to pulsate in the depths of glassy bodies, enemies leaped at one another's throats (or whatever they possessed in lieu of such a region), and on the instant of watery liberty, feathery-footed males danced and whirled in courtship ecstasy about their less ornamented mates. These are no meaningless, flowery phrases, for within a minute after dilution, the jelly mass under my binoculars exhibited every emotion known to invertebrates.
>
> (1926: 350)

Emotions link Beebe to organisms. He had a 'pulpit' built, a wooden platform, so he could stand almost clear of the ship and scan the ocean surface for life. On the *Zaca*, one day he scooped up 'a bit of something' drifting past. Under a microscope it proved to be a cork raft full of barnacles. Beebe was puzzled, because young barnacles get one shot at attaching, usually gravity-assisted downwards. 'It was as reasonable as if a geranium, not caring for its place in the shade, should move across a flower bed to the sunny herbaceous border' (1938: 222). Garden metaphors, usually helpful, get stuck because the barnacles are so animate, 'a fringe of frantically beckoning beings planted exactly where they should be, reaching out eager fists which unfolded into clutching fingers' (1938: 223). This cluster, gradually individuated, have smaller barnacles growing on them. And the raft has other creatures: a shrimp skeleton; a grazing herd of nudibranchs, milky grey, varying sizes; a flatworm and an amphipod. 'Something in the whole setting made my mind leave the silly fears and worries of this earthly life.' Beebe goes up on deck, looks at the black stormy ocean, then returns to his lab and fauna of the cork.

> I watched its ceaseless energy and movement, its hopes and desires, its successful adaptation to the small environment. From this my mind went on past my six-foot self and my world to some supercorkland, and I looked down at the *Zaca*, a tossing chip on whose surface and in whose interior were a score of little beings, all somewhat naked mollusks under the skin, all bustling about their various importances. The barnacles and the snails and the lonely amphipod grew in significance, and my world of human beings took its rightful place as only one among a host of many sizes and dimensions of other worlds.
>
> (1938: 227)

Beebe adjusts scales of time and space so that humans and marine beings co-exist equally. His microscopic view is microcosmic, then cosmic, making equal coexistence into equality: we are all somewhat naked molluscs under the skin. The microscope mirrors how 'thought of the Other is sterile without the other of Thought', as Édouard

Glissant puts it (1997: 36). In a tender comic coda, Beebe reports that the corkland inhabitants have slowed down; when he drops salt water into their dish, they speed up, oxygenated. He marks the moment as privileged, 'to watch and share with enthusiasm and complete absorption in a momentary cross section of the little lives.' In a humorous nod to Buddhism, because they have 'acquired merit' he returns them to the ocean – and goes to bed.

Beebe's ocean is full of encounters in which species become individuals. *Zaca's* dredge brings up two *Mazatlania hesperia,* turreted snails with beautiful shells. On these 'more often the lower three-fourths of the whorls were vividly stencilled with rich red-brown zigzags, arrows, Vs, and abbreviated lightnings' (1938: 54). He compares the markings to Sanskrit. 'Later, on board, I devoted half an hour to them, whereupon they became distinct recognizable individuals with marked personalities'. But his idea of a distinguishable individual came under pressure. Catching a blue shark, he dissects it and realizes it is a she, with embryos. He counts up other creatures attached: remora, pilot fish, crustacea, a total of 106. 'My great blue shark was less a fish than a mother, an aquarium and a zoological garden combined' (1928: 180). Single organisms also differed within a species. 'I saw, under a hand lens, differences, tears in the jelly, slight disproportions of size and parts, which made of each an individual, – a jelly separate and apart, with its own endurance and weariness, its preferences, achievements and failures. All this too, without in any way embarrassing it with anthropomorphic characteristics or abilities' (1928: 21). Telling jellyfish apart can be so difficult that Elizabeth Agassiz recommended using touch to feel for fractional differences of thickness and smoothness, complaining 'One's vocabulary is soon exhausted in describing the different degrees of consistency in the substance of Jelly-fishes' (1865: 60). Beebe saw individuals within species, connected by subjectivity including his own; for him this was not compromising scientific objectivity but refining it.

HELMETEERING

Writing of a mid-ocean dive on breath-hold, Beebe recorded how human individuality could be tiny and lonely:

> I dived a second time and sank as low as my stored-up breath permitted, and then before I turned and kicked upward, took one long look beneath and tried to imagine that unimaginable world of life down, down in the ever blackening, ever greater pressured depths. No ship or companion was visible and my sense of devastating isolation, of cosmic awe can never again occur with equal force in this life.
>
> (1926: 36)

In contrast, helmet diving on a coral reef seemed initially tame. With vision restricted by his helmet to 60° of visual field and unable to take notes to steady himself, he surrendered to surge and responded to oceanic space:

The sun's rays filtered down as though through the most marvellous cathedral ever imagined – intangible, oblique rays which the eye could perceive but no lip describe. With distance, these became more and more luminous, more wondrously brilliant, until rocks died away in a veritable purple glory. No sunset, no mist on distant mountains that I have seen, could compare with this. One had to sit quietly and absorb these beauties before one could remember to be an ichthyologist.

(1926: 83)

Helmet diving opened up perception of atmospheric topographies – 'I am eclipsed, and change planets' (1926: 300). Stacy Alaimo has written of how the 'alien' trope, recurrent in oceanic writing, relieves humans of embodiment and responsibilities on this planet (2013: 194). But Beebe made correspondences to experiences on earth. Dropping into 'a city of giant mushrooms', he saw analogies with oriental places. 'In the middle distance I saw the palace of the Dalai Lama at Lhasa with its majestic down-dropping lines, beyond it the corals had wrought a fairy replica of the temple of the Tirthankers at Benares' (1926: 300). His extensive land travels in Asia (when working on pheasants) provided comparisons. 'Invariably the architecture of the East was brought to mind ... light, uplifted pagoda roofs, curving domes, and stalagmite minarets, together with the scroll-work which is lace-like but never gingerbready' (1926: 300). Orientalist architecture links coral and humans as equal makers.

Helmet diving gave Beebe new perspectives and interactions. Until you have seen 'eight hundred pounds of sea turtle floating lightly as a thistledown overhead', you have not properly seen a turtle, he suggests. He then imagines how the turtle might see him: 'this strange, copper-headed, white-skinned, worm-like being, with an enormously long, curving tentacle from the tip of its nose, forever pouring forth a mass of white, bubbly gas, and which idiotically kept standing up and sitting down' (1926: 180). Changing points of view, Beebe locates himself as an observed object too. When a large school of yellow-tailed surgeonfish, his favourite fish species, goes by, 'It was an amusing sensation to have these hundreds of fish file past, all rolling their eyes at me as they went. I felt almost embarrassed' (1926: 183). Characteristically he deals with this social discomfort by closer engagement. The species (known as *Xesurus* to Beebe, and now as *Prionurus punctatus*) is treated to a chapter exploring 'the image of a personality, the *raison d'être* of some fish' (1926: 283). It begins in media res: 'I had made probably forty submersions in my diving helmet, and on my last ascent sat shiveringly on the dripping thwart and with water-wrinkled fingers scrawled damp notes on what I had seen' (1926: 282). Metaphor helps to translate its strangeness. 'I tried to parallel that day's notes with corresponding items which a Martian, dropped into Fifth Avenue or Regent Street, might glean in a few minutes' time'. Little fish are newsboys, sea urchins are swarms of people, a hieroglyphic fish is a curious old man, a wrasse is a lady in a green dress, watched by a tiger shark as suspicious as a policeman. Oceanic lives become refamiliarized into city conviviality, but anthropomorphism quickly gives way to a discussion of surgeonfish spines. Anatomical functionality was safe descriptive ground whereas urban imagery had limited uses given Beebe's belief in 'sham, insincerity, deceit, illusion, veneer as dominant notes in civilization' (1919: 23).

On later expeditions, Beebe increasingly used a waterglass to view underwater from a small boat. Alfred Alcock, surveying coasts and islands of the Indian Ocean, had also found this very useful in water down to twenty metres. It comprised

> a wooden funnel, with a window of good plate-glass in the broad end and a pair of hands about halfway up. Taking a good grasp of the handles, you run the funnel overboard, push the window well below water, and put your eyes to the narrow end, and then a perfect picture of the bottom is before you, free from all the distortions caused by ripples and surface reflection, and free from glare.
>
> (Alcock 1902: 49)

Like Beebe, Alcock associated this view with magical imagination. 'And what a picture it is to a man who comes from museums and books. Looking back after thirteen years, I can only remember visions of fairy groves and glades, lit by a strange ethereal light, half moon half sun, where, among Christmas-trees of purple and blue and golden green, fishes painted like butterflies flitted and hovered' (1902: 49-50). Although Beebe became an enthusiastic user, a waterglass was technology predicated on distance. In contrast, helmet diving gave

> the feeling of intimacy and identity with this water world, [and] added a reality which never be conveyed in spoken or written words. Looking through the waterglass one is still in the upper light and air; here, both body and mind were transmuted into the actual cosmos of these fish. My body was bathed by their atmosphere, they were close, surrounding me, looking at me as a friendly stranger. … As I landed on the rock, it seemed to me that most of the biggest ones [fish] had gathered at that exact spot to greet me, I have never seen such fearlessness. I was assuredly the first human being to walk the bottom about this island, and the fish attested this by coming as close as they could get.
>
> (1938: 268-9)

In this instance, friendliness or conspeciality is unspoilt by Beebe's violent methods – netting, trapping, harpooning, dynamiting fish in the name of science. He found fish sociability touching: underwater off Bermuda he encounters a school of chub so big it blots out the light. Shock subsides into delight in their 'milling around and around me, apparently absorbed in interest in this being new to their cosmos' (1932: 47). It is an optimistic version of 'first contact', the moment of encounter between two communities who have not met before; in colonial contexts, oppression follows. Jill Tarter who directed SETI, an organization devoted to the Search for Extraterrestrial Intelligence, proposes that encountering other beings enables the idea of a Cosmic Mirror, 'the mirror in which all humans can see themselves as the same, when compared to the extraterrestrial "other". It's the mirror that allows us to alter our daily perspectives and see ourselves in a more cosmic setting. It is the mirror that reminds us of our common origins in stardust' (Tarter 2010). Beebe tilts a cosmic mirror not only to fish, but even to the sand. An account of 'Almost Island', off Bermuda, includes a passage where he lies down to watch for life in the shifting grains and becomes beguiled by the sand itself:

The crests of the furrows beyond me loosened, thousands of glittering motes rose a little, then tumbled down the slope and up the flank of the succeeding furrow. I stopped calling them furrows and recognized them as new and strange waves, tuned, like my own actions, into slow-motion imitations of our corresponding activities in another world.

(1932: 44)

Robert Gibbings was comparably absorbed by sand in the Red Sea:

Sand, whether rippled by wind or water, takes the same forms; traceries of miniature dunes, seemingly parallel, get interwoven in endless variations. In one case silver dust fanned by the lightest airs, in the other a heavy conglomerate moulded by tons of water. I sometimes wonder if it isn't the same with most of us. Whatever the circumstances, whatever the guiding force, mightn't the pattern of our lives have been the same? We like to think differently, but are we right?

(Gibbings 1946: 92)

Where Gibbings reflects on sand to think about fate and destiny, Beebe makes sand ridges metaphysical, a cosmic mirror tilted back to himself and humanity, stripped down to form and movement and united by an ancient music of the spheres: 'I am sure if I had a microphone I could hear the sand grains singing together' (1932: 44). No component of underwater life was too small to convey a vision of harmonious coexistence.

FAIRYLAND

One of the jacket blurbs for *The Arcturus Adventure*, from the *Brooklyn Daily Eagle*, says 'More than any other man writing in English he has the faculty of making laboratory research read like a fairy tale.' Beebe invoked fairy tales often, both in his lab and underwater. 'The general impression of hours and days spent at the bottom of the sea is its fairylike unreality. It is an Alice's Wonderland, where our terrestrial experiences and terms are set at naught' (Beebe 1928: 204). Natascha Adamowsky thinks *Alice's Adventures in Wonderland* was Beebe's favourite book (2015: 27); he also regularly mentions Verne, Conan Doyle and H. G. Wells. Other authors invoked Lewis Carroll to help with strange encounters. Alfred Alcock refers lightly to 'the wonderful "jabberwocky" animals that the deep-sea trawl brings up' (1902: 27). But more evident in Beebe's books is a complex weave of fantasy literature of two kinds: fairy tales, and the sinister stories of Lord Dunsany. Edward John Moreton Drax Plunkett, 18th Baron Dunsany, wrote in various genres; his tales, usually described as fantasy (subsequently influential on science fiction), had a growing band of devotees. Best known perhaps are *The Gods of Pegana* (1905) and *The Book of Wonder* (1912). Beebe's allusions create an imaginary world which has romance (often oriental, as for Dunsany); variations of the human, or humanoid forms (goblins, elves, fairies, supplemented by gnoles and mipts from Dunsany); creatures of legend (dragons), and atmospherics especially of malice, mystery, the sinister and inexplicable. On Clarion Island, about five hundred miles west of Mexico, Beebe and his companions found a tide pool. 'From its surface rose eight monsters, temporarily quiescent in lava, their black heads protruding in a sort of fearful school. The most ordinary was amazingly like the head and snout of a bull elephant seal while the nomenclature of the rest would tax the imagination of a Syme *cum* Dunsany. One was unquestionably a mipt!' (Beebe 1938: 243). Robert Gibbings also turned to phantasms to image a recurrent feeling, here in sea caves on the island of Mangaia, that 'Anything may change at any moment': 'Huge caverns, their ceilings dripping stone. Monstrous pillars, in semi-human forms, weep through a thousand generations. Gnome-like bodies lie contorted on the floor. Gorgon masks glare from the aisles. Gargoyle faces grin from the calloused ceilings' (1946: 176). Visualizations of strangeness came to hand through illustrators like Sidney Sime and Arthur Rackham. Of Bermuda reefs, Beebe proposed 'If we desire an image of their beauty and their strangeness, I must demand a mental melange of the moon, a primeval jungle in the youth of the world, and a Rackham landscape packed with scarcely visible gnomes and hobgoblins' (1934: 77-8).

There was an explicit link between fairy tales and marine biology, in Jørgen Moe and Peter Christen Asbjørnsen. Collectors of Norwegian folklore, they published tales from 1837 to 1852 which, like their precursors the Brothers Grimm, they put into memorable common language. A complete collection in 1852 was translated into English in 1859, adding Nordic to the English-speaking imaginary. Asbjørnsen, a forest-master, had extensive natural history interests that included marine species. *Brisinga*, a genus of starfish named by Asbjørnsen in 1859, honours the jewel made by dwarves for the Scandinavian goddess Freya, or the Brisingamen, Freya's coveted necklace (Alcock 1902: 286). Raiding myths was not uncommon in science; life writing could give it personal inflection. Fairyland was for Beebe a trope succinctly evoking an accepted otherworld in which the imaginable includes the unimaginable. 'To my delight I found that I could duplicate or actually improve upon every character of dragons or gargoyles. After one has become acquainted with the everyday inhabitants – villagers, aristocrats, commoners – living today in the deep sea, Dunsany, Barry, Blackwood, Grimm, Sime – all these lose force as inventors of fairies, hobgoblins and elves, and become mere nature fakers' (Beebe 1926: 340). But he held on to fairyland as a figure for beauty and disturbing strangeness. In the same book he discussed eel larvae whose elusive migrations were not yet fully known. 'As *Leptocephalus* is strange as any dragon in a fairy tale, so its life history equals the unreality of any fairy tale itself' (1926: 21). Dunsany provided a peg for 'spectral eels which seemed more suitable adornments of a fairy tale – intimates perhaps of deep pools beyond Mluna, – pale, slender eel wraiths' (1926: 382).

Mluna invites a closer look. It appears in Dunsany's 'Probable Adventure of The Three Literary Men' in *The Book of Wonder* (1912) illustrated by Sidney Sime. The peak of Mluna overlooks the Dubious Land, from which three thieves come to steal an enchanted box holding songs to revive their tribe. They move through a terrifying landscape in which much is inexplicable and some threats are all too clear:

> Something so huge that it seemed unfair to man that it should move so softly stalked splendidly by them, and only so barely did they escape its notice that one word ran and echoed through their three imaginations – 'If – if – if.' And when

this danger was at last gone by they moved cautiously on again and presently saw the little harmless mipt, half fairy and half gnome, giving shrill, contented squeaks on the edge of the world.

(Dunsany 1912; https://victorianweb.org/authors/dunsany/wonder/4.html)

Though here the mipt proves harmless, Dunsany's worlds pivot on dangerous imagination. Some stories feature London clerks entering visionary worlds, as if real, to rule them or steal some magic object. Dunsany's antithesis between daily drudgery and free imagination, between capitalism and romance, helped Beebe situate underwater as 'the edge of the edge of the world' where questions of value, labour, purpose and escapism could hover between real and imaginary. Illustrators like Sime and Rackham, packaged into the allusions, depicted how fairy dream could easily become nightmare. Paul McCann points to Dunsany's interest in 'problems of the future and the past, problems of scale and problems of futility' – all relevant to Beebe as a writer (McCann 2008). Fairyland was Beebe's shorthand – and longhand – for underwater magic which writing struggled to convey. In speech, and on the page, even his lush descriptions of underwater helmet diving might collapse: 'you suddenly find yourself wordless. You exclaim something bromidic which sounds like Marvellous! Great! Wonderful! then relapse futilely into silence … as if fairyland had not intervened in your life' (1928: 6). Fairyland recast anthropomorphism whilst supplying a life writing template of enchanting and unpredictable lives.

Fairies were much invoked in late nineteenth-century nature writing. In 1898, *Half Hours in the Deep* quoted Kingsley on liveliness and colour of creatures in coral gardens: 'Nothing so odd, nothing so gay, even entered your dreams, or a poet's, as you may find alive at the bottom of the sea, in the live-flower gardens of the sea-fairies' (*Half Hours* 1898: 215-16). Thirty years later, another instructive book described the Angler fish as 'a most beautiful object after hatching. Its fins are drawn out into filaments of fairy-like delicacy' (Russell and Yonge (1928) 1949: 84). Fitting both delicate species and colourful environments, fairyland was a metaphor for beautiful otherness. Yet Beebe's generation knew a very particular kind of fairyland. Anne Chassagnol has pointed out that 'Darwin's theory is quite a fairy-like concept' because it involves metamorphosis and small creatures; both appear in Charles Kingsley's *The Water Babies* (1863) where fresh-water fairies turn water into something spritely (Chassagnol 2010: 1). By the early twentieth century, fairy tales were a rich and widespread genre. Collecting tales by the Grimm brothers, Andersen, Perrault and from countries like Norway, Russia and America, from 1889–1913 Andrew Lang's *Fairy Books* appeared, each with their own defining colour. Lang's series, edited with Leonora Alleyne, was immensely popular. Lang was a powerful influence on L. Frank Baum, author of the *Wizard of Oz*, who kept Lang's portrait in his bedroom and wrote an underwater fantasia *The Sea Fairies* (1911). The *Fairy* series was much reprinted (Bacchilega 2013; Hines 2013). It was also gorgeously illustrated, mostly by Henry Justice Ford. Illustrating other collections, early twentieth-century artists like Walter Crane, Arthur Rackham, Edmund Dulac and Kay Nielsen (who worked for Walt Disney from 1937–1941) visualized magical worlds in exquisite and striking ways. Marine subjects appear in, for instance, Walter Crane's 'Neptune's Horses' (1910); Arthur Rackham's mermaids, 'They Have Sea-green Hair' (1922); Edmund Dulac's 'Portrait of a Woman, Eleanora' (1907) and illustrations

EPISODE X.—"HOW ONE CAME, AS WAS FORETOLD, TO THE CITY OF NEVER."

"When they came to the heights, that venturesome rider saw, huge and fair to the left of him, the destined city of Never, and he beheld . . . the cliffs of Told a-glistering in the twilight like an alabaster statue of the Evening. Towards them he wrenched the halter, towards Toldenarba and the Under Pits; the wings of hippogriff roared as the halter turned him. . . . There watched him ceaselessly from the Under Pits those eyes whose duty it is; from further within and deeper th[at] dwell there arose when they saw the surprise in the eyes. . . . Even so he came, as foretold, to the city of Never, perched upon Toldenarba, and saw late to on those pinnacles that know no other light. All the domes were of copper, but the spires on their summits were gold. . . . Then, as he neared the city's [rampart . . . he suddenly saw far off, dwarfing the mountains, an even greater city. Whether that city was built upon the twilight, or whether it rose from the c some other world, he did not know. He saw it dominate the city of Never, and strove to reach it."

After the Drawing by S. H. Sime. [For Lord Dunsany's Story, *see Facing Page.*] Page 72.

Figure 3 Sidney H. Sime (1867–1941), 'How one came, as was foretold, to the city of Never', in Lord Dunsany, *The Book of Wonder* (1912). Image courtesy of the Sime Gallery.

for *The Little Mermaid* (1911), and Kay Nielsen's illustrations for *East of the Sun and West of the Moon* (1914). The golden age of fairy tale illustration, roughly 1880–1930, coincides with the impressionable age of underwater life writing.

Margaret Cohen establishes how early twentieth-century 'filmmakers create underwater imagery that hearkens back to pre-existing fantasies' (2022: 10–11). Beebe's fairy tale repertoire, more familiar to readers then than now, provided a template of imagination for his scientific adventuring. Recuperating it increases the entanglement of science, popular science, underwater exploration and diver impressions that characterize Beebe's underwater writings. But it also simplifies. Cohen locates 'pre-Romantic and Romantic aesthetics for celebrating nature' (2022: 10) as prominent tropes in underwater film. Beebe's use of fairyland and supernatural tales shows he borrowed from his era too – a useful reminder that sciences and humanities share cultural space.

This imaginary of fairyland, legend and supernatural tales involves genres in which beings are different from humans, yet have contact, communication and interactions with them. They are worlds that humans do not control. Forceful laws govern. Settings and activities are often dark. Fairies were conventionally light, transparent, delicate beings who, like bubbles (discussed in Chapter 11), are mobile in often uncontrollable ways. Symbols of magic and enchantment, they are miniatures of transparency, diaphanousness and evanescence. They are naturals on camera – hence the excitement at the Cottingley fairies who 'appeared' in 1917 in photographs taken by two girls in Yorkshire. Sir Arthur Conan Doyle believed them genuine. Like chiffon (invented in 1938), fairyland in this period has a gossamer aesthetic useful for the insubstantiality of underwater. Its darker side of gnomes and horrid creatures gave cultural ballast to fears that prowled underwater too. Fairyland was a readily available cultural hinterland for Beebe – and other underwater writers. It positions humans as outsiders who can enter in, conditionally, and it provided characters, plot and topography recognizable to a general reader. That readability was important to some scientific figures.

> The great naturalist Agassiz used to say that a student did not know his subject until he could present it successfully in four different forms: first as a technical monograph, second as a scientific lecture, third as a popular lecture, and fourth as a simple child's tale. Probably the scientific men of our day would flinch or flunk the fourth of these tests.
>
> (Crowder 1935: i)

Beebe succeeded by separating out scientific monographs and using life writing to join the rest. Adamowsky, focusing on his bathysphere dives, concludes that Beebe's writings reveal 'the insight that the deep sea resists the parameters of scientific construction, because it is also a mighty ocean of discourse and a mythological echo-chamber' (2015: 174). The echo-chamber prosaically included Beebe's collaborators, with whom he worked closely. 'Almost all the pronouns "I" in this book should be considered as divided into four', he wrote in *Half Mile Down* (1934: 230) acknowledging John Tee-Van, Gloria Hollister and Jocelyn Crane, all permanent staff of the Department of Tropical Research. They, and illustrators like the painter Else Bostelmann, helped shape the content of Beebe's writings, and perhaps the transparency of his ego on paper. His biographer thinks 'the very breadth of Beebe's knowledge and vision have worked against him in the recent era of specialization' (Gould 2006: 408). That breadth can be understood again through life writing in much of which, paradoxically, he decentres himself into a representative of his species: 'to the aquatic devotee, the oceanic fan, surprise after surprise is vouchsafed' (1926: 197). He shared the role with his readers.

2

Adventurous Aquanauts

'We must not make a mess of the first stages of man's relationship to a new element.
Experimental psychology should guide us through the traps laid on the sea-bed.'
(Diolé 1954a: 21)

The 1950s is probably the richest period of underwater life writing: besides image-makers Hans Hass and Jacques-Yves Cousteau, discussed more in the next chapter, almost all the French pioneer divers turned out a book. Among Cousteau's intimates, Dumas, Tailliez, even the strong-man Falco produced memoirs; Diolé wrote several, all genre-bending. Along with first-person accounts were many generalist books that laid out histories of underwater exploration, usually going back to the ancients and encompassing a long history of diving machines and suits. Most of these used the liberating invention of scuba, particularly the Cousteau-Gagnan valve which made air supply assured and safe, as a turning point to adventuring in the present and its future possibilities. These generalist books were marketed to appeal to a readership that explicitly included new divers and general readers open to new ideas about underwater exploration's influence on human destiny. Comparisons with the emergent space age are made, but less often than one might expect: this underwater literature has a confidence in the significance of its own subject, dropping anchor in the past precisely because it is secure in the present.

With such a wealth of material, I discuss several themes and one author in depth. The change from goggling to scuba produced three currents to follow. One is how diving reconfigured natural history. The second is how underwater archaeology became a subject. The third is underwater metaphysics, exploring diver subjectivity through life writing. For this I go deep with Philippe Diolé who made it his speciality. 'Already, up there on the surface, the sceptics, the cavillers, the fanatics, are busy commenting, each in his own way, upon the great adventure. "Just another form of snobbery," say some; "a literary affectation", "a new sport" – and others, "a revelation". Maybe it is still too soon to say exactly what it is' (Diolé 1957: 189). Others too wrote of strange beauty, eerie solitude, fear, loneliness, wonder and elation. Some had read Beebe, mostly his bathyscape account in *Half Mile Down*, where humans dangle in a tiny sphere in unearthly deeps; many drew on their own experience in shallower water to convey adventurous thrills.

These thrills were radically new. Thanks to scuba's rapid popularizing, a new species of large mammalian fish have been observed in the last few years one eyed monsters shaped and colored like nude human beings with green rubber tail fins, gills of metal, and tubular scales on their backs. They are called Cousteau Divers. They swim around sportively at hundred-foot depths, examining sunken ships, taking photographs, and harpooning big fish.

(Dugan 1948: 16)

'[T]he "fish-man" is a reality ... a wonderful story' wrote Gilbert Doukan (1957: 14), who wrote nine admiring pages on the workings of the Cousteau-Gagnan apparatus in his generalist book. Then he turned philosophical:

Man is an insatiable animal. It is only recently that he has penetrated the secret of the seas: his erstwhile great enemy now welcomes him to her bosom. There he can breathe for hours, without fear, without weight, moving freely among the host of the fish and living like them. He no longer fears the Kraken, the Maëlstrom, or the ferocious divinities who rule the undersea kingdom. But still he is not satisfied. Tempted now by those glaucous blue depths, which seem so infinite and so attractive, he seeks to challenge their mystery, to violate with his presence the unexplored abysses of Neptune's stronghold.

(Doukan 1957: 169)

This is prose soaked in a multiplicity of myths. In its phallocratic fantasy – to penetrate, tempt, violate – and a jumble of legends, classical gods and transcendental rivals, it appeals to transgression and conquest. Restlessness is made purposeful: humans can go anywhere.

Much has been made of the overlap between underwater and space exploration, for instance by Helen Rozwadowski, who tracks a frontier metaphor common to both (2018: 202–5). Even myth-saturated Doukan alluded to divers as men and women of the jet age. But Doukan's model of his species is interestingly unmodern: it is feudal, fighting, fortressed. It both recognizes and refuses fear, specifically an anxiety that something else – figured as someone else – is more powerful than Man. Technological innovation is often described as a leap forward but backward-looking shadows it underwater. Cousteau and his comrades make these sorts of claims much more than other underwater writers: what Falco referred to as 'the spirit of Calypso' adds at least a dash of grandiosity to their writing. They promoted French notability chauvinistically, comparing national success in the air to pioneer French achievements underwater. In Doukan's drolly grandiose claim,

When it comes to exploring the depths, priority must be given to Rouquayrol and Denayrouze, Boutan, Le Prieur, and Cousteau. Perhaps there is some argument that would prove that the French mind, often taxed with levity and superficiality, is, in fact, naturally inclined to try to get to the bottom of things rather than to remain on their surface ...

(Doukan 1957: 255)

Yet Doukan acknowledged the inescapably inter-national and international reach of scuba. One American complained, 'I have always been irked that Cousteau gets credit for inventing scuba when we had ours in 1937' (Tillman and Perry 2001: n.p.). Even the acronym S.C.U.B.A. (Self-Contained Underwater Breathing Apparatus) was contested; diving pioneers Albert Tillman and Zale Perry attribute it to a fellow American, Christian J. Lambertson in 1954 (2001: n.p.). The *OED* attributes first use to Lambertson and Hahn in 1952. Cousteau's gear triumphed through wider marketing, especially by René Bussoz, another skinny Frenchman, who sold Aqualung sets. Two million pairs of fins along Corlieu's design were sold in US by 1954; sadly it was little known that Benjamin Franklin had experimented with hand fins, in the form of painters' palettes (Dugan 1960: 24–5). But there was less life writing about underwater adventures in the United States, and little archaeology. 'New World activity in this area cannot compare in volume or scope with the work carried out in the Mediterranean' (Goggin 1960: 348).

THE MEDITERRANEAN

The Mediterranean is a crucial frame for reading French underwater life writing of the 1950s. Scuba enabled a sort of underwater imperialism in which engagement with archaeology created continuity with ancient civilizations. Underwater books cast the Mediterranean as an organic entity, almost a literary character, that gave a context both familiar and fresh to discoveries. Writing of 'the dawn of historical civilisation', an undated moment, Pierre de Latil and Jean Rivoire propose 'What the sea was then to Phoenician or Cretan seamen it still is today both to poor fishermen toiling to secure a living from its depths, and to rich men who sail over its surface for pleasure' (1956: 22). They were in tune with Fernand Braudel's immense and magisterial history of the Mediterranean which he drafted in a German prisoner-of-war camp and published in 1949. It became a highly influential book in the Anglophone world when translated into English in the 1970s. Braudel's Mediterranean is not limited to the sea, but uses the sea to link 'three levels of time and their contingent realm of inquiry – the long term of geography, the conjuncture of structures, and the short term of events' (Marino 2004: 639). The sea was a connective element, argued Braudel:

> The Mediterranean as a unit, with its creative space, the amazing freedom of its sea-routes … with its many regions, so different yet so alike, its cities born of movement, its complementary populations, its congenital enmities, is the unceasing work of human hands; but those hands have had to build with unpromising material, a natural environment far from fertile and often cruel, one that has imposed its own long lasting limitations and obstacles.
> (Braudel 1976: 1,239, quoted by Horden and Purcell 2006: 724)

Two historians reconsidering Braudel agree with him that the Mediterranean can be considered individual: 'its distinctive historical regimes of connectivity actually turn out to be very unusual, and notably hard to parallel in other parts of the world' (Horden and Purcell 2006: 738).

Take the example of the movement of people and goods. In traditional Mediterranean history, what was visible was high commerce, the glamorous movement of high-value cargoes. This is also what was most prominent in the evidence from antiquity, and it was regularly marginalized as 'only' luxury trade, small-scale and of interest primarily to the elite. Even for the early modern period, Braudel had to insist that high-value cargoes mattered economically, too.

(Horden and Purcell 2006: 738)

Underwater archaeology revealed the significance of low-value, high-bulk cargoes too. Writers stressed a trade involving mass production – thousands of amphoras! – by nameless workers who left traces of their lives in wrecks with on-deck smelters and cooking pots, and who shipped goods between places not famous as ports, nor for glamour or luxury. The Annales school to which Braudel belonged has a tagline, 'history from below'. The phrase is from E. P. Thompson (1966: 279). History from below the waves could materialize everyday life as well as recuperate glittering statues intended for temples. Casting finds as part of Mediterranean identity, diver-writers filled out blanks in the *Mare incognitum* and joined them up to what one book reverentially called 'the Miracle of the Mediterranean' (de Latil and Rivoire 1956: 22). Although Cousteau and Hass took diving to other seas, many first-wave scuba authors saw the Mediterranean as their marine terroir: 'The Mediterranean, fortunately, is the sea most favourable to divers and most fruitful to historians' (Diolé 1954b: 159).

Besides a Mediterranean prepossession, much underwater life writing of this era flags up species-interest in its book titles. *Man and the Underwater World* (de Latil and Rivoire) could stand as a generic, or *Man Explores the Sea* (Dugan), or *Men and Sharks* (Hass). Ostensibly Man stands for *Homo sapiens*. It also, obviously, defines species through masculinity. Hardly any women feature. De Latil and Rivoire's French title, *À la Recherche du Monde Marin* (1954), had a Proustian nod lost in translation. They position scuba as inclusive: 'in recent years there has been a great change. Today I can, you can, he can – and that very definitely includes she! – they can, in fact we all can, go down safely and freely into the depths of this erstwhile forbidden world' (1956: 17). This comes after an offensive remark about the ugliness of Englishwomen. One Englishwoman – whose good looks made her in demand to model diving suits – shows how *she* very definitely could dive. Rowena Kerr, a pottery lecturer in the West Midlands, was celebrated in the local press for singlehandedly raising a sunken boat. She was also an expert demonstrator for the British Sub-Aqua Club. BSAC's early promotional films star women who led the way underwater and treat diving as a way to have fun on equal terms with men (BSAC *c.*1960; Wilson 2022). You would never guess this from the relentlessly masculinist books. A rare glimpse comes from 1966 when Cousteau addressed the annual conference of the British Sub-Aqua Club, with a film and talk about his underwater living project, Conshelf III. But 'the laugh of this Conference was provided by the British girl who got up and asked Cousteau why all his underwater livers were men – weren't women welcome down there?' (McKee 1967: 276). Cousteau was floored for a reply.

A few women did write, notably American ichthyologist Eugenie Clark, discussed in the next chapter. Photographer Anita Conti went with a trawler from Brittany to document the world of cod fishing in Newfoundland, sharing her tiny storm-tossed cabin with an auk and writing a gripping account, *Racleurs d'océans* (1953), translated into English as *Deep Sea Saga* (1955). Sharing the tough conditions of the trawlermen, even she does not escape masculine symbolizing. The captain has what he thinks is a magnificent idea for her first film: 'I was to climb into the belly of the shark [a gigantic Greenland shark] which would be hoisted up by the tail above the deck, and he, Captain Richer, would slit open the belly of the Beast to deliver the Daughter of the Sea' (Conti 1955: 157). Ever a good sport, Conti and her pet auk were pushed into the greasy, stinking shark cavity, then valiantly delivered. Conti's friend Philippe Diolé used some of her fine photographs in *The Undersea Adventure*. Although not a diver, she was emphatically a pioneering oceanographer, publishing in 1957 *Géants des mers chaudes*, 'giants' being mostly sharks encountered on the coast of West Africa. Much of her work presciently exposed the destructive consequences of overfishing (Lefebure 1995).

But most men's diving literature erased women as participants in underwater activities. Supervising Roman columns being raised from the waters of Saint-Tropez, Professor Henri Broussard went down in a helmet, amid a crowd of onlookers underwater.

> He smiled indulgently behind the glass pane of his 'port-hole', like some paternal and friendly sea-god in a group of half-naked immortals. But when he noticed that one of the ladies of the group was preparing to pass to him one of the slings, which tear the hands and break the nails, a reproving bubble escaped from his helmet, and it was clear from the faces he pulled that he thought this was no work for women.
>
> (Diolé 1957a: 119)

With annoying irony, one edition's paperback cover shows a shapely young woman in scuba gear bringing an amphora to the surface. One might laugh at face-pulling professors, especially if you are Rowena Kerr refloating a boat singlehanded, but the sexism is hard work. Even Diolé, who writes frankly about diving with two clearly capable women, is seduced by language loaded with bias. Discussing sirens and mermaids, he opines

> All the carnal weight of the women entrusted to the sea does not evoke either the scales, or the fins of marine monsters. Women divers show the softest, the smoothest femininity. They belong to a foreign voluptuousness, voluptuousness of another world which has nothing to do with a clash of scales and a fish spawning.
>
> (Diolé 1954a: 189, my translation)

This sentiment appears in a book whose cover shows an attractive young woman diving, in a tight swimsuit. Other covers are full of male images, from Glaucus with trident and beard to Ley Kenyon on a diving ladder, patriarchal counterweight to inclusive aims like Diolé's in a different book: '*I have tried to make diving an intimate, friendly affair ... I have wanted, if nothing else, to show that life underwater is within the reach of everyone*' (Diolé 1954b: 6, his italics). Much more common is the sort of stereotyping found in a caption to an illustration of Aqualung scuba kit: 'The face of this modern siren is invisible [behind her mask], but somehow we know she is beautiful' (de Latil

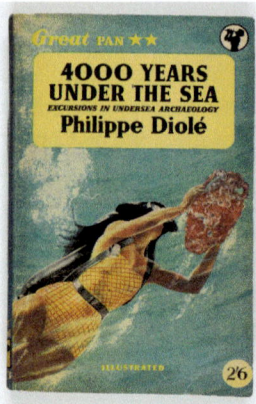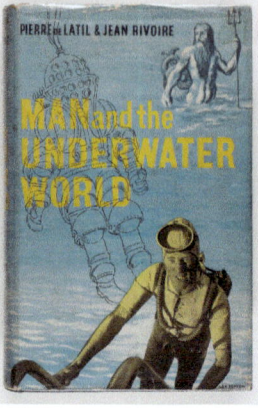

Figure 4 Gendering by book jackets – note the bubbles!

and Rivoire 1956: 240). Modern sirens had some outstanding skills: a film about a pioneering excavation in 1960 off Cape Gelidonia (near Bodrum in Turkey) shows Susan Woolmer making impeccable drawings; she sits midwater with perfect buoyancy control and all the calm of a levitating fakir (Duthuit 1962: 11'52; Green 2016: 476-8).

FROM GOGGLING TO HUNTING

The Mediterranean had divers before scuba – besides Greek sponge divers, some of whom were helmeted, there were free divers, who were hampered by not being able to see properly underwater. This liability was soon resolved. Between 1935 and 1940 along the Côte d'Azur, inventors were busy. 'We pooled our ideas and efforts in the same brotherly crucible. Very curious contraptions came out of it: weird-shaped harpoons, spring guns, rubber propelled harpoon guns, watertight cameras. We concocted goggles out of car inner tubes mounted over small circular or oval glasses – Cousteau had cut out a standard model to fit all faces' (Tailliez 1954: 19). Alex Kramarenko, a Russian who had spent three years in Japan where divers had goggles, hit on the idea of a single pane, set in moulded rubber, and patented it in 1937. Maxine Forjot, based in Nice, extended the mask to cover the nose too, making equalizing a simple matter of pinching your nose and breathing out. 'With this the "classic" underwater mask had been found: eyes and nose enclosed in the mask, mouth in contact with the water' (De Latil and Rivoire 1956: 234). Rubber fins were patented by de Corlieu in 1935, though divers could make their own from gluing two slices of rubber together (Tailliez 1954: 19). 'We must indeed confess that there was nothing very impressive about our tackle. Small welder's goggles edged with black rubber gave us the popeyed appearance of a turbot', wrote one pioneer (Doukan 1957: 19). Splendid biographical research by David Wilson recovers other names, like the four Pulvénis brothers. They had relocated from Mauritius to Nice; Roger and Raymond were famed for spearfishing. With Paul and Edmond, they were endlessly inventive. Roger combined a spring-action Eureka pistol with a metal tipped dart, a bicycle pump, steel spear and spring to fashion a deadly underwater gun. He also designed a mask with rubber enema bulbs to relieve pressure on face space. Between them they devised a breathing tube, to be fitted at the end of their garden hose air supply, which they called a 'tuba' (Wilson 2021). Known everywhere else as a schnorkel, then snorkel, it shows how inventions appeared, converged and travelled in multiple, merging histories which underwater life writers reported variously.

The whole enterprise of home-made self-sufficiency was popularized by an eccentric American, Guy Gilpatric, who popped up in the waters near Cannes to astound locals. In 1938 he published a book, *The Compleat Goggler*. Tailliez gave a copy to Cousteau. Mimicking Izaak Walton's *The Compleat Angler* (1653), Gilpatric cheerfully set forth '*the Proper Manner of Making the Goggles, Spears & Other Needful Gadgets Together with Descriptions of Many Marvels Witnessed Upon the Bottom of the Sea And Fully Exposing the Author's Cunning Methods of Swimming, Diving and Spearing Fish & Octopi*' (1938). One account says Gilpatric heard from a Yugoslav who heard from a Greek in Italy that Japanese divers in Naples were wearing single-plane masks (Dugan 1960: 22). In this frenzy of inter-nationalism, 'Everybody on the Riviera seems to have thought of tucking the nose inside at the same time' (Dugan 1960: 22). This was despite there being a full face mask refined by Yves le Prieur from a breathing apparatus designed by Maurice Fernier in 1925. It was allegedly Tailliez who discovered if you rub spit on the glass interior and rinse it off, a mask won't fog.

Gilpatric's goggling catalysed interest among hunters. 'I believe that there was not a single ship of the Mediterranean Fleet, from the cruiser to despatch boat, in the years 1937-9, on which some fanatical junior officer was not secretly constructing, with the complicity of the ship's workshop staff, a powerful harquebus designed for mérou hunting', wrote Philippe Tailliez (1954: 20). By 1938, hunting inventions proliferated: 'Piano wires, double, triple, quadruple; barbs which open cruelly in the flesh and secure the unfortunate prey; winglike appendages, encased in innocent-seeming grooves, which open out wickedly to form a cross – every sort of device is pressed into service by man in order to affirm his domination' (Doukan 1957: 30). It became so popular France introduced a law that forbad hunting with breathing equipment; even so, 'In 1941, no fewer than four different underwater hunting equipment manufacturers operated within the city of Nice' (Wilson 2021). The Second World War gave underwater fishing new meaning: Albert Falco was one of many who later told of slipping past German guards to hunt fish or lobsters for much-needed food or income.

The rush of hunters had contradictory consequences. On the one hand, it seriously depleted fish populations, especially grouper, the Med's big fish. 'The brutal fact was there: in forty-eight hours, after only four contacts with humans, a mass of fishes of very diverse species, careless and without any mistrust, had become almost completely unapproachable by two underwater hunters, experienced ones at that' (Doukan 1957: 102). Fish became mistrustful and moved into deeper water where possible. On the other hand, hunters became knowledgeable about fish habits, and some turned their interest to natural history, swapping spearguns for cameras. One described his conversion: 'when their little eye seems to stare at me in their last convulsion of agony, I have a horrible impression that they are judging me, that they feel sorry for me, and I am ashamed' (Doukan 1957: 92). Scuba came too late, thought Diolé, to change fish suspicion of humans: 'I can remember the time when fish were less frightened for their lives and would come up to nose my harpoon. Now their education is complete, they know we are murderers and flee at sight. I believe we have missed a wonderful opportunity, a possible friendliness such as the birds gave to Saint Francis' (Diolé 1954b: 51-2). A film by Cousteau, *Ten Fathoms Deep* (1952), which combined footage from several early films, showed a fearless diver entering the water and exploring a wreck from which he takes a souvenir amphora and modern crockery. As he leaves, the voiceover proclaims that the fish return to their home, adding 'And who knows what swift monster, with a shark's hunger and a thousand teeth, uses this for a private game preserve?' The rhetorical question had an answer clearly shown: Man, hunting. 'Captain Cousteau, passionately fond of the sea, does not deny that he has acquired an untiring curiosity about everything that lies in its depths through the practice of underwater hunting' (Doukan 1957: 160). Underwater hunters did contribute to understanding fish behaviours. Léon Bertin, professor of ichthyology in France's Natural History Museum, praised their observations: 'it goes without saying that *the diving hunter is the only person in the world who is able to give us information* ... When a Gorsky brings me a real-life account of some of his observations on fish, and a Cousteau moreover illustrates that data with remarkable photographs, I consider that they render science an exceptional service' (Doukan 1957: 46-7; his italics). Some professors learnt to dive, reporting that the study of live fish, rather than dead specimens or drawings, was transformational. The sea was still an unread book, it was agreed, but divers were filling in blank pages (Doukan 1957: 92).

For the proper study of underwater environments, 'one state only need be acquired – that of being, in the water, able to see, to move with as much ease as on land, to look, to compare, to capture, to comprehend the situation directly' (Doukan 1957: 8). Above all it was fish who attracted human scopic regimes, power through looking.

> Does not the exploration of the seas attract you more than the perusal of dusty books in gloomy museum libraries? Of course nomenclature, classification, and characteristics are of undoubted interest, but who alone gains those revealing glimpses of the true life and habits of a species, who is able to intercept those glances, cunning or it may be baleful or icy, from the creatures' living eyes, who if not the underwater hunters and explorers?
>
> (Doukan 1957: 52-3)

Old books said squat lobsters were rare and lived in sand; divers proved they were abundant and made homes in rocks. 'A few more books like this, and we will begin to think that aqua-lunging is really a useful means of obtaining biological information after all,' wrote a reviewer of Pierre de Latil's *The Underwater Naturalist* (Hedgpeth 1956: 143).

UNDERWATER ARCHAEOLOGY

Writers of diving history in the 1950s knew about earlier treasure hunting. Researching his book, James Dugan met up with Captain Damant who had led the long and dangerous recovery of £5 million in gold bars from the *Laurentic*, a White Star liner sunk by a U-boat in World War One. Damant knew he was history, saying 'why don't you write about these new chaps, the frogmen, all lashed up with T.V. sets?' (Dugan 1960: 90). Between the two points of helmet and camera-assisted diving was a period of extraordinary development and the birth of a new subject: underwater archaeology.

First, some thoughts about shipwrecks. All sorts of objects and people are lost at sea, but it is shipwrecks that produce the strongest hauntology, the persistence of elements from the past in ghostly form. The concept is Derrida's, in *Specters of Marx* (1993). Sarah A. Rich has adapted this to hauntography, the literary placing of underwater haunting, arguing that 'like ghosts in a flooded and forgotten storm cellar, shipwreck realities are so far removed from our own that they exist in a kind of ontological void' (2021: 14). Rich proposes that because of the ship's symbolic relations to the human body, wreck investigation is analogous to resurrection, especially in the early modern period, but also now through digital technologies, so that the scientist becomes a kind of saviour enabling spiritual as well as material restoration. Fascination with the *Titanic*, a wreck finally located in 1985 by a joint French–American expedition led by Jean-Louis Michel and Robert Ballard, lends credence to this idea of hauntography. It is animated by continuing arguments about whether the *Titanic* should be respected as a mass grave and left alone, or skimmed of objects including personal articles that can be lucratively displayed in a touring museum. Hauntography amplifies in the melancholy disappearance of the wreck itself, steadily consumed by iron-eating bacteria. But in the 1950s, a less romantic attitude is also evident. Wreck-exploring was simply one of many things to do underwater, as demonstrated in Cousteau's film *Shipwreck* (*Épave*, 1943), and the everyday activities of groups like the Club Alpin Sous-Marin of Cannes. Its programme for 1946 offered excursions, explorations, submarine archaeology, swimming, nautical sports and underwater hunting. Three years later it changed hunting into ichthyology (Dugan 1960: 285–6).

Although two world wars spread interest in wrecks around the world's oceans, the Mediterranean had a special hauntography. Dugan quoted Flaubert, who as a young man was moved by the thought of Roman keels cutting across the sea in front of him: 'here the absence of tides which divide time in regular periods seems to make you forget that the past is far distant and that centuries separate you from Cleopatra' (Dugan 1960: 226). It was not the return of the repressed so much as awareness of interlacing times, in which the present held new conditional futures. 'The Mediterranean is an underwater museum still awaiting its visitors. … The secrets of 4000 years lie in these undredged waters. … All we need is a compressed air-flask, method and financial backing' (Diolé 1954b: 164). For Diolé, retrieving objects was secondary to hauntology: 'Bringing fragments of amphora or anchor out of the sea seems to me to be a trivial job compared to the task of conjuring up the ghosts of the marine past' (1957a: 30). Yet archaeology, he thought, could join in: 'There is much in common between the loneliness of diving and the loneliness of ruins … In both there seems to be hidden some secret close to man's heart' (1957a: 174). Channelling Gaston Bachelard, who wrote of the soul's past as deep water and indeed all description of times past requiring terms of depth, Diolé thought underwater challenged how historians described culture. 'Speaking of civilisations they use, uneasily, words drawn from the vocabulary of architecture –

fragility, solidity, collapse. In the water we think no longer in terms of buildings, but of currents, vibrations and alluvial deposits. Is all this just … a quarrel over words?' (Diolé 1957b: 152).

The obscurity of many wreck locations was part of hauntology, surviving the joy of discovery. At Grand Congloué, where a Greek galley laden with pottery was excavated by Cousteau in 1952, Jean Rivoire embraced spectrality. 'From the moment I left the world of the sun and the air the world of shadows, phantoms and mystery down below obsessed me' (de Latil and Rivoire 1956: 287). Even pragmatic Dumas responded to the haunting effects of everyday objects, and complained archaeologists were too interested in art objects (1976: 57). The distinction was tricky. One item brought up at Antikythera proved to be half an astronomical clock – later studied by Derek Price, it might have related to a mechanism retrieved there in 1901, which Price identified as a planetary computer dating from *c*.80 BCE (Turner 1984). Tensions between archaeologists trained on land and divers learning archaeological skills were mostly resolved through agreement on methodical mapping techniques, though university-funded George Bass savaged Honor Frost in print for preferring divers to those (like himself) whom he saw as professional archaeologists (Bass 1964). Dumas, who liked Honor Frost and worked cheerfully with her at Bodrum, noted the status squabbles: 'The archaeologists alone remain in the status of poor relations. They produce nothing of commercial value and their study of warfare is rooted so far in the past that military men living in the atomic era are not interested' (Dumas 1976: 78). He admired their persistence. 'Joan [Throckmorton], Honor, and Bass spent hours, sometimes even whole days, trying to piece together, with the help of their sketches and underwater photos, the jumble of ingots and other little objects.' But he also got bored by their 'interminable discussions … [and] seemingly endless deliberations' (Dumas 1976: 94).

Wreck-finding stories often follow a pattern. A fisherman finds something. Objects appear in the market. Authorities are alerted and the hunt becomes officially approved. Despite difficulties of weather and equipment, the wreck is found, often buried in thick mud, investigated, emptied if possible and then left to marine life. Politics complicated the destination of objects, split between souvenir-hunting, black market and legitimate museums, usually local and underfunded. The tensions are central to David Devine's novel *Boy on a Dolphin* (1955) made into a film starring Sophia Loren and Alan Ladd. It features a sponge-diver who finds a classical statue of a boy riding on a dolphin, which may go to either a millionaire collector, profitably, or to the Greek authorities, patriotically. Fact followed fiction: two years later, a bronze statuette of Artemis was uncannily found near Delos, the novel's setting. It was swiftly claimed for the National Museum.

Dumas, who had a Roman bath and other antiquities in his own garden, deplored other divers raiding wrecks. A wrecked tile ship at Ile Pomègues attracted hunters: 'despite their lack of commercial value, the tiles still attracted divers, the urge to pilfer being so strong that a goodly number of tiles were hauled off to be used as table tops and as brick for a garden wall or patio' (Dumas 1976: 112). Dumas devoted a chapter to 'pillage'; he blamed foreign visitors, 'hordes of pink, chubby little divers from Germany, Belgium, and Switzerland [who] set out in feverish pursuit of nautical souvenirs' (1976: 72). Amphorae adorned restaurants, nightclubs and shops along the coast, soon to be glamorously transformed thanks to Brigitte Bardot and Roger Vadim who came to Saint-Tropez to film *And God Created Woman* (1956). Bardot knew something of underwater archaeology. Aged seventeen and wearing skimpy bikinis, she starred in a 1952 film *Manina, the Girl in the Bikini*, shot partly in Cannes and Nice, in which Gérard, a student, discovers a fragment of Phoenician amphora in Corsica. Several years later he embarks on a smuggling boat, looking for the treasure he thinks he has found. Then he falls in love ... but underwater archaeology drives a desire equal to sexual passion.

Underwater memoirists were honest about mistakes, and lessons learnt. If marine archaeology was 'a science founded without scientists', in Dugan's phrase (1960: 239), divers tried hard to design approaches to sites and materials that were physically sensitive. It was arduous, exhausting work. At Mahdia the divers lay in thick slime, stirring it up with their bodies, digging into it with their hands, or wrangling high-pressure air lines which churned up more mud (Tailliez 1954: 96). 'Clouds of mud have plagued me on almost every archaeological project', wrote Dumas (1976: 71). Divers agreed it was important to construct context as fully as possible. But working underwater changed what a context could be, profoundly. 'For once one has become involved with the sea one finds oneself dealing with one branch of knowledge after another', said Tailliez (1954: 68). In all the underwater disturbances of time, authors underwater excavated their own depths. Diolé dives deepest, so I dive with him next.

HAUNTING PSYCHOLOGIES

Strange things happening underwater were often attributed simply to narcosis. Celebrating a coral reef near Grand Congloué profuse with varied sponges, Tailliez felt inarticulate, then remembered some lines from Rimbaud's 'Le Bateau Ivre' ('I dreamed the green night of extravagant snow;/Kiss of the ocean ...'). He became euphoric and began to sing the Marseillaise, loudly. Cousteau hurried him upwards to recover from evident narcosis. But was it narcosis? Tailliez endorses a visionary dimension of underwater here, despite usually favouring plain prose. 'Words, paltry words – not even those that poets create have the power to suggest the sight of a deep underwater rockface in this vision', he wrote (Tailliez 1954: 62). Damien Bright and Roy Kimmey have argued that scuba's success turned on seeming to slip the tethers that bound man to earth, figuratively, or to a support vessel, literally (2021). Cousteau's sales prospectus put the challenge: 'Have you realized that the great depths are now accessible to you?' (Doukan 1957: 202). This sales pitch for scuba promoted physical freedom, appealing to novices. To more experienced divers, however, there was metaphysical freedom and of a kind not encountered before or available elsewhere. Especially for the solitary diver, solitude underwater made it possible to enter what was gradually being called 'inner space'. The phrase comes from British author J. B. Priestley, who was critiquing stories of space exploration and aliens; he thought them symptoms of men hurrying away from inner life and the unconscious, and recommended several centuries of matriarchy as an antidote (Priestley 1957). Rhetorics of mastery and conquest associated especially with Cousteau sound loudest, but other voices explored subtler, inner forms of depth – for instance, 'the proud moment when one's personality, left on its own, is confronted with an unknown world, a confrontation that remains thrilling no matter how experienced one becomes' (Doukan 1957: 202).

Diolé had read Bachelard's book on water and dreams, and it was in the language of dream that he bravely engaged to explore underwater's inner effects. 'Diving means not only the sure handling of our most valued images, but coming face to face with our dreams' (1957: 8). His category of dreams, like Bachelard's of reverie, turned not on conscious aspirations, though he did include those, but on poetic, psychoanalytic thresholds. 'This porosity of the spirit, so sensitive in the sea, could well have its equivalent in the night, in the dream' (1954: 177; all my translations). Psyche was more important to him than body, though he was eloquent about the body underwater and uncertain about what name best fitted his investigations – possibly 'fossil psychology', a mash-up of ancient and modern, or 'psychological paleontology, a region still to obscure to travel'. It was, he admitted, a 'strange programme which I have drawn up for myself, a mixture of archaeology and dream, an attempt to get closer to the essence of the universe through the medium of the sea' (1957: 135).

> My suitcases contain a kind of marine humanism also, projected sciences which I have been trying for several years to test under water: I have not only dreamed of an archaeology and history of the deep, but also of taking psychology to the sea-bed, away from the shore where it flounders about in the pools like a nervous algologist.
>
> (Diolé 1957a: 20)

Diolé made an extensive collection of seaweeds, so his simile is self-knowing. Where J. B. Priestley deplored science fiction's raids on fables and legends, Diolé argued modernity had moved from fable to image but needed marvels, magic and myths from the Greek and pre-Greek world to make modern understanding of the depths less clumsy (1957: 21–2). The sea, he thought, spiritualized those open to it. 'As to the mystic symbols born of the sea – the spiral, the fish, the sea-fan and the anchor – they are endlessly persistent. They are older than gold, older than minted money' (1957: 165).

Diolé shared some attitudes of his time, but he is the most imaginative of all the divers; his writings test orthodoxies and dissolve boundaries. Where Cousteau was multimedia from the start, keenest on making films, Diolé, whose life was quite restless (he travelled in India and Africa), thought of underwater as philosophically entrancing, metaphysically rich and strange. He understood Mediterranean history as a binding force – one he explored in depth through Sicily, a criss-crossing point of civilizations. 'Along those sea lanes, Egypt, Crete, Phoenicia, Athens, Carthage, Rome, Byzantium, Vandals, Arabs and Normans lost their ships. And now we know that the sea preserves their remains' (Diolé 1954b: 160). Archaeology needed hauntography's attention to immaterial histories:

> A diver going down to a wreck must bear in mind the names of all races whose ships may once have sailed these seas, must conjure up their Gods, their skill, their aims and wealth, and bring all this to bear upon the ghost ship plunged in

mud, overgrown with seaweed, and only a dim outline in the blue half-light of under water.

(Diolé 1954b: 160)

Where others created timelines of diving inventions as a history of stages on the way to conquest, he handled diving as a combination of physical and inner movement, filtered through first-hand observation which was timeless because poetic. 'Poetry is the medium through which we grope at expression' (1954a: 129). That medium was open to anyone open to it, as 'a favour that the sea accords right away to a diver of sensibility. He only needs a minimum of gifts; a certain skill in the water, a quality of awe, curiosity. A submarine sensibility will one day become one of the attributes of the cultivated man, like taste or an ear for music' (1954a: 137). He was suspicious of photography; despite the difficulties of underwater language, he suggested '[p]erhaps the world of water is more naturally accessible to the writer than to the artist. This shadowless light, spilling out in all directions, these congealed back drops, with their melancholy impressiveness, can be painted with words' (1954a: 141).

Diolé's title *The Undersea Adventure* was cleverly not about adventures, in a narrative sense; his opening line is 'I have no "stories" to tell.' Instead he gives a presentist sense of presence, 'breaking the surface of the sea, roaming about in the deep waters of the ocean, going down slowly, eyes open, watching the flicker of mullet and the dance of sea-bream, the butterflies of these liquid skies: this does not make up a "story"' (1954a: 11). Though studying marine life was pleasurable, he pursued a deeper seriousness. 'To lose one's head over diving is only the beginning: the next step is knowing how to get the most benefit, once the sea has closed over you, out of this state of being a live, drowned man. One has to learn to be worthy of one's position as a "melted body"' (1954a: 18). Benefit came through heightened senses, attention to light, to fish, to words. 'But who thinks down here? Who speaks? Alone? Not quite.' He self-narrates a self that overspills a first-person pronoun – as many of this underwater life writing generation do. But where others make the collective identity of divers into aspirational Man, Diolé hunts for inspiration to understand the limits of the human condition:

I have known for a long time that the monologue of underwater wandering was in fact a dialogue. And sometimes an impassioned dialogue. … What should one seek down here? Rest? Life? The purlieus of death? Limbo? Dreams? A mystical communion with the universe?

(1957: 117-19)

Words become ghosts of what they refer to on land. Rather than mastery and conquest, Diolé brings a sense of the uncanny: man is not at home here. 'We remain mere creatures of the earth, intruders into, obsequious and awkward visitors in, a world where we do not belong. The Sea has conquered Man' (1957a: 9). Yet the mind, cut loose from a solid world, could develop new imaginative reflexes by being open to a stream of images. Solitary diving was more conducive to this than the companionable kind:

I love nothing so much as setting out, dressed in an old sweater, and diving when and where I will. My chief enjoyment is to move slowly through the water, or to stand stock still with leisure enough to mutter over to myself, down there beneath the surface, all the words that have become so mightily enriched by their sea-associations, that I may compare them with my memory-distorted dream.

(1957a: 96)

What one might call autohauntography, the Diolé diver-dream in which unconscious elements disturb conscious language-making, including that about the unconscious, could be stabilized by Gestalt psychology, which explores how humans make sense of experience through pattern, association, context (thus you grasp a sentence, not a sequence of letter forms). Gestalt was popular in the 1950s, then rather displaced by 1960s neuroscience. It brought attention to how the whole is different from the sum of its parts. 'I have tried to use my eyes and understand the meaning of what was before me, and to fit together where I could the pieces of a vague jig-saw of the sea' (1954a: 12). Hence Diolé's focus on slow, careful descriptions – 'Dreams float up very slowly from the sea' – and aesthetic pattern: 'I swim between the huge pages of an illuminated manuscript. Now I am dazzled by the purity of the light, the luminous beauty of the deep' (1954a: 14-15).

Diolé's present-tense interiority expresses a preference for monologue, interesting given that he dialogically co-authored life writing with Cousteau and Falco. Gestalt methods could stabilize autohauntography by organizing impressions:

when I dive, my equipment consists of a camera, a salad basket for specimens, a weighted drawing-board, a pencil, carefully sharpened so that the lead does not come away from the wood, a notebook. That's a heavy load, but worth while for the joy of being able to list at leisure the plants on rocks below the surface or the creatures clinging to the walls of caves.

(1954a: 72)

Descriptions needed to include shape, colour, position – a classic Gestalt approach, which he described elsewhere as straightforward: all he had to do was settle on the pattern and write in the water (1954: 10). And yet even that had limitations. 'Try it and you will see how illusive the accurate, illuminating adjective can be, even with the time you get with self-contained diving gear and with the help of pencil and drawing-board' (1954a: 72).

The fluid elusivity of language, itself a kind of hauntology, meant Diolé continually crossed genre lines. He wrote two novels set underwater; they too dissolve conventions. One, *Au Bord de la Mer* (1954), announces it is neither a documentary nor a novel but the confession of a diver. Diolé's autofiction grapples with nuances of mood, sensation, desire, and how the philosophical ambience of underwater enables reflections on identity. A self in the water reaching out to another becomes an unstable construction, open to exhilaration and doubt. What Diolé calls enchantment is an erotic pattern of thought emanating from the flow of water, of narrative, of subjectivity, which all share a fluidity expressed through and found by diving. Noting that not everyone understood his evocation of underwater sensibility, he persisted in trying to articulate what he calls a psychological truth from the world of water that does not yet have a language. This is more important to him than describing the difficult resonances of a nearly-love affair, and a near-death dive. Underwater, the self's deep layers can be revealed – a haunting thought.

Diolé's deathly bond of a dive that runs out of air has analogies in Jean-Luc Godard's 1960 crime film *À bout de souffle*, 'Out of Breath', in which the man dies. Godard told Francois Truffaut, who began the project based on a newspaper story he had read, that "'Roughly speaking, the subject will be the story of a boy who thinks of death and of a girl who doesn't'" (Fotiade 2013: 29). Breath and death interwreathe. Diolé took up hauntography again in *L'Eau Profonde* (1959), a story about a diver clearing a dangerously sunk submarine who finds a body wedged in his way and who becomes immersed in trying to return the body to the man's wife. 'Nothing is erased in the Sea nor in ourselves. Is deep Water that of Death or that of Love?' (blurb). The same question drives *Au Bord de la Mer*, which can be described in several ways: as the story of a summer love triangle, a liaison made possible through the romance of diving; as the unfolding of a relationship in difficulties in which danger of death underwater heals love; as an account of intersecting subjectivity constructed through a riskily shared pursuit. Most of all it is a love affair with underwater, its atmospherics, powers of transformation and play of light and shadow upon human senses, including the sense of self in relation to others. In Diolé's poetic, philosophical and very French style, one can see weight falling on particular words, which carry psychoanalytic import, possibly consciously. One pattern involves light on bodies: '*lueur*', gleam, and '*chair*', flesh, indicate his attraction to the young woman, Jaky, who becomes attached to him and his partner, Marthe. In English flesh implies raw meat; we put flesh and blood together, and talk of fleshpots, disparagingly, as places of resort to carnal pleasures. In English skin and body are the usual words of erotic locus; there is something lost in translation. Rimbaud's poem 'Sol et Chair' (1870) makes flesh female and earthly; Diolé also embodies his women. But they too are open to '*le cheminement de l'eau*', the flow of water, which dissolves distinctions between body and spirit and transforms subjectivity: '*ils changent de densité jusqu'au coeur*', they change density to the core, the same word for heart.

'The direct physical and visible properties of water can provide a clear way of conceptualising and understanding the most abstract of feelings and emotions' (Walsh 2017: 49). Exploring Bachelard, Linda Walsh helpfully explains that he 'describes a series of vibrations associated with reverie, which stem from what he describes as *resonances* which are dispersed onto us from the object, *repercussions* which draw us deeply into ourselves, and *reverberations* which give us poetic power' (Walsh 2017: 61). The fluidity of water changes what Diolé might call the density of relations between these aspects of the process of the imagination, but since diving is a physical activity, often strenuous, in an environment unnatural to humans, the diver is unusually alert to the interplay of body and mind. Diving when upset is dangerous; you need psychological equilibrium. Depth can affect mood and the sea is also changeable. Underwater, human properties of fluidity interact with those of the sea.

You might uncharitably read Diolé's account as Rousseau-inflected confessions of a middle-aged man neglecting his partner in order to ogle a young woman in an underwater world that provides unusual and transparent cover. But where Rousseau's *Confessions* (1782) asserted a unique selfhood (Treadwell 2005), Diolé wants to explore the fluidity of underwater subjectivity. In other words, every dive makes interiority different, sometimes as simply as where you dive and with whom. Where others took up technologies as transformative, Diolé's underwater life writing engages with profound issues of relationality – and without quest or conquest narratives to provide easy explanations. Because underwater dangers make literal the possible death of the subject, hauntology shadows its literary expression.

HEALING MODERN MALAISE?

Diolé thought of scuba as a psychological advance, not a technological one. Modernity was not self-evidently progress. Between 1885 and 1910, he argued, 'curiosity about sea life was considerable', evidenced in many books and large audiences. That had gone. 'In less than 50 years ignorance of, and indifference to, marine life has become almost incredible' (1954a: 182). Yet scuba widened access to underwater. 'Civil servants and housewives, as soon as summer comes, put on goggles to gaze into the waters and to sample an enchantment which ten years ago was reserved for initiates. For children the magic of the sea is as commonplace as television and radar. I am not one of those who deplore it' (1954a: 19). But Diolé searched for something deeper than commonplace magic, as antidote to alienation. 'Like many others I do not feel in perfect harmony with our age and the solitude of diving lulls and stays a deep-rooted dissatisfaction. Down below, where dream and action move silently forward through the dense waters, side by side, man feels for a moment in tune with life' (1954a: 11). One of Freud's friends told Freud of a sensation of eternity, a feeling of something limitless, 'oceanic'. Freud was unsure where it fitted in his psychic inventory. At the end of *Civilization and Its Discontents* (1930), he suggested that mastery was problematic: 'Men have gained control over the forces of nature to such an extent that with their help they would have no difficulty in exterminating one another to the last man. They know this, and hence comes a large part of their current unrest, their unhappiness and their mood of anxiety' (Freud 2005: 53). The jet age was for some an exciting rush; for others, it brought ennui. 'The more lucid and literary will explain to you that this western world is dead ... everything is tamed and domesticated', complained Gilbert Doukan: even pygmies have seen the cinema and at the foot of Annapurna are posters advertising Coca-Cola. From this perspective, 'the universe of the depths is a world in which there is still something to know, to discover, to dream about' (Doukan 1957: 344). Doukan's terms here are not ones of conquest. He imagines a depressed friend who could find happiness by diving. Malaise would disappear in a dazzle of new activities – hunting, exploration, photography, cinematography, observation, applied biology – whose brilliance and beauty would stay with him throughout long winters in town. By diving, the friend can shed modern drudgery and defy its effects. In Freudian terms, he can return to infantile pleasures, satisfying primal needs:

The sea, from whence he came, has recognized him again as her child. He feels himself caught up in her rhythm and her spaciousness, linked to her by a thousand intimate bonds. And in the slow futile gnawing of the terrestrial hours in some administrative office or at some managerial desk, he will catch himself writing on his blotter, with a strange smile on his lips: 'O sea, infinite sea, O splendour of the depths!'

(Doukan 1957: 345)

Diolé too saw much at stake psychoanalytically. 'For me the stake of this sea-victory is no less than 20th-century Man, a creature so richly equipped with tools, yet so confused, so fragile. In the deep places of the waters he can find a refuge' (Diolé 1957b: 189). Cousteau and his confederates – of whom Diolé was unexpectedly one – treated underwater explorations as empowering adventures for an emergent *Homo aquaticus* who would be triumphant. Action beat reflection because 'The sea ... isn't the ideal place to think' (Dumas 1976: 157). Diolé made an underwater poetics that was unsettled, psychologically, because for him underwater was an ideal place to think.

3

Shark Lady, Shark Lords

Expectations about the oceans changed after the Second World War, as Helen M. Rozwadowski establishes: 'References to the ocean as frontier appeared soon after the war's end, most frequently alluding to either economic potential or new scientific knowledge' (2018: 163). 'Frontier' as a term is not obviously downwards, but underwater writers recognized they had a role in creating new knowledge. In this pioneer phase, there was a great surge of diving life writing – also of photography and film, so the books about underwater are emphatically part of a wider cultural nexus. But the literature is important for explaining its representations, including images; its plotlines explore distinct psychological depths. In this chapter I discuss a selection of texts – from a large corpus – that feature sharks. 'There is unquestionably an effect of physiological shock when, ascending from the bluish night of the depths, which impresses even the most hardened diver, into the submarine field of vision glides the powerful, massive, and savagely beautiful bulk of a shark' (Doukan 1957: 79). How divers responded was various. Discussing Hass's films for television, *Diving to Adventure* (1956), 'the first miniseries about the underwater realm', Margaret Cohen notes 'Footage of sharks swimming exhibits their power and authority ... along with a recognition that humans are not their preferred prey' (2022: 132, 145). Hass's books describe how he came to this recognition, and how meeting sharks created uncertainty about human power and authority underwater. The texts I take up were all translated into English, another mediation to consider, but a sign of their international circulation. They include: Hans Hass – *Men and Sharks* (1949, English edition 1954) *Diving to Adventure* (1952), *Under the Red Sea* (1952), *I Photographed under the Seven Seas* (1956); *We Come From The Sea* (1959); Lotte Hass, *Girl on the Ocean Floor* (1972), and Franco Prosperi, *Lord of the Sharks* (1955). Cousteau has a chapter in *The Silent World* (1953) 'Shark Close-Ups', which I draw on, and a later volume (1970) dedicated to sharks, co-written with his son Philippe.

European divers were keen to explore warmer waters like the Red Sea, the Caribbean, the Indian Ocean and the Pacific. Drawn by the cinematographic allure of colourful coral, they sought encounters with megafauna like the whale shark, newly recognized as gentle and beautiful, and the manta ray, also transforming from monster status. But most of all the diver-writers focused on sharks, whom many assumed to be a threat to their activities and hostile to human dominion underwater. At stake was human freedom and supremacy. 'Two rival lords cannot share the same domain', as Philippe

Cousteau put it, describing sharks as the Cain of the aquatic world, evil brother to the dolphin's Abel (1970: 49). The term 'shark lords', widely used, represents competitive engagement with sharks: in this chapter I track its significance. It is not an even story – the Cousteaus never liked sharks, and sharks suffered again from human paranoia when *Jaws* (1975) re-terrorized the seas (Hunter and Melia 2022). I read Eugenie Clark, known as the 'Shark Lady', for a more scientific, more humane approach to sharks. 'Shark lords' assumed masculinity in humans *and* sharks, a prejudice serving male chauvinism and human egotism. Clark, who worked on other species besides sharks, redresses the imbalance. I discuss her after a section on Hass and associated writers; ironically she rejoined the shark story as it became vicious again in the writing of Philippe Cousteau. Unlike his father, whose feelings towards sharks mellowed a little in the 1960s, Philippe invested heavily in antagonism. The full story is too big to cover here – Margaret Cohen discusses other parts of it on film (2022). It includes the activities of macho Australians like Ben Cropp in *Shark Hunters* (1964) which jubilantly records the poisoning, stabbing and shooting of all kinds of sharks – slaughter which in his words, and images, was 'Australia's most saleable subject' (Cropp 1965: 95). Cropp won Underwater Photographer of the Year in 1964. In a human-staged competition between the whale, majestic, artistic monarch of the seas, the friendly, playful, intelligent dolphin, and the heartless, vicious, man-eating shark, the shark won only a loser's prize in terms of fascination for humans: 'what maritime subject is more fascinating to everyone than the shark?' (Cousteau and Cousteau 1970: 5).

SHARK LORDING

Hans Hass is now overshadowed by Jacques Cousteau as underwater pioneer, but it was Hass rather than Cousteau who was originally associated with underwater thrills. 'For Adventure, the name is Hass', as *The Evening News* put it catchily in a blurb that became a tagline. Diving with rebreather apparatus rather than scuba, his dive-ography flagged up sharks:

> Diving Activities and Expeditions of Hans Hass: 1939, first expedition to tropical waters … 4000 underwater photographs … First pictures of sharks; 1942, in the Aegean, 'observation of sharks', 3000 underwater photographs; 1949, First expedition to Port Sudan on the Red Sea … 1500 underwater photographs … First pictures of sharks and mantas in the Red Sea; 1950, Second Red Sea expedition … 2300 underwater photographs. First pictures of whale-shark. … 1952, Great Barrier Reef, 1800 photographs, and 1953-4, on the *Xarifa*, to the Azores, Caribbean and Pacific, 3700 underwater photographs … First pictures of cachalots [sperm whales], hammerhead-sharks and tiger-sharks.
>
> (Hass 1956: 68)

In his second book, *Men and Sharks* (1942; film also 1942), Hass concentrated on sharks. Although Cousteau devoted a volume of his ocean series to sharks – *The Shark: Splendid Savage of the Sea*, co-written with Philippe Cousteau, 1970 – and the first episode of his internationally successful TV documentary series, *The Undersea*

World of Jacques Cousteau (1966–1976) was titled 'Sharks', it was Hass who first gave them equal billing, and more than twenty years earlier. Lotte Baierl, who had been his assistant and became his wife, was said in the 1950s to have a book in preparation (Hass 1956: 68), though *Girl on the Ocean Floor* was not published till 1970 (in German; translated into English two years later). It draws on a diary she kept at the time. Wikipedia notes, with no citation, that some critics 'mockingly titled "Lotte Baierl" as "Lotte Haierl"', or Lotte Shark. Franco Prosperi was a young Italian naturalist explicitly inspired by Hass, evident in his books *Lord of the Sharks* (1955) and *Vanished Continent* (1959) about Sri Lanka and the Comoro Islands respectively.

When Hass died in 2013, innumerable tributes referred to his nickname, 'Lord of the Sharks'. I have been unable to pinpoint who first used that nickname and when; it is ubiquitous now. By the mid-1950s, he was an obvious authority on sharks:

> *I have observed sharks of almost all species in the various seas I have visited. They only seldom made any serious attempt to attack me. Of course one should never show any fear of them, for the instinct of any beast of prey is to pursue fleeing game. Most sharks are timid and it is hard to get near them with the camera. In order to attract them it is necessary to await their approach quietly or else feign flight. ... Many species can be frightened by shouting at them through the water. Several are so sensitive to sound that they make off as soon as the shutter clicks.*
>
> (Hass 1956: 133; italics in original)

A consistent interest in sharks throughout his life and work runs alongside attention to all marine life forms. 'Not one of them could be understood without all the rest' (Hass 1954: 56-7).

One day in the Aegean Sea, Hass makes eight dives and triumphantly gets all the shark footage he wants. One sequence features a shark who is 'absolutely a born film star', despite his 'crafty look'. He is joined by a giant ray to munch fish peacefully together, as if in a zoo (Hass 1954: 174). A potentially dangerous cast turns out to be placid. But Hass also writes a wilder sequence about sharks which uniquely takes a shark point of view:

The shark is the concentrated essence of felinity. His whole body is in motion. His mighty tail fin barely sweeps the water, and he's gliding effortlessly along. For him there is no resistance. Eight or ten quick fin strokes, and he is flying through the sea at thirty-five, fifty, perhaps sixty miles an hour. And then a little turn and he swings aside. There's a fish before his maw: he surveys it with both eyes before he bites. Of course he does not turn over on his back, as people are always saying. There is something jolly in the way he snaps, in his pointed nose, in his supple motions. Something tremendously frolicsome – but the next moment he is lofty again, superior, almost arrogant. You approach him, and he never even notices. He swims quite casually on. What cares he for the vulgar herd? He is king of the sea, plays when he feels like it, takes what he wants, and swims on his way with no one knowing where it leads.

(Hass 1954: 214-15)

Here Hass recognizes that the shark, so perfectly adapted for ocean life, is king of the sea, not he. The description is remarkably free of the brute and monster terms that appear elsewhere. It gives the shark – always *he* – jouissance, and it makes humans insignificant.

Hass was unsentimental about his production cycle. A diver with a camera finds a subject, presses a button, makes photographs or films to sell. 'And with this money I pay for camera, ship, and expedition, and immediately we swim off somewhere else and the cycle beings anew' (Hass 1954: 215). Supplemented by public lectures, Hass's books also contributed to funds. Underwater writing supplied additional material for those interested in the films, and reveals a cycle of dive, film, book, or dive, book, film, connected by still images and descriptions of filming. 'Everything we see we are seeing not for ourselves alone, but equally for the cinema audience we hope will share our expedition' (Hass 1954: 64). This principle continued in *Diving to Adventure* and *Under the Red Sea*. Meeting hammerheads off Cocos, Hass was prepared, choosing the right positions to record them. 'Lotte had photographed and I had filmed a scene we had been waiting for through fifteen years' (Hass 1959: 236). Success came from intense preparations. After a strenuous day filming manta and whale sharks in the Red Sea, a diary-writing Lotte interprets Hass's silence as absorption in thoughts about shots, editing and cinema audiences. '*Only Hass is concerned with the whole scheme the whole time and to the exclusion of all else. For him this giant shark and we ourselves are figures on a chess board which he is using for his purpose, a purpose that is more important to him than all of us and his own self*' (Lotte Hass 1972: 59; her italics).

Margaret Cohen argues that 'After 1956, underwater documentation for a general public occurred increasingly in filmic media and dwindled in print, a trend that has continued to the present' (2014: 122). Readers of print, however, could be let into the process of making films. If the films made exploration seem easy, the books stressed it wasn't:

> What is not apparent on the screen is the almost insurmountable difficulty of such an enterprise: the years of technical preparation, of research and documentation; the financial obstacles involving substantial personal sacrifices for a crew of one hundred and fifty men; the thousands of dives in conventional diving suits, the hundreds of dives in the saucer, the hours passed shivering in the cold water or in the decompression chamber, the nights spent repairing a piece of essential equipment or a flooded camera, the tempests of sand, the tropical cyclones, the accidents that occur in a ship in the middle of an ocean, the agonies we experience when we lose trace of a diver or a saucer – and lastly the most direct of all these risks, those which Philippe is writing here – those which always accompany any meeting with sharks.
>
> (Cousteau and Cousteau 1970: xii)

Those using new technologies upheld old ones: 'Undersea television is totally incapable of replacing direct human observation' (Cousteau and Cousteau 1970: 160). And film would not tell you what Lotte does in the episode above, which is that the participants were tired, mentally exhausted and afraid. Shark lords could also be fallible humans.

Through shark encounters, Hass developed theories. In Curaçao he met a blue shark: 'I don't know what got into me. From everything I knew about sharks I should really have been afraid. But this creature was so handsome, so graceful ...' He swims towards it, 'armed only with the camera'; the shark comes closer and closer, then it spins round and disappears. 'The shark, the king of the sea, had fled before a small, unarmed human being. How could that be?' (1952: 128-9). Hass thinks the shark is frightened by meeting a creature simply not afraid of it, a psychological theory that instates human dominance. This theory accompanies another, that yelling at sharks can deflect and scatter them. Here he reasons that flapping fish speared on diver harpoons attract sharks by their vibrations; underwater yelling produces bigger vibrations so the sharks are deterred. Physiology of shark organs – the sensitivity of their lateral organs, principally – explains human-shark dynamics. '"Would be" and "probably", remember. For so far, with all its logic, this is merely a theory' (Hass 1952: 225). Here the latent question is whether a shark is merely a somatic creature or one with a mind. Where shark intelligence is ambiguous, human intelligence is assured. This reassures readers: they too could be shark lords.

Being eyed up by a shark or fixed with a fast-approaching stare made the shark gaze actively disturbing. Writers repeatedly notice shark eyes, regularly describing them as cold and evil. Hass's writing pays explicit attention to the gaze – his, the camera's, and any shark's gaze. Off Curaçao he is tracked by twin sharks, 'always close together, with wily, wicked eyes ... I grew so nervous that I finally thought I saw the sharks where they were not' (1952: 131). Hass's photographs of sharks are usually full body side view; it is difficult to make out eyes and their expression – or the presence of claspers to indicate a male. In *Diving to Adventure*, figures 26 and 27 split images of approaching shark and Hass into separate pictures united on the same page, with an overlap to suggest the same water. Over the page, figure 28 is an image of Hass in a strange pose – one leg back, like a tailfin, left arm down, like a shark's pectoral fin in threat mode, right arm up, holding a weapon, and the caption 'Why did the shark flee from me?' An image incorporated into the cover design, it shows Hass copying the body language of sharks, but with three important differences. He is armed, he is unafraid and his cheeks are distended, as if readying to shout. This is how a shark lord looks.

Franco Prosperi's *Lord of the Sharks* (1955) crowns him insecurely. The episode that gives rise to his nickname locally is emphatically ironic: the young divers are panicked by sharks, glad to get out uninjured, and happy to receive acclaim they know they don't deserve. His penultimate chapter, 'Are Sharks Man-eaters?', is careful and full of nuance. Hass's shouting deterrent can work on young sharks but not all. Shark behaviours vary with times of day, place and species. 'It follows that when researching on the behaviour of sharks, one should beware of drawing general conclusions, and should limit one's remarks to the area where the field-work has been carried out' (Prosperi 1955: 198).

Lotte Bairl went to the Red Sea as Hass's assistant and film eye-candy, a girl on the ocean floor. On one of her first dives she finds herself alone – Hass has gone back to the boat to sort his camera, her buddy Gerry has disappeared. Then she sees her first shark. 'It was as if I was hypnotized – I could neither move nor take my eyes off this creature that was coming towards me' (Lotte Hass 1972: 35). It approaches her, staring at her. She remembers Hass's advice – don't show fear and swim straight at it. But she

Figure 5 Book jacket design of Hans Hass, *Diving to Adventure: Harpoon and Camera under the Sea.* No shark is in view on the cover image.

is immobilized by fear. It comes closer, 'fascinatingly beautiful', then calmly departs. She thinks it just wanted to investigate her, and feels almost sympathetic: 'Never before had I seen such a harmonious combination of concentrated power and graceful movements.' Safely back in the boat, she writes in her diary about this close encounter, and her return to what she terms 'unreal life': '*Everything has become terrifyingly clear, and yet it is like a dream. I think I am very happy and simply a little afraid of being happy*' (Lotte Hass 1972: 37–8; her italics). Fear, terror, happiness: the dreamworld prompted by sharks is bewilderingly intense, and self-aware. 'As I wrote I saw the shark again clearly in front of me. The picture of his eyes full of interest, watching and waiting, was branded on my memory.' The shark is now he, not it, no longer cold and evil but cunning, curious, calm, majestic. What one might call the written shark is different from the underwater one: it has a symbolic presence, a masculine gender and a gaze at least equal to hers, full of curiosity. Like a photograph, 'the picture of his eyes' has lasting power.

Though Hass was bitten by a shark he tried to catch by the tail, Lotte implies fear of sharks is about symbolic power. As she quotes from her diary, '*Today O-Sheik told me that people think Hass must have had a letter from his God for the sharks, and that's why they don't do him any harm ...*' (Lotte Hass 1972: 148). In a later episode, supernaturally protected Hass is filming as usual when ten sharks show up. Lotte has company too:

> To my right was a fairly large shark coming straight at me. It was swimming a bare eight inches away from the coral. Like a gust of wind, it shot round my rock. Although it was considerably larger than I was, I felt myself superior, as though it were no more than a dog with which I was on very friendly terms. I had thrown it a stick and it was now bringing it back to me. One voice inside me said: Are you mad? Another said: Come on, I'd like to see you from really close to! This shark was not a stranger to me but a friend.
>
> (Lotte Hass 1972: 157)

Rather than convert an 'it' shark to a 'he', this time Lotte turns an emphatically 'it' shark (thus eight times in five sentences) from an object to a subject, and one with whom she wants intimacy: 'I'd like to see you from really close to!' It has the eroticism of mental undressing; it is also a form of address, a vocative. Her two voices, ego and id, seek fidelity, trust and play in which the shark is a companion species, like dogs, subservient to men. It is a version of shark lording tempered by a wish for intimacy.

On a reef off Cosmoledo, Franco Prosperi and his friend Stanis watch a great old turtle, a placid, barnacle-encrusted female, when in sweeps a group of ten large orcas. The young men look on 'petrified with horror' as the orcas tear the turtle to pieces (Prosperi 1959: 187). Luckily the orcas move off, not seeing the lads dangling above. Prosperi was so shocked by this reminder of human vulnerability that his life changed. 'From that day forth I was never again able to relax in the sea' (1959: 188). The orcas replace sharks as the principal enemy. 'Orcs are the most cruel of the great creatures that inhabit the sea. Their appetite is insatiable' (Prosperi 1959: 188). Though called killer whale, *Orcinus orca* is a species of dolphin. Tolkien denied any linguistic connection between orcas and orcs, the brutish malevolent monsters in *The Lord of the Rings*; he said he got orcs from ogres in *Beowulf*, not sea-beasts. In Italian, *orco* is an ogre in fairy-tales who feeds on human flesh; we lose Prosperi's resonance in translation.

Like Lotte Hass, Prosperi wanted intimacy, and achieved it in a strange way. At this point nobody had seen sharks mate. Diving in a lagoon in the Comoro Islands, he and Fabrizio stop close to some branching black coral: 'one had the impression of peering through the curtained window of some fantastic submarine chamber.' Then he sees two nurse sharks, eight-feet long. 'The sharks lay on the bottom, completely relaxed, the one resting its head on the body of the other, like two lovers exhausted after an embrace. There was about the two figures an air of contentment and mutual devotion, a disarming gentleness which I should never have thought to see in such ferocious creatures' (Prosperi 1959: 163). Prosperi's cameraman arrives and begins to film what seems to be renewed action.

> With a sensuous movement the male sought his partner's head. Hungrily he pressed his mouth to her branchial aperture. Trembling beneath his caress, the female writhed voluptuously. The two creatures rolled over, their tails entwined ... The

sharks' contortions grew more and more violent ... And now, casting discretion to the winds, we threw ourselves excitedly on the two creatures. Frantically I grabbed the male shark by the tail and held the two lovers by their great pectoral fins. But they did not seem to have noticed our intrusion, and they continued to roll about the sea-bed. Minutes, unforgettable minutes passed thus. Then the lovers separated. They seemed at last to have become aware of the presence of their unwelcome visitors. For a moment they paused in bewilderment, then, with rapid strokes of their tails, they disappeared from our view.

(1959: 164)

From its peeping Tom start, his account climaxes with joining in, as if he wants to jump a species barrier. Converting touching distance to touch was normally one way humans made a connection that could also be a simulacrum of control. Philippe Tailliez described a shark-tail-pulling competition in terms of 'a revenge complex. Man tends to bear malice towards his dead gods' (1954: 116). In contrast, Prosperi is simply yearning for contact that connects.

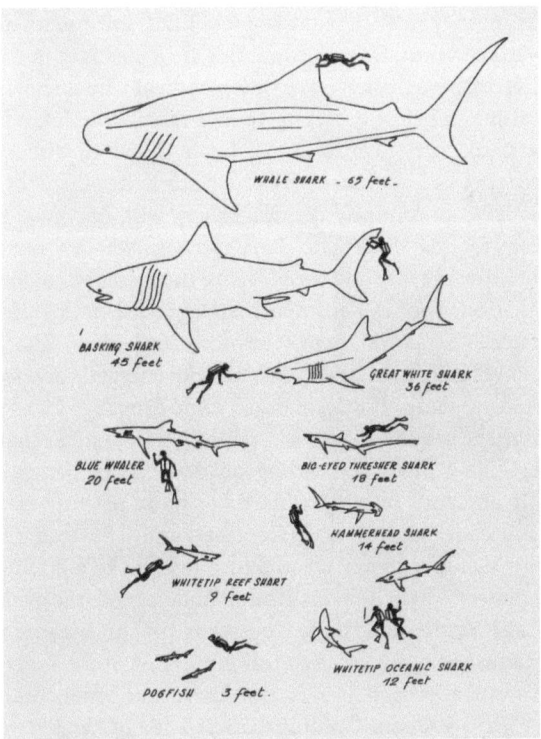

Figure 6 Shark-touching guide: line drawing by Jean-Charles Roux from Jacques-Yves Cousteau & Philippe Cousteau's *The Shark: Splendid Savage of the Sea* (1970).

SHARK LORDS

Human superiority was also achieved simply by representing sharks as inferior to men. Cousteau and Dumas were underwater off the Cape Verde islands when they saw a great white approach. Cousteau describes his feeling as 'ice-cold terror ... What we saw made us feel that naked men do not really belong in the sea.' His usual disparagers apply: 'The brute was swimming lazily.' But 'Then the shark saw us. His reaction was the last conceivable one. In pure fright, the monster voided a cloud of excrement and departed at an incredible speed.' The jubilant humans proceed with self-confidence, convinced that 'all sharks were cowards. They were so pusillanimous they wouldn't stay still to be filmed' (Cousteau and Dumas 1953: 117-18). They devise an experiment to prove this. They harpoon and tether a porpoise as bait:

> The sharks circled the porpoise as they had circled us. We stood on deck remarking on the cowardice of sharks, beasts as powerful as anything else on earth, indifferent to pain, and splendidly equipped as killers. Yet the brutes timidly waited to attack. Attack was too good a word for them. The porpoise had no weapons and he was dying in a circle of bullies.
>
> (Cousteau and Dumas 1953: 124)

This makes sharks morally weak, like the shark voiding shit supposedly from fear. We talk of abject cowardice; accusations of cowardice are a means of making sharks abject, cast out beyond norms. More recent observation of great whites shows they move their bodies in a vertical spasm before excreting, to help faecal flow; 'pure fright' is a human projection, not a shark fact (Keartes 2015). Dean Crawford discusses the language around sharks: 'No species is as destructive or vicious in its pursuit of its desires as our own, so it's ironic how we routinely connect sharks with our most reviled traits.' He notes one etymology for 'shark' relates to *shirk*, 'someone who was not only indolent but a parasite and scoundrel preying on others'. Hence the metaphor of loan sharks: 'sharks might conclude that our species has unfairly maligned theirs by projecting our own villainous and despicable traits on them' (Crawford 2008: 98-9). That also explains the recurrent accusation of laziness, a quality at odds with energetic dive expeditions. Shark lords could not emulate shark effortlessness, so some disparaged it as moral weakness.

The whole language around sharks is – still! – oddly feudal: sharks are majestic, lordly, powerful. 'Like a duke descending on some petty baron, the great ocean shark occasionally descends on his less hardy or more fearful vassals. ... I thought of him with a kind of secret jealousy' (Cousteau and Cousteau 1970: 88, 95). The frequency of terms like monster, brute and lord testifies to a fascination with shark power in uneasy dialectic with humans aiming to dominate the oceans. Harpooning a whale off the Cape Verde islands, the Cousteaus spot an oceanic whitetip coming in: 'Lord Longimanus, or as we came to call him, Lord of the Long Arms ... not in the least afraid of our approach' (1970: 29). There was other interest in lords and lording in the 1950s – William Golding's novel *Lord of the Flies* (1954) concerns a band of boys on an island facing a beast who embodies their own dark drives, and whose threats they respond to in dreams. More lording appears in J. R. R. Tolkien's trilogy *Lord of the Rings* (1954–1955), in which the rings are associated with new powers, subjugation and total dominance of other societies – all relevant to underwater ideas of conquest. Most relevant to shark lording is a historical model for a dominant ruling class found in the medieval period, feudalism, much debated in the mid-twentieth century. In 1933 (English translation 1961), Marc Bloch argued in *Feudal Society* that peasants got lordly protection in return for labour, a reciprocal arrangement countered by the research of Georges Duby that suggested lords were more likely to strong-arm peasants and use violence to impose power (Duby 1953). Although historians' debates about feudalism were taking place far from underwater, their visions of lordly power engage with archetypes relevant to sharks – and shark lords. Even the new global medium of television could be cast in medieval terms: thus Philippe Cousteau described the *Calypso* expedition in an unexpectedly historical metaphor:

> Our only task, our profession, was to see. In a time of superspecialization, we became the farseeing eyes of all those who could not or would not journey themselves. We were akin to those knight-errants who travelled across the world and returned to tell the king the news of the Holy Land or of Mauretania. We were different in the sense that we would bring the story of our adventures not to a solitary king, but to millions of people.
>
> (Cousteau and Cousteau 1970: 13)

The appeal of the 'lord' persists. 'With the occasional exception of humans and killer whales, the shark rules among all the myriad life forms of the sea' (Crawford 2008: 47). Rule, power: these are qualities given to apex predators, at the top of a trophic pyramid. Rather like the Great Chain of Being, being at the bottom has lower status. Technology kept humans on top, as Hass observed: 'A crane, an airplane, a gun or microscope are, biologically speaking, artificial organs which man has created to increase his possibilities and power. … these implements far transcend anything which on a living organism can be formed and maintained' (1959: 263). Four hundred million years of shark history and evolution was leapfrogged by human ingenuity, itself part of nature but armed with tools.

In the 1950s, morality, psychology and history all provided paradigms of power that enabled humans to represent themselves as dominant in their rivalry with sharks. Relentless masculinity reinforced this: sharks are almost never *she*. Underwater life writing of this mostly post-war period is progressive in undoing some of the terror around sharks as man-eaters, and regressive in positioning humans as, after all, lords of the deep. Reflecting on human assumptions of progress, Hass thought it less obvious underwater: 'we appear to have gone right off the tracks. With almost unbelievable brutality and presumption we grab for ourselves everything in the realm where we had our origins.' Yet diving could put us 'into a solitude from which a lot of things in the world above look somewhat different' (Hass 1959: 275).

SHARK LADY

Eugenie Clark looked differently at sharks, starting as a child on Saturday trips to the New York Aquarium, a story made much of in biographies of her for younger readers. As the blurb for one puts it,

> Before Eugenie Clark's groundbreaking research, most people thought sharks were vicious, blood-thirsty killers. From the first time she saw a shark in an aquarium, Japanese-American Eugenie was enthralled. Instead of frightening and ferocious eating machines, she saw sleek, graceful fish gliding through the water. After she became a scientist – an unexpected career path for a woman in the 1940s – she began taking research dives and training sharks, earning her the nickname 'The Shark Lady'.
>
> (Lang 2016)

Clark published *Lady with a Spear* (1951) aged only twenty-nine; based on letters to her family, it became a Book of the Month choice (Balon 1994: 124). The title riffs faintly on iconography defining women (thus Lady with an Ermine, or the Lady with a Lamp), radically recast in the memoir, where Clark is a cheerfully enthusiastic scientist who spears fish so as to study them. Her studies had a consistent theme of fish reproduction, panning out across plectognaths (a group including mola, puffer, porcupine blowfish, triodon, boxfish, unicorn or filefish and Hawaiian triggerfish): 'they seem to represent the most heterogenous assortment of bizarre marine creatures that a taxonomist could possibly gather together' (Clark 1953: 22). She devised ways to sex her subjects without killing them, to milk them of eggs and sperm and inseminate them. Friends asked if she was compiling the Kinsey Report on fishes (1953: 46–7). She also worked on fish optics, particularly how eyesight and memory might be linked. She was frank about facing prejudice – she lost one job because 'E. Clark' was assumed to be a man – but obstacles are not simple sexism. 'It amused me that when I did do some of the things (e.g. diving in caves with "sleeping" sharks) considered "macho male accomplishments" that I was given more credit than males for doing the same thing they did. It helped to balance some of the prejudices against females' (Balon 1994: 122). Hierarchies between the Navy and civilians, and within science, were also powerful. 'I think I started a new category', she wrote wryly (1953: 86).

In 1955 Clark opened the Cape Haze Marine Laboratory on the west Florida Coast (now the Mote Marine Laboratory and Aquarium). Initially a small enterprise, funded by a local philanthropist inspired by Clark's first memoir, it attracted a growing flow of visiting scientists (Mahadevan 2010). Clark expanded facilities to include sea pens, where she studied captured sharks. Misunderstanding journalists thought she speared sharks like she speared fish. Even when she was able to correct their copy, artwork reinstated her as the lady spearing sharks: 'they sketched a picture of me diving, with a one-rubber arbalete spear gun that would barely hold a mullet, about to shoot the spear into a gigantic shark. This came out as a two-page spread in the magazine' (Clark 1969: 88). Popular culture here flirts with the monstrous feminine, a concept established by Barbara Creed in relation to horror films, in which horror turns on women's power to castrate or kill. 'The image of woman as castrator takes at least three forms: woman as the deadly *femme castratrice*, the castrating mother and the *vagina dentata*.' Terror of a toothed vagina, Creed argues, explains *Jaws* as an instance of 'aquatic dentata' (Creed 1993: 7, 150). Where big teeth – shark jaws, vampire fangs – evoke fears of castration in men, a spear-armed woman is mildly, safely, taking on a symbolic order in which sharks enact and shield the threat of women. Clark pointed out with amusement that the only shark bite she sustained was from a set of tiger shark jaws in her car which snapped on her arm in a traffic incident. Otherwise her shark encounters 'all had happy endings' (Clark 1969: 115).

Clark liked younglings – she had four children of her own, whom she folded into her underwater and lab world, and she responded warmly to little girls whom she met on her travels. Motherhood was real to her, naturally part of the natural world. Dissecting a mako shark, she found six embryos inside it: 'pickled in formalin, these chubby little fellows – with their characteristically sharply pointed noses, large eyes, rudimentary second dorsal and anal fins, and symmetrically crescent unsharklike tail – looked cute. But their mama! Her monstrous set of teeth, each like an elongated curved spearhead, dwarfed those on the mounted twelve-foot tiger shark' (Clark 1953: 232). Unlike shark lords who could see only masculinist competition, Clark acknowledges the existence of mama sharks. She pointed out gender blindness among her fellow men too. On a field trip across Pacific islands, the only woman on a Navy boat, she resists the erasure of women: 'Ngulu did not sell copra. Its major products were sculptured wooden figures which the Island Trading Company called "frogmen." Actually they were heavy-browed, triangular-faced pregnant women symbolizing fertility' (1953: 157-8). Though Philippe Diolé thought about 'the terrible and suspicious kiss of sharks' (1954a 103, (mis)quoting Michelet 1861, XI 222, 'A terrible and suspicious embrace'), shark lords are notably silent about female sharks and fecundity. The monstrous feminine here is too terrible for them even to imagine. In contrast, Clark nurtured shark embryos and built up new knowledge. 'Our shark dissections, especially on pregnant females, supplied fascinating information on the reproductive habits of some large species of sharks about which little was known previously' (Clark 1953: 90).

Pregnant with her fourth child, Clark continued diving almost till due, joking 'even if it did make me feel like a "Lady with a Sphere"' (1953: 122). Researching poisonous fishes in the Pacific, Clark's idea of danger underwater was unusually relaxed: 'misinformation often leads the person unfamiliar with sea creatures to form an unfair opinion of it. A diver can swim among most "dangerous" fishes, even tickle the belly of many a shark without being bitten, but unfortunately it is always the exceptional case that makes the news' (1953: 206). A pregnant lemon shark started Clark on a shark-training project. At the time the US Navy was keen to find shark repellents that worked. It was also secretly developing Project Headgear which aimed to convert sharks into torpedoes, remote-controlled by headgear, who could ram and blow up ships (Roach 2016). In contrast, Clark's experiments were designed to explore shark vision, intelligence and memory. She set up targets in the sea pen; through conditioning, or the use of associated stimuli, in this case a ringing bell, the sharks learnt to press those targets to get food. Made famous by Pavlov's work on dogs, conditioning theory flourished in psychology between the 1940s and 1960s, when it was challenged by humanists who doubted the relevance of animal behaviour to human subjects. Animal behaviourists continue to be interested in it, for instance in dog training. Using stimuli,

Figure 7 Smalltooth sand tiger (*Odontaspis ferox*) pregnant female swimming in shallow waters, El Hierro, Canary Islands, Spain, Atlantic Ocean. Photo and caption by Jordi Chias. Nature Picture Library.

rewards and punishments, it is still upheld by aquaria like Seaworld who train animals to perform.

Clark's Cape Haze Lab pioneered scientific study of local underwater life – besides sharks, she took a special interest in a hermaphroditic and self-fertilizing fish, *Serranus subligarius*, the belted sandfish. Florida was also home to popular attractions which exploited dolphins particularly. By the 1960s, 'Silver Springs was a household word', staging underwater dramas alongside fortune-telling chickens and other animal performers (Hollis 2006: 23, 28). It was here some scenes of the *Tarzan* movies were filmed, and where Howard Hughes's film *Underwater!* starring Jayne Mansfield (and a few sharks) was premiered in 1955. Marine Studios, which opened in 1938 and became Marineland, was billed as the world's first oceanarium: it held Flippy, who entertained thousands in an act whose tricks climaxed 'when the dolphin star towed a woman and a little fox terrier around the tank on a surfboard' (Mitman 2009: 166). Gregg Mitman has admirably tracked the unsteady relations between science and spectacle at these and other aquaria. 'War-weary Americans looked to nature for wholesome entertainment for their children', says Mitman – hence Flippy's enthusiastic masturbation was kept quiet – and dolphins had a major role 'as simultaneous experimental subject and popular celebrity' (Mitman 2009: 177, 205, 168).

Since trainability was taken to be indicative of intelligence in both science and spectacle, Clark's experiments were not entirely free from human-interest performativity. Her lemon sharks proved adept learners, and in 1965 she took one as a present for the Crown Prince of Japan, a keen ichthyologist. The little shark travelled as hand luggage in a special box on the airplane seat next to her. Duly decanted into a tank, he went through his trained responses to be rewarded with a slice of lobster, offered in mother-of-pearl chopsticks from an exquisitely arranged dish held by a palace servant (Clark 1969: 217–21). Apart from this short episode of shark celebrity, Clark's research concentrated on understanding shark abilities so as to understand sharks better, not exploit them. In 1968 she was able to join the Cousteaus on their shark-hunting voyage in the Red Sea. She recognized the power of the Cousteau name, and they were respectful of her credentials. Chapter XII of *Splendid Savage* covers her experiments, which aimed to test shark responses to visual and sound stimuli by setting up differently fish-dispensing targets on a reef. It seems she was not diving but watching a television feed in the wheelhouse with Jacques-Yves Cousteau, and the chapter is oddly illustrated only with photographs of a giant school of squid. Nonetheless, Philippe Cousteau describes how the sharks come to differentiate between two targets:

> By the time we left, the sharks were coming regularly to the target with the horizontal stripes, in search of their meals. Throughout the entire experiment, I had never seen a shark brush against the vertical target. In comparing these results with those of Doctor Clark's earlier experiments, it would seem that sharks at liberty – the *Albimarginatus*, [silvertip] as [sic] least – learn more rapidly than their captive relatives.
>
> (Cousteau and Cousteau 1970: 227)

Clark has been credited with changing the shark's reputation from savage killer to intelligently complex. Although *Jaws* attributes intelligence to its great white, in terms of being able to plot absurd revenge attacks, it reinstated the shark as monstrous and fearsome. But before *Jaws*, the Cousteau narration – on television and in print – puts the shark squarely as a savage, even with Clark on board the *Calypso*. Her credo of 'Love fish. Love sharks' seems wholly at odds with that of the Cousteaus, bent on casting sharks as murderers (Balon 1994: 124). A review on the back flap – by the *Daily Telegraph* – praises the book's 'electrifying accounts of skirmishes between the "splendid savage" and the gentlemanly dolphin', as if a colonial or class victory was at stake. For underwater lords, shark power was a deep affront to male egotism. Meeting a blue shark, Philippe Cousteau acknowledged shark power resentfully. 'His configuration is perfect. Suddenly, the idea that he deserves killing comes to me like a shock and instantly shatters the spell. Murder is the real function of this ideal form' (Cousteau and Cousteau 1970: 2). This is savage, inverted logic: shark perfection, a spell-binding idea, is rerouted into shark murderousness to justify sadism as a response. Morality – somehow the shark deserves killing – defends against enchantment and a shark lord's deep fear that sharks are more perfect than humans.

"'Everyone has a lot to say about sharks attacking people," thought Eugenie sadly. "But what about people who attack sharks?"' (McGovern 1987: 51). Philippe Cousteau was visceral in his hostility to sharks. He never seems to think how his interventions create behaviours – how the flapping of speared fish would attract competing, hungry sharks. 'I think it is the irrationality in this frenzy of sharks that strikes me most. It gives me a feeling of complete impotence such as I never experience in any other

Figure 8 Eugenie Clark's experiment: line drawing by Jean-Charles Roux from Jacques-Yves Cousteau & Philippe Cousteau's *The Shark: Splendid Savage of the Sea* (1970).

circumstances. The shark is the most mechanical animal I know, and his attacks are totally senseless' (Cousteau and Cousteau 1970: 69). A feeling of complete impotence points to fear of castration. Un-natural imagery is also used by his father about 'the killing machine that is a shark'. The violence of human intentions is camouflaged by shark violence: a shark is 'a killing machine ... a malignant and terrifying symbol imagined by some Aztec sorcerer ... just a mean-looking, dangerous killer' (Cousteau and Cousteau 1970: 35, 45). At the end of the book he asks himself, what have I learned of the shark? Very little, it seemed: 'The beauty of a supple line, the thought of possible menace, the exaltation of a combat in which I know nothing of the rules ... but what more than that?' (Cousteau and Cousteau 1970: 229). So much for the new knowledges of the ocean frontier! Others studying sharks were also frustrated. 'The more we found out about the display of the gray reef shark, the less we seemed to know' (Starck 1979: 216). Reason is baffled by sharks. 'The further we advance in our knowledge of sharks, the more evident becomes the futility of any attempt to understand them completely' (Cousteau and Cousteau 1970: 124). Shark enigma reinforced an impasse of contempt that made the murderous great white of *Jaws* more possible – and, predictably, sadly, licensed the venting of murderous revenge on sharks after the film, when big game fishermen targeted all sharks along the eastern US coast.

SHARK FRIENDS, THEN AND NOW

Bucking the trend for interspecies friendships with dolphins and reviling sharks, an unusual novel of 1951 by Clément Richer, a novelist from Martinique, has a plot featuring shark taming. In *Ti-Coyo and His Shark*, an uneducated, opportunist lad wants to be the only diver for coins thrown by passengers from docking steamers. He has a plan: to train a shark to eat his competitors. He succeeds in this, and the shark, as it grows, becomes his friend. Ti-Coyo rescues it from capture by local fisherman, and it in turn saves his life, twice – once from a volcano's eruption, and once from a cyclone. The book's inside flap is frank about the challenge of classifying the novel – in 'this queer, idyllic, heartless, lyrical story … terror becomes a tamed denizen of fairyland, and the basest of human motives live in a curious shimmer of innocence'. It is possible to read it as an allegory of colonialism – after the volcano erupts, the sea is clogged with corpses which the British authorities want to expel as undesirable immigrants; the shark grows big feasting on those bodies. But simple symbolism is smaller than the shark, who is given a name, Manidou, and a consistent role as trusted friend. Ti-Coyo trains Manidou through appetite, providing fish and being careful about species difference: 'a shark – whether a baby or not – is still a shark, and it is well for human beings, even those as clever as Ti-Coyo, to keep such creatures at arm's length. Besides, the training of a shark is an extremely complicated business. … Ti-Coyo was playing a difficult game, and he knew it' (Richer 1951: 30-2). As the shark grows, it is described as a monster. It is also a companion conscious of friendship, expressing joy in reunions and delight in swimming together. 'The shark was his very life, his best and only friend, a friend who had brought wealth to him and his relations, a friend who loved him and had proved his love in a hundred different ways' (Richer 1951: 53). An interviewer reported that although Richer gives a voice to entities like the volcano, he 'never allows his animal characters to talk because he despairs of attaining Kipling's proficiency in this kind of dialogue' (Cook 1953: 39). Some mysteriousness thus informs shark subjectivity, but there are several scenes in which the 'monster' gazes into Ti-Coyo's eyes in ways one might recognize as love. Shark gaze here is bonding and beautiful. It coexists with shark appetite, including a taste – acquired thanks to a human – for human flesh. Shark lordliness is diffused into animal companionship, mutually caring and protective.

When the novel was made into a film, adapted by the writer Italo Calvino, no less, one reviewer criticized its shark-handling. 'With its fairy tale background, the film often has a heady airiness, a pungent gentleness; but it could and should have saturated itself with the friendship with the shark alone, as a symbol of an escape from time' (Pestelli 1962). The bond between boy and shark – *his* shark – is grammatically unpersonalized, to *the* shark: *Tiko and the Shark*. In publicity the shark is described as a pet. Extraordinary friendship between human and shark is possible: there is a striking instance in the mutual affection of diver Jim Abernethy and Emma, a fourteen-foot tiger shark resident at Tiger Beach in the Bahamas (Viewable at https://www.youtube.com/watch?v=iPGb9FMLl8g). They have been best friends for twenty years. Abernethy argues that sharks respond to kindness. 'Trying to describe what it's like really makes me believe that the English language isn't good enough. To have a connection that lasts the entire time you're in the water is so moving and so impactful. One of the best things that's happened to me is this discovery of the affectionate side of sharks' (Mukundarajan 2022).

Ignorance about sharks made them big in underwater literature, but with little examination of the human arrogance that turned encounters into a contest for supremacy. Although 'the question of sharks and their habits is one that might occupy us indefinitely' (Doukan 1957: 70), new knowledges of those habits were patchy. They still are, making it hard to rescue the shark from mostly Western paradigms of supremacy. Pacific peoples have long had shark gods who protect and guide, in Hawai'i and Fiji for instance, where sharks also help fishermen and dispense justice (Gibbings 1949: 200). White men still cast sharks as opponents whose fearsomeness lends aura to conquest. The phrase 'shark lords' was revived by two Australian brothers for a 2020 TV series marketed as 'a dangerous mission to dominate man's oldest foe', arrogating the title of shark lords to humans and repeating crude violence against sharks. Despite the many books pointing out that sharks are invaluable and irreplaceable in keeping reef ecosystems healthy, ocean writing for children still casts them as enemies. Thus *Scuffle In Coral Reefs* (Zerarki 2023), a supposedly moral tale, uses the outdated binary of friendly dolphins and terrorizing sharks, and *SpongeBob and Friends Adventures* has a psychotic Shark Lord who commands an 'entire army of shark supervillains' (*SpongeBob*). For some, there is still an ideological battle in which the shark must be cast as terrifying and then killed so as to reassure humans of their supposed superiority. For others, the greater terror is in losing sharks altogether, from the human violence of overfishing and finning. As Carl Safina reflects (2010: 224), with some guilt after killing a mako, 'The shark does only what it needs, and needs only what it does. Of the burden of needing to make an impression, the shark is free. Yet we cause the whole world, even the sharks of the blue ocean, to bear the burden of our egos.'

4

Coral

'Indescribable! Indescribable! *Sensational! ... Absolutely in-des-crib-ab-le!'* Jacques-
Yves Cousteau's words on emerging from a first dive in the Red Sea

(Tazieff n.d.: 38)

Like a reef, coral literature has been steadily built up by divers and scientists. From
prized magical substance to imperilled ecosystem, coral arouses passions. Coral
challenges writers about how to write reef life, to convey its physical complexity,
biological diversity, metaphysical specificity and cultural entanglements. 'Some words
hold magic, so that when they are uttered the mind loses itself in mists of enchanted
reverie ... Such a word of wonder is "coral"' (Clarke 1956: 13). In this chapter, I take
coral as a connective thread through an underwater world of abundance to one of
destruction. Given the powerful idea of coral reefs as Eden, a paradise of variety and
pristine beauty, how did divers respond to places where damage became painfully
visible? Life writing on coral, like corals themselves, takes many forms.

'The complexity and interdependence, richness and diversity, of the reef have
meaning for human lives that is intellectual, spiritual, and aesthetic', says Rosaleen
Love (2001: 55). Ann Elias identifies three themes in the visualization of coral, starting
in the 1920s: 'the mediation of vision of the underwater and manipulation of truth by
modern technologies; the racialization of coral reef environments and subordination
of coastal peoples in colonial modernity; and the objectification of marine animals
as source of knowledge and entertainment' (2019: 1). These themes appear in the
corresponding literature, but they do not overpower literary drives which are different:
to celebrate the beauty of coral; to understand better the organisms that compose reef
life; to explore subjective possibilities for humans which reefs catalyse, and to warn of
coral's imminent disappearance. In a grim twist, scientists began to write in frustration
about indifference to their warnings. From sacralization (in myth, jewellery, tropes
of paradise) and romantic escapism (the coral island), corals have become a carrier
of consequences, doom-laden, deathly. 'As a scientist who has researched reefs
for nearly 40 years, I do not want my work to be merely a post-mortem of what reefs
once were. Unfortunately, this is all too likely to be the case' (Sheppard 2014: 113).
Scientist-memoirists glue elegy to coral eulogy.

EDEN

The Garden of Eden was originally an oasis in a desert, says biologist Steve Jones; he blames filmmakers of the 1930s for transposing it to a coral atoll. 'A remote island can soon become a tiny but terrifying nightmare ... Even so, the universal obsession with a sun-drenched Garden of Eden lives on' (Jones 2007: 190-1). In the words of a 1955 handbook to the Great Barrier Reef, 'CORAL ISLAND. What a wealth of romance there is in the words!' (Serventy 1955: 1). Two elements combine: pristine abundance, and analogies with gardens.

> I was tingling with subdued excitement, fired with keen anticipation of the natural wonders I had so often heard about – palm-fringed coral islands; sheltered lagoons with water clear as crystal, sparkling, glittering in the sunlight; animal life infinite in its variety, absorbing, thrilling in its interest; coral gardens of great beauty; fishes gaudily coloured, amazingly patterned; fishing unrivalled in its productiveness; sunsets, peaceful, majestic, awe-inspiring.
>
> (Roughley 1941: 1)

Coral paradise supplies physical and metaphysical escapism. 'The reef offers beauty, wildness, and rest for the weary citified soul' (Love 2001: 5). It gives a vision of spiritual promise: 'as we watch the dolphins play we feel that here we have the very spirit of happiness, that *joie de vivre* which we poor humans, born into a world of strife and rumours of strife, are far too seldom able to enjoy' (Roughley 1941: 2).

These forms of the Eden concept – coral islands, lagoons, coral gardens, escapism and redemption – don't change much over the eighty-plus years since that was written. Although Stephen Torre proposes that '[o]ver two centuries the sublime power of the Great Barrier Reef is gradually diminished in discourse, as naturalists become scientists and ecologists' (Torre 2008: n.p.), the beauty of coral reefs became a kind of sublime. Descriptions regularly allude to paradise and gardens. Diving off Zanzibar in 1954, Frank Talbot reported 'it was like diving in an underwater paradise. The rich and varied coral beds were like luscious planted gardens' (2012: 14). Images reinforce this. Photographic books present tropical reefs as colourful, lush, teeming with life. In reefs, says one,

> that most wondrous and mysterious of all natural phenomena, life, has found its fullest expression. Nowhere else can one find so many diverse creatures living so closely together in such abundance. Complementing and enhancing this extraordinary intensity of life is its exquisite beauty of form, colour, and motion. This is nature's richest realm ...
>
> (Steene 1990: 21)

The genre of coral reef photographic books is indeed rich. They usually feature seascapes and close-ups, and a range of tiny, unfamiliar creatures whose colour is enhanced by back backgrounds.

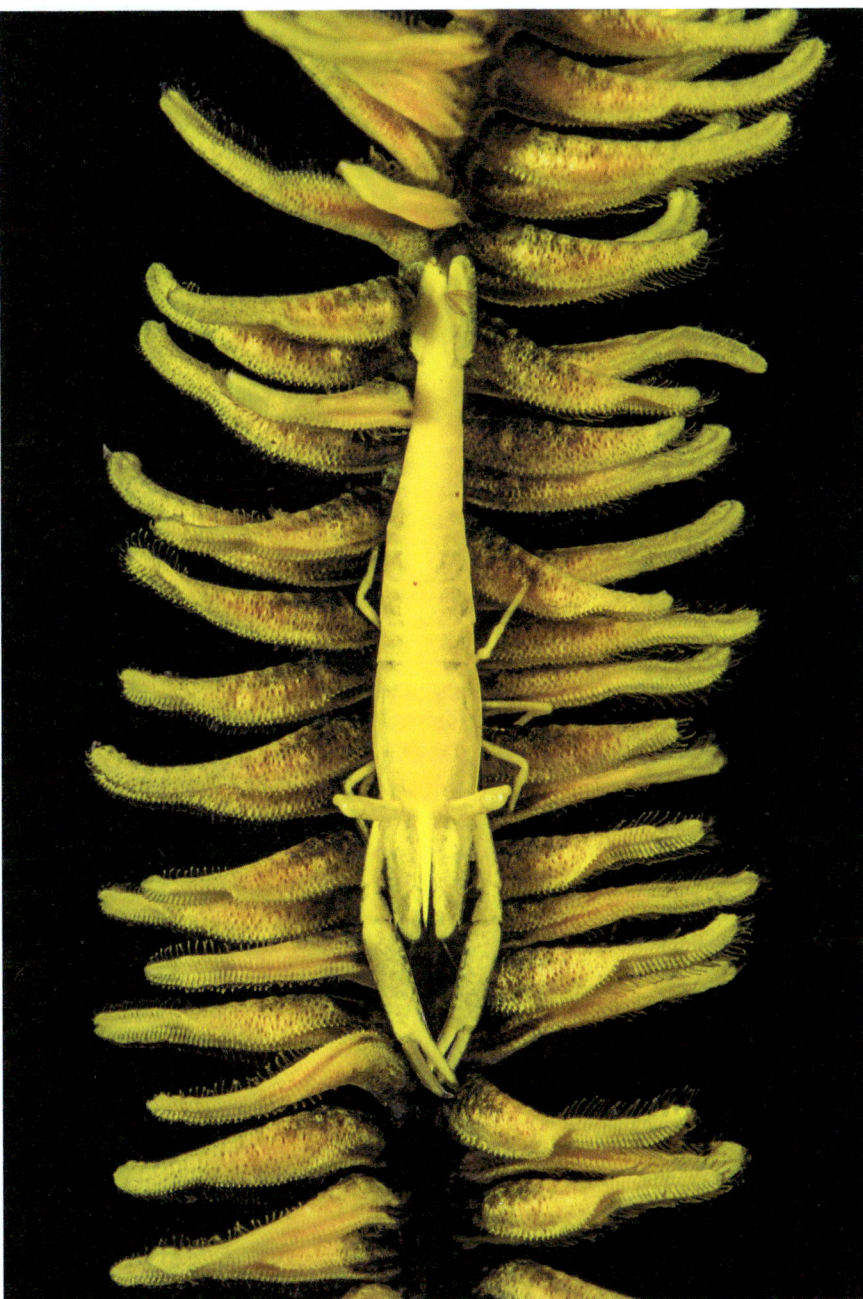

Figure 9 A yellow crinoid shrimp (*Laomenes* sp.) on an arm of a Bennett's feather star (*Anneissia bennetti*) on a coral reef. Anilao, Batangas marine protected area, Luzon, the Philippines. Verde Island Passages, Tropical West Pacific Ocean. Photo and caption by Alex Mustard.

Figure 10 A tiny (0.5 cm) 'Shaun the sheep' slug (sap-sucking slug: *Costasiella kuroshimae*) crawls across an *Avrainvillea* sp. alga on the seabed. Bitung, North Sulawesi, Indonesia. Lembeh Strait, Molucca Sea. Photo and caption by Alex Mustard. The 'sheep' is no bigger than a freckle.

There are also richly illustrated cultural histories of coral. J. Malcolm Shick's *Where Corals Lie* is one such: a typical double page includes a photograph of a Yemeni bride wearing an elaborate veil of coral beads, and a nineteenth-century Tibetan cloth showing a monk praying in front of an array of auspicious symbols and prized gems, of which coral is one of the Precious Seven (2018: 158–9). These books are beautiful in a double sense: they have high production values and photogenic subjects. Depending on their date they also include text and images about threats to coral. From the 1990s on, most authors have chapters addressing bleaching, overfishing, plagues of starfish, diseases and the material and philosophical consequences of reef collapse. They feature witness accounts, like Shick's first dive on the Great Barrier Reef: 'the most striking sight as I neared the bottom was a front of these sea stars [crown-of-thorns, *Acanthaster planci*] advancing across healthy plating acroporid corals, leaving behind digestively denuded, deathly white skeletons' (2018: 230). Photographs make seeing part of reading. Large format photo-books were promoted by David Brower (who oversaw the Exhibit format book series for the Sierra Club 1960–69). He argued they needed '"a page size big enough to carry a given image's dynamic. The eye," he explained, "must be required to move about within the boundaries of the image, not encompass it all in one glance"' (Dunaway 2005: 120). This 'moving about' gives readers freedom of movement akin to diving's fluidity. In conjunction with a 'wealth' of images, and the 'richness' of coral, it accords readers the immersive privilege of access to abundance.

I discuss photography more in Chapter 10; here I stress the importance of photographs for amplifying words. As Roughley puts it, 'No description can adequately convey to the mind an impression of the beauty of the coral and the life associated with it' (1941: v). Hence he included colour photos. Their captions reinforce the association with gardens: Plate 7, 'Branching coral, like trees in blossom'; Plate 23, 'Like a delicate

flower this small anemone spreads its tentacles in a garden of coral and seaweeds.'
Others life writers pick up the conjunction of garden and colour. 'I doubt if it is
possible to describe the wonder of such a scene. The background of living coral reef has
a beauty all its own. The colours of the coral, while not gaudy, are lovely in the mingling
of many soft colours: they are like trees, shrubs, and flowers exquisitely sculptured in
coloured stone' (Monkman 1956: 51). Flower-like animals add to category confusions.
In the Caribbean, looking at 'an informal garden of maize-coloured flowers whose
petals unfolded in a long graceful spiral', Gilbert Klingel was startled to see them
retract, a sensation 'the same as one would have in a garden should one try to pick
a daisy or a nasturtium and have it suddenly yanked into the ground.' These 'worms'
he thought 'all lovely. Why they should be so exquisite is hard to answer unless it is
because everything else on the reef is so gorgeous that to be ugly would seem out of
place' (Klingel 1942: 230-1). The worm may be *Spirobranchus giganteus*, the Christmas
tree worm, indeed lovely.

Memoirs match images to garden-related words, filling out Shakespeare's tag for
coral (in *The Tempest*) as 'rich and strange'. Diving in Martinique, Bernard Gorsky's
description covers both registers. He dives a jade-green reef with

a strange luminosity and in this a profusion of mineral wealth, other-worldly
corals and madrepores in shapes drawn by an opium-smoker of genius at a peak
of ecstasy and harmony, a calcareous fairyland, porcelain of every possible hue
fixed for ever in liquid light. Then, from what might have been a giant ear carved
in pomegranate-red jelly spangled with lapis lazuli, there emerged a parrot-fish, a
phosphorescent Matisse creation, draped in the freshest of almond greens, barred
with Empire green, bottle green, pond green, English green, blue-green, Cardinal
violet, vivid orange, chrome yellow. A living thing, its fins pulsating, incessantly
changing position, taking up new stances against a background of gorgonian
seaweed (which is an Andalucian fan trembling between a young girl's fingers and
thumb), thus the fish, behind sentient lace, creating a spectacle of surrealist beauty.
And under all the flowers and under-water plants whether living or miracles of
mineral, there was in every nook and cranny, in the rock cloisters and the rock
faults nothing but scintillating colour, through which the endless passage of all
the small fish life of the corals, at play, at pasture, at combat, or withdrawn into the
floating obscurity of their caverns.

(Gorsky 1956: 80)

This description, like many others, draws on art tropes – fairyland, Matisse,
surrealism, paint colours, portrait props – to convey nature. On the H.M.S. *Beagle*
voyage (1831–36), Darwin often consulted a book, *Werner's Nomenclature of Colours
Adapted to Zoology, Botany, Chemistry, Mineralogy, Anatomy and the Arts* (1814)
which gave thirteen colour palettes and 110 swatches with suggestions for where they
were found in nature among the animal, vegetable and mineral world. Underwater
writers faced reefs that had all of those colours and in ways hard for a human eye to
distinguish. Stephen Harrigan thought of 'a chaotic, benevolent, overgrown garden.
The coral blinded me with its variety, its seemingly random shapes and textures and

colors, its immense patternless bulk' (1992: 43). References to art helped to organize visual chaos: hence life writers allude to Chinese painting, Japanese watercolours, nursery school paintings, van Gogh, Matisse, Picasso, 1960s posters, even the Sistine Chapel. Impressionism is useful: 'To drift with a gentle current over a coral reef is one of life's great thrills. The world that unfolds below is crowded with bright dappling colors in constant motion. It feels like gazing at a Monet painting in which every brushstroke has come to life and is swimming around the canvas' (Roberts 2012: 85).

The garden analogy embraced organisms as well as seascape. 'As a garden on land has its butterflies, so these coral groves had their legions of gorgeously coloured fish' (Clarke 1956: 81). Its prelapsarian echoes underpin reef as pastoral, pumped up:

> The reef blends into open sand fifteen metres down. Corals blossom like drifts of flowers in some glorious English garden, all self-arranged. Giant clams half a metre wide sprout from limestone ledges like gladioli. Their velvet fleshy mantles are as richly colourful as prize garden blooms: deep-dyed indigo, mauve, blue and imperial purple, flecked and curled with twists of bumblebee yellow or dragonfly blue. It feels as if this garden should be heavily scented …
>
> (Roberts 2019: 270)

Yet reefs are not a simple Arcadia. 'A coral reef is not, as most of the world imagines, a place of perpetual sunlight and crystal seas. It has weather – plenty of it' (Clarke 1956: 70). It also has violence – 'the coral reef is a cauldron of carnivory, every day lived a small miracle of luck and instinct' as inhabitants prey on each other (Roberts 2019: 82). 'The reef is a battleground of ceaseless warfare, with a slogan of "eat, or be eaten"', where at night one might hear 'the anguished shrieks of the myriads dying and the harsh triumphal cries of the victors!' exclaimed Noel Monkman (1956: 75, 92). More common than Homeric epic are urban metaphors that make reefs busily peopled. Beebe had imagined himself 'a Martian, dropped into Fifth Avenue or Regent Street' (1926: 282); Roberts uses a similar simile. 'The reef was a confusing swirl of movement, like Grand Central Station at rush hour' (2012: 1). Reef activity felt overwhelming to

Figure 11 A lettuce leaf sea slug (*Elysia crispata*) on a coral reef. Jardines de la Reina, Gardens of the Queen National Park, Cuba. Caribbean Sea. Photo and caption by Alex Mustard. Image courtesy of Alex Mustard.

some, resistant even to Edenic metaphors. Harrigan was impatient with himself 'for trying to reduce all this alien grandeur to something comprehensible and comfortable. I longed for my pedestrian imagination to fall away, because finally it was what barred me from truly perceiving the reef' (1992: 147). Reef life overspilled its templates.

CORALS AND SCIENCE

'Scientific knowledge grows like the reef itself, through accretion and erosion. … Science itself is the process of weaving disparate strands of information into a braid we call knowledge a plait that is ceaselessly unwoven and rewoven' (Davidson 1998: 103). Although much weaving has been done in laboratories, especially in the twenty-first century, 'an ecological understanding of [coral] function principally followed the advent of diving apparatus' says marine scientist Charles Sheppard (2014: 9). Coral authority Charlie Veron stressed how important that was: 'without scuba these experts had never seen corals as I was seeing them' (2017: 80). Sheppard emphasizes the significance of coral reefs in time and space. 'Their scale is enormous; the Indo-Pacific coral reef province, for a start, is the largest ecosystem on Earth, and probably its most diverse, at least at higher taxonomic levels' (Sheppard 2014: 2). There were reef-building predecessors, stromatolites; some still survive, living fossils. The great Permo-Triassic extinction event saw perhaps 90 per cent of marine species disappear, 250 million years ago; scleractinian corals, the main reef-builders now, arrived 240 million years ago. 'The riot of life seen on healthy reefs today is the result of a very long heritage', says Sheppard (2014: 15).

The Eden paradigm of tropical reefs tends to blot out other kinds, like *Lophelia pertusa*, 'a cold-water, reef-forming coral, [which] has a wide geographic distribution ranging from 55°S to 70°N, where water temperatures typically remain between 4–8°C' (Maddock 2008: n.p.). They can be found off Scotland, Scandinavia and Nova Scotia, among other places, down to 2775 metres; unlike most tropical corals they do not host zooxanthellae, and feed carnivorously by catching plankton. 'The development of tools ranging from acoustic mapping systems to mini-submarines has allowed scientists to visit cold-water corals in their natural habitat. Scientists have now recorded over 1,300 species living among coral reefs in the north-eastern Atlantic, proving them to be among the most important and diverse ecosystems of the world' (Lophelia 2025). Their remoteness from view keeps them out of popular imagination, though advocates promote them as a poster species for deep ocean conservation (Braverman 2018: 191, 194). Temperate water corals also have less recognition than tropical ones. 'Overall, cool-temperate species inhabiting the Great Southern Reef – the interconnected network of kelp-covered rocky reefs that extends from northern New South Wales to southwestern Australia – are generally declining in number more rapidly and are more threatened with extinction, than tropical species' (Edgar 2023: n.p.). Leafy sea-dragons, red velvet fish and handfishes live in these reefs, or did.

Coral is properly corals, plural. The Octocorallia, named because they have eight tentacles around the mouth, include sea fans, sea pens and soft corals. The Hexacorallia, with multiples of six tentacles around the mouth, include stony corals, black corals, sea anemones and others. The peculiar status of hard coral in premodern science, puzzlingly neither animal nor plant, possibly insect, was resolved into understanding it as a curious arrangement of polyps and algal cells. The animal polyps can survive without algae for a while, but the partnership suits both: the algal cells, or zooxanthellae, draw on light to make sugars that support the polyp, which also feeds, often at night, on plankton. It is the polyps who deposit calcium carbonate beneath them to accrete into a reef. Settled coral may have a neural network connecting daughter and parent polyps. They reproduce two ways: asexually, by budding off, and sexually, by broadcasting eggs and sperm, often in astonishing synchrony, a sight first witnessed by scientists on the Great Barrier Reef in 1981. The fertilized eggs or planulae can swim short distances before settling; they can absorb algal partners from the water, or travel with them. Different water and light conditions give colonies a bewildering variety of shapes initially misunderstood as distinct species. *Acropora*, for instance, a hard coral genus currently with 120-140 species including table coral, elkhorn and staghorn corals, can be branched, in thickets, domes, columns or flat shapes. Visiting a coral nursery near Honolulu, Irus Braverman reported that 'although many of the corals are extremely rare, they have not been listed as threatened because it is unclear whether they are separate species or are part of a spectrum of morphological variability' (2018: 167). As Braverman explains, 'Corals confuse and destabilize our categories: they are a cross between animal, plant, rock, microbe, and ecosystem', a confusion she inventively resolves: 'corals are, in fact, "coralations" – bundles of constantly changing assemblages that shape and reshape their ways of being in the world' (Braverman 2018: 11). This biological elasticity creates category confusion. One strand of coral science now sees most species as hybrids, creating complications: laws protect species but not hybrids (Braverman 2018: 156).

Charlie Veron is an Australian coral scientist whose life's work has been to identify and sort out the species of world corals. In his autobiography, he described it as 'like trying to put together a dozen great big jigsaw puzzles all at once, with the majority of the pieces missing' (Veron 2017: 86). Wrestling with palaeontology, taxonomy, biological oceanography, ecology, systematics and molecular science, he invented a concept of 'reticulate evolution' that was all and none of the above (Veron 1996: 6). Most simply, corals dissolve binaries.

> In addition to challenging the distinctions between life and death and the very concept of aging, corals undermine basic human assumptions about the relationships between plant and animal, individual and colony, fixed and mobile, male and female, hybrid and pure, sexual and asexual reproduction, and organic and inorganic matter.
>
> (Braverman 2018: 255)

Corals are multiplicities. Working on coral infections, Eugene Rosenberg and Ilana Zilber-Rosenberg argue that coral is not only polyp plus algae, but coral plus algae plus bacteria, archaea, dinoflagellates and other organisms – hence it is a superorganism, a hologenome, one combining a host genome and a microbiome (Braverman 2018: 208), or a holobiont, a host and microbial community. Like the multispecies human (Haraway 2008), a coral is a community. Genetics may seem remote from life writing, but both disciplines come to agree that 'a coral reef is an erratic process rather than a thing' (Sale 2021: 14).

Before holobiont and hologenome featured from the 1990s onwards, scientists tended to explain the relationship between coral polyp and algae in simple metaphors: as host and guest, or tenant and landlord, or marital partners – recently, ones who divorce because global heating makes the relationship impossible to sustain (which raises questions of agency in terms of whether a polyp makes algae leave, or the algae walk out). There are political variants, like Kropotkin's worker and slave, or Beebe's 'socialistic, standardised equality of the coral builders' (Beebe 1928: 44; Jones 2007: 100-3). Nineteenth-century America cultivated coral metaphors for both a just society and one dependent on slavery (Navakas 2023). Such anthropomorphic metaphors still saturate reef literature, even though a posthuman turn in academia calls for 'a more respectful and responsible "living-together" with the nonhuman both "big like us" as well as "small and not like us"' (Beck 2021: 373). Besides the corals themselves, reefs are homes to innumerable lives that are tiny, hidden and cryptic – like the female gall crab who inhabits a minute dwelling that closes around her as the coral grows (Van der Meij 2014: 1008). The much smaller male crabs 'visit' females to mate – a difference in life cycle to which many writers apply stereotypes of male wanderlust. Noel Monkman's is typical. 'Evidently the spirit of adventure has departed from the female of her species, and mere existence has taken the place of living' (1963: 154). Nobody thinks of anchorites as analogy, just as mysteriously motivated.

For many writers, anthropomorphism increases accessibility. Late twentieth-century underwater life writing, however, includes authors who think explicitly about the place of humans and their relations to reefs. They did so the more readily because television took over much documentary work, and because the growth of scuba diving as a holiday activity meant observers wanted to distinguish themselves from tourists. Easier access brought increasing damage to reefs. Unlike destruction from climate change where causes can appear remote, this damage is immediately traceable to humans. Writing of underwater tourism in the Red Sea, Callum Roberts nails the paradox. 'These reefs are like boxers, struggling on, bruised and bleeding but still on their feet. Their mistreatment is not deliberate. They are simply loved too much' (2019: 181).

REEF OTHERNESS

Stephen Harrigan's *Water and Light* is an account of really getting to know a reef. He chose Grand Turk in the Turks and Caicos Islands, an archipelago south of the Bahamas, in part because it had no Club Med. A water-baby childhood, combined with reading Beebe, Cousteau, Dugan and – crucially – Diolé, inspired him to attempt metaphysical immersion. 'The waving tentacles, the darting fish, the ceaseless secret business of the reef filled me less with wonder than with anxiety. My desire to comprehend this place was a sort of panic.' Logbooks, the usual on-the-spot records of a scuba diver, were too like haiku or diary entries, not full enough to constitute, 'as I once hoped they would, the autobiography of an underwater pilgrim' (Harrigan 1992: 13-15). Going to the reef with local dive operators, this pilgrim distances himself from diving *hoi polloi*:

Homeward-bound divers – in T-shirts bearing florid likenesses of dolphins or manta rays or the simple logo of a diving equipment manufacturer – stood about sipping beer and waiting to board. The hair on their forearms was bleached white, and the skin on the back of their necks was peeling off in sheets as crinkly as parchment. The divers appeared at ease, played-out, sated. They may have been wage slaves back home, but here in Grand Turk they had the languorous bearing of aristocrats. …

This was not yet a major dive resort, where the cattle boats disgorged forty or fifty underwater tourists at a time; where the coral was broken and bruised by the careless swatting of fins; and where the fish, ruined by handouts, swam up to the divers expecting an aerosol burst from a can of Cheez-Whiz. 'Yeah, this is pretty great,' a paper salesman from Seattle told me one day as we headed in from a dive. 'Come back in ten years, it'll break your heart.'

(Harrigan 1992: 37)

Seeking 'the rapture of belonging' (Harrigan 1992: 91-2), related to Freud's oceanic feeling, Harrigan improved his diving skills and knowledge of reef creatures. But those competences perversely countered rapture. 'After a while I found that without consciously meaning to do so, I had peopled the reef with my own creations. One by one I had given each fish a personality' (Harrigan 1992: 146-7) – an anthropomorphism at odds with posthuman connectivity.

Part of me, it was true, wanted to insinuate myself into the lives of the creatures on the reef – to touch them, incite them, ride them, make them pay attention to me. But every time I gave in to this impulse I felt shut out from the true life of the reef and sealed once again into my outsider's bubble. … In a way, I thought, I had what I wanted: I was living underwater. My imagination was soaked in undersea thoughts and imagery, and here on the surface world it operated with a perceptible lag – refactoring, reconfiguring, purging itself of an endless store of aquatic references.

(Harrigan 1992: 177-8, 219)

Well-read in underwater literature, he planned to add his own immersive book to it. Philosophical solitude clashed with literary sociability. 'I stopped in mid-note, suddenly aware that the book I was writing was an invitation for others to join me in overwhelming the reefs of the world with our smiling curiosity. The reef, I knew, would probably be better off without me or my book' (Harrigan 1992: 247). At the end, he outlines all the risks to coral reefs – already happening, in 1992 – including divers who, by sheer numbers and careless damage, destroy the beauty they come to see.

For Harrigan, television is a competitor and it also makes wondrous things commonplace. 'Run through the cable channels on your television, and at any given time you may come across a documentary showcasing the beauty and fragility of coral reefs or the endangered grandeur of the humpback whale' (Harrigan 1992: 241). Writing, on the other hand, can explore inner space and the way a reef can change it according to different weather, moods, times of day or night, company. Harrigan sought revelation:

> I wanted the impossible: to be noticed, to be invited in, to be taken down into a coral grotto and shown the secret handshake. But there was no secret handshake. Nobody was invited. Everybody was just here, no more or less welcome than I. One of the problems humans have always had with the rest of creation is that we insist on seeing ourselves as either superior to it or unworthy of it. What I wanted now was to know what it felt like simply to take my place in it, to accept what it had to offer and to stop pining for gifts of revelation that were beyond my reach.
>
> (Harrigan 1992: 247)

One episode demonstrates how difficult it is to shed cultural paradigms. Harrigan, now diving confidently, explores solo:

> Caverns were everywhere. I stuck my head into a crevice to have a look around, expecting an indentation in the coral of only a few feet, and saw instead that the whole bank was honeycombed with corridors and tunnels. It was irresistible, and I swam inside. Rooms and rooms opened ahead of me, the kind of ever-expanding interior space one encounters – full of rapturous expectation – in a dream. The floor was clean sand, with precise ripples that charted the direction of the water flow. Light came in skittery beams from holes in the ceiling. And every room I entered led to some deeper chamber, from which tunnels radiated in all directions, leading either to more rooms or to an exit marked by a pane of blue ocean light. The walls, scoured smooth by the relentless pulsing of the water, were festooned with algae and coiling sea whips and tubular sponges.
>
> (Harrigan 1992: 129)

This is a fine description. It is also a version of uterine space, an idea developed by Roger Dadoun. He tracks the 'universal theme of the descent' through shrinking spaces in relation to the architecture of vampire castles, where Gothic turrets partner (rather than oppose) underground vaults in evoking an archaic mother, a figure of primal terror (Dadoun 1989: 38–61). This pre-Oedipal mother 'is that in which everything is engulfed, the oceanic thing … that calls for fusion – thereby putting the subject in touch with his own terror of fusion and formlessness' (Dadoun 1989: 39). Uterine space constricts, whereas here there is free passage for the diver. But what happens next is startlingly sexualized. Harrigan remembers a scene in a novel where the protagonist, alone in a room, pulls down his pants and masturbates. Harrigan thinks that's a great idea, because 'I saw the strange romance of it, the compulsion to release one's seed into this coral womb, to watch it float upwards in ropy strands, one more hopeful clutch of waterborne protoplasm searching for its destiny' (1992: 131). If the ocean is felt to be feminine, ejaculating in it forces masculinity back into significance. Harrigan's buddy, less poetic, turns up and wants to stab a giant grouper. By Dadoun's model, their violation and violence can be understood as unconscious hostility to a still more archaic mother, 'a totalising and oceanic mother … evoking in the subject the anxiety of fusion and dissolution' (Dadoun 1989: 54–5). The frighteningly boundless ocean is too full of oceanic feeling, so patriarchal mastery yanks cosmic significance away from reef sensitivity.

Rosaleen Love's *Reefscape* (2001) reflects on the Great Barrier Reef. It is not an immersive memoir like Harrigan's, but she is interested in underwater states of mind and their socially constructed filters. The Great Barrier Reef is a political construct – its protected area and geographical area are not identical – and it is a powerful brand. 'By 1996 tourism on the Great Barrier Reef would be worth $750 million annually to Australia' (Love 2001: 98); twenty-five years later, annually, 'the Great Barrier Reef is valued at $56 billion as an Australian economic, social and iconic asset' (Great Barrier Reef Foundation 2025). That's $55 and a quarter billion value added; $32 billion of that is related to tourism. A whiff of profitability attaches to coral health; the beauty of corals is marketable. Hence some environmental organizations have partnered with big companies to share media attention and social reach. For the Australian Open tennis tournament in 2022, the sportswear brand Adidas installed on the Great Barrier Reef a floating tennis court made of recycled plastic, as was its new collection of tennis clothes. The founder of Parley for the Oceans which partnered Adidas argued the initiative got people's attention. 'Doing so in a positive and graphic way helps us reconnect to the most important mission that is so deeply programmed into our genes: our own survival' (Ravenscroft 2022). Such partnerships between ocean campaigners and big brands lend products the metaphysical value of 'caring for Nature'. Thus the brewer of Corona beer backed an outfit replanting corals, through the sale of coral seedlings (Corona 2021). After purchase, every coral owner received a certificate with their name and a QR code showing the location of their coral. Otherness here disappears into feel-good consumption and personal possession. With a tag line of 'Gift the Ocean', the sales campaign invited people 'to gift their loved ones a meaningful present that lasts'. Quite how regrown corals can survive ocean acidification is unclear. In 2021 a leading cat food brand, Sheba, owned by Mars Incorporated, sponsored a replanting effort in writing, literally: 'the letters H-O-P-E spelled with regrown coral' (Ads 2021). Writing in coral makes the reef a billboard for messages to humans. Otherness is exploited for marketing or simply eliminated.

THE LIFE WRITING OF CORAL DISASTER

In 2012 British marine biologist Callum Roberts published a book about ocean life, starting with a 'timeless and primordial' dive on the Great Barrier Reef in 1987. Time quickly proves not to be timeless:

> I wonder what I would have thought if on return to shore we had been greeted by a curmudgeonly sage who prophesied that in one hundred years this magnificent reef would be a crumbling ruin, that its bright coral escarpments would be replaced by green fuzz, and that the ranks of fish would have thinned and given way to swarms of jellyfish and gelatinous plankton. I would probably have thought him mad. Nothing could have seemed less likely. And yet less than twenty-five

years later most serious marine scientists predict just such a fate. We can already see it happening.

(Roberts 2012: 2)

Eden is now dystopia for reefs:

A few years ago I swam through the remains of what had been a glorious reef there. It was a scene of devastation. The seabed was strewn with chalky fragments, like a field of bones in the aftermath of massacre. Here and there a mound rose above the wreckage where once some mighty coral had stood.

(Roberts 2012: 86)

This war zone is created by one species. Scientists point out that corals have had extinctions before their Anthropocenic collapse; they also point out that corals war with each other, especially at night. 'Peaceful-looking coral gardens are anything but peaceful; there are war zones everywhere' (Veron 2017: 91). Article II of the UN Convention on the Prevention and Punishment of the Crime of Genocide, adopted in 1948, has as its third defining clause 'Deliberately inflicting on the group conditions of life calculated to bring about its physical destruction in whole or in part' (United Nations n.d.). The Article does not extend beyond humans. Some think it should. In the words of Ben Cropp, underwater photographer and film-maker, 'Coral genocide by humans is taking place all over the world' (1993).

Scientist memoirs hover between memory and history: descriptions of diving on healthy reefs appear alongside witness accounts of dying reefs and the historic disappearance of coral. Pierre Nora weighs the significance of the acceleration of history, a mood music for the present:

An increasingly rapid slippage of the present into a historical past that is gone for good, a general perception that anything and everything may disappear – these indicate a rupture of equilibrium … Indeed, it is this very push and pull that produces *lieux de memoire* – moments of history torn away from the movement of history, then returned; no longer quite life, not yet death, like shells on the shore when the sea of living memory has receded.

(Nora 1989: 7, 12)

Nora's marine metaphor can be extended from shore to underwater: corals, so consistently now between life and death, can be read as their own *lieux de memoire*. In 2010 Callum Roberts dived with Sylvia Earle in the Galápagos Islands in a marine reserve where protection assured some richness of fish life, though not of coral. 'At the end we surfaced unsure whether to laugh or cry. If this were my first ever dive I could not have been happier at the wild exuberance of life. But Celine [Cousteau's granddaughter] and I were burdened by the ghosts of the disappeared' (Roberts 2019: 120).

Nora proposes that history books 'inscribe a neat border around a domain of memory' (1989: 21). Diver memoirs struggle against neatness because older divers remember Eden and younger divers do not. The difference can be explained by shifting baseline syndrome, by which abundance diminishes but still looks like abundance. Imagine you have a garden and a bird table. In the first year you have thirty birds visiting each day. In the fifth year you have twenty visitors a day. Twenty years on, you have five visitors a day. Five can seem plenty to watchers who never saw the thirty. Commenting on the 'bombshell' that the Great Barrier Reef lost half its coral between 1997 and 2012, Callum Roberts asks 'When will there be too little cover to warrant the name "coral" reef, I wonder? Already the average coral cover hovers at around 14 per cent, whereas once it ranged from 40 to 60 per cent' (2019: 254).

Was coral disappearance heeded? 'Increasing numbers of scientists have given increasingly urgent warnings, but what can be done about it? Coral reefs as a whole have been described as being the canaries in the coal mine – they are the part of the ecosystem that will be the first to succumb to overexploitation and abuse' (Sheppard 2014: 18). It is peculiar that a fossil-fuel related metaphor represents a crisis caused by fossil fuel use. Nonetheless, the canary is firmly established as an other-species Cassandra (Schrope 2009). What is the canary's deathsong? In 2014, it was that 'about a quarter of reefs that existed 50 to 100 years ago are now largely dead, and another quarter or even third (depending on the area) are in critical condition; only about a quarter of the remaining reefs are in a healthy, robust state' (Sheppard 2014: 84). A relatively new field in academia brings history, anthropology and ecology together to explain 'collapse', borrowing 'from the literature on networks, systems, and complexity. In these fields, collapse refers to the disaggregation and breaking apart of a connected network. A collapsing complex system breaks down or fragments', as dying reefs do (Centeno et al. 2023: 9). Covering collapses as various as Mayan civilization and bee colonies, collapse studies has sadly rich ground in coral reefs. In fact reefs signal several collapses: one of climate and ocean stability, hence another of coral, which anticipates a third, the collapse of human society.

The difference between climate crisis and other disasters that wiped out earlier civilizations is that evidence for climate crisis is clear and its causes preventable. Or they were. Alarm was sounded by Rachel Carson in *The Sea Around Us* (1951) and J. J. McCoy in *A Sea of Troubles* (1975) who warned especially about human pollution of the marine environment. Those warnings redoubled from the 1990s on as marine biologists encountered unmistakeable signs of system collapse, painfully visible on coral reefs. What Callum Roberts calls 'the five horsemen of the apocalyptic loss of biodiversity that is sweeping the planet' – habitat loss, pollution, climate change, overkill by hunting or fishing, and invasive species (Roberts 2012: 195) – were all in evidence, especially after the bleaching event of 1997–1978, so severe on the Great Barrier Reef that some coral scientists publicly wept. In spite of media attention, they were lonely conduits: 'scientists emerge from these emergencies as the sole witness to coral death: monitoring, documenting, recording, measuring – and weeping' (Braverman 2018: 75). In Peter Sale's analysis, 'the prognosis is dire – many of us see little chance that reefs resembling the 1960s will persist past 2050. If this future comes to pass, we will have witnessed the elimination of an entire ecosystem and the regional or global extinction of many thousands of species within a single human lifetime' (2021: 170).

One notable study of collapse genres identifies 210 explanations for the end of the Roman Empire (Ward-Perkins 2005: figure 3.1). There is a similar abundance of explanations for climate inaction and a similar pattern in the explanations themselves, particularly political and psychological, updated to include the complex influence of digital connectivity. Analysis of coral collapse involves many strands from this braid; Peter F. Sale discusses them at more length. Hubris is one big reason: 'Getting people to understand that we are one species of animal is a first step in building some humility in the face of nature. ... if there is one thing *Homo sapiens* needs, it is more humility' (Sale 2021: 67). Osha Gray Davidson also condemns species arrogance. 'We have given ourselves the grand name *Homo sapiens*, "wise man." But that's mere bravado. Until we understand who and what and where we are, we will remain a distant second best: *Homo versutus*, "clever man"' (1998: 222). Sylvia Earle's widely cited formulation invokes humility and wisdom: 'What we must do is acknowledge a sea change in attitude, one that acknowledges we are a part of the living world, not apart from it.'

One account renders coral reef destruction in miniature. Osha Gray Davidson went to visit Nyamuk Besar, one of many islands off Jakarta, weekend getaways for the rich. He wanted to see the coral which a description of the 1930s praised for 'the splendour and wealth of forms and the delicate tints of coral structures'. What he found was hell, not paradise.

> There is no living coral at all. There are no fishes. The only 'delicate tints' and 'brilliant colours' in the water come from the multitude of plastic bags, chunks of Styrofoam, and liter soda bottles that float around the island. Oil slicks add an iridescent dash of color to the surface.
>
> (Davidson 1998: 119-20)

Of ninety-six species of hard corals noted in the 1930s, there were sixteen left, all sickly.

> Nyamuk Besar is just one well-documented site in Jakarta Bay, a body of water that went from being a coral paradise to what can only be described as an algae-choked sewer in the span of a few decades ... Another scientist put it more succinctly: 'We've come up with a good word to describe these reefs,' he told a colleague after returning from Jakarta. 'Fucked.'
>
> (Davidson 1998: 120-1)

Invasive sea urchins, *Diodema*, complete Davidson's apocalyptic cast. 'Human waste. Heavy metal pollution. Sedimentation. Coral mining and dredging. Overfishing. What killed Jakarta Bay? That's like asking who killed a man executed by a firing squad' (Davidson 1998: 126). Archaeologist Guy Middleton explains the appeal of collapse stories as that of quest romance, tragedy and parable (2017: 5). In each of these forms, fate is writ large. In tragedy and parable, actors are agents of their own downfall; in tragedy they admit it. In coral collapse, life writers hunt for genres that do more than patiently explain. They want genres that rouse.

Steve Jones observed in 2007 that 'scientists, like novelists, have become pessimists in what once appeared to be an earthly paradise' (2007: 6). Are scientists like novelists? In a book on Anthropocenic fiction, Adam Trexler argues that

> the novel has become an essential tool to construct meaning in an age of climate change. The novel expands the reach of climate science beyond the laboratory or model, turning abstract predictions into subjectively tangible experiences of place, identity, and culture.
>
> (2015, publisher summary)

But coral scientists had long been beyond the laboratory: many were underwater, and writing about subjectively tangible experiences. Why does fiction trump life writing? Peter Sale thinks the genre of story – one shared by fiction and life writing – is crucial. 'Most readers see the prevailing coral reef message as "reefs are being harmed, scientists are making discoveries, there is concern, but there is also reason for optimism." That is a story that is not particularly interesting, certainly not a story that will keep *everyperson's* attention' (Sale 2021: 183). Sale thinks about his own practice in terms of story-making, claiming 'it is the stories that make a piece of science memorable' (2021: 176), though without wider reference to other Anthropocenic locales and sciences which have attracted different kinds of writers – the poets of disappearing ice, for instance (Cox 2026; Farrier 2019).

Sale tells a 'story' – or he narrates an experience mediated through memory, discourse and genre – about being in Dubai, where a construction project of huge hubris, Palm Island, was concreting over a reef with exceptional possibilities. I condense his narrative to two sentences: that reef 'was composed of some of the most heat-tolerant corals on Earth'. 'They were buried to build sand islands' (Sale 2021: 163-4). It seems to me that what's powerful here is the symbolism – living things sacrificed to a simulacrum of a living thing, a sand island shaped like a palm tree. That has narrative, but it serves to point the moral of hubris. Palm Island is in fact three islands, one shaped like a palm tree, all made of sand dredged, dumped and compacted as the (now leaky) base for luxury development, including a hotel so luxurious it services only one occupant at a time. The corals and other marine life killed off in consequence – a token handful were relocated – were a community, one destroyed for an economy of extreme exclusivity. 'Modern Western-style nations have built economies in which nature has no rights other than the right to be used by people', Sale observes (2021: 211). Callum Roberts has a similar story of being asked to assess the marine life of a bay soon to be concreted over so that the city of Doha can expand. 'It feels ... that I am documenting a world condemned, like a linguist sent to record a tribal language before its last ageing speakers die' (Roberts 2019: 105). Both writers point the moral of their stories – because stories by themselves are not enough.

Scientist life writers try other metaphors too, representing reef death in singular human terms. 'Watching reefs decline has been like watching a parent age. Little by little they lose strength. The changes, hardly perceptible at first, mount up to rob them of mobility, independence and even dignity. The love you feel is now sadness' (Roberts 2019: 247). After a 2016 survey of the Great Barrier Reef showed that on twenty-four of eighty-four reefs surveyed, 50 per cent of corals had died, Joanie Kleypas said 'It feels like a very special person whom you just started to get acquainted with suddenly dies on you' (Braverman 2018: 38). Logically extending this metaphor of reef as person, an obituary of the Great Barrier Reef appeared in 2016. It went viral:

> The Great Barrier Reef of Australia passed away in … after a long illness. It was 25 million years old. [...] The reef was born on the eastern coast of the continent of Australia during the Miocene epoch. Its first 24.99 million years were seemingly happy ones, marked by overall growth.
>
> (Jacobsen 2016)

The obituary, written by Rowan Jacobsen, used Charlie Veron's work, especially his elegiac talk in 2009 to the Royal Society about how the world's largest living structure is dying and is likely to have gone – dissolved by acid seas – by 2030. The reef 'provided some of the most thrilling marine adventures on earth to humans who visited. Its otherworldly colours and patterns will be sorely missed. [...] To say the reef was an extremely active member of its community is an understatement' (Jacobsen 2016). There was a big response on social media, not all of it positive: some missed the satire, some denounced the piece as clickbait. Others insisted on the value of hope. Terry Hughes put it bluntly: 'You don't write the obituary of a loved one when they are diagnosed with a serious illness – you help them fight for their life' (Urry 2016).

Jacobsen's obituary was not the first. The *Guardian* posted a multimedia obituary of the Great Barrier Reef (Milman 2014) which drew attention to the massive impact of the mining industry, exporting coal from big ports on the reef. But it didn't catch on. Why did Jacobsen's? Its success comes from how impeccably it grasps the conventions of an obituary, even down to its grammar. It repurposes the anthropocentrism which has caused the Anthropocene, and how obituaries assign social significance to their subject. Critics disliked parody applied to something deadly serious, but irony underlined that deadliness.

Arguments about exactly how dying coral reefs are lead to a double bind. 'If humans can fix nature, there is no reason to change our damaging ways; at the same time, if all is hopeless, there is still no reason to change our ways' (Braverman 2018: 250). Alongside are visions of coral reefs as 'zombie ecosystems' (Bradbury 2012) and a critique of the idea of pristine nature as a baseline for restoration. 'This idea that we go out in nature to conserve things back to the way they were is a gone concept', says Ove Hoegh-Guldberg (Braverman 2018: 59). Pristine nature is a concept that mirrors fine art – what is pristine, what is fine being agreed cultural constructs. Charles Sheppard has twice ended books with a comparison between the destruction of coral reefs to stripping a Rembrandt for its canvas (Sheppard 2014: 114). Hoegh-Guldberg invokes van Gogh's *The Starry Night*. 'I say, well, what if we decided we're just going to burn this painting? Get rid of it. There'd be a huge outcry because of its uniqueness. So why are we doing that with species?' (Braverman 2018: 59). The value of fine art comes from markets, which have long treated the ocean as natural capital. 'What price can be put on wonder? How much is a species worth?' asks Callum Roberts (2019: 339).

The Great Barrier Reef has a managing authority (GBRMPA) that translates natural capital into financial worth. In 2015–16, the Great Barrier Reef was valued at $56 billion as an Australian economic, social and iconic asset (Great Barrier Reef 2025, using 2015 figures). 'Managing the reef is a highly political activity' observes Rosaleen Love (2001: 194). Scientists too have turned to modern portfolio theory to identify reefs which, so far escaping catastrophic losses, would maximize returns (Beyer et al. 2018; Coral Reef Rescue Initiative 2020; Hoegh-Guldberg et al. 2018). Adopting the language of business that some argue fixes nature within extractive capitalism shows coral scientists in a frantic hunt for persuasive genres besides life writing.

Life writing by diver-scientists overlaps with analyses of Anthropogenic causes and consequences by environmental writers and journalists. An older trope of protest as voice, revived in podcasts and TED talks, calls writing into question as the best medium. Irus Braverman's book *Coral Whisperers* (2018) uses interviews, speech put into writing, as a means of giving equal weight to voices and to show difficult divisions among the coral science community. Rebecca Roach and Anneleen Masschelein propose that 'interviews in the social sciences might well be conceived as a life writing practice' (2018: 172). And in the sciences, since the coral scientists speak autobiographically, and Braverman situates them biographically in the history of coral science. This clever weave, which also includes herself as autobiographical subject, creates what Masschelein and Roach call 'a collective, impersonal viewpoint that exceeds subjectivity, turning the interview into an assemblage of "voice[s] without organs" … that results in a living body of thinking' (2018: 173). All Braverman's participants are passionate voices for coral, spread across despair and hope, and newly realigning around possible practices of repair. Arguing for moving beyond obituaries, Nancy Knowlton acknowledges 'negative stories are stickier' (Braverman 2018: 3). But the interview genre allows negative emotions to be aired, disputes acknowledged and common aims affirmed. 'The emotional layers in the work of the coral scientists are arguably just as meaningful as their analysis, if not more so' (Braverman 2018: 14). Coral scientists become not only gatherers and interpreters of data, but also distressed humans who find strength in staying with the trouble, to use Donna Haraway's far-echoing phrase (2016a).

GARDENING AFTER EDEN

Braverman identifies a literary challenge for coral scientists: tone.

> Their task is tough: they must both witness their beloved corals dying out and at the same time narrate this death to the world. They must be careful not to sound too gloomy, lest their warnings be labelled alarmist, nor too hopeful, lest they be dismissed as Pollyannaish or even as denialists.
>
> (Braverman 2018: 16)

A recent generation of coral scientists propose a sweet spot which is also practical: restoration. As Braverman's interviewees explain, this means growing corals on ropes, nets, cages or plastic trees which are then transplanted back onto a reef. 'Bleaching is bad but giving up is worse', as Nancy Knowlton tweeted (Braverman 2018: 35). Propagated by asexual and sexual methods, corals can be selected for heat tolerance or disease resistance or ideally both. Ruth Gates promotes assisted evolution, or breeding to aim for supercorals; Mikhail Matz argues for assisted gene flow, in which humans transplant potential winners to let them reproduce, a process also known as assisted migration or genetic rescue (Braverman 2018: 43, 148). Hopeful tones here clash with sceptical ones. If the alternative to coral graveyards are human-made coral gardens, what ecology applies? Hoegh-Guldberg believes restoration will fail unless the climate is stabilized and planting locations freed from diseases. As with plants, he told Braverman, planted coral needs tending 'because you don't have the grazing fishes any more, you've got to pull up the seaweeds. So it's very much like a garden. In fact, it *is* gardening, it's underwater gardening' (Braverman 2018: 58).

Other scientists point out that corals are animal, and breeding raises ethical questions about their destiny. Jeremy Jackson invokes coral genocide:

> But to raise a bunch of beautiful, innocent corals and have them be healthy, young studs, and stick them out in the reef where they died in the first place is like sending them to a concentration camp. If you can't clean up the environment, if you can't make the water good, then what the hell do you think you are doing? You're either a fool or a sadist.
>
> (Braverman 2018: 104)

Purity is difficult in this messy world. Braverman interviewed a coral nurseryman from Florida, Ken Nedimyr. He expanded his breeding business to plant on reefs. New arrivals were tagged, but storms broke up corals so 'you had no idea where they came from … Eventually, we just outplanted a reef of one thousand unknown corals. We have no idea which ones they are, but we have a reef' (Braverman 2018: 142). By the gardening analogy, it seems no worse than throwing a packet of mixed seed onto bare ground. But a reef of randomly human-installed corals may be eco-anarchy, or worse.

The restorers have taken up life writing too. Juli Berwald's *Life on the Rocks* follows other nature writing that folds in human trauma or misery as counterpoint narrative. Berwald's text features an illness memoir of her daughter's anxiety and recovery from OCD as analogies for damage to corals and their possible repair. 'Coral restorations will be the lifeboats sheltering the corals until we get control of our carbon emissions' (2022: 287): Berwald's metaphor invokes rescue, a prospect others doubt or critique. Life writing on corals has spanned their vibrant life, collapse and grim death. Yet despite their expertise and accessible autobiographies, the biographers of this charismatic underwater life find their testimony not powerful enough to secure its future.

Part Two

Species

5

Fishy Knowledges

'It is generally believed that calling a spade a spade helps towards clarity and understanding. It is most regrettable that such a course is not possible when mentioning fishes.'

(McMahon 1946: 33)

'The Atlantic spadefish, Chaetodipterus faber *is known by numerous other colloquial names, including angelfish, white angelfish, threetailed porgy, ocean cobbler, and moonfish.'*

(Wikipedia)

Our knowledge of fish is decidedly fishy – piscine-centred and questionable. This chapter explores how fish and other marine beings present challenges in terms of their names, their taxonomy (schemes of classification) and what sorts of knowledge ecologies we bring to them – 'we' being also a problematic category. Western science is undergoing major rethinks, spearheaded by multispecies ethnographers, decolonizers, feminists and queer thinkers, animal studies scholars and many scientists including marine biologists. These rethinks join up variously, along with a rapidly evolving vocabulary for how life writing contributes to the posthuman by attending to nonhuman lives (Braidotti, Jones and Klumbyte 2023). In this chapter I look first at the Linnaean system, then at recent alternatives – clades, DNA, e-DNA – to sketch scientific models of naming marine beings. Writers about underwater life draw on those namings, which are also a form of life writing. Besides giving an internationally agreed and regulated identity to a marine being, a name may carry traces of life stories. These are visible especially in eponyms, things named for a person. Eponyms and etymologies can signify social values and power structures which are being challenged by decolonizers. Western science underpins marine biology, but it coexists with vernacular and local knowledges which have quite different names and import. I show this through two regions, Pacific and Arctic. Western scientific naming involves a web of relations between scientists; non-Western Indigenous understandings of fish may incorporate mythological genealogies, local topographies and folk beliefs. So too do Western vernacular knowledges. Noting in the 1980s that on Scottish fishing boats it was unlucky to name a salmon, one name collector commented on current alternatives. 'A glance through the dialect names for salmon given in the glossary would seem to indicate that the folk memory of Finn mac Cumhail's great Salmon of Wisdom may still be with us, in that it is still safer to call the deity the Red Fish or the Queer Fella rather than its true name' (Watt 1989: 1).

The naming of marine beings is an important topic because the natural world does not 'arrange itself into the categories we set for it', says the biographer of a marine taxonomist (L. Miller 2020: 176). Relatively few creatures have the same word for their scientific and common name; marine ones include dugong, manta, nautilus, octopus, remora. What Jane Pilcher identifies as the 'names-bodies-identity nexus' (2016: 766) is even more unstable for marine beings than for humans.

LINNAEUS AND LINNAEAN NAMES

'What does a fish care if some taxonomist, walking a few feet above him, happens to label him a "fish." With or without his name, he is still a fish ... ', says Lulu Miller (2020: 64). In an obvious sense this is true, though her assumption of gender may not be. Labels matter: in a human-dominated planet, marine beings acquire legal categories, for instance protection, or lack of it, under international law. The law also governs what species of fishes and how many can be fished for food. The sardine, for instance, *Sardinus pilchardus*, has been at times synonymous with pilchard. Confusable with an anchovy, which has a bigger mouth, and a herring, which has smaller scales, 'deciding what is and is not a sardine is not straightforward ... as to which of the clupeid species is actually a sardine, it depends to whom you speak', says Trevor Day who spends four pages outlining the complexities of identifying a sardine, even though it has an agreed, fixed name (2018: 11). A vernacular name change affected *Hoplostethus atlanticus*, a fish that lives 600-m deep. Like many deep water organisms it grows slowly, lives long and reproduces late. Once known as slimehead because of mucus-producing canals on its head, it began to be fished in the 1970s by deeper trawls, and sold as the more appealingly named orange roughy. Its populations crashed. Total Allowable Catches (TACs) were set at zero in 2010; in 2025, it is classed as Near Threatened on the IUCN Red List of Threatened Species.

It is possible to follow the disaster that befell *Hoplostethus atlanticus* because nature-governing bodies recognize its Linnaean name (and its commonest synonym, orange roughy). Tracking it through the plankton-bloom of acronyms around those international bodies and agreements (like IUCN International Union for Conservation of Nature, and CITES, the Convention on International Trade in Endangered Species of Wild Fauna and Flora), informed guesswork about its surviving numbers depends on historically consistent identification. In this globalized world, classification and naming are based largely on the system established by Linnaeus in his *Systema Naturae* (1735). In this system, organisms have two names: genus and species. It may help here to recall King Philip Could Only Find Green Socks, memnonic for Kingdom, Phylum, Class, Order, Family, Genus, Species – the big picture of Linnaean-based organization. Ironically Linnaeus's own name was newly systematized. His father, Nils Ingmarsson, had to find a family name to be admitted to university, and dropped his patronym for *Linnaeus*, Latin for the Swedish *lind*, commemorating a giant linden tree that grew at his home – a witty invocation of a family tree. Hence his son Carl, Latinized to Carolus, was also Linnaeus (printed with a ligature, æ). Linnaeus proposed three Kingdoms, divided into classes and they in turn divided into orders and genera (the plural of genus); a genus was divided into species. Modern taxonomy added Phylum and Rank, and some extra categories – Subclass, Infraclass, Superfamily. Now Domain rules above Kingdom, and there may be five or six Kingdoms depending on how you see bacteria.

In comparison, Linnaean classification seems simpler. Its binomial nomenclature gives a genus name, capitalized, and an epithet or further name which identifies the species. Both are italicized: thus *Homo sapiens*. So far binomialism has survived questions about the unsingular nature of species, or their possible hybrids. You might say that species are holosymbionts, an assemblage of a host and species which live in, on or around it (Haraway 2008; Margulis 1988). Every human incorporates viruses, bacteria, intestinal flora, skin mites and so on: we may distinguish them as different species, but they make up who each one of us is. You might say too, as Gertrude Stein did, that a rose is a rose is a rose, but if you say *Rosa rugosa*, many people will know exactly and at once which one you mean, out of thousands of possibilities. The Linnaean system is still handy and relatively stable. It has migrated comfortably into digital resources: FishBase, launched in 1996, specializes in finfish, and SeaLifeBase, covering all forms of aquatic life, launched in 2006, are authoritative databases which include information about names including rejected names (often because of misspelling). The World Register of Marine Species or WoRMS, launched in 2008, lists names of marine organisms. Under its umbrella, DecaNet, a portal for decapod informatics, launched in 2023. One analysis reports 'marine biota continue to be discovered and named steadily at a current average of 2,332 new species per year … At the current pace of discovery and characterization, it will take several hundred years to describe the remaining 1–2 million unknown marine species.' It takes approximately 13.5 years for identification to be formalized: of 600 species investigated in this study, eighty-five were sampled by scuba divers. Amateurs contribute significantly to taxonomy. 'New marine species description is still very much a cottage industry that relies on basic sampling techniques and the observation of morphological characters' observe the authors (Bouchet 2023: 6, 12).

Hoplostethus is a subgenus of Roughies, officially the family Trachicthydae; its name (introduced by Georges Cuvier, leading French naturalist, in 1829) uses Greek words for armour and chest to evoke its bony abdominal plates. The Atlantic group became *atlanticus* in 1889, identified by Robert Collett, a Norwegian zoologist. Following a Swede, a Frenchman and Norwegian fixed a name on a type of fish, refined by its typical place (there is also *Hoplostethus japonicus,* found off Japan). It has other names in for instance German and Mandarin. Such rigorous collation reduces the muddles Cousteau complained about, like 'angelfish', applied variously to four genera by different nationalities. 'Somewhere, somehow, there must be a system established that will enable an American diver to know what a Frenchman means when he says "sea angel," and a Japanese or German or Indian to understand what species an American means when he says "angelfish."' (Cousteau and Diolé 1971: 271). One advantage of the Linnaean system's bedrock in Latin and Greek is that description is stabilized by the classics. Cousteau complained that Americans call *Abudefduf saxatilis*, a silvery fish with black stripes, the sergeant major, which made sense in relation to the American Army. 'To a Frenchman, however, "sergeant major" conjures up the image of a brand of pen. ... it becomes almost impossible to develop a popular international vocabulary of marine life' (Cousteau and Diolé 1971: 270). Even so, the sergeant-major, as FishBase lists it (hyphenated), has eighteen different names in Brazil alone.

Complexities arise not just from vernaculars. Peter Sale explains:

> Ecologists working on coral reefs in the 1960s and 1970s got used to talking about *species a* and *species b*, because even quite common creatures remained undescribed; we also got used to the species for which we used the correct name in one paper becoming known by a different name by the time we wrote a follow-up paper about its ecology. That situation has improved, but taxonomy of reef organisms remains a work in progress – too many species, not enough taxonomists.
>
> (Sale 2021: 52)

Sale follows the bumpy history of *Abudefduf zonatus*. In 1825 Quoy and Gaimard had called it *Glyphisodon biocellatus* (thinking of its eyespots). In 1830 Cuvier called it *Glyphisodon zonatus* (thinking of its saddle). Then *Glyphisodon* became part of *Abedefduf*, so the damselfish was for a while *Abedefduf biocellatus*; in the 1980s, damselfish were reorganized, so it became *Chrysiptera biocellata*. Tidied-up Latin prevails for this damselfish: its two spots, *biocellata*, now agree with the gender of its genus name. Studying butterflyfish and damselfish on the Great Barrier Reef, Callum Roberts reported that 'learning the fish feels like a new language, or reading hieroglyphics perhaps, every species a unique cartouche'. Tidy Latin can be difficult. 'Several species of seaweed-munching damselfish are ignored. They go by tongue-twisting names like *Plectroglyphidodon leucozona* and *Chrysiptera unimaculata* that seem to have been devised as an ichthylogical test of sobriety' (Roberts 2019: 52-3).

Fish would seem to be an obvious category, but it isn't. 'The tendency to add fish to any animal that lives in the sea has given us a number of incorrect titles', observed one author (Serventy 1955: 16). Analogies abound. As Stephen Harrigan put it, 'Doctorfish, trunkfish, cowfish, boxfish, butterflyfish, lizardfish, hogfish, squirrelfish, parrotfish – their names reinforced the perception that always took hold of me underwater, that I was in a kind of counter-world, where every feature and principle of surface life had its alien obverse. Including me, the manfish' (1992: 32). Even these analogies wobble: fire fish, lion fish, scorpion fish described the same creature. 'To prevent confusion science has only one name for this fish – *Pterois volitans*' (Monkman 1956: 79). Analogical thinking, however, lessens the unfamiliarity of underwater. The doctorfish, for instance, is a vernacular version of *chirurgis*, meaning surgeon, which is part of its Linnaean name. Surgeonfish have two sharp blades like scalpels; hence the comparison. Enlightenment thinking valued analogy – Joseph Priestley praised it as 'our best guide in all philosophical investigations' (1775/1966: 14). Comparisons link a name to the known-already world. In 1670 John Winthrop, Governor of Connecticut, sent a specimen to the Royal Society. It had five limbs whose subdivisions he calculated amounted to at least 81,920 branches; out of water, it coiled up into a shape like a wicker basket. In an accompanying account, he wrote

> This Fisherman could not tell me of any name it hath, and 't is in all likelihood yet nameless, being not commonly known as other Fish are. But until a fitter English

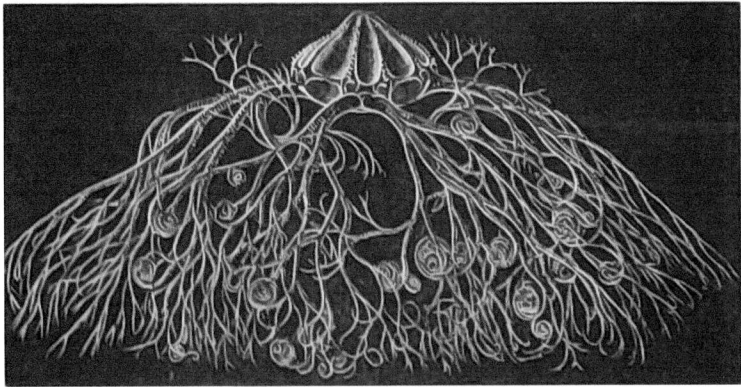

Figure 12 'Basket-fish': from Elizabeth Cary Agassiz and Alexander Agassiz, *Seaside Studies in Natural History: The Marine Animals of Massachusetts Bay* (1865), 118.

name be found for it, why may it not be called (in regard of what hath before been mentioned of it) a *Basket-Fish*, or a *Net-Fish*, or a *Purs-net-Fish*?'

(Agassiz 1865: 120)

We now know it as a basket star, an Ophiuran, a relation of starfish. Neither starfish nor basket stars are fish. The latter's Linnaean genealogy looks like this: Animalia (Kingdom); Echinodermata (Phylum); Ophiuroidea (Class); Euryalida (Order); Gorgonocephalidae (Family); *Astrophyton* (Genus); *Astrophyton muricatum* (species, if this was the one the Governor met).

AFTER LINNAEANS

New technologies mean it is possible to identify organisms according to their DNA. Environmental DNA, or e-DNA, can identify species from the traces they leave, even in water. Non-invasive, the technique has many benefits and some limitations (Beng and Corlett 2020). Two scientists discovered a natural e-DNA collector: sponges (Mariani et al. 2019: 402). Able to filter up to 10,000 litres of water a day, sponges retain e-DNA traces left by other beings. A small chunk of sponge, which the organism can repair, lets those traces be recovered. E-DNA has important uses: it can reveal what species are present; estimate population, abundance and distribution of those species; identify life history stages; detect aquatic invasive species and species at risk. It can also identify the constituents of fishily labelled products, with legal consequences. E-DNA tests on fish balls sold by supermarkets and restaurants in Singapore proved a startling percentage were made of pork and contained little or no seafood (Ho et al. 2020).

The most exciting use of DNA for many biologists is in classification. Where the Linnaean system rested on exact observation and linguistic facility to tell species apart, DNA identification can uncover different relationships. For seahorses, for instance, where fossils and details of body shapes helped establish homologous characters, or features evolved in the same way, genetic evidence can now establish how closely related one species is to another. There are different ways to analyse seahorse DNA: via mitochondrial DNA (inherited through the mother) or nuclear DNA (inherited from both parents). GENBANK holds more than 2000 *Hippocampus* gene sequences, mostly from mitochondrial DNA; the Barcode of Life (BOLD) prefers the gene cytochrome *c* oxidase. Rather than use Linnaean groups of ordering, genetic analysis prefers to group into clades. A clade is a grouping of organisms composed of a common ancestor and all its lineal descendants. Relationships are represented on a phylogenetic tree. This can be visualized in a stick diagram, with each branching representing a lineage splitting off, usually marking an evolutionary turn. The International Society for Phylogenetic Nomenclature runs Phylocode, a set of rules for phylogenetic naming. It explains: 'The groups of organisms or species considered potential recipients of scientific names are called taxa (singular: taxon). The only taxa whose names are governed by this code are clades. However, species, whose names are governed by the rank-based codes, are frequently used to define clade names in this code' (International Society for Phylogenetic Nomenclature 2020). For the Sygnathidae – seahorses, pygmy pipehorses, seadragons, pipehorses, pipefish and, arriving late at the biologists' party, a pygmy seadragon (2007) – genetic analysis shows some features, like a grasping tail, may have evolved independently in different groups, not necessarily from a single common ancestor (Lourie 2016: 9, 44-5). DNA analysis turns up surprises: some species once thought to be separate prove genetically very close. One of the largest studies of the Sygnathidae confirmed the old division into tail-brooders and pouch-brooders, but radically shook up evolutionary relationships between them (Hamilton 2017: 388-403). In practice, what does this change?

For Sara Lourie's guide to seahorses, it means that *Haliichthys taeniophorus* gets a different genealogical place – one more exact than its bet-hedging vernacular names. 'Known as the Ribboned Seadragon, Ribbon Pipehorse, or Ribboned Pipefish, *Haliichthys taeniophorus* is not in fact closely related to either the seadragons or to the pipehorses. Instead, it is a Urophori (tail-brooding) pipefish', related to the Bent Stick pipefish, the pygmy pipehorses and the seahorses (Lourie 2016: 144). It looks quite like a seadragon in having leafy filaments along its body, but two of its three vernacular names assume that kinship wrongly. The Sygnathidae are endangered: seahorses are commercially valuable for Chinese traditional medicine. This lovely leafy creature which is found on the north-west and north coasts of Australia has striking resemblances, think some scholars, to the Rainbow Serpents in the rock art of Arnhem Land. The Rainbow Serpents are 'great composite beings with supernatural significance, [who] appeared on rock shelter walls and ceilings. These fantastic works of rock painting are the oldest known surviving forms of one of the world's most powerful mythological creatures. Indeed, they are evidence of one of the oldest continuous religious traditions' (Taçon et al. 1996: 103). Crocodile and snake morphology feature too, but in Yam-period art (4000–6000 BCE) there are definite similarities to pipefish, in particular a likeness to *Haliichthys taeniophorus*. Whatever its taxonomic wobbles, it has cosmic importance.

Figure 13 A male weedy seadragon (*Phyllopteryx taeniolatus*) carries eggs through a kelp forest (*Macrocystis pyrifera*) in Tasmania, Australia. Tasmania is the only part of Australia with giant kelp forests. The kelp is a variety of the same species found on the other side of the Pacific Ocean in California. Tasman Sea. Photo and caption by Alex Mustard. Image courtesy of Alex Mustard.

WHAT'S IN A NAME? ETYMOLOGIES AND EPONYMS

Writing of proper names, Foucault proposed 'Obviously, one cannot turn a proper name into a pure and simple reference. It has other than indicative functions: more than an indication, a gesture, a finger pointed at someone, it is the equivalent of a description' (Foucault 1998: 209). To figure in science, roughly two thousand marine species a year need a distinguishing name. Some will be unlike anything else; many will be like organisms already named. Taxonomists oversee the process of naming to ensure accuracy, consistency and conformity to some rules. 'Without taxonomists, entire fields wouldn't exist. We'd be working in darkness', says biologist Terry McGlynn, who in 2013 on what he describes as 'a half-whim' established March 19 as Taxonomist Appreciation Day (McGlynn 2013). Why does taxonomy matter? 'The nonidentifiable becomes the unnamable', said Paul Ricoeur; conversely, the unnamed becomes the nonidentified (1992: 149).

Richard L. Pyle has joked that taxonomy among his college friends was redefined as 'The perpetual re-classification of mis-named species' (2008). Ensuring consistency means more stability for names and knowledge exchange. Accurate communication between databases also adds to consistency (Pyle 2016: 261-81). Taxonomists explain that species' names change for various reasons – for instance, if a juvenile that looks wildly different from a parent is mistakenly thought to be a different species. That would be a case of synonym, or different names for the same species; also targeted are homonyms, or the same names for different types of organism. Zoology has different conventions from botany for recording the history of such changes. Humans naturally err too, usually by misspelling Latin (Remsen 2016: 214).

Fish have an exceptional etymologist at their service: Christopher Scharpf, who in October 2013 announced his ETYFish Project, a website devoted to etymologies of fish names. The total in 2023 was 42,708. Then he embarked on revisions. He explains his motivation in terms of human interest: 'when a taxonomist assigns a name to a species – the name by which the species will always be known – this is the one time the scientist can be creative, personal, poetic, whimsical, and sometimes enigmatic or mysterious. I'm fascinated by that. I'm fascinated by the intersection of science and creative self-expression that biological nomenclature often represents' (personal communication).

Scharpf identifies eight ways an ichthylogist can name a fish: descriptive, names that refer to a physical characteristic; biological, names that refer to an aspect of biology; systematic, names that refer to taxonomy, classification or phylogenetic relationship; anthropocentric, names that refer to a fish's importance to humans; commemorative, names that honour people, cultures, ships, institutions and more; toponymic, names that refer to places; vernacular, names derived from historical, local or Indigenous vernaculars; nonsensical, coined or borrowed names with little or no significance. As he explains, name formations must obey IUCN rules, which are that a name must be in the Latin alphabet; at least two letters long; pronounceable; not offensive, and unique. A name must be identified as new; a type of it must be identified in relation to the museum or fish collection where it is housed, and it must have a description that distinguishes its taxon from other taxa. Publications giving new names need to include the date of publication and be registered in the Official Register of Zoological Nomenclature (ZooBank) with evidence of such registration (a ZooBank number) appearing in the text (Scharpf 2023: 2). Around four hundred new fish species are currently named each year with additional names changing or needing correction, as biologists' knowledge of Greek, Latin and their grammar can have mistakes, and taxonomy protocols change. Scharpf's ETYFish Project is an impressive lifetime's work and a treasure-house for the etymologically minded.

Eponyms are namings after people. An *Eponym Dictionary of Fishes* (Beolens et al. 2023) has entries for everyone after whom a fish has been named. It runs to 1463 pages. Its last entry is an eleventh-century king of Croatia and Dalmatia, Zvonimir, for whom a blenny found on the Dalmatian Coast in 1892 was possibly named: *Parablennius zvonimiri* (G. Kolumbatović 1892). Most entries are unconjectural and there are patterns. Namers commemorate teachers (and occasionally students), patrons, colleagues, partners, illustrators, helpers, suppliers of specimens and children. Some names adapt better to Latin than others. A searobin, *Lepidoptrigla jimjoebob* (Richards 1992), combines the first names of the identifier's three sons (Beolens et al. 2023: 661). Not everyone warms to eponyms. William Beebe wrote a little outburst about 'a round-bodied herringlet with a silver stripe, but with the terrible name of *Jenkinsia*. No matter how wonderful a professor of physiology Dr Oliver Peebles Jenkins and how splendid a man – I resent the name of anyone of my race being given to the genus of a brave, individual, end-product member of the wild fauna of our globe.' He then added, not very convincingly, 'hurrah for Jenkins' (Beebe 1926: 247). The *Eponym Dictionary* records two genera and five species named for Professor Jenkins, who worked for a while with leading ichthyologist David Starr Jordan, after whom three genera and thirty-two species are named. One of the latter is *Myctoperca jordani*, a Gulf Grouper, named by Oliver Peebles Jenkins and B. W. Evermann in 1889. Barton Warren Evermann had three genera named after him and eight species; of those, David Starr Jordan was one of the namers in five cases. How, when and why Jenkins, Jordan and Evermann pay each other compliments points to relationships that can be tracked by life writing. Such interlacing of connections in a professional field can be represented in digital biography by graphs of social networks; known as social graphs, they show links between people in rhizomatic ways, spreading without evident hierarchies (Arthur 2014). Social graphs are rather less good at distinguishing different emotions in professional rhizomes – David Starr Jordan's biographer describes his collecting expeditions as payback. 'The men get increasingly creative in their naming. They name ugly fish after their enemies, pretty fishes after friends' (L. Miller 2020: 57).

Gratitude, however, is assumed to be the dominant motive. Personal patronage patterns have been affected by changes in how science is funded – fewer philanthropists, more institutions. A sailfin jawfish *Opistognathus fenmutis* (Acero and Franke 1993) commemorates not a person but the Mutis fund of the National Electric Finance Company, FEN, in Columbia which financed the senior namer's work. The Coral Reef Research Foundation becomes an acronym, *Trimma corerefum* (Winterbottom 2016); its founders, Pat and Lori Colin, give their surname to the fish's vernacular name, Colin's pygmygoby. *Dana* and *Galathea* inscribe not mythological figures but Danish research vessels that have supported ichythyology. Names that commemorate the person who collected the holotype show how important Indigenous and local helpers were and are; new variants on that include scuba divers who spot and report new sightings. Thus ETYFish records that *Rhamphocottus nagaakii* (Munehara, Yamazaki and Tsuruoka 2022) honours Nagaaki Satoh, 'a professional diving instructor, who first observed the reproductive behavior of this species underwater and informed the authors of his observations' (ETYFish). Christopher Scharpf detects a trend, Chinese ichthyologists coining toponyms for new species, 'presumably because the "place + -*ensis*" construction is the easiest way for Chinese ichthyologists to correctly coin names using a language and alphabet so different from their own'. Toponyms may instate national pride, he adds: '380 or so Chinese fishes have names such as *guangxiensis*, *lancangjiangensis* and *qiongzhongensis*, to list but three' (personal communication).

Mellifluous naming still matters to some. *Paraliparis kadadakaleguak* (Stein and Mundy 2021) is a species of bathyal (200–2000-metre deep) snailfish (Liparidae) from the Mariana Islands. Schoolchildren in Guam were invited to suggest names for it. 'Alyssa Roces from Okkodo High School suggested the name *Paraliparis kadadakaleguak*. ... Dr. Stein, who has described or co-described ~125 snailfish species, says a goal when trying to coin a name is for it to be "euphonious." "You want a name that sounds good,

and I particularly enjoy *kadadakaleguak*," he said. "I just love it'" (ETYFish name of
the week 2021, 5 May). It also happens to be descriptively precise, recognizing the
fish's short ribs; in Chamorro, *kadada' kaleguak* means short rib bone. Democratizing
naming by competition is another way to engage a younger public.

A recent call to decolonize science by replacing Western eponyms has stirred up
debate (Guedes et al. 2023). Eponyms should have no place in twenty-first-century
biological nomenclature, argues one paper, because 'many of those honoured are
strongly associated with the social ills and negative legacy of imperialism, racism and
slavery. Moreover, nineteenth-century and early twentieth-century taxonomy was
largely dominated by white men who, by and large, honoured other men (funders,
colleagues, collectors and so on) of their own nationality, ethnicity, race and social
status' (Jost et al. 2023). Others argue that resources to purge taxonomy of these taints
take away from urgent work needed to identify species disappearing forever because
of climate crisis. Defenders argued too that eponyms are now better representing non-
Western people's input to science. 'Using eponyms, local scientists can now fund their
work, honour local scientists, recognize Indigenous leaders and policy-makers, and
help to save their study organisms from extinction. It is unfortunate and discriminatory
that some members of the scientific community want to take away this tool just at the
moment that non-European biologists are becoming its main beneficiaries' (Jost et al.,
2023). The International Code on Zoological Nomenclature Commission has said it
will not remove eponyms nor revise the Code in decolonizing ways.

'The global spread of western cultures, to which universities have made a huge
contribution, may be compared to the spread of monocultures in agriculture where
imported, hybridized, fertilizer-dependent seeds, produced at a profit for multinational
corporations, crowd out indigenous local varieties', says Konai Helu Thaman (2003: 7).
This powerful metaphor from a poet who is also an academic is applicable to a raft
of names taken from popular culture, largely American in origin, applied informally
to new species. In the deep sea, an abyssal octopus found worldwide was dubbed the
Dumbo octopus because it has extended ear-like fins like the big ears of the elephant
in Disney's 1941 film *Dumbo*. In the film Jumbo is mockingly called Dumbo for those
ears, but being able to fly with them he turns ridicule into triumph. Its genus name
is *Grimpoteuthis*, which combines the Greek word for small squid (*teuthis*) with the
name of a distinguished cephalopod researcher, Georg von Grimp (1889–1936).
Disney beats Grimp on recognition factor, for sure; a neutral global term, umbrella
octopus, also describes this group (Collins 2003: 93-4). Grimp's eponym is used by
specialists; Dumbo is used by the media.

Some scientific databases release 'top ten' species lists each year as a way to connect
scientific and public interest. The World Register of Marine Species list released in 2021
included 'The E.T. sponge', formally *Advhena magnifica*, Latin for 'magnificent alien',
chosen because the shape of the organism echoed that of the extra-terrestrial E.T.'s
head in Spielberg's 1982 film. WoRMS second choice was a starfish, *Astrolirus patricki*
(Zhang, Zhou, Xiao and Wang 2020). It is named for Patrick Star, a character from
the cartoon *SpongeBob Squarepants* who hangs out with his best friend SpongeBob.
Specimens of this species were all found attached to sponges. Also in the list was one of
the *Peinaleopolynoe*, deep-sea scaleworms found at methane seeps, hydrothermal vents

and whalefalls. 'The authors had for many years nicknamed these sparkly scaleworms "Elvis worms" because their scales resembled the sequins on Elvis' signature attire. This nickname is honoured by the naming of one of their new species as *Peinaleopolynoe elvisi.*' How far does one culture stretch before becoming global? And what about species colonialism in the Anthropocene? In a chilling precedent, in 2014 a new species of amphipod (a small crustacean) was found in the Mariana Trench about 6900-metres deep. Close inspection revealed it had plastic in its gut. The lead researcher said: 'We decided on the name *Eurythenes plasticus* as we wanted to highlight the fact that we need to take immediate action to stop the deluge of plastic waste into our oceans.' (Newcastle 2020). Is that name a stronger catalyst for environmental action than a study two years before (using 2009 data) which analysed Gentoo penguin scat in the Southern Ocean? The study found plastic in 20 per cent of them. One estimate suggests 'that about 25.5 billion fibers of synthetic origin are potentially entering the Southern Ocean per decade from clothes laundering, making a substantial contribution to the local levels of microplastics' (Bessa et al. 2019). How many species are not *plasticus*?

UNNAMINGS

In phylogenetics, the term 'fish' disappears. Underwater writers record curious disappearances of names for unscientific reasons. One term for shark was *requin*, derived from *requiem*, a mass for the dead. Cousteau wrote

> Aboard the *Calypso,* we rarely hear the word *requin* (shark). Divers prefer to speak of sharks as *les barbus* – the bearded ones; or as *balaises* (which has no English equivalent, or, for that matter, any particular meaning in French), or as *Jean-Louis.* The name Jean-Louis is a traditional one for sharks, and is of long standing in the French Navy.
>
> It is hard to pinpoint the reason why we prefer these circumlocutions. It may be superstition, or it may even be a mark of respect for these redoubtable beasts of the sea. Or, more likely, it is simply the 'in' language of an exclusive society. It is impossible for thirty men to live at close quarters and to share dangers and projects every day without evolving some kind of special vocabulary for themselves. A clever psychologist, no doubt, could divine our darkest secrets from the words that we use aboard the *Calypso.*
>
> (Cousteau and Diolé 1971: 139)

Cousteau then records his men's eagerness to name animals they worked with or brought aboard. Thus a whale calf was Jonah, two sea lions were Pepito and Cristóbal; the film star grouper was Ulysses. 'The very act of giving a name to an animal is a sign that contact has begun and that the animal is regarded as a member of the group rather than an outsider', explained Cousteau. First contact, used in anthropology and science fiction to describe the moment of encounter between two groups, is traditionally wary. In Murray Leinster's short novel *First Contact* (1945) which perhaps established the term, biped aliens and humans discover they share laughter. Naming animal captives is a kind of game; humans bond over ideological inferences. Not all of those are conscious. Alfred Alcock, a thoughtful namer, nonetheless described *Lucina spinifera* as 'A British bivalve that also lives in the Bay of Bengal', rather than an Indian bivalve that also lives off Britain (Alcock 1902: facing 280, caption for Figure 77). William Beebe wondered whether names guided or blocked engagement:

> A passing swell, coming out of the black night, would fill the lighted circle with a mêlée of jetsam – porpita, ocyropsis, ianthinas and salpa, which, if you do not know them by these names does not matter, for if you will allow your imagination full play, and try to think to what strange and beautiful beings such names might apply, your mental images will yet fall short of the strangeness and beauty of the reality.
>
> (Beebe 1926: 65)

Discarded signifiers merge with jetsam; the signified is reader-produced. Eugenie Clark also abandoned words, favouring sand drawings which even upside-down were readily identified by fishermen:

> ask a strange fisherman to help you find a specific fish (the harder and rarer the better) and you will immediately get his interest and eventually his whole-hearted help. You don't have to know his language; just draw a picture of the fish, gesticulate for his help, and let him lead the way. In doing so you have told him three important things: you have not come just to stare at him and his people, you have a specific interest in common with his; you respect his judgment and recognize his superior knowledge of local conditions (and a native fisherman knows more about his water than the most highly trained ichthyologist); and you trust him.
>
> (Clark 1953: 186-7)

INDIGENOUS KNOWLEDGES: OCEANIA

Many writers describe Indigenous skills underwater with admiration and respect. Playing truant from brutal relatives, Noel Monkman met kindly Māori boys; he was taught to swim underwater by Rangi, their leader (Monkman 1963: 21, 34). Eugenie Clark described at length the diving skills of Siakong, 'the best spearfisherman in the Palaus – or maybe in the whole world, I sometimes think now' (Clark 1953: 109).

> A small red loincloth and homemade goggles formed Siakong's diving outfit. The rest of the time he wore an old pair of khaki shorts over his loincloth, a dirty handkerchief around his head and a decrepit straw hat over the handkerchief. When he took these off to go into the water he was suddenly metamorphosed from a bum into a Greek God.
>
> (Clark 1953: 110)

He would lie on a reef ten- or twenty-feet down and wait for the fish to come to him. In Fiji, Basil Thomson was impressed by how Fijians perfected sidestroke for long-distance swimming: 'they can swim at greater speed than all but the best European swimmers' (Thomson 1968: 316). Like other Westerners, he was intrigued by a different style of descent:

> When diving he [a Fijian] does not plunge head first from the swimming position, but draws his head under, and reverses the position of his body under water without creating a swirl. If the water is not too deep, when he reaches the bottom he lies flat with his nose touching the sand, his hands being behind the back, and propels himself with incredible speed by digging his toes into the sand.
>
> (Thomson 1968: 317)

Taking a lesson in underwater swimming, Thomson felt inept in comparison.

The ease of Indigenous peoples in the ocean was incontrovertible. So too was their knowledge of fish in the waters around their lands. Robert (Bob) E. Johannes, a tropical marine ecologist, reported on this in depth; his life's work was to incorporate it into marine conservation. For one project he was based on Tobi and its sister islands Sonsorol and Pulo Anna (three hundred miles south of Palau). He noted 'The significance of these islands in the global scheme of things is such that no one in the West has ever bothered to give them a collective name' (Johannes 1981: 86). Seeking out Indigenous knowledge was an approach

> so inconceivable to his professional colleagues that he was pegged by some as having dropped out, or 'gone troppo' to use the Australian term. The Palauans Bob worked with were more favorably impressed. In several villages people commented that while fisheries researchers had visited them before, Bob was 'the first one who ever asked us about our knowledge; the others only told us about theirs'.
>
> (Pew Trust 1993)

Johannes' *Words of the Lagoon* is a fascinating study of Micronesian marine culture. He was not looking for a system of naming but listening to what mattered to local people. 'Biologists devote as much attention to the naming of rare species as they do to naming common ones. Pacific islanders, in contrast, give specific names only to those species that are important or otherwise interesting to them' (Johannes 1981: 125). Names were a practical element of fishing, incorporating knowledge about habits. As one islander told Johannes, 'We perhaps cannot name as many fishes as our forefathers, but the fishermen of my generation know more about their habits' (Johannes 1981: 16). There were gender divisions, though the authority on spelling Tobian fish names was his interpreter's wife, the aptly-named Marina, because women's fishing took place mostly in the lagoon rather than reefs, and required different fish knowledge.

Tobi was not untouched by the wider world: a legacy of Palau employment in Japanese fishing fleets meant various tuna had Japanese names. Johannes did not enquire into myths, legends and spiritual beliefs because he was not an anthropologist. But he attended carefully to the devotional care given to fishing by those who need to catch fish for food. Naming was a practice of attention. 'Sounds made by various

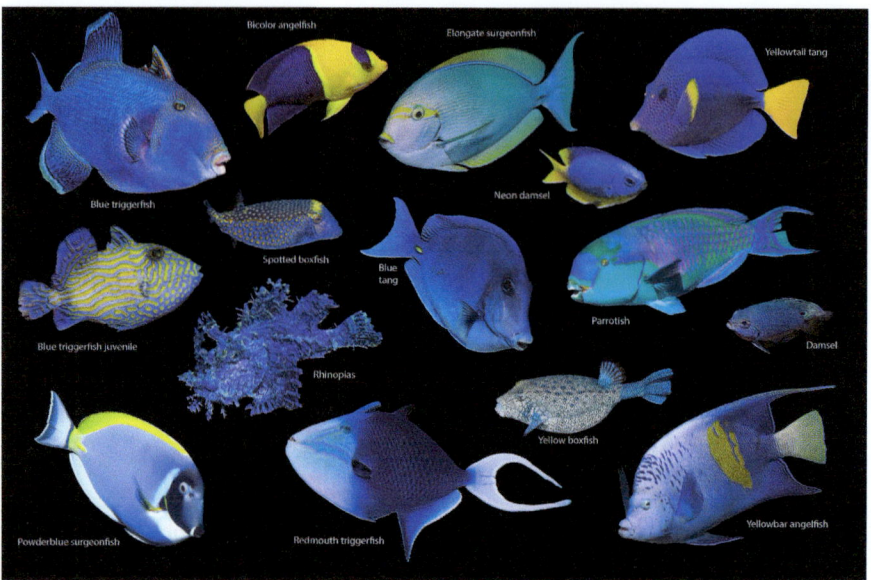

Figure 14 Blue tropical reef fish composite image on black background, Blue triggerfish (*Pseudobalistes fuscus*), Bicolour angelfish (*Centropyge bicolor*), Elongate surgeonfish (*Acanthurus mata*), Yellowtail tang/surgeonfish (*Zebrasoma xanthurum*), Neon damselfish (*Pomacentrus coelestis*), Spotted boxfish (*Ostracion meleagris*), Blue tang (*Acanthurus coeruleus*), Greenthroat/Singapore parrotfish (*Scarus prasiognathos*), Nagasaki damsel (*Pomacentrus nagasakiensis*), Rhinopias scorpionfish (*Rhinopias eschmeyeri*), Yellow boxfish (*Ostracion cubicus*), Powderblue surgeonfish (*Acanthurus leucosternon*), Redmouth triggerfish (*Odonus niger*), Yellowbar angelfish (*Pomacanthus maculosus*), Indo-Pacific species. Blue tropical reef fish composite image and caption by Georgette Douwma. Nature Photo Library Image.

reef fishes are sometimes employed by the underwater spearfisherman to locate or attract prey. Several species of angelfish bear the onomatopoetic Palauan name, *ngemngumk*. When said quickly with an emphasis on the vowels, the word reproduces the percussive grunting sound these fish make when alarmed' (Johannes 1981: 19). Palauan names had some patterns, literally: '*Bub*, a word roughly equivalent in meaning to "parallelogram" in Tobian, is in widespread use in Micronesia, including Tobi, as both the family name for triggerfish and the constellation we call the Southern Cross, both of which approximate a parallelogram in outline' (Johannes 1981: 129). Western grouping by anatomical similarity mattered less than similarity of relevance. Snappers and damselfish, different families in Linnaean terms, were *ricoh*, 'closely related in Tobian minds, and quite logically so. They look fairly similar, taste similar, live in similar habitats, eat similar food, and are caught by the same methods'.

Habits rather than anatomy explain Tobian fish names.

Chera is the name applied to a woman who dotes on a man and will not let him out of her sight. The name is also applied to remoras and alludes to their habit of following or actually adhering by means of an adhesive disc on their head to larger fish and turtles. Another fish that is well known for its habit of accompanying a larger fish is the pilot fish, *Naucrates ductor*. Its name in Tobian, *yetam*, means 'travels with a father.'

(Johannes 1981: 128)

Resemblances that underlie analogies are carefully observed. '*Paip* is the name given to hollow bone straw through which infirm Tobians used to suck water from coconuts. It is also the generic name for butterfly fish and refers to the protruding tubular mouths of many species' (Johannes 1981: 130). These instances are anthropomorphic, projecting human culture onto fish; they are also imaginative, even sympathetic. 'The nurse shark, *Ginglymostoma ferrugineum*, is called *sabacho*. The name is derived from two words meaning "sleep" and "awkward" and refers to the ungainly swimming motion of this fish and its habit of resting motionless for long periods on the bottom' (Johannes 1981: 128). Habit and habitat are words that came into English at different times. Habit joined Middle English from Latin *habitus*, 'condition, appearance'; originally it meant dress (as in a nun's habit). Habitat, 'it dwells', comes from Latin *habitare*. Its first use, according to *OED*, was in 1796 by a British botanist, William Withering, to describe the natural place of growth of a plant in its wild state. For the Tobians, habit and habitat intersect naturally: how a fish looks, what it does and where it lives are cohabiting concepts. Squirrelfish retire to caves during the day; their generic name was *mor*, a word for 'in mourning', an analogous withdrawal. Johannes's study shows the reasoning in Tobian names and how it draws on a vocabulary richer than Western equivalents. Phases of the moon, for instance, have perhaps a dozen terms in English; in Palau, there were words for every day of the lunar cycle. That was important given how phases of the moon govern spawning, and hence affect the availability of fish, present and future, for fishing. An edible annelid worm, *palolo* in Palau or *mbalolo* in Fiji, kept such exact lunar time that in Fiji its seasonal appearance gave names to two months – October and November, small and large swarm respectively (Thomson 1968: 324). It rose on the night of the third quarter of the moon, exactly – which meant that to do so at the same time every year (a measure in solar time) it had to adjust its lunar clock. 'For two years it rises after a lapse of twelve lunations, and then it allows thirteen to pass, but since even this arrangement will gradually sunder solar and lunar time it must intercalate one lunation every twenty-eight years in order to keep to its dates' (Thomson 1968: 325). It is still a mystery as to how a worm can do this. Its name combines *pa*, meaning 'to burst', and *lolo* 'fatty or oily', describing the oily mix of body segments shed after spawning (Burrows 1955). *Palolos* were scooped up, boiled, wrapped in banana leaves and sent, like wedding cake, all round Fiji; according to one European author initially reluctant to try them, 'They taste like caviare' (Thomson 1968: 325). Imagery made some bridges between Indigenous and Western descriptions; it also shows up uncrossable gaps.

ARCTIC KNOWLEDGES

The cold, ice and darkness of underwater in polar regions makes them exceptionally challenging to dive. Hardy souls have done so, from Willy Heinrich in 1902 in Antarctica (Brueggeman 2003), to the French explorer Alban Michon who in 2022 planned to set up Biodysseus, a Cousteau-style base, for six months under Arctic ice. Understanding sea, ice and underwater life differently with help from Indigenous knowledges, Barry Lopez's *Arctic Dreams* (1986) mediates between cultures of science, history and imagination, engaging respectfully with Indigenous knowledge – known now as Inuit 'Traditional Knowledge', Inuit Qaujimajatuqangit, sometimes shortened to IQ. 'Inuit Qaujimaningit refers to Inuit Traditional Knowledge as well as Inuit epistemology without reference to temporality' (https://www.inuitcircumpolar.com/about-icc/icc-political-universe). Knowing the sea in this region is essential for human survival. I follow Lopez along a few of his knowledge-trails – he covers a great many – which establish contexts for namings that shape understanding of Arctic life, including underwater. Lopez insisted that

> the element in the ecosystem at greatest risk is not the bowhead but the coherent vision of an indigenous people. We have no alternative, long-lived narrative to theirs, no story of human relationships with that landscape independent of Western science and any desire to control or possess. Our intimacy lacks historical depth, and is still largely innocent of what is obscure and subtle there.
>
> (Lopez 1986: 11)

Writing in the 1980s, Lopez refers to Indigenous peoples as Eskimos; I adjust that to Inuit-Yu'pik, those peoples' preferred term now. '[Inuit-Yu'pik] who sometimes see themselves as not quite separate from the animal world, regard us as a kind of people whose separation may have become too complete. They call us, with a mixture of incredulity and apprehension, "the people who change nature"' (Lopez 1986: 39).

Place names are as important for manifesting Indigenous knowledge as species names – and they merge. As the *Canadian Arctic Marine Atlas* explains,

> many of the names still used and found on official maps of the Arctic today were given by European and Euro–North American explorers. They often named places they 'discovered' after themselves, places in their home countries, European royalty, or the financial backers of their expeditions. The use of these names has obscured the naming traditions of the Arctic's Indigenous peoples. The Inuit practice of naming places reflects their ongoing interaction with and observations of their environment. The names identify distinct geographic features; concentrations of game, fish, or edible plants; strategic sites for fishing or hunting; sources of raw materials; efficient and safe travel routes; landmarks for navigation; and superior or strategic campsites. They also mark sites of historical and legendary importance and areas of spiritual significance. As Inuit culture was until very recently strictly oral, place names were and continue to be an effective means of retaining and passing on knowledge about the landscape.
>
> (Oceans North 2018: 12)

Like Lopez, the Atlas explains how a different outlook changes the meaning of words. To the Western mind, ice is an obstacle, freezing up ships; to Inuit-Yu'pik peoples, it is a highway and a bridge connecting people, enabling movement not restricting it (Oceans North 2018: 11). The sea's surface changes in winter: whipped up by strong winds and storm waves, ice ridges form and shift, making a new vocabulary. Open areas of water, polynyas (a word from Russian) and leads (more variable, linear ice-free areas) are merging points for above and below water. 'Flying creatures here at Admiralty Inlet walk on ice. They break the pane of water with their dives to feed. Marine mammals break the pane of water coming the other way to breathe' (Lopez 1986: 123). Polynyas are good places to watch for marine life: 'when you see a polar bear surface quietly in a lead [passage in sea ice], focus its small brown eyes on a sleeping bearded seal, draw breath soundlessly, and submerge without a ripple, you wonder at the insouciance with which we name things', writes Lopez (1986: 86). He learns from his Indigenous friends that watching requires long stillness. 'The [Inuit-Yu'pik] have a word for this kind of long waiting, prepared for a sudden event: *quinuituq*. Deep patience' (Lopez 1986: 176). In contrast, Western watching is connected to making lists, collecting up names. 'We move at such a fast clip now ... At a snap ... We name everything' (Lopez 1986: 172). Understanding behaviours, like the Palauans' focus on habits, needs more than one sighting. 'It not only takes a long time of watching the animal before you can say what it is doing; it takes a long time to learn how to watch. This point is raised, deferentially but repeatedly, in encounters with [Inuit-Yu'pik]' (Lopez 1986: 96). Watching is a staple of Western engagement with nature – as in birdwatching. But it can be cursory compared to Indigenous practices of long observation. Waiting for a lead to close, Lopez reflects on better understanding:

> The indigenous rhythm, or rhythms, of arctic life is important to discern for more than merely academic reasons. To understand why a region is different, to show an initial deference toward its mysteries, is to guard against a kind of provincialism that vitiates the imagination, that stifles the capacity to envision what is different.
>
> (1986: 176)

One Arctic animal whose difference has supplied Western imagination with a whole visionary category is the narwhal, whose tusk gave rise to legends of the unicorn. Its blubber is an Inuit-Yu'pik delicacy, *muktuk,* which Lopez described as tasting like hazelnuts. When he first saw a narwhal, 'I knew that no element of the earth's natural history had ever before brought me so far, so suddenly. It was as though something from a bestiary had taken shape, a creature as strange as a giraffe' (1986: 125). Lopez writes in 1982 when oil explorations represented narwhals as an environmental nuisance; he celebrates them simply for existing. 'In those moments the animals did not have to mean anything at all.' But he is soon enmeshed again in cultural histories, and they turn on the narwhal's name.

The Chilean poet and essayist Pablo Neruda wonders in his memoirs how an animal this large can have remained so obscure and uncelebrated. Its name, he thought, was 'the most beautiful of undersea names, the name of a sea chalice that sings, the name of a crystal spur.' Why, he wondered, had no one taken Narwhal for a last name, or 'built a beautiful Narwhal Building?'

(Lopez 1986: 128)

Part of the answer, thought Lopez, was that the narwhal's name had associations with death. 'The pallid color of the narwhal's skin has been likened to that of a drowned human corpse, and it is widely thought that its name came from the Old Norse for "corpse" and "whale," *nál* + *hvalr*' (1986: 128). *OED* confirms that etymology. And if the unfortunate resonance of that name stuck, like *requiem* for sharks, further knowledge of the narwhal was elusive. 'The obscurity of narwhals is not easily breeched [*sic*] by science', Lopez observed (1986: 129) though it is now possible to find narwhals by infrared flukeprint tracking (Florko et al. 2021).

The narwhal's scientific name, *Monodon monoceros,* meaning one tooth one horn, describes the species through their tusk. It is now thought they use their tusk not for sexual display or combat but for communication of information. An expert in marine dentistry at Harvard who has researched the narwhal's exceptional tooth for decades argues its physiology shows it has considerable sensory ability (Nweeia et al. 2014). 'In Inuktitut, the narwhal is described as *qilalugaq qernertaq*, which translates as the "one that is good at curving itself toward the sky"' (ELOKA). Inuit dialects have at least nine words to describe differences between narwhal tusks. Etymology, history and science define the narwhal in different ways, by different names. Lopez reflected on the persistence of legend. 'Animals are often fixed like this in history, bearing an unwarranted association derived from notions or surmise having no connection at all with their real life. The fuller explanations of modern field biology are an antidote, in part, to this tendency to name an animal carelessly' (Lopez 1986: 129). He concluded it was also a task of literature to take animals out of storage and bring them to life. His own life writing does that most thoughtfully.

6

Fish Biography

'If fish were all just alike, writing about them would be a great deal easier than it is. They differ, sometimes radically. It is impossible to make universal statements about fish; it is impossible to use the words "always," "all," "never," "none," when talking about them.'

(Curtis 1949: 5)

'One fish two fish red fish blue fish': Dr Seuss's incantation neatly invokes fish plurality and diversity (1960: 1). Some purists will tell you there is no such thing as fish. Strictly speaking, they have a point: the reorganization of biological relationships into clades means fish can't be separated from reptiles, mammals or birds who also descend from a common fishy ancestor – unless you argue everything is a fish, including humans. 'Perhaps to be called the great-great-great-etcetera-grandson of a sturgeon is so grotesque as to be beneath notice, whereas to be called the grandson of a gorilla is too close for comfort', writes one fish author, who then offers a simpler definition (Curtis 1949: 11). 'Fish, then, are backboned animals which live in the water, breathe through gills, and have fins. As usual, there are exceptions. Some breathe with lungs, and some have no recognizable fins. Lung-fish and eels are fishes, but whales and porpoises are not' – they are mammals (Curtis 1949: 13). Within this category of aquatic vertebrates there is an important distinction between bony fishes, *Osteichthyes*, and cartilaginous fishes, *Chondrichthyes* (ones whose skeletons are made of cartilage not bone); these include sharks, rays, skates, chimaera and the biggest fish in the world, the whale shark – a placid giant about whom we know little, though more than we did. Ichthyologists like to divide bony fish into *Actinopterygii*, ray-finned fishes, and *Sarcopterygii*, fleshy-finned ones, whose lobed paired fins evolved into the legs of the first amphibians, or tetrapod land vertebrates. For most people, a fish is a fish by means of its fins, gills, scales and swim bladder, even if there are many exceptions. The halibut, for instance, has no swim bladder but is unequivocally a fish.

But what are two fish? Should the plural of fish be fishes? Some say yes if you mean two fish of different species: thus red and blue fish together could be fishes. Writing a book explicitly '*on behalf of* fish', Jonathan Balcombe favours the plural 'in recognition of the fact that these animals are individuals with personalities and relationships' (2017: 6). In this chapter, I explore first what one might call generalist writing about fish lives, with an eye on what Balcombe calls their 'inner lives', to consider fish sentience: does this constitute subjectivity? Habits, behaviours, aptitudes and abilities establish them as biographical subjects in life writing. That fits into animalographies, a genre of life writing that affirms other species besides humans are subjects who matter, and whose interests can be voiced. 'It isn't easy being a fish, especially in an age of humans' (Balcombe 2017: 211).

GOGGLE-BOGGLE

In a poem by Leigh Hunt, 'The Fish, The Man, and the Spirit' (1836), a man addresses a fish:

> O scaly, slippery, wet, swift, staring wights
> What is't ye do? What life lead? eh, dull goggles?
> How do ye vary your vile days and nights?
> How pass your Sundays? Are ye still but joggles
> In ceaseless wash? Still naught but gapes, and bites,
> And drinks, and stares, diversified with boggles?

The Fish replies in an answering sonnet that turns strangeness back onto man – 'Long-useless-finned, haired, upright, unwet, slow!' before turning into a Man, then a Spirit, to equalize the two in their difference: Man is warm, glad, sad; a fish has 'A cold, sweet, silver life' (Manning-Saunders 1962: 184-5). In spite of this imaginative shape-shifting dialogue, generalist writing on fish still has to contend with an impression of them as goggles, joggles and boggles. 'No pity or gratitude or love or excitement is stirred in us by the sight of a fish' wrote one author, although he identified a specific latent admiration. 'No one who has ever watched fishes can help being aware of the fact that they have a control of their own bodies in their own element unequalled by any other animal' (Curtis 1949: 30, 59). But although basic needs are 'much the same for humans as for fish: oxygen, food, water, mates, and shelter from enemies' (Curtis 1949: 243-4), there is little empathy. 'Most people think of fish as dull, uninteresting creatures, leading monotonous lives', wrote Francis Ward, who determined to prove otherwise by building a fish observation chamber, sadly dismantled in case invading Germans made use of it, and made underwater photographs with lively captions such as 'Pike rigid with excitement' and 'Perch becoming pale from fear' (Ward 1911: ix, 4, 6).

'Because their lives are more difficult to observe than most terrestrial animals, fishes are not easily fathomed', Jonathan Balcombe observes (2017: 15). Estrangement is compounded by apparent fish muteness and a lack of detectable facial expressions, though neither apply to live fish underwater. 'Their place in human culture falls almost universally into two entwined contexts: (1) something to be caught, and (2) something to be eaten. We think of them as "cold-blooded", a layman's term that has little credibility in science', says Balcombe. 'I do not see why having a built-in thermostat or not should have anything to do with an organism's moral status' (Balcombe 2017: 19), especially since fish have sophisticated mechanisms for keeping muscles, nerves, brains and eyes at the right temperatures for optimal functioning. Swordfish can heat up their eyes twenty to thirty degrees Fahrenheit above the water temperature, thanks to a special organ in an eye muscle that runs a countercurrent heat exchange, enabling them to track prey without being slowed by cold (Balcombe 2017: 290). Icefish, who live in freezing Antarctic waters, don't have haemoglobin in their blood; rather than red blood cells to transport oxygen round their bodies, they have myoglobin, which stores oxygen in muscle tissue (Bo-Mi Kim et al. 2019: 469–78). If that sounds too goggly, one can think of icefish as splitting off seventy-seven million years ago from a stickleback lineage and developing an antifreeze adaptation. Cold-blooded can be clever.

Balcombe's biography of fish has a conventional scientific framework that relates fish perception to morphology: their bodies explain their being. A hinge with life writing begins to appear in his link between the senses and subjectivity. 'Central to empathy – the capacity to place oneself in another's shoes, or in this case, fins – is an understanding of the experiences of the other. Central to that is an appreciation of their sensory worlds' (Balcombe 2017: 22). We don't often think of humans through this prism of sensory worlds. We might. Eminent Victorians, say, evolved bushy facial hair as an adaptation to a need to assert masculinity in an immediately visible way (Oldstone-Moore 2005: 7–34). Those with big beards presumably experienced their manly crinosity as a sensual social force, and hence felt better about themselves. When Charles Dickens first grew moustaches, as he pluralized them, he wrote to a friend, 'The moustaches are glorious, glorious. … They are charming, charming. Without them, life would be a blank' (Lloyd 2012: n.p.). Glorious and charming – doubled so that each moustache gets full praise? – is still mysterious, despite Balcombe's argument that 'How a species' senses work goes some way toward understanding the mysteries of its felt experiences' (2017: 26).

Balcombe proposes we think of fish *Umwelt*, Jakob von Uexküll's term for an organism's unique sensory world, a world mediated by biological characteristics that can be analysed by science but which also has subjectivity and agency, more elusive aspects. An eel is incapable of keeping a diary, Freud observed (Svensson 2020: 37): in the apparent absence of fish autobiography, fish-friendly authors try to construct the inner-pointing components of umwelt to establish fish as full feeling subjects. Balcombe recognizes the limitations: 'what we know about fishes is only a tiny slice of what they know' (2017: 38). Dominating interpretation is the human model of consciousness and intelligence: he quotes a crocodile expert, Vladimir Dinets, who complains 'When people use the word "intelligence" what they usually mean is "being able to think the same way I do"' (Balcombe 2017: 108). Defining species' intelligence turns on tests which humans devise based on their own capacities, like the ability to use tools. Fish can use tools: in 2009 off Palau, a researcher saw a tuskfish carrying a clam to a rock to smash it open; like a thrush using an anvil stone to break up a snail, it is proof of planning and conscious tool use. But goggle-boggle prejudice is deep-rooted. 'I believe that the main source of our prejudice against fishes is their failure to show expressions that we associate with having feelings' says Balcombe. 'We hear no screams and see no tears when their mouths are impaled and their bodies pulled from the water' (Balcombe 2017: 232). Muteness is assumed to be lack of sentience. Similarly brain size becomes an index of intelligence attached to personhood, even though 'you don't need a big brain with a neocortex to feel petrified or pissed off' (Balcombe 2017: 88). Balcombe is generous in his insistence that sentience is enough for subjectivity: 'being aware involves having experiences, taking notice, remembering things. An aware creature is not merely alive; she has a life' (2017: 18).

Three examples based on relatively recent studies show fish life has intricate sociability and organized structure. Intricacy is in part related to place: complexity is best seen on coral reefs, home to many species who occupy interconnected spaces. 'A SCUBA diver's view of Red Sea coral reefs inevitably reveals an intricate and varied, apparently haphazard, arrangement of surfaces created by a wide range of species' (Vine 2019: n.p.). First impressions register gorgeous confusion. In the Red Sea in 1982, a young Callum Roberts reports: 'Shock blossoms into wonder. Fish throng a labyrinth of coral: fat fish, slender, spiny, smooth, bulbous-eyed, serious, striped, barred, spotted, dotted, ringed, plain, lemon peel, orange, aquamarine, black; a mind-bending confusion coming and going' (Roberts 2019: 17-18). Dazzle makes it hard to see relationships, further confused by coral's textural jumble, described by Jay Griffiths as 'a phantasmagoria of the spiny, the prickly, the feathery and spirally; fiddle-headed, pronged, whorled, tubular, spotted, dotted, spiky, gauzy, gossamer and crusted' (2006: 196). Where to look? In the 1970s, diver-scientists established that some damselfish grazed particular patches of algae that they defended vigorously. Described as 'farming', this grazing contributes to reef health, structure and social arrangements. Roberts studied this underwater. 'The long days watching their lives unfold have revealed an exquisite pattern of resource sharing, mutual benefit and parasitism among a loose collective of fish that all depend on the algal lawn for food. Big and aggressive surgeonfish keep out sticky herbivores such as parrotfish, but tolerate small and aggressive damselfish that drive away small grazers, saving them work' (Roberts 2019: 94). Also investigating damselfish and their territories, Peter Sale established that each had neighbours and intruders – and a third kind of interaction, a sort of rapid socializing, like saying hello to a neighbour (2021: 80). Sale thought damselfish might behave like bulldogs or gang members, but that was 'partly because you – big, black, lumbering, noisy, bubble-spewing – have just arrived on the scene.' He instanced more peaceable socializing. An old turtle with algal turf on its shell would float past most afternoons; the damselfish would stop patrolling, come over and feast as if from an ice cream truck (Sale 2021: 84). Aggression is usually explained as competition for space, but findings point to intricate social factors. Damselfish are less aggressive near islands with rats, because rats kill seabirds whose guano enriches algal turf, so there's less to protect. They maintain larger territories to compensate (Gunn 2023: 82-91). What you see depends on where and where else you look.

Roberts thinks about analogies. 'It was suddenly astonishing to me how visible it all was. What if the terrestrial world were like this? What would it be like to take a stroll in the forest, and find, within an arm's-length radius, a similarly teeming display of woodland creatures: beavers, robins, woodpeckers, deer, squirrels, chipmunks, rabbits, foxes ... ?' (Roberts 2019: 140). Suppose a beaver and a fox hunted as a pair? A second surprise about fish sociability concerned teamwork. In 2006 Redouan Bshary and colleagues described roving coral groupers 'using a rapid, full-body shimmer to recruit giant moray eels to hunt with them. The two teammates swim off over the reef like friends on a stroll' (Balcombe 2017: 166). The eel pursues fish into narrow places; the grouper works open water. Between them, they flush out or trap prey, sharing opportunities to feed. In 2013 researchers saw coral groupers and leopard coral groupers using a headstand signal to engage potential hunting partners, who include giant morays, humphead wrasses and octopuses. Unlike a shimmer, a headstand is a referential gesture; it shows fish have intentions and can point to them, an ability previously attributed only to great apes, ravens and humans. The groupers were patient, waiting as long as twenty-five minutes until their potential partner responded. Balcombe sees this as a kind of thinking. 'It is two fish minds working in concert to translate and transfer desires and intentions into favourable outcomes' (2017: 168-9).

A third instance of social skills evident on reefs are cleaning stations, to which all sorts and sizes of fish and marine animals go to be relieved of parasites and enjoy some light grooming. Five species of cleaner wrasses of the genus *Labroides* are the best known; they use different postures to signal availability to clients. A Great Barrier Reef study showed 'that a single cleaner wrasse serviced an average of 2,297 clients each day. Some individual clients visited a specific cleaner up to an average of 144 times per day.' Unsurprisingly perhaps, cleaners recognize regular clients and adjust their schedules to fit in late-comers. An instance of mutualism, the cleaner nips out fish mucus, which it feeds on, but returns a service, removing parasites; they prove to be extra careful with new clients, so as to establish trust (Balcombe 2017: 156). Bshary thinks cleaner wrasses can recognize more than a hundred individuals and remember previous interactions – much like an owner of a beauty salon.

> The cleaner-client fish mutualism phenomenon represents one of the most complex, well-studied social systems in nature ... the system encompasses long-term relationships built on trust, crime and punishment, choosiness, audience awareness, reputation, and brownnosing. These social dynamics support a degree of awareness and social sophistication quite out of keeping with our cultural impression of fishes.
>
> (Balcombe 2017: 157)

Reefs with plentiful and busy cleaning stations are healthier than those without; thriving stations increased fish numbers, health and species diversity. 'The large-scale effect of the presence of the relatively small and uncommon fish, *Labroides dimidiadus*, on other fishes is unparalleled on coral reefs.' The small, not-very-numerous wrasses had 'remarkable' and 'disproportionate' positive influence on local fish community health (Waldie et al. 2011: x). They are a powerful instance of 'elusive co-enchantment, seeing the oceans as a spirited place, alive with character and emotion' (Griffiths 2006: 187).

The sensibilities of fish society are clearly more than simply sense-based, and show how sensing is a relational process. 'For cultural studies of the sensory, it may well be an unsatisfactory premise to portray the senses as some sort of universal bio-physical faculties of the human race (and by extension, of the whole of fauna) that are materialized in the discrete sensory organs of the individual being' (Järviluoma and Murray 2023: 5). One sense organ that fish have which humans do not is a lateral line, a pressure-sensitive line along a fish body, made up of specialized scales containing neuromasts, cells with hair-like projections that react to changes in pressure, usually from water movement, and relay information to a fish's brain. It provides hydrodynamic imaging so that even visually impaired fish can navigate around objects (Balcombe 2017: 59; Mogdans 2019: 53-72). One might describe it as a language for presence and change. Equally different from us are systems of fish communications, often written in light which we barely understand. Discussing the huge range of fish illumination, Helen Scales calls fish 'the uncontested champions of bioluminescence' (2018: 124). Using either luciferin molecules or glowing bacteria taken in as food, fish can use light to make themselves visible or invisible – especially in the twilight zone, where subtleties of blue light enable hiding and socializing. 'Barreleyes, also known as spookfish, write messages to each other on their bellies' (Scales 2018: 128). They have 'enormous green, tubular eyes that swivel around beneath a clear bubble like an astronaut's helmet'; they also have a second pair of eyes with guanine crystals – 'the only animals that have mirrors for eyes' – so as to detect 'the dim blue glow of other bioluminescent animals, including other barreleyes' (Scales 2018: 128). The appreciative wonder of fish authors is lost in translation: online reports reductively describe the barreleye as a 'deep-sea weirdo' (Pare 2023). The strange-to-us appearance of species cast as 'weirdos' may be alien, but to fish authors that strangeness is not alienating:

> What many of these people like about fishes is not that they are like us. What is beautiful about them, and equally worthy of respect, is how they are not like us. Their different ways of being in the world are a source of fascination and admiration, and cause for sympathy. We can connect across the great divide that separates us ….
>
> (Balcombe 2017: 233)

PLURALITY AND SINGULARITY

Generalist authors tend to tackle the immense diversity of fish by breaking it into themes based on physiology and behaviour. Common behaviour is evident loosely in a shoal, tightly in a school. A shoal is a group in which individuals swim independently, says Balcombe, whereas a school is more disciplined. Shoals forage; schools migrate. The collectivity of a school is usually presented as uniformity – whatever individuality might be accorded to a single fish disappears into the unity of collective movement.

> Diving in the coral reefs off Sulawesi, I once found my vision completely filled with fish. I was swimming in five shoals: blue and gold fusiliers, pyramid butterfly fish, big grey snappers, lunar fusiliers and striped fusiliers. They swam together, then separated out into their own shoals, then swam together again. The vivid powder-blue lunar fusiliers remained longer than the others, then the whole shoal was suddenly skittish and rang out for a different angle, swimming a blue streak. Soaring and falling, they shot vertically downwards like a thousand shooting stars plummeting together down a mercurial plumb line. Shoals of fish, alerted by a movement or a flicker of a shadow, turn around on a fin-instant as a flock of birds can turn on a wingtip's timing. They move as if fluent in the languages of striations of light and the confluence of waters ….
>
> (Griffiths 2006: 192-3)

Shoals have poetics for Osha Gray Davidson, also off Sulawesi. 'Looking up is even more compelling. It's like staring into a shimmering blue sky that, as if in a dream, is filled by great flocks of birds with iridescent wings moving in unison and in slow motion: more fishes' (Gray Davidson 1998: 62). The biodynamics of shoals are intriguing – how is it that fish don't bump into each other? Complicated mathematics explain that, but so do social factors: 'shoals comprised of familiar individuals show more efficient schooling behaviour than those comprised of strangers' (Brown, Laland and Krause 2011: 6). Shoalmates know their places, integrate individual abilities and observe dominance rankings. 'In schooling species, for example we often find that fish that are strongly left-eye-biased in social contexts will take up positions on the right side of the school so they can monitor the behaviour of conspecifics with their preferred eye and vice versa for right-biased fishes' (Brown, Laland and Krause 2011: 7). Defensive actions have names like fireworks: the fountain effect, splitting into two clusters that reassemble behind a predator, or flash expansion, when all the fishes dart away from the centre (Balcombe 2017: 136–7).

A school of fish images fish abundance, convenient for humans. 'Plenty more fish in the sea', a phrase used to console those disappointed in love, has been condensed in a dating app, Plenty of Fish. Abundance is now a wrecked fiction, given relentless hunting, bottom trawling and overfishing. Different species have acquired historians, like Jennifer Telesca whose searing study of the giant bluefin tuna exposes the terrible failures of ICCAT, the International Commission for the Conservation of Atlantic Tunas (Telesca 2020). Schools of giant tuna, now scarcer, are one way to image carefree abundance: 'imagine a team of stampeding horses or a pack of lions on the chase below the ocean surface', says Telesca, one of the very few writers who chooses female fish as protagonists.

> One of the fastest fish at sea, cheetah-like … she clocks over fifty miles per hour (eighty kilometres per hour). In fact, the Bluefin can cross the entire Atlantic Ocean in forty days, and somehow find the nine-mile (fourteen kilometres) stretch of the Strait of Gibraltar at its narrowest point to enter the Mediterranean Sea. She enjoys one of the longest migrations of any fish on the planet.
>
> (Telesca 2020: xiv–xv)

Another biographer offers *Swordfish: A Biography of the Ocean Gladiator* (Ellis 2013), whose publisher says it 'provides a complete history of the fish from prehistoric fossils to its present-day endangerment, as our taste for swordfish has had a drastic effect on their population the world over.' Charles Clover argued in *The End of the Line* (2004) that fishing technology is comparable to that of war: sonar, GPS, cameras, sensors, computers prowl the oceans. Now drones, AI and smart boats extend human reach (Environmental Defense Fund 2021). Ironically some success has been had with albatrosses fitted with radar detection tags that signal back to New Zealand fisheries officials whether the boats they check out have their positioning systems turned off (Roy 2020). How the Ancient Mariner would have stared.

Figure 15 Group portrait: Bigeye yellow snapper, *Lutjanus lutjanus*, Raja Ampat. Photo by Clare Brant.

In *Eating the Ocean*, Elspeth Probyn investigates consequences of 'the overwhelmingly masculine framing of the relation of fish and human', and how 'Framing the fisheries in totally gender-blind ways that naturalize fishing as an entirely masculine problem is part of the problem, not the solution' (Probyn 2016: 104). Sylvia Earle puts *Homo sapiens* in the frame. 'We should have learned with wildlife on the land that we have the power – through both our numbers and our technologies – to be able to find, kill, extract and market, to decimate, anything that swims in the ocean' (Earle 2009: n.p.). Bycatch (or by-catch as the *OED* has it, with first use 1962) is a neutralizing word for carnage. The unintended catch of non-target species means dolphins, sharks, turtles, birds, fish and many other beings are killed as a result of indiscriminate fishing, legal and illegal. Most editions of Clover's *The End of the Line* have a cover image featuring a single, small fish on a plate or in a fish crate, an iconography of depletion. Fish literature includes older accounts of abundance – Anthony Netboy quotes a Russian ichthyologist who in 1926 witnessed a massive run of chum salmon, at least a mile long and 100-metres wide, thundering upriver 'making a very loud noise, as if a new river had burst into the Bolshaya' (Netboy 1980: 273). As a commodity, fish made fortunes for businesses including fishing, processing, packing, canning, distributing and selling (Day 2018); the Bodleian Library in Oxford was funded by profits from pilchards that accrued to Ann Ball, a widow who married Sir Thomas Bodley. Mark Kurlansky's book *Cod* is subtitled 'A Biography of the Fish that Changed the World'; as its synopsis explains, 'Wars have been fought over it, revolutions have been triggered by it, national diets have been based on it, economies and livelihoods have depended on it. To the millions it has sustained, it has been a treasure more precious than gold' (publisher website description). In *The Most Important Fish in the Sea: Menhaden and America* (2008), H. Bruce Franklin shows 'how menhaden have shaped America's natural – and national – history, and why a single company now threatens their crucial ecological mission. The same pudgy little fish that once saved the Pilgrims from starvation and helped power the industrial revolution are today being ground up by the billions and turned into everything from linoleum to lipstick' (publisher website description). Biographies of species that support humans as food and commodity are increasingly elegiac – and angry. Mark Kurlansky's *The Last Fish Tale: The Fate of the Atlantic and Our Disappearing Fisheries* (2008) takes depletion to its logical end for humans: the extinction of fishing as a way of life. Tropes of 'the last fish' may be increasing. In *The Last Fish Swimming* (2019), Gohar A. Petrossian shows how illegal fishing worsens apparently unstoppable depletion, for instance for totoaba (*Totoaba macdonaldi*) whose swimbladders, known as maws, are often described as aquatic cocaine for their illegal value. Totoaba share waters with vaquita, small porpoises who live in the Sea of Cortez too and get entangled in the nets set to catch totoaba. 'The intertwined fates of the vaquita and the totoaba have given rise to the term "dual extinction," highlighting the fact that both species are teetering on the edge of oblivion' (Hutchins 2025a). In 2025, fewer than ten vaquita are left.

In life writing terms, biography is one way to focus attention on the fate of species whose populations have crashed. Decline and fall narrative arcs reveal these are interspecies biographies, the other species being humans whose greed and carelessness wipe out abundance. Fish also carry their own autobiography in two physical forms. They have otoliths, ear stones in a fluid-filled chamber which vibrate against sensory hairs and send signals to a fish's brain. As they sink under gravity they tell the fish which way is up. 'There's a chemical story written into every fish's ear-stone that records details of its life' (Scales 2018: 266). They vary between species. 'Ray-finned fish have six otoliths; lampreys have four, hagfish have two. Sharks' otoliths are the size of sand grains' (Scales 2018: 265 note). Fossil otoliths have been found at prehistoric settlements; otolith microchemistry studies can reveal fish travels. Like tree rings, otoliths indicate age: Francis Ward explains how to extract an otolith from a plaice's head, and then how to read its age by counting light and dark rings (Ward 1911: 118). Also like tree rings are scales, to which a fish adds many rings each year, farther apart in summer when growth is faster. 'No other animal known to man carries about it such a complete autobiography' (Curtis 1949: 25).

The push-pull of plurality and singularity applies to other groups besides fishes. Pets have some subjecthood: a dog's life can be told both as a dog story and a personality story. But fish individuality has been realized more slowly and patchily. The oceanic manta ray, for instance, is a species identified only in 2009 by Andrea Marshall, 'Queen of the Mantas', who proposed a third, the Atlantic, recently confirmed (Hutchins 2025b). Individuals can be identified by their unique markings, like a fingerprint on their bellies: each one is different. These ventral patterns can be seen – and photos lodged – at a database (Manta Trust). Hence Balcombe infers an interior life: 'each fish is a unique individual, not just with a biology, but with a biography. Just as each sunfish, whale shark, manta ray and leopard grouper has a distinctive pattern from which you can recognize individuals on the outside, each has a one-of-a-kind life on the inside too' (2017: 8). Each human has unique fingerprints but conferring that uniqueness on interiority is a form of humanism, even if it's cartilaginous fishes who get to be special. Interiority is also constructed through identity politics which colour fish life writing.

INVISIBLE FEMALES AND QUEER FISH

Many fish are gender fluid. 'More than one-quarter of all fishes on a reef can transition from male to female, or vice-versa … Other fishes opt for a unisex approach, assuming both male and female identities simultaneously, or sequentially' (Balcombe 2017: 182). Riffing on an American bumper sticker popular with diehard heterosexuals, 'God created Adam and Eve, not Adam and Steve', Osha Gray Davidson suggests one for fish would read 'God created Adam and Eve, Adam Who Becomes Eve, Eve Who Becomes Adam, and Adameve' (1998: 90). And EveAdam, or EVEadam, or EVEadamadamadam in the case of anglerfish whom I discuss shortly. Studies suggest some bony fishes 'have a sexually bipotential brain that can manage two types of behaviors, unlike most other vertebrates' who manage one (Balcombe 2017: 183). Some double up with impressive versatility. 'Chalk Bass in the Caribbean have both male and female sex organs at the same time, and use both throughout life-long partnerships. Pairs of bass live together, often inside old conch shells, and swap gender roles, male to female then back again, up to 20 times a day' (Scales 2018: 171).

Writing about sexism in birdwatching, Jasmine Donahue exposes how identification handbooks favour males, shown as bigger in pictures even when females of that species are larger (Donahue 2023). There may well be a similar bias in fish guides. There certainly is in fish life stories: I have found no instance of any female-focused salmon journeys upriver, and only one of down, a fleeing parr put at the end of a study which begins with a heroic cock salmon leaping his way inland (Shelton 2009: 201-4). Human models of sexuality are rarely far away. 'Reef fishes have such diverse and inventive sex lives that they make pornography see as bland and unimaginative as … well, as it really is' (Davidson 1998: 90; his ellipsis). Even Balcombe makes sexual action seem masculine. 'Depending on his sexual playbook, a male fish may keep a harem, defend a territory, spawn in a group, engage in sneak copulations, bide his time as a satellite male, or commit acts of sexual piracy' (2017: 181). A new gender fluid language is evolving: as one Tik-Tok post puts it, 'Holy Shit Fish are Trans Icons????' (26 September 2023). They are. Females are still less visible. Their erasure can be seen in Disney's *Finding Nemo* (2003), featuring an anemone clownfish father and son. Clownfish, *Amphiprion*, have a matriarchal society. They live in groups headed by a big female, with a breeding male and smaller male subordinates. If the breeding female dies, the breeding male becomes female and the next largest male moves up the hierarchy to be a breeder. 'The largest and oldest individual of a group is always female and dominates the male, subadults and juveniles' (Fricke 1977: 831). When Nemo's mother died, his father would have become his mother. But not in Disney, which also managed to misrepresent matriarchal meerkats as patriarchal.

There is some strong language around clownfish arrangements. 'Low ranking males are psychophysiologically castrated'; it is 'Monogamy by force' (Fricke 1977: 831) even though for reproductive purposes it has efficiency. A large female produces more eggs; a smaller male can fertilize and guard them perfectly well. Clownfish feature as an instance of 'the Strangest Family Lives' for father and son Stephen R. Palumbi and Anthony R. Palumbi, who then move on to anglerfish, also on the book cover (2014: 141-2). What is strange, other than strange to us? Anglerfish feature repeatedly in fish literature as almost unbearably strange, the discomfort arising from human gender models. I look first at life writings, then science, then queer ecotheory to explore angles on anglerfish.

Most of the simultaneous hermaphrodites live in the deep sea. 'Being able to fertilize yourself is a very useful adaptation where the daily prospects of finding another of your kind are almost as dim as your surroundings' (Balcombe 2017: 182). Anglerfish – a large group with variations – are not hermaphroditic. The reproduction method adopted by most, though not all, is for a dwarf male to latch on to a female many times his size, onto whose body he is then permanently fixed, partially absorbed and sustained by her resources. 'The union is so remarkable that there is no simile or metaphor with which to introduce it', wrote William Beebe (1942: 278). He saw a murderous melodrama: 'From now on, the gentler sea-devil sex swims on her way with the tattered remains of her suitor dangling from her body' (Beebe 1942: 289). It horrified him:

> But to be driven by impelling odour and light headlong upon a mate so gigantic, so impersonal, so unconscious of any emotion, in such Stygian darkness, and wilfully to eat a hole in her tough hide, to feel the gradually increasing transfusion of her blood throughout one's veins, to lose everything that marked one as superior to a worm, to become a spineless, brainless, senseless thing that was a fish – this seems sheer fiction, absurd beyond all belief unless we have seen the proof of it.
>
> (Beebe 1942: 289)

Beebe's oneness – like others – is with the male. He doesn't think about it from the female's point of view – how a bite in the dark might be understood as a love-bite, or how the irritation of a suitor's grip would be known to be something not to be shaken off, even welcomed, or how donation of energy, of vital forces, might feel to the donor. The position of attachment among anglerfishes varies – upside down, on belly, anywhere on body, on head (Pietsch 209: 307) – perhaps akin to intercourse position preferences among humans? What varies less are human reactions to anglerfish fusion, out of which anthropomorphism creates strangeness and estrangement.

There are two recurrent issues. The first is identification, or not, with the tiny male. 'His jaws sink in. And he never lets go again. By and by his skin grows together with her skin. Her blood-vessels make connection with his blood-vessels. His mouth degenerates and becomes functionless. He literally becomes one with her' (Curtis 1949: 263). Diolé called the males dwarfish and degenerate, but found consolation in their virility. 'The only organ which they have managed to keep is a huge testicle'

(Diolé 1954a: 107). Balcombe is more relational: 'It looks like a lurid form of sexual harassment.' He sees fidelity assured. 'In exchange for the male being the ultimate couch potato, the female never has to wonder where her mate is on a Saturday evening' (Balcombe 2017: 17). Lurking closely is a fear of female agency: the anglerfish presents 'an awful warning provided by nature of what can happen when feminism is allowed to run away with itself' (Carrington 1960: 142).

The second issue is the spectacle of the couple. Metaphors of marriage turn up in accounts of the anglerfish in interestingly historicized ways. Brian Curtis admires the couple as an ethical sight:

> of unswerving masculine devotion to a single spouse this is unquestionably the world's outstanding example. Here is conjugal faithfulness carried to the ultimate degree. Here are no puny words about 'till death us do part.' Not even death will part this little fish from his mate. If she dies, he at once dies also. Here is marital fidelity beyond the powers of the most virtuous of the human species. Poor fish, indeed!
>
> (Curtis 1949: 263)

A more maritally relaxed Robert Gibbings was droll. 'Then the jaws and gills become atrophied, and from that on the whole system of the male is an integral part, a mere appendage, of the female. Such conditions are an ideal of matrimony to *some* people' (Gibbings 1946: 17). Jay Griffiths goes for nightmare. For her, ocean depths

> seem to represent the lower depths of the mind, our subconscious fears made flesh and living beneath us. With suggestions of incubi, small male angler fish bite into the much larger female's belly until the two become fused and her circulation takes over for both, so he is a permanently attached sperm supply. There are deep-sea creatures that look like half-slaughtered, gashed ghosts vengeful and near to death, but ready to devour.
>
> (Griffiths 2006: 219)

Beebe's last paragraph returns to musing over the process.

> Did she know he was there? When did the last vestige of sight and smell, of heart-throb, of individual instinct and sensation, leave the little being? What theory or combination of theories of evolution can explain the gradual development through past ages, the first male to attach himself, culminating in this wholesale self-immolation on the altar of generation?
>
> (Beebe 1942: 290)

It's noticeable that anglerfish accounts often come at the end of a chapter or book, as if the finality of absorption was shared with blank space, and as if human questions collapse into silence.

The ichthyologist who knows most about anglerfishes, Theodore W. Pietsch, points out how obscure they are to us: 'living ceratioid anglerfishes are totally inaccessible by all reasonable means of observation. Their behavior is therefore almost completely unknown, and what we may assume about their life-style is … "armchair biology"' and the study of a few hauled-up specimens (2009: 249). Fixation on anglerfish reproduction masks other aspects of their interesting lives. They have an unusual immune system, which accounts for female absorption of another body without triggering rejection (Lu 2020: n.p.). Only the females have a luminescent lure or *esca*. Sight is limited in the vast dark ocean; many think males find females by following pheromone or scent trails, though some species have tiny nostrils. Attached males grow bigger than unattached ones. 'In all probability the males are incapable of free development, and it is likely that the great majority of them fail to find a female and perish', thinks one expert (Bertelsen cited by Pietsch 2009: 280). Underwater writers represent anglerfish attachment as singular, to make it singularly grotesque. But females can and do acquire multiple attached males. 'The current record is now held by a 316-mm female with eight males ranging in size from 35 to 56 mm' (Pietsch 2009: 290). One thinks of this large She moving jauntily along with fertility assured by her attached handbags. Or manbags. Writers imagine the extinguishing of consciousness in the male: why is there no imagining of its possible expansion or alteration in the female?

Pietsch says anglerfish adaptations are 'almost beyond our ability to imagine' (2009: 64). Morphology here does not help infer subjectivity. Unimaginability depends on typologies of imagination, how you categorize possibilities. For Timothy Morton, 'life is catastrophic, monstrous, nonholistic, and dislocated, not organic, coherent, or authoritative' (2010: 275). Comprehending the mesh of liquid life is difficult: 'it defies our imaginative capacities and transcends iconography' (Morton 2010: 276). Queer ecology can help. 'To contemplate ecology's unfathomable intimacies is to imagine pleasures that are not heteronormative, nor genital, nor geared to ideologies about where the body stops and starts' (Morton 2010: 280). Since queer theory argues that 'sexuality is never a case of a norm versus its pathological variants', the startling relations of anglerfishes can be accepted. Morton says cheerfully, 'It's life, Jim – but not as we know it' (2010: 278). Anglerfishes seem a perfect species group for queer theory as well as feminism. 'Acknowledging the zombielike quality of interconnected life-forms will aid the transition for an ideological fixation on Nature to a fully queer ecology' (Morton 2010: 279). Stressing relationality rather than individualism, Morton offers an alternative to a populist language of 'deep-sea weirdos'. 'Queer ecology may abandon the disastrous term *animal* and adopt something like *strange stranger* – my bad translation of Derrida's *arrivant*. … Strange strangers are uncanny, familiar and strange simultaneously. Their familiarity is strange, their strangeness familiar' (Morton 2010: 277). Best of all, such uncanniness applies not metaphorically but uncannily literally to anglerfishes. 'They are composites of other strange strangers.'

It might be said that *strange strangers* subtly, queerly updates an old language of science as discoveries and mysteries. One group of anglerfishes take strangeness even further. Pietsch reports that the mechanism by which males and females of *Neoceratias* find each other remains a mystery. Although free-living males are unknown, the eyes and nostrils of all known parasitic males of this genus are especially small and degenerate, and besides these apparent deficiencies, the females lack an illicium and esca and any other known bioluminescent structure.

(2009: 330)

So if neither scent nor vision leads a male to a female, how on earth, how underwater do they find each other?

Figure 16 Richard Ellis: 'Triplewart Seadevil and Anglerfish'. Science Photo Library.

7

Fish Autobiography

I am a bream, and I swim around the stone walls at Iluka, where I eat oysters, and crustaceans. When I was young and innocent I used to do many foolish things. One day, as I was politely swimming along, I saw a nice piece of mullet lying on the bottom. My appetite being very good, I at once took it up to eat: but as I did so a naughty boy gave a pull. I at once knew what had happened, but I must say that my luck was in. I chanced to be so small that the boy let me go. Now, when the amateur fishermen come here I play many tricks on them. They try me with fine silk lines and precious baits. But still I decline. They say I can read and write. – Bert Paddon, 5th Class, Iluka.

(Paddon 1917: 4)

This autobiography was written by an Australian boy aged ten and published in 1917 in his local newspaper. He grew up to become a fisherman like his father (Pittwater 2016). What if a fish could read and write? In this chapter I explore a selection of texts which are autobiographies, animalographies and above all migration stories, genres entirely familiar in life writing terms – except when starring a fish. How does life writing help us read fish literature?

Salmon and eel are properly fishes, multi-species. There are more than eight hundred species of eel; the ones discussed here are *Anguilla anguilla*, the European eel and *Anguilla rostrata*, American. Salmon too are various: Atlantic salmon (*Salmo salar*) and Pacific (Northwest) salmons, who include king or chinook, silver, pink, chum, steelhead, coho and sockeye or red salmon, and the cutthroat, also known as sea trout (Salmon 2013). The misfortunes of Atlantic salmon include being farmed in the Pacific, where escapees from fish farms have led to the Atlantic salmon being tagged an invasive species in the Pacific Northwest (Shore 2017). Conversely, Pacific pink salmon who escaped from Russian farms established in the 1950s are now an invasive species in the river system shared by Norway and Finland. Also known as humpheads, these fish have so overwhelmed Atlantic salmon that AI facial recognition systems have been put in place to try to catch them early on their routes up Norway's Storeva river. In 2021, pink salmon, *Onchorhyncus gorbuscha*, amounted to 57 per cent of all salmon caught in Norway; in Finland, native wild salmon have declined by a comparable figure (Marzouk 2022). In 2023 the UK Government issued a public warning notice because pink salmon have spread across the North Sea (Environment

Agency 2023). Surveillance technology to guard borders gives fish migrations a politics analogous to that of humans.

FISHY TALES

In 1994 Umberto Eco published an essay, 'How to Travel with a Salmon.' His salmon is dead; the essay ruefully recounts Eco's attempts to keep it refrigerated in a malfunctioning hotel. The salmon's journey, from Sweden to London, in and out of a hotel room minibar fridge, is the pivot for Eco's discomfiture with modernity. It is the last, least written part of a journey for many salmon: to a plate. Smoked, plastic-wrapped and increasingly malodorous, Eco's salmon is a consumer object. Despite being inert and mute it haunts Eco's short essay, inviting an imaginary salmon narrative, 'How to Travel with a Postmodernist.'

I take up a handful of salmon narratives to think through who they travel with and how. I go back to George Rooper's *The Autobiography of a Salmon* (*Salmo Salar*), its title simplified in the second edition (1886). Roderick Haig-Brown's *Silver: The Life Story of an Atlantic Salmon* (1931) and Henry Williamson's *Salar the Salmon* (first published in 1935) likewise follow the return of a salmon to its birthwaters and back to the sea. Rachel Carson's *Under the Sea-Wind* (1941, her first book) features a mackerel and a female eel migrating to the sea. Pacific Northwest salmon literature has different configurations of place, people and meanings: as Svetlana Seibel summarizes, 'salmon literature creates textualities of care aimed not only at criticizing the colonial economies, but at narratively restoring the threatened lifeworlds of both the people and the fish' (Seibel 2022: 39).

Life writing scholarship includes much about migration writing, entirely focused on humans. The migration literature of marine beings deserves critical attention, especially as hotter oceans compel more creatures to move. What concepts can one use for species migration narratives? Surveying the field, Joanna Kosmalska offers a broad-brush typology that sweeps some paths through very thick plantings. One cluster she identifies is where authors are bicultural or multicultural. 'The permeation of one culture by another forces the writers to explore identity issues. In the very act of writing, the authors analyse and reformulate both their individual and group identities. Their investigations into identity construction help them invent new, alternative conceptions of home and belonging' (Kosmalska 2022: 337). In one sense this doesn't fit fish migration literature very well, because fish are at home in their waters. But it is helpful if you turn it inside-out: home and belonging are conceptions that are stable in fish migration literature. What writers invent are threats to that belonging, from predators in the open ocean to predators in estuaries and on the riverbank. Belonging too is not so much a cultural category, as it is for humans, but an environment in which the main narrative drive is survival of threats to life so as to arrive at a meeting point which is also a mating point that ensures the existence and migratory cycle for a future generation. Reproduction renews the species, and has its own poetics – in Henry Williamson's final words in *Salar the Salmon*, 'the star-stream of heaven flowed westward, to far beyond the ocean where salmon, moving from deep waters to the shallows of the islands, leapt – eager for immortality.' That final chapter is titled 'End and Beginning'; spawning produces death and life in a mythic circle (Williamson 1944: 186).

Salmons fascinate us with their unerring navigational ability. Migration for humans is usually about going to countries whose strangeness is fearful or disorientating – ironically 'fish out of water' is a phrase recognized in criticism for the state of displacement often felt by new arrivals (Butcher 2010: 23-36). Especially for anadromous fish, those like salmon who move between salt and fresh water with accompanying physiological changes, going home may not be the end of the journey – or, the journey can end with a return to sea, which is also home. Atlantic salmon may make this journey up to five or six times. Their auto/biographies cover transitions between ecologies humans tend to keep separate (stream and sea) but which for the salmon are fluidly connected; their differentness is imaged through changes to the fish body, though with sensory continuity and a growing weight of experiences (Bratton 2004: 1-22). Metamorphosing from fry to parr (juveniles), to smolt (ready to migrate to sea) to grilse (after one winter at sea, ready to spawn) to hen and cock (mature) to kelt (post-spawn), salmon have distinct life stages, all with their own perils.

George Rooper's *Autobiography of a Salmon* is a … curious fish. Its chapter headings mimic the first-person summary common in the nineteenth-century novel, as if it was a Dickensian bildungsroman. 'I volunteer the story of my life and commence it before I was born' – like *David Copperfield* (1884) whose chapter 1 is headed 'I was born'. Rooper's story begins on a train: he shares a carriage with a strange-looking gentleman wittily clothed in a tweed, or Tweed, overcoat who launches into his life story. The story's supposed editor, a keen salmon fisherman, also uses first person to interject in footnotes that elaborate views on fishing. The narrative covers birth, growth, migrations, encounters with fishermen involving injuries and escapes, pleasurable feeding seasons in the sea, and a final return to the Tweed river. For a while the salmon has a female companion, older, wiser, but also gendered in a dispiritingly Victorian way as a helpmeet: 'her presence was an aid and consolation to me, and I felt cooler and stronger for her sympathy' (Rooper 1886: 51). Her death is gendered too: after 'wantonly' biting at a 'butterfly', actually a fishing fly concealing a hook, she is caught and killed with a gaff, a barbed stick. Being a teeming mother is no protection, even for a modest hen salmon.

Rooper's anthropomorphism is erratic. At one point the salmon takes on the appearance of an old river-keeper to complain about fishing legislation and river management, at length in dialect speech. The story's river topography is real; somehow the salmon knows Sir Walter Scott is buried at Drysdale Abbey, just above his current pool, and the whole text is a defiant apologia for anglers and the value of their salmon-knowledge. And it was all a dream, from which the author awakes. It does though have a remarkable moment, one which startlingly upends that contract between writer and reader which Philippe Lejeune sees as necessary to autobiography's projection of truth-telling (Allamand 2018; Lejeune 1971). Normally the narrator and protagonist share a name with the author. Rooper's ending defies that identification: 'the elderly gentleman in the straw-coloured paletot [overcoat] resolved himself into the straw-enveloped salmon, the victim of my prowess but yesterday afternoon' – hence 'the Narrator was killed by the Author' (Rooper 1886: 79–80).

Rooper was soaked in blood-sports, and his metaphors in Victorianism – smolts are like schoolboys, young kelts like married men escaping from their wives. His anthropomorphic conversion of salmon to elderly gentleman imports obvious ideologies. Twentieth-century writers were more careful in their establishing apparatus and more interested in accounting for migration as sensory longing that could not be fully explained. Roderick Haig-Brown is halfway between Rooper and Williamson's approaches. He was officially Canadian but grew up in England on his grandfather's estate in Dorset where shooting and fishing were the norm. His story *Silver: The Life Story of an Atlantic Salmon* (first published in 1931) is dedicated to a boy with similar expectations, and it gets underway with child-friendly language. After hatching, eating, growing and evading predators, Silver spends the winter sleepily, like lying in bed longer than you ought, before spring arrives and hunger rouses him. Spring heralds 'the greatest event of Silver's life – the beginnings of his silver jacket' (Haig-Brown 1947: 20). The water sings a song, 'Down to the sea', which the parr find irresistible. Heading downstream Silver evades more predators – heron, pike – and feasts on flies; he is caught by a Good Fisherman who tags him and returns him to the river. Migration instinct is explained by several drives: 'he felt the blood of his thousands of generations of roving ancestors, the urge of his silver jacket, the mystery of the vast salt waters and the Great Feeding-Grounds that lie somewhere under the edge of the North Pole' (Haig-Brown 1947: 32). Haig-Brown is clear about fish sentience and sensibility; in his transformation from parr to smolt, Silver feels stronger, lighter, freer, able to swim and think faster. He leaps for joy, introducing 'a very difficult question. Can salmon talk or not?' (Haig-Brown 1947: 33). Here the frame of children's literature, with its tolerance of fantasy, supports the question; the author-narrator says confidently

> I'm certain that all animals talk, some of them perhaps more than others, but all well enough to understand one another. That doesn't mean that all of them talk with their mouths: some talk with little twitches of their tails and other movements of their bodies, and this is the way fish talk. Silver must have been able to talk at least a little, or many of the wonderful things that he did would have been impossible.
>
> (Haig-Brown 1947: 33)

Fish communication is presented as real. A sea trout tells Silver which way to go – follow the kelts. Haig-Brown has another drive to explain – how is it the salmon know the way to the Great Feeding-Grounds? Class privilege explains it: 'he was one of the chosen among salmon – one of those favoured ones that are born of noble, healthy parents, and leave the river at the end of their first year, having always fed on an ample supply of the best of everything' (Haig-Brown 1947: 38). As a grilse Silver feels restless, which in 'some curious way' is connected with finding a mate, the graceful Grace; they return to fresh water where 'The Voice of the River was repeating over and over again ever so faintly but ever so clearly, "Come up and spawn, come up and spawn"' (Haig-Brown 1947: 42). They leap the falls; after spawning Grace is weak and feeble, so

Silver leaves her, is taken and released again by the Good Fisherman, returns to sea and finds another beautiful mate, a sort of salmon Bright Young Thing. 'And she probably watched and admired, and sometimes jumped out of the water or swam nearly as fast as he did, just to show that she could. These modern girls who can play tennis and golf so well are not really so vastly different from the old order of things' (Haig-Brown 1947: 61).

After several runs, Silver meets his end at the hands of the Good Fisherman who appeared at the start of the story, watching salmon:

> What the Good Fisherman thought or said as he looked at the battered glory that had been Silver and thought of the wonderful heart of the great fish, I do not know. But his hands were very clumsy as he sought to remove the hook from Silver's jaw, and his eyes were rather sad when he turned uphill to the lodge.
>
> (Haig-Brown 1947: 94-5)

Salmon heroes are destined to die. The foe that a salmon faces is usually singular, a fisherman, though these fishy tales do recognize collective human threats to salmon. Haigh-Brown's final sentence evokes the slowing down of the classical elegiac couplet (conventionally, a hexameter followed by a pentameter). Like the stuffed specimens of big fish still viewable in riverside pubs, triumph is attended by melancholy.

Figure 17 A female (in front) and male Sockeye salmon (*Oncorhynchus nerka*) over eggs in their spawning river. Adams River, British Columbia, Canada, October. Photo and caption by Alex Mustard. Image courtesy of Alex Mustard. Note the dead salmon below the female.

Candice Allmark-Kent proposes the term 'speculative representation' to describe attempts by authors to represent nonhuman animals realistically. As she observes, fish literature is neglected in animal studies (2021:170). Using Jonathan Balcombe's evidence of knowledgeable fish to push against boggly-goggly prejudice, Allmark-Kent explores fish literature looking for empathy. Grouping Haig-Brown with other Canadian authors, she thinks Henry Williamson's *Salar* 'bears a striking resemblance to this style' (Allmark-Kent 2021: 176). I would trace a different line of influence, through Sir John Fortescue, who wrote an Introduction to Williamson's *Tarka the Otter* (1927) and to whom Williamson paid tribute as a predecessor. Fortescue's *The Story of a Red Deer* (1897) like Williamson's fiction is mapped onto real Devon places by endpaper maps, his river has a beguiling song and his animals talk to each other – though in forelock-tugging, deferential, country-folk speech. He too follows hunts with implicit criticism of their cruel and inventive methods of killing.

Henry Williamson is a difficult figure. Discredited for fascist sympathies – he joined Oswald Moseley's British Union of Fascists in 1937 – Williamson is nonetheless a nature writer with lasting influence. Rachel Carson wrote that Williamson's work had deeply influenced her, and that his *Tarka the Otter* (1927) and *Salar the Salmon* would be two of three books she might take to a desert island (Rodda Quaratiello, 2004: 29). *Tarka's* subtitle, *His Joyful Water-Life and Death in the Country of the Two Rivers*, establishes water-life as a medium in which fish have emotions. Allmark-Kent observes his fishes 'experience excitement (as well as thrills and exhilarations) at a similar frequency to fear … Williamson also uses more overt language of positive emotions, such as "pleasure," "joy," "elation," "glee," and even "jubilation"'. He extends senses of smell, touch, hearing and sight to assert fish perception of waters as pleasant or unpleasant, and he gives fishes sociable, communicative lives (Allmark-Kent 2021: 178–81). Fish character is developed well beyond the cold-blooded language of science. 'At present, researchers restrict discussions of fish personalities to a dichotomy between "bold" and "shy" fishes … Salar, who seems to be strongly affected by outside forces, fluctuates between boldness and shyness' (Allmark-Kent 2021: 185). Salar finds a mate, Gralaks, and travels too with a sea trout, Trutta, who is injured when he tears through a fishing net at sea. 'Representations of fish personality, friendship, attraction, and affection may seem to straddle the line of uncomfortable anthropomorphism', says Allmark-Kent (2021: 185). But Williamson's handling is careful: 'He [Trutta] was a sick fish, and Salar was piloting him. Salar was unaware of Trutta's weakness and pain, but he knew he was being followed, and was content thereby. His tail was guarded. Also he knew Trutta for something like himself, a familiar form accompanying his life, making the same journey' (Williamson 1944: 58). 'What a fish knows', in Balcombe's phrase, comes as sense perceptions and emotions, but it goes beyond embodied cognition to invite empathy. 'What a fish knows' is more than you think.

After the international success of *Tarka the Otter*, readers were eager for Williamson's next work. 'A Salmon Is To Be the "Hero" of a Novel' announced the *Daily Mirror* on 26 September 1935, adding 'Stream as Scene of Story' (Henry Williamson Society, Salar: 'Critical Reception'). The report quotes Williamson on his research – over 5000 hours of river watching. Given that salmon literature has a basic plot – variations on upriver and down – Williamson focuses on what he calls 'the "feel" of the water' as it might feel to fish. 'The book took a long time to write, as the strain of keeping "under water" for so long was naturally terrific – the descriptive passages, for instance, had to be true and yet have variety. They had to make the reader know the bed of the river and its changing moods' (Henry Williamson Society, *Salar*: 'Critical Reception'). Science refers to ecotones, a transition area where two biological communities meet, like a shoreline or estuary; they have a literary equivalent, ecotonality, sensitivity to shades of place. Williamson uses four intertitles to indicate an ecotonality which is both place and time-defined: Tideways, Spring Spate, Summer River, Winter Star-Stream. Life stages are defined by the different feel of water.

Writing about Rachel Carson's ethics in *Under the Sea-Wind*, Susan Bratton stresses movements that are not migrations, and indeed challenge the migratory as dominant (2004: 1-22). Important here are movements between different ecosystems – ocean and shore, coast and river pool – and between different places in the sea, which have different significance for different organisms. Williamson fills his rivers with creatures who live alongside fish, adapting scientific names for species – a method Carson adopted too. There are many birds who have hop-on parts, like Hackma the woodpecker whose nestlings are chissiwissing in a dead alder while Salar lies lethargically below (Williamson 1944: 123). Details are extraordinarily fine: after ponies come to drink, 'The last of the hoof-frog scent was carried past the hiding place of Salar' (Willliamson 1944: 121). Human and creature characters are both narrowed down – intent on striking, intent on escaping – and widened out to symbolize bigger meanings of species' drives.

Bratton sees a contrast between human predators, who brutally harvest or overharvest with no care for continuity of populations, and animal predators who take only what they need. Williamson has fuzzier boundaries on that: his fishermen are demotic types whose dialect speech sets them apart from the literary English of the narration, though with explicit sympathy and an understanding that for a rural labouring class, economic need can be pressing. Humans can be constructive if they intervene to remove impediments to fish travel: the Board of Conservators maintains the Two Rivers without the weirs and traps that obstruct free running of the fish (Williamson 1944: 60). Both sea and river creatures become aware that humans are dangerous. Human-made entities – nets, ghost gear, hooks, gaffs, fishermen's flies, guns – regularly threaten the narrative subjects. It is also possible for humans to be kind: putting youngsters back is self-interested because the fish may return larger, but it is a gesture of recognition of natural cycles. It does not question the entitlement assumed by anglers to take salmon for sport. In these auto/biographies of third-person subjectivities, fish lives are subservient commodities.

The British salmon texts do recognize, to different degrees, that rivers are part of property networks that discriminate in favour of landed gentry and against the rural working class. Old ways are caught in new regulatory nets (set by the Conservancy Board); the rural underclass is constrained by laws from which the rich are free. 'I ban't no water-whipping rod-and-line gentry', Old Shiner tells the water-bailiff (Williamson 1944: 91). 'Since Shiner had come to watch salmon for their own sakes, Shiner had appointed himself a sort of honorary elusive water-bailiff ... Water-bailiffs were enemies of the other half of himself' (Williamson 1944: 162). His character has a precedent in a real water-bailiff in Lancashire, Old Moon, quoted by Francis Ward as 'a born naturalist, who has learnt his natural history entirely from observation' (1911: 51). Old Shiner is a kind of animal, stalking the riverbank for possible catches and bycatch. In *Tarka* he is a poacher who hates otters as competitors for salmon; in *Salar*, he is salmon-sympathetic. He opens a sluice so trapped fish can progress and he lifts a fungus-doomed Salar off a silt of mud and sticks to deeper water where he may recover enough to continue back to sea. "'That's right, midear. Shiner knoweth." And talking to himself, the old man ambled away along the river bank, peering into the water, seeing almost everything that happened' (Williamson 1944: 162, 184). That's a convenient literary device for staging incidents and interactions, for crossing the gap between air and water which is also the gulf between these two species. 'Knoweth' can be read as Biblical – Old Shiner intervenes like a benevolent God – or loosely rural. He is also a figure representing authorial empathy, the only human in the book who cares about fish 'for their own sakes'.

It is not to detract at all from Rachel Carson's *Under the Sea-Wind: A Naturalist's Picture of Ocean Life* (1941) to see in it much that Williamson had originated. Her biographer quotes a letter of 1953 in which she wrote that her style and thought were deeply influenced by Williamson (Rodda Quaratiello 2004: 29). The book has three stories: Edge of the Sea; The Gull's Way; River and Sea, featuring protagonists with genus names – Rynchops, a black skimmer; Scomber, a mackerel and Anguilla, an eel. When mackerel spawn, 'They leave in their wake a cloud of transparent spheres of infinitesimal size, a vast, sprawling river of life, the sea's counterpart of the river of stars that flows through the sky as the Milky Way' (Carson 1965: 94). Scomber is born from one of these eggs:

> He came into being as a tiny globule no larger than a poppy seed, drifting in the surface layers of pale-green water. The globule carried an amber droplet of oil that served to keep it afloat and it carried also a grey particle of living matter so small that it could have been picked up on the point of a needle. In time this particle was to become Scomber, the mackerel, a powerful fish, streamlined after the manner of his kind, and a rover of the seas.
>
> (Carson 1965: 95)

Flowing between different scales, tiny and vast, vulnerable and powerful, Carson's mackerel grows in the plankton, encountering predators: comb jellies, glassworms, porpoises, petrels, gannets, menhaden. In a sheltered harbour there are more threats from squid; the yearling mackerel tune their movements to the rhythms of the tides. The feel of water controls the narrative: in September, 'there came a night when the flood tide stirred in the young mackerel Scomber a strange uneasiness, and on that night the ebb tide, running to the sea, drew him with it' (Carson 1965: 127). The sea bottom has distinct topography: a gully, a horseshoe ridge, all with predators – haddock above, crabs and stingray below. Carson's sea is full of marine beings at different depths and habitats. Like William Beebe, to whom she dedicated *The Sea Around Us* in 1951, she is attentive to protozoa, who in autumn light up the water with waves of liquid fire. The mackerel come across an abandoned gill net lit up by their light:

It was as though all the myriad lesser fry of the sea – the plants small as dust motes and the animals tinier than a sand grain – drifting from birth to death in an ocean of infinite size and endless fluidity, seized upon the meshes of the gill net as the one firm reality in their uneasy world and clung to it with protoplasmic hair and cilia, with tentacle and claw.

(Carson 1965: 144)

This net, and the trawls, seines and lines of hooks which are regular threatening obstacles, can be read in terms of smooth and striated space, that is, marked with long thin parallel lines. Gai Farchi models this idea from Deleuze and Guattari's *A Thousand Plateaus* (1988). 'In Deleuzian thought, the ocean – just like literature – is considered to be a "smooth space" through which change and becoming are made possible' (Farchi 2020: 190). Smooth space is nomadic, which suits a mackerel's journeyings; it is also a medium of constant becoming, one whose intensive sensations are not graspable by human minds. Farchi suggests 'each intensity, unbounded in terms of known human measurements, is new and never experienced before. Therefore, this experience is the product of a singular connection between the human and the nonhuman, which actually renders this opposition irrelevant' (2020: 190). The opposition is however fatally reinstated by nets, trawls and longlines, because nets impose striated space in smooth space. Tiny animals cling to it like an anchor protecting them against the nomadic force of smooth ocean space, but for mackerel caught in the net, their journey ends. Death is also disappearance into striated space, the toothed or bristled maw of a predator.

Smooth space needs some redefining for underwater. The sea is a mobile medium where fluidities are perceptible through currents, waves, wind and weather. So it is not a static smooth space. Carson combines it with an old trope in travel, the roads of the sea, to give directionality to where the mackerel go. Underwater roads smooth the way, but also roughen it with dangers. The romance of travel through smooth space is expressed by a curious fisherman, a sort of young Old Shiner:

He sometimes thought about fish as he looked at them on deck or being iced in the hold. What had the eyes of the mackerel seen? Things he'd never see; places he'd never go to. He seldom put it into words, but it seemed incongruous to him that a creature that had made a go of life in the sea, that had run the gauntlet of all the relentless enemies that he knew roved through that dimness his eyes could not penetrate, should at last come to death on the deck of a mackerel seiner, slimy with fish gurry and slippery with scales.

(Carson 1965: 161-2)

This philosophically minded fisherman is 'seeing in imagination what he could not see in fact – the race and the rush and downward whirl of thousands of mackerel. He suddenly wished he could be down there …' (Carson 1965: 163). Scomber escapes this seine net and its harrying by a pack of dogfish. He 'was swimming down through deepening green along sea roads new and strange to him … He was going to a place he himself had never known – the deep quiet waters along the edge of the continental shelf' (Carson 1965: 166-7). The story ends on that note of disappearance into unseeable oceanic smooth space. Carson 'transports her reader into a world where the idea of human "belonging" or "home" is quite foreign. We cannot be full-time residents in the light-depleted depths', says Susan Bratton (2004: 18). But we can be readers who journey part-way there through fish auto/biographies.

SALMON IN THE PACIFIC NORTHWEST

Salmon literature in the Pacific Northwest is a genre in which myths, stories, economics and politics converge. Svetlana Seibel explains that

> as the region's keystone species, salmon is widely recognized as one of its most defining inhabitants and, consequently, it became one of its most potent cultural symbols. Author and journalist Timothy Egan goes so far as to define the region through the movement patterns of the fish: "The Pacific Northwest is simply this: wherever the salmon can get to".
>
> (Seibel 2022: 22)

Every interpretation of salmon lives moves through ideological waters, often passionately. At stake is a vision of precontact relationship in which salmon sustained people and people's respect for the land and its beings ensured the thriving of salmon.

That vision, conveyed in myths, stories and cultural practice, was torn apart by colonial violence, enforced by an 1855 Treaty; the 1887 Dawes Act (which broke up traditional tribal landholding arrangements); imposition of industrial agriculture, and overextraction of fish. The figures are shocking: on the Columbia River, where the Nimiipuu (Nez Perce) people live, ancestral salmon runs of more than ten to sixteen million a year have shrunk to as few as two hundred thousand in some years – this in spite of nearly eighteen billion dollars being spent on restoration programmes (Lichatowich et al. 2018: 5). Salmon advocate Jim Lichatowich argues that fish management has proved to be mismanagement because it turns fish into commodities valued only financially:

> The value of commoditized salmon leaves no room for wonder at the diversity of life in nature, no concern for other sentient beings, no recognition of the ecological attributes that sustain wild salmon across generations, and therefore, no concern for the legacy future generations will inherit. It's just dollars and cents and wild salmon and steelhead be damned.
>
> (Lichatowich et al. 2018: 10)

'We must return the wild salmon story', he argues. For him, place is central to that story because wild salmon like Indigenous peoples have strong attachments to place, and because place is a place-holder for salmon diversity and resilience. Salmon who return to their birth waters help maintain genetic strengths. Salmon from hatcheries, who have a much lower survival rate, have no genetic bond with place; they are 'ecologically placeless' (Lichatowich et al. 2018: 86), breaking the bonds between habitat and life history. Some Indigenous peoples who run their own hatcheries disagree, preferring a principle that welcomes fish whatever their origin, hatchery included, in the hope it will keep some salmon going (Johnson 2004: 69–70).

Place is a fragmented concept in this conflict. On the one hand, the ocean-estuary-river-tributary complex can be taken as an ecosystem, a big place with local places within; on the other hand, agencies governing that ecosystem constitute a maze of boundaries. Returning fish may cross as many as seventeen different management areas, each with different governance, policy and authority over physical barriers to fish movement (Lichatowich et al. 2018: 17). A simple route for salmon – downriver to the sea, upriver to spawn – is impossibly complex in its Anthropogenic version. Its mythic version was beautifully simple:

> the salmon were a race of supernatural beings who dwelt in a great house under the sea. There they went about in human form, feasting and dancing like people. When the time came for the 'run', the Salmon-people dressed in garments of salmon flesh, that is, assumed the form of fish to sacrifice themselves. Once dead, the spirit of each fish returned to the house beneath the sea. If the bones were returned to the water, the being resumed his form with no discomfort and could repeat the trip next season.
>
> (Drucker 1965, quoted by Netboy 1980: 241)

In other versions, Salmon was one of the Myth People who inhabited the land from the beginning of time. The Myth People created all the landforms, animal and bird peoples, fish and plant peoples to prepare the world for the coming of the human peoples (Frey 2000: 10). Salmon were so plentiful 'that for many of the tribes of the region the salmon contributed up to 40% of the entire aboriginal diet', and were given homage in a First Salmon Ceremony lasting five days (Frey 2000: 10). In contrast to Anthropogenic exploitation, where 'Wild salmon are the road kill of the industrial production system' in Lichatowich's phrase (2018: 42), traditional ecological knowledge, sustenance and reverence braid together.

Exploring recent salmon literature of the Pacific Northwest, Svetlana Seibel notes 'an upsurge of Indigenous literature that features salmon prominently in its storylines, or focuses on them as protagonists' (Seibel 2022: 39). Salmon are cultural kin, representing an original compact between people and animals, and ecological balance. 'Following tenets of Indigenous thought, kincentric autobiography affirms personhood and peoplehood of both human and other-than-human subjects' (Seibel 2022: 49). Anthropomorphism in Western writings troubles critics whereas personhood in Indigenous stories does not. There is a logic – if salmon and humans are both a people in their own right, they can swap in and out of a common personhood. With few ancestral stories left to anchor personifications in myth-making, the gulf between species is greater for Western writers to cross.

Horace Axtell, a Nimiipuu elder, commented in September 2008 on the relationship between water and salmon and Nimiipuu culture: 'According to our spiritual way of life, everything is based on nature. Anything that grows or lives is part of our spiritual life. The most important element we have in way of life is water. The next most important element is the fish because the fish comes from water' (Colombi 2012: 77). In the traditional story 'A Meeting between Creator and the Animals', as told by Allen Pinkham, a Nimiipuu tribal elder, the Creator asks all the animals how they can help soon-to-be-created humans:

> Salmon and Steelhead came forward and said, 'We can help the human beings with our flesh.' Salmon said, 'When we come up the river we will die, so the human beings will have to catch us before that happens. I'll come up only on certain times of the year, and that's when they'll have to catch me.' Then Steelhead said, 'I want to come in the wintertime, but I'll give them something special. That will be the glue from my skin. This glue can be used to make bows and spears. I'll be in the water all winter long.' So Creator let Steelhead become qualified. Sockeye Salmon came forward and he said, 'I don't want to be big like Chinook Salmon and Steelhead, and my flesh will be red because I will eat different foods.' Then Trout came forward and he said, I am going to look like Steelhead, but I am not going to go down to the ocean. I'll just stay here in the waters even in the winter, and if these human beings can find me they can have me for food. But in the wintertime I will be down in the gravel and if they can find me that's where I will be. Then Eel came out and said, 'I don't want to look like the Steelhead or Salmon or Trout. I want to be long, and when I rest I want to put my mouth on the rocks. But I'll come up the river every year, and they can use my flesh for food.' So this is how the fish became qualified.
>
> (Landeen and Pinkham, 1999: 7; also quoted by Colombi 2012: 85)

This is a gift economy of volunteering and mutualism, not dollars and cents. It is also an economy of auto/biographical futurism in which the fishes' desires shape their bodies, lives and after-lives.

Seibel argues that 'Salmon literature unfolds its power precisely by emphasizing the inseparability of the people, the land, the waters, and the fish, the deep entanglements that cannot be torn asunder without a high cost and a heavy loss' (2022: 46). Not all the texts are literary: two that combine stories and visual imagery are the Nimiipuu film *Commentary of the Salmon People* (2022) and Hayley Austin's photo-essay *The Body of the Snake; fighting to save Snake River salmon* (2022). Austin points out that other species besides humans suffer from salmon loss:

> The Southern Resident orca population consists of only 75 animals [73 in the 2025 census] and is on the endangered species list along with Snake River salmon. These whales require 400 pounds of food per day. They eat only Chinook salmon. In the past, a Snake River salmon weighed 100 pounds, and the whale only needed to catch 4 per day. Today, salmon weigh an average of 12.5 pounds. The whales have to search farther and longer and suffer as a result.
>
> (Austin 2022)

Kincentricity dissolves the hierarchies of a common food web where humans are always at the top and ignore the needs of other species. Pacific and Atlantic salmon life writings put the case for redress.

EEL DAYDREAMS

In 2023 searchers for eels in the drainage channels of the Somerset Levels could find no traces of them, not even by e-DNA. These ancient wetlands overlap with Thomas Hardy's Wessex. Their northern section curls round Glastonbury; forty miles eastward is Stonehenge, one of the world's most famous prehistoric monuments. Eels inhabited this marshy country before Stonehenge was built, a date notionally 3000–2500 BCE. Like Glastonbury festival goers, they create a community simply by arriving, not necessarily because they are related to previous years' arrivals. The Somerset Eel Recovery Project (SERP) is trying to reverse local extinction; they also collect eel stories and ingeniously promote eel husbandry in schools (https://www.somerseteels.com). In helping eels past barriers to upstream, SERP activists recognize the symbolism and narrative power of home.

That segment of eel migration has resonance in life writing with the poetics of primary place described by Gaston Bachelard. In *The Poetics of Space* he argued that memories of home, particularly a settled first home, shelter our dreams in powerful ways – 'I should say: the house shelters day-dreaming, the house protects the dreamer, the house allows one to dream in peace' – and proposed topoanalysis, 'the systematic psychological study of the sites of our intimate lives' (Bachelard 1994: 6-7), as a productive route for critics. For Bachelard, memory and imagination are connected, 'each one working for their mutual deepening. In the order of values, they both constitute a community of memory and image' (Bachelard 1994: 5). We cannot know if eels have daydreams, but we do know that they, like salmon returning to their birthing pools, have something so powerful they navigate from these places to a faraway ocean, from where they find home by drifting, seeking and settling in a place by choice. Life writing can describe that as a migration daydream, though eels favour nocturnal travel so their daydream is active at night.

Some writers recognize the magic of migratory species whose life cycle depends on a story of place from whence they came and to which they must return – a story of two places as home. In this section I discuss a selection of eel life writings that engage with migration cycles, place and personhood. From the Sargasso Sea eels divide into two groups, one heading to North America, *Anguilla rostrata,* as in Rachel Carson's eel story, and one to Europe, *Anguilla anguilla*, as in Patrik Svensson's *The Gospel of the Eels* (2020), described on its inner jacket as 'a memoir of grief, an exploration of masculinity, and a riveting journey through the life of the world's most mysterious fish'.

Eels are catadromous: they live in fresh water and breed in the sea. Eel and salmon are complementary opposites. Salmon return to the fresh water of their birthplace to breed; eels also return to their birthplace, to breed – a sight nobody has yet seen – and then die, somewhere in the Sargasso Sea. 'All eels from throughout their range, Greenland to Central America, converge on the spawning waters at about the same time. This is remarkable considering the vastly different distances they must travel. Northern fish leave much sooner to arrive "on time." Despite the enormous geographic range of the species, all American eels comprise a single breeding population' (Nedeau 2005: n.p.). Like salmon, eels change body shape profoundly along the way. Eel eggs hatch into larvae known as leptocephali, meaning slim head, their tiny transparent bodies always compared to willow leaves in shape. They float on currents toward

Europe, or to America – somehow they know which flow to join. Arriving as glass eels, also termed elvers, they spread out among rivers and tributaries. They grow into yellow eels – males are smaller and venture less far upriver than females – then become silver eels who, when the time is right, make their way down the rivers to the sea, out to the Atlantic and on to the Sargasso Sea where they mate and die. Their loop between ocean and river used to be thought inexorable, though recent studies have found that not all eels proceed in the same way. 'We need to be aware that the behaviour of eels can be very diverse in the early stages of spawning migration': some pause, some stop for a while, some go back temporarily to fresh water – movements of a two-step migration which it is thought are fine tunings to the best conditions for their long 6500-kilometre journey (Tambets et al. 2021: 6). Going the other way, an eel chooses a suitable river in which to live – not, as with salmon, determined by where it was born. Choices are now blocked by man-made obstacles and pollutants.

Comparing the cyclical lives of eels and salmon, Patrik Svensson finds in the eel a modesty which makes it a hero. 'The salmon comes off as a self-absorbed, vain fish' he says, because it sparkles and shimmers and makes wild jumps. 'The eel seems more content. It doesn't make a big deal of its existence' (2020: 129). For Svensson, 'Every eel seeks its place in the world without a guide, without inheritance or heritage and existentially alone' (130). It is a philosophical entity, he proposes: 'The eels' mystique becomes an echo of the questions all people carry within them: Who am I? Where did I come from? Where am I going?' (Svensson 2020: 73). One might suggest that the eel has answers to those questions in a way that humans do not; people's uncertainty of their place in the world is why they project mystery onto eels. In a book about eel mysteries around the world, James Prozek concludes, 'With the eel … intuition and spirituality have braided with the science' (Prozek 2010: 277). Steve Ely who has written an epic poem about the European eel explains the attraction for poets: 'because so much of the lifecycle and ecological context of the European eel is unknown or merely hypothesised – that is, as much defined by absence as by presence – it leaves lots of space in which the imagination can roam … *They can't tell me what I want to know*' (Ely: 2021b, italics in original).

The mysteries of eels have intrigued many. Aged nineteen, in 1876 Sigmund Freud had a job sexing eels in Trieste, in the employ of an eel-focused professor of zoology (Svensson 2020: 37). He was looking for male eels, who were so rare as never to show up in his samples. The potency of genitals and the power of the invisible possibly sculpted psychoanalysis accordingly. An eel is a mysterious entity, slippery, moving at night, vanishing into land or water or in-between. 'Origin to an eel is not about family or biological belonging, it's simply a location', says Svensson (130). Hence he weaves place-based eel reflections into his relationship with his father and mourning for his death. Childhood homes are important, as Bachelard understood; growing up in the same place, and a good place, gives stability. Svensson's autobiographical fusion of boyhood, father and river is secured by the eel who tethers all three to a bond that has both love and distance. For Svensson, the eel is Romantic: 'seeking your place in the world on your own: Surely that is, at the end of the day, the most universal of all human experience?' (2020: 130). That interpretation angles away from the migration story to the bildungsroman; it makes the young eel romantic rather than the mature one.

An eel is a difficult hero, thought Carson. She explained in a letter to her publisher: 'I know many people shudder at the sight of an eel.' But she related to it as a purposeful wanderer:

> To me (and I believe to anyone who knows its story) to see an eel is something like meeting a person who has travelled to the most remote and wonderful places of the earth; in a flash I see a vivid picture of the strange places that eel has been – places which I, being merely human, can never visit.
>
> (Svensson 2020: 137–8)

Carson's tale starts at Bittern Pond, where Anguilla arrived as an elver ten years earlier. 'She knew every crayfish burrow that ran in honeycombing furrows through the mudbank under the hill. She knew her way among the swaying, rubbery stems of spatterdock, where frogs sat on the thick leaves' (Carson 1965: 73). A 'strange restiveness' impels her to leave, so she follows the stream by night. 'Often she was aware of dark forms moving in the water near her. They were other eels' (Carson 1965: 177). From here on the narrative becomes collective, with only one more mention of Anguilla as an individual. That's odd, given the opportunity to feature a female protagonist and her 200-mile journey to the sea. Steve Ely's long poem rejoices in a 'little eel' who is female and epic (Ely 2021a); why does Carson sink singularity into collectivity? This is not an individual fishography. Even at the beginning Anguilla is species-defined: 'like all eels she was a lover of darkness', 'like all eels she was a lover of warmth' (Carson 1965: 173). Personhood slips into a plurality of eels, whose path nobody knows: 'probably … Perhaps … somehow' they passed 'to the deepest abyss of the Atlantic. There the young were to be born of the darkness of the deep sea and the old eels were to die and become sea again.' Now the eels become focalizers. 'Billions of young eels – billions of pairs of black, pin-prick eyes peering into the strange sea world that overlay the abyss' (Carson 1965: 207). It is through their eyes we see the twilight zone, with copepods, jellyfish, winged snails, ghostly shrimp, hatchetfish, nereid worms, sea spiders and prawns singled out as species. Mysterious eel personality gives way to eel perception of reassuringly identifiable beings. Eel migration begins again after spawning, the American leptocephali passing outward-bond adults heading to spawn and die. 'They must have passed without recognition – these two generations of eels – one on the threshold of a new life; the other about to lose itself in the darkness of the sea' (Carson 1965: 215). Indeed there are several generations of eels drifting in stages on their way, which dissolves the temporal certainty of migration that is notionally annual. At the end of the last section, also the end of the book, time expands:

> As the waiting of the eels off the mouth of the bay was only an interlude in a long life filled with constant change, so the relation of sea and coast and mountain ranges was that of a moment in geological time. For once more the mountains would be worn away by the endless erosion of water and carried in silt to the sea, and once more all the coast would be water again, and the places of its cities and towns would belong to the sea.
>
> (Carson 1965: 218)

The eels can outlast drowned civilizations: 'once *more*' (my italics) connects eel cycle to a bigger life cycle that is also cyclical time, as fluid as water. 'To disappear into deep water or to disappear toward a far horizon, to become a part of depth or infinity, such is the destiny of man that finds its image in the destiny of water', says Bachelard in *Water and Dreams* (Bachelard 1999: 12). The eel lives that image literally. Eel life writing imagines its subject's vanishing.

'An eel is never allowed to simply be an eel. It's never allowed just to be. Thus, it has become a symbol of our complex relationship with all the other forms of life on this planet', reflects Svensson (2020: 95). Listed as endangered on the IUCN Red List in 2013, numbers of silver eels leaving Europe have halved, and glass eels arriving from the Sargasso Sea are only 5 per cent of their 1970s numbers (Svensson 2020: 205). Anthropogenic heating of ocean waters changes currents and salinity, meaning drifting eels cannot count any more on ancestral migration routes. Both Svensson and Ely list other endangering factors – parasites and viruses from escaped captive eels; hydroelectric works, which kill more than two thirds of eels trying to pass through; dams, weirs, traps; extractive and illegal fishing; smuggling – 350 million glass eels were trafficked in 2018 in the UK (Weston 2021); polluted, contaminated, chemical-laden waters … no wonder eels struggle in the Somerset Levels. Eels do live in local imagination: a folk singer from Somerset, Kitty Macfarlane, wrote a song, 'Glass Eel', 'about the eels that have migrated across the world to European waterways for as long as we know, and it's about people moving too, and freedom of movement for both' (Macfarlane 2019). For as long as we know … eel life writing braids migration with ancestral time as one vanishing point becomes another.

8

Other Bodies, Other Minds

In this chapter, I take up life writings on marine beings other than fish (except for a guest appearance by whale sharks), featuring seals (pinnipeds), sea turtles (marine reptiles), some whales (marine mammals) and octopuses (cephalopods). I follow three themes: infancy and motherhood; hapticality, a way of thinking about touch; datafication, or practices of naming, numbering and biologging, which represent marine animals in science and its digital offshoots. These themes are a narrative form of Donna Haraway's tentacular thinking: they push, wreathe, loop into movements of argument.

YOUNG THINGS

Animal autobiographies incline to one of two poles, says David Herman.

> At one end of the scale are methods for presenting animal experiences in relatively summative, globalizing terms – as refracted through human-centered practices and values. At the other end are accounts designed to anchor interpreters in a conception or model of what it is or might be like for nonhuman agents to interact with their environment on a moment-by-moment basis; these accounts project nonhuman experiences in a more detailed, granular way.
>
> (Herman 2016: 82)

Herman proposes a wobbly axis of sympathy which nonetheless builds empathy:

> animal autobiography can be used to create oscillating human–animal alignments via (different sorts of) acts of speaking-for. Some life stories told by nonhumans can be read as co-authored acts of narrating in behalf of equally hybrid (or humanimal) principals; these experiments with narration beyond the human afford solidarity-building projections of other creatures' ways of being-in-the-world.
>
> (Herman 2016: abstract)

Animalographies that start with infancy have a particular narrative footing. For a very young creature, experience comes as a sequence of new things. What one might call 'the feel of how to feel it' is filtered through an animal's sensorium, species-specific, so a reader learns how such an animal may learn. Secondly, primal drives and simple emotions build solidarity by expressing needs and desires that a human can share. Hunger, pleasure and fear dissolve species' differences. Yet out of the protective shelter of maternal care, a young animal is vulnerable to dangers, including dangers from humans. Reader solidarity with young vulnerability then acquires dissonance when humans intrude on an animal's security.

Victor B. Scheffer (1906–2011) was an American zoologist who came to specialize in marine mammals. He wrote a textbook on pinnipeds and became an expert on fur seals. Then a publisher asked him to write 'a lively book about whales' (Scheffer 1980: 175). Hence *The Year of the Whale* (1969), which tells of the first year of life for the Little Calf, his mother and their group. Lyrical whale-narrative is interspersed with sections, in smaller font, which expand, sometimes autobiographically, on scientific questions of anatomy, morphology and human activities, principally hunting. Scheffer published before the International Whaling Commission's moratorium on almost all whale hunting in 1986 – Japan, Norway and Iceland still continue to hunt whales. 'It is difficult to think about whales without thinking about men ... As I write about one particular whale, I try to show, too, how men feel about whales and what they do to whales, and what whales do to men' (Scheffer 1969: 7). Hunters and scientists are differently invested in whale knowledge, but at times they overlap. Keen to acquire foetuses for dissection, Scheffer participates in whale slaughter in ways that read uneasily according to how much moral elasticity you give to the production of new knowledge.

> When any whale is brought to a commercial whaling deck there is little time for biology; business is business; profit is profit; the carcass must be turned into meal and oil and frozen meat without delay. If the whale is a pregnant female, the government biologist, present with his measuring tape and specimen jars, is itching to have his hands on the fetus for just an hour. If the whaling foreman says okay, he can; if not, the unborn baby will go into the cooking pot along with the mother, or over the rail into the sea with the entrails.
>
> (Scheffer 1969: 13)

Embryos give evidence about cetacean evolution. Scheffer though wants science to be humane. At the surface, the Little Calf sees a research vessel collide with a small whale, mortally injuring her.

> She sends out a wild, ragged call of distress and two of her companions move in. They defecate in sympathy. They put their shoulders under her body on either side and try to support her at the surface. Other whales come from all sides, showing the instinctive care-giving behaviour of cetaceans that biologists once scoffed at but now accept as real.
>
> (Scheffer 1969: 34)

Care-giving begins in the mother's tender concern for her newborn. An emotional, even sacred pairing for some people, mother-baby closeness, expressed as physical closeness, is imaged in the text's 'decorations'.

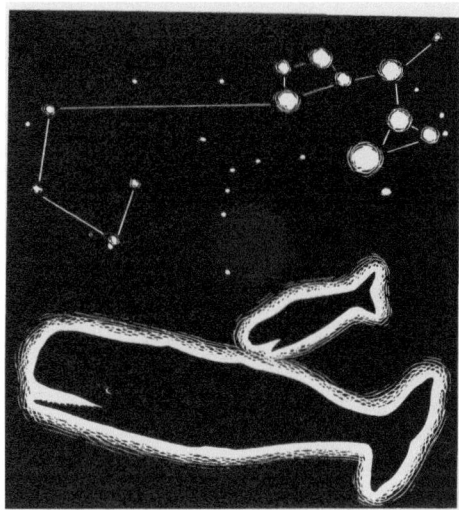

Figure 18 'November', from Victor B. Scheffer, *The Year of the Whale* (1969): mother, the Little Whale and the constellation of Scorpio above. Illustration by Leonard Everett Fisher.

Each chapter has a headpiece showing the Little Calf and companions under the constellation for that month. Whales and stars co-exist in cosmic time. Night-sky and ocean deeps unite as a black background to intimacies in motion, changing like the stars. 'The great creation and the small creation move in silence as a double whale' (Scheffer 1969: 91).

Mother-love is naturally wordless; it is based on loving touch and presence, qualities to which human infants also respond positively. The Little Calf is swept away from his mother by a gale:

> His mother senses the trouble and makes a lee for him with her great, comforting back. He spouts air and water for several minutes, then breathes more freely, falls in with the smashing rhythm of the seas, and feels secure. All that day and night his mother stays with him.
>
> (Scheffer 1969: 16)

Scheffer calls the story 'fiction based on fact' (1969: vii); factually, many mammals practise mother love. One reason reviewers were enthusiastic may be that the Little Calf acts for powerful psychoanalytical drives in readers – drives all with good outcomes, as being well cared for turns into independence.

One challenge for Scheffer was narrative variety. A whale's year consisted of adventure and routine, stress and rest, food and hunger, potentially repetitive. Scheffer tackles reader impatience: 'The year of the whale resembles the year of man a thousand centuries ago, when life was plain and brutish and progress was measured in simple terms of staying alive' (1969: 180). Yet entering ancient time is part of the attraction of whale narratives. So too is slow gigantism.

> Softly the Little Calf sinks. He has no limits. He is in balance with time and space. Infinite time and planetary space are nothing. He stares sleepily into the soft blue

growing darker blue and purple black. The pressure gains. He stops. He moves a
lazy tail and gently rises to the top. He breathes a dozen drafts.

(Scheffer 1969: 170)

Scheffer was interested in art and thought both zoology and art deepened wonder. The
ending fuses animalography and the Little Calf's oceans in 'a swirling punctuation, a
blend of liquid and life' (1969: 195).

After worldwide success with *The Year of the Whale*, Scheffer wrote *The Year of
the Seal* (1970), in which he himself features as a character in the Alaska fur seal's life
narrative, anonymized as a biologist. Episodes match with those in his memoir, though
in the autobiografiction, Max Saunders' term for life writings whose authors are also
characters, Scheffer is more rueful (Saunders 2010; Scheffer 1980). *The Year of the Seal*
puts emphasis on seal physiology. Especially striking is Golden Seal's V-shaped uterus
in which an embryo arrests its development for several months while she recovers
her strength from the last birth. The seal does not have thoughts but consciousness
articulated through senses, especially smell and taste; her actions are conscious,
intuitive but directed. In between seal scenes are episodes of activities by the seal-
killing gangs and scientists on the Pribilof Islands, raising ethical questions about
human knowledge of animals, human control of animals, human violence to animals
and other humans. What is acceptable in the name of conservation, Scheffer asks? How
best to resolve competing national claims over seas and seals?

> In the 1930s we supposed that we could "manage" nature and "improve" or
> "reclaim" the earth's ancient, time-tested organic systems. Now we are less sure.
> We spoke of living animals as "resources." In the interest of science, and with a
> clear conscience, we hot-iron branded them, trapped them in painful devices, and
> shot, clubbed, or harpooned them.
>
> (Scheffer 1970: xiii)

By 1972 when the Marine Mammal Protection Act was passed in the US, the goal of
maximum sustainable yield was replaced by another, optimum sustainable population.
But unresolved questions continued: how could animal value to humans relate to value
of animal life in itself? Fur seal treaties between the US, Russia, Japan and Canada
negotiated trade-offs so that those nations whose fisheries might be depleted by seal
appetites were compensated for not killing them at sea. At St Paul in the Pribilofs,
50,000 salted skins were put in barrels: fifteen in every hundred went to Canada and
Japan, seventy to the US. Besides the value of seal skins as a luxury good, principally
for women's coats, seal parts had particular markets. Their whiskers were found to be
ideal for cleaning opium pipes. Their penises went to Chinese medicine markets. Their
carcasses could be chopped up for animal feed.

> Zoologists of the 1940s were prone to ask: How can we use this resource? How
> can we harvest or crop it? Nowadays, the question is more apt to be: How can we
> profit from it as it is, within its ecosystem? The next question will be: Why should
> we expect to profit financially from it?
>
> (Sheffer 1980: 59)

Scheffer's tale interweaves economic preoccupations, ethically complicated science and the life narrative of seals – besides Golden Seal, the female protagonist, he features her newborn pup for his first few months, and some individualized bulls.

> A year in the life of a seal is an ordinary year; repetitive, ritualistic, undramatic. In summer the female gives birth on land, copulates, nurses her pup; in the fall she goes to sea for many months, returning to land in the summer, again to give birth and copulate. How does a writer work this stuff into a story containing the central message that humans are richer for sharing a world with seals?
>
> (Scheffer 1970: ix)

As for whales, Scheffer works this stuff around a calendar. The story unfolds over months that have different activities, locations, physiological changes and social interactions. For the pup, he creates sweetness without sentimentality. After the pup feeds, 'His belly again bulges with milk; he is a neat, round package of content' (Scheffer 1970: 49). His coat moults from black to silver; he puts on weight; he explores, plays and teaches himself how to swim. Compare that to a scientific life history: 'The life history of an individual is the pattern of allocation of resources to maintenance, growth, and reproduction throughout its lifetime. Life history analysis attempts to explain the scheduling of the allocation process throughout an organism's life which maximizes fitness' (McKnight and Boyd 2018: abstract). Contented sucking is evocative in a way that allocation of resources is not. Scheffer treats 'resources' imaginatively – a seal's mammary gland, he says, is shaped like an apron, running along her underside, and he colours feeding with poignant emotions:

> When a pup's mother has been long at sea and the pup is very hungry, it may seek a pacifier – another pup in the same stage of distress – and the two will then engage in a mutual sucking bout. Curled like Yin and Yang, each will suck the dry fur of the side, or armpit, of the other.
>
> (1970: 40)

Scheffer agreed with reviewers that his seal tale was less successful than *The Year of the Whale* because

> It seems that I had known *too much* about seals! Although the seal book was more factual and complete, it was less image-provoking. As I had written in the whale book: "Moving through a dim, dark, cool, watery world of its own, the whale is timeless and ancient; part of our common heritage and yet remote, awful, prowling the ocean floor a half-mile down under the guidance of powers and senses we are only beginning to grasp." While the seal sits on a rock in its own filth, scratching its molting fur.
>
> (Scheffer 1980: 176)

But *The Year of the Seal* succeeded in presenting the world of pinnipeds as one badly fractured by colonial humans. It also establishes deep foundations for pinniped poetics.

Unsanitary filth and itch are opposites of mystic powers not because marine mammals make such distinctions but because humans do.

Older readers may remember television scenes from Canada of white harp seal pups being clubbed to death. Despite protests and partial bans of seal-pelt products (by the EU in 1983 and Russia in 2011) the practice continues, with animal welfare organizations estimating that in the 2001 'harvest' about 40 per cent of the pups were still alive when skinned (International Fund for Animal Welfare 2001: 8, 10). Seal clubbing invites the term 'horrorism', Adriana Cavarero's term (2008) for forms of violence that offend the human condition at its ontological level, like violence inflicted on the unarmed and defenceless. Clubbing seal pups is an instance.

Literary hinterlands do exist for some seal species.

> The seals living closer to our societies have become wrapped in our myths and legends: there are tales of seals who have sought out human society, following the sound of children's voices, or the music of the pipe and flute; and there are darker stories of selkies and other seal-like creatures that take on human shape for purposes of both good and ill.
>
> (Dickenson 2015: blurb)

Two British texts show seal life writing addressing human threat. Susan Richardson's *Where The Seals Sing* (2022) is a land-based account of seal-watching, interspersed with managing her father's ill health. A recurring preoccupation is about disturbance to seal places, from screaming RAF jets over Lincolnshire beaches to the Farne Islands' throng of tourists. The principle of non-disturbance, which Richardson firmly upholds, wriggling to cliff edges to watch with binoculars, conflicts with engagement. Britain's coasts are relatively developed: hence people see seals 'both as cohabitants of the coasts, and uncanny spirits of a world they cannot begin to imagine' (Dickenson 2015: 55-6). Many human cohabitants of coasts, however, see seals as competitors, not uncanny spirits. Imaginatively inhabiting seal subjectivity, like Scheffer, Niall McKillop's *Rondo One-Eye* (2000) is set around Loch Shiel in the Scottish Highlands; it features harbour or common seals (*Phoca vitulina*) and cohabitants.

Figure 19 'A pup harp seal and mother keep close on the ice floes on 3 March 2008, off the coast of the Magdalen Islands, Quebec, a few weeks before the annual seal hunt.' David Boily/AFP via Getty Images. Seal whiskers, or vibrissae, are highly sensitive.

Seal, eagle and man, and all other living things had formed, forged on the anvil of time by fire and flood, to change, to adapt, to hide or to hunt. And in that ancient time all shared in matters of the earth and lived by the Ways and Laws of The Ages under a common rule of survival.

(McKillop 2000: 2)

The Ways and Laws of The Ages folds bodily instinct into cultural myth. It connects species so that behaviours which further their survival are shared and differentiated. The story features first Rainha, then her (fifth) pup Rondo who is horribly wounded and loses an eye but survives. Localism is important: Rondo comes to know what places are good for rest, for feeding, for safety. Dangers are everywhere, principally from Eye-Peckers, gulls and crows, and from humans. Threat, injury and exhaustion recur: there are dangerous weather events; predators on the beach and in the air; humans who want to shoot seals as competitors for salmon. There are also careless and ignorant people, represented by a couple who long to get close to seals and in doing so, frighten them. 'Each time a seal was spotted the man shouted, and his wife, pink and naked, leaned perilously over the side with a camera as he drove the boat, its engine straining and pouring blue smoke, straight for the seal' (McKillop 2000: 11). Faculties of vision acquire powerful symbolism. Rainha helps her pup negotiate swimming – and seeing – underwater by becoming a shadow whose movement can be sensed and followed. Rondo the pup is at first mystified:

She had seen nothing above her and now, her young misty eyes scoured the water below. Something moved, not directly beneath her but down to her left; it was hardly discernible, – a flicker, but she went after it almost without thinking, hardly noticing that she was totally immersed for the very first time, moving easily into a strange, new world.

(McKillop 2000: 22)

Getting to the right place for safe, recuperative sleep is a regular mission. Rondo is half-blinded because the couple in the boat block a route to safety. Such human interference is hapless and, in other incidents, malicious – nylon fishing net cuts deep into Rondo's head (McKillop 2000: 111–16). A sinister new threat emerges. Phocine distemper virus, now known as *Phocine morbillivirus*, swept through harbour seals in 1988, killing more than eighteen thousand; in 2002, another outbreak along North Sea coasts killed twenty thousand, almost half the seal population. Its cause is not known, though Anthropogenic stresses are suspected. The stink of death frightens Rondo, 'bringing a growing awareness that all was not as it should be; that once again her life, somehow, was under threat' (2000: 121). In McKillop's animalography, 'where the Kind of Rondo and Rainha had lived in peace before men stood straight, seals died in their thousands, swept by the plague like blossom before a spring gale. Predictably, men denied that the problem had been caused by them' (2000: 132). A sympathetic deerstalker, akin to Old Moon and Old Shiner in salmon tales, is puzzled and concerned. 'In his heart he felt that he had seen the last of the natural world as nature had meant it to be' (2000: 134). His rescue helps Rondo return to the sea. There she recovers, thrives and mates. Returning to her own birthing waters where salmon cages have been newly installed, she is shot by a guard with a rifle. She dies.

Development of loch waters for holiday rentals and salmon aquaculture change the environment for marine residents. McKillop's narrative, like some salmon tales, is sad, fearful and clear about how money-making drives those changes which also distress many local people. Anthropogenic damage is everywhere – an oil tanker runs aground, poisoning the seals' seas; financiers build a jetty for holiday boats, dynamiting the seals' resting rock. His animalography builds a picture of disturbance that is deeper than Richardson's – literally, because he describes a seal's underwater life. Disturbance is not only sightseer harassment, but destruction of organic old ways connecting habits and habitats. The Ways and Laws of The Ages is species-specific, in that his seals know when to do what, and how to do it; it is also open to humans, who benefit from it too. It is unsentimental. A pair of eagles take the live young of other species to feed their own large chick. The Ways and Laws of The Ages naturalizes such predation, making capital-driven human rapacity more starkly unnatural.

For Richardson, close encounters too often show human disrespect, enabled by mobile phones and their insatiable flow to social media. A seal warden on one Norfolk beach tells her of 'people venturing ever closer to the seals: most shockingly, a man recently had to be stopped from sitting his toddler on the back of a pup so he could take a photo' (Richardson 2022: 302). Victoria Dickenson proposes that 'Books about seals may begin as wild animal studies, but will end somewhere in the queer, uncomfortable place where distinctions between human observer and animal subject waver and cloud, and the lens becomes a mirror, the enquiring gaze returned' (2015: 10). She thinks seal eyes are pivotal to boundary dissolution: 'the eyes, the windows of the soul, are large, exceedingly lustrous and expressive'. Seal eye memes confirm the attraction. But many proponents of connection with other species focus on eyes. Looking into the eyes of a pyjama catshark, Ross Frylinck says 'It felt like I was looking from space into a storm system blazing on the surface of an alien planet. How could such a simple animal have eyes like this?' (2021: 21). Writers about octopus repeatedly comment on reciprocal eye contact and an equal gaze. 'When you look eye to eye at an octopus, something clicks. You feel it staring at you, taking your measure, *thinking* about you. There is a disturbing, almost unspeakable recognition' (Harrigan 1992: 73). An octopus can not only return an enquiring gaze, but impose its own metaphysics. Haptics are central: some marine beings take your measure.

HAPTICS

The usual rule in scuba diving is Look – Don't Touch. Some authorities won't let you dive wearing gloves; touch is associated with damage to sea life and imperfect buoyancy control. Yet the surrounding feel of water gives a diver continuous haptic sensations, says Elizabeth Straughan, and they 'mobilise a complex of emotions' (2012: 20). Touch is a powerful human instinct. The information we get from looking doesn't always satisfy curiosity: by touching something, we sense its reality. Meeting a dead whale, Kathleen Jamie wanted to touch it – and she is not the only one with this reaction:

It was the heaviest creature I had ever seen, dead and out of the water's buoyancy, a massive failure. I thought about touching it, with just one finger, furtively, the way a gull pecks, and I wish now I had, because I've never touched a whale and probably won't get the chance again. I should have touched the skin because it looked almost like black leatherette … some gesture seemed required and I didn't know what …

(Jamie 2005: 57–8)

Sensual information – how does whale leatheriness feel? – comes second here to symbolism, touch as connection to another entity. The haptic has a potential circuity of completion, like Michelangelo's Adam and God stretching out their fingertips across the Sistine Chapel. It gestures to required gestures. Underwater, the sensorium of touch is both more and less than in the world above: water alters sensation, but adds to its haptic significance.

In this section I focus on life writing about other species that explores touch as a medium. Impressions through touch can be as powerful as visual experiences: we have tactile propensities, especially in infancy, which can inform encounters, especially with creatures with highly tactile sensitivities themselves. Life writing about octopus is particularly alert to touch and its meanings, because octopuses are. Terms are slippery here: besides touch, we have kinaesthesia, your body's ability to sense movement, action and location. That sense of position, often termed proprioception, comes from sense organs, proprioreceptors in our muscles and joints. It gives us a sense of balance, which divers have to relearn underwater. 'Sense (sensation) literally means recognising a single specific type of stimulus as, for example, touch or warmth. Perception on the other hand is a cerebral process designed to clarify the nature of the source of a stimulus or stimuli' (Stillman 2002: 667). There is some fuzziness about how these words are used, to which I will add the concept of haptic, to evoke perception of touch. Claire Colebrook observes that 'there cannot be an immediate grasp of touch itself; to *think* about touch is already to be in relation, to be distanced, to no longer be present' (2009: 25). Being-in-relation is much in evidence in underwater life writings where humans make tactile contact with other species and touch expresses co-presence. The haptic is a useful idea here: it connects touch, thinking about touch and *writing* about touch. A reader can't literally grasp what a diver touches, but the haptic's sensual figuration means you can grasp what touch conveys underwater.

Octopus literature over the last seventy years has seen renaissance and reinvention. Monstrous to nineteenth-century writers, octopuses slowly shook off revulsion. For instance, writing in 1952, Arthur Grimble, an otherwise genial person, thought *Octopus vulgaris* was disgusting. 'You feel that if only the creature would stick to its grubbing on the bottom, the shocking ugliness of its shape might even win your sympathy, as for some poor Caliban in the enchanted garden of the lagoon' (1952: 114). Grimble's skulking Caliban is akin to a Kraken monster: 'once its scores of suckers, rimmed with hooks for grip on slippery skins, are clamped about their prey, nothing but the brute's death will break their awful hold' (1952: 115). Unexpectedly, Grimble reported that children of the Gilbert and Ellice Islands could kill this fearsome beast simply by turning it inside out. Twenty years later, Cousteau and Diolé admired the cleverness of otherwise timid octopuses in the Mediterranean. 'In the course of many encounters they have given ample demonstration of either humor or of a surprising understanding. With an octopus, one must always be ready for anything' (1973: 24). They also appreciated octopus mysteriousness, for instance in the giant octopus, *Enteroctopus dofleini*, which they filmed off Seattle. 'When a diver sees a giant octopus in the dim water, its great eyes fixed on him, he feels a strange sensation of respect, as though he were in the presence of a very wise and very old animal, whose tranquillity it would be best not to disturb' (Cousteau and Diolé 1973: 45). These octopuses had, they thought, a 'divinatory sense' and 'an appearance of *knowing*' (Cousteau and Diolé 1973: 48, 54). Handling octopuses for Cousteau's film crew was Joanne Duffy, diving instructor, karate expert and octopus aficionado, a combination clearly unnerving for Cousteau: he described her as 'The most surprising thing that we found in the waters of Seattle' (1973: 55). Duffy explained her affinity with octopuses. 'What I like about them is that they seem to be very intelligent and sensitive, and yet very different from us. It is not sympathy that I feel for them, but an emotion' (Cousteau and Diolé 1973: 74-5).

Intelligence, sensitivity, difference and emotion are fundamental to octopus life writing of the next generation. Sy Montgomery's bestseller *The Soul of an Octopus: A Surprising Exploration into the Wonder of Consciousness* (2015) and Craig Foster's documentary *My Octopus Teacher* (2020), a big hit on Netflix, elevate the octopus to the status of sage. Peter Godfrey-Smith's book, *Other Minds: The Octopus and the Evolution of Intelligent Life* (2017) sandwiched between them, also repositions octopuses as philosophically fascinating beings. 'This is probably the closest we will come to meeting an intelligent alien. … When we imagine the lives and experiences of simpler animals, we often wind up visualizing scaled-down versions of ourselves. Cephalopods bring us into contact with something very different' (Godfrey-Smith 2017: 9-10). Around three hundred species of octopus are currently known, with recent new additions. The mimic octopus, *Thaumoctopus mimicus*, which can conjure itself into the shapes and movements of other animals, was discovered in 1998 off Sulawesi; the deep-sea ghost octopus, nicknamed Casper after a friendly cartoon ghost, was first spotted at 4290 metres off Hawai'i in 2016. A new species of *Muusoctopus*, nicknamed the pearl octopus, was identified at 2800 metres off Costa Rica in 2023 (Schmidt Ocean Institute 2023). Scientists found females congregating in huge nursery groups near a hydrothermal vent, where warmer water could incubate their eggs faster. These discoveries reinforce notions of octopuses as surprising.

Sy Montgomery's book acknowledges species difference from the start. 'It's hard to find an animal more unlike a human than an octopus. Their bodies aren't organized like ours. We go: head, body, limbs. They go: body, head, limbs. … Octopuses represent the great mystery of the Other' (Montgomery 2015: 1-2). She cultivates relationships with a series of octopuses and people at Boston's New England Aquarium; towards the end of the book she learns to dive and meets some octopuses in the Pacific. Their situation 'in the wild' is a small counterweight to the 'in captivity' state (a phrase not used by Montgomery) of the aquarium octopuses, whose situation is endorsed because they are well cared for and loved by an assortment of people, including Montgomery. These humans learn that octopuses are sentient beings with personalities, intelligence, needs, extraordinary abilities – and a soul. As with its close relative the cuttlefish, *Sepia officinalis*, 'Assessing the mind of a creature this alien demands that we be extraordinary [*sic*] flexible in our own thinking' (Montgomery 2015: 13, 50).

Athena is the first octopus Montgomery gets to know. 'Athena's is an exceptionally intimate embrace. She is at once touching and tasting my skin, and possibly the muscle, bone, and blood beneath. Though we have only just met, Athena already knows me in a way no being has known me before' (2015: 5). Mutual caressing pleases Athena and entrances the humans, who thereby enter Octopus Time, 'liquid, slippery, and ancient, flowing at a different pace than any clock' (2015: 23). After Athena dies, Montgomery starts again with Octavia whose differences prove octopuses are individuals. Octavia is playful, squirting humans for fun with jets of water. So does a young octopus, Kali, who is keen to socialize and clings to human arms 'as if she is eagerly reading us by using an octopus Braille system' (2015: 68). Mutual haptic pleasure leads to reveries. 'To share such a moment of deep tranquility with another being, especially one as different from us as the octopus, is a humbling privilege. It's a shared sweetness, a gentle miracle, an uplink to universal consciousness' (2015: 90). Reverie is comically doused as Kali hoses them, using her funnel like a squirt gun, swinging it around. 'It's as surprising as if you saw a person stick his tongue out his mouth, and next out his ear – and then out his other ear' (Montgomery 2015: 91).

Octopus character is clearly established. It is also developed beyond the science model of bold/shy personality into nuances of curious, gentle and playful. Besides having a dominant eye, like being left or right-handed, an octopus's tentacles favour different activities – 'each arm may have its own personality, almost like a separate creature' (Montgomery 2015: 160). Over several weeks, Octavia lays pearly strings of eggs which, like female octopuses in the wild, she tends assiduously. Octopuses can store sperm for months and thereby choose a time of reproduction. But mating means approaching mortality for the female: she stops eating and fades, fanning oxygenated water over her progeny until they hatch. Then she dies. Much as octopus anatomy muddles up human ideas of bodies – their heads do grow beneath their shoulders – octopus maternity confusingly twists natality and fatality. Life-giving will end in death. 'Caring for her eggs is the job that will last a female octopus to the end of her life. ... The proper end of any female octopus's life *should* be laying eggs': thus her death will be 'an act of love' (Montgomery 2015: 95-6, 119). Underwater in her tank, 'Octavia will give us a close-up and detailed view of her most intimate, ultimate task, far more than would be possible to see in the wild' (Montgomery 2015: 99).

Anthropomorphic projections about motherhood are big in underwater literature. On cephalopods, Cousteau and Diolé proclaim that 'The females among cuttlefish, squids, and decapods are, to all appearances, bad mothers in most cases. They do not watch over their eggs, nor defend them against predators, or show any interest in the fate of their young' (Cousteau and Diolé 1973: 182). In contrast, an octopus is exemplary. 'She definitely wins the Mother of the Year award!', says one of Octavia's human friends (Montgomery 2015: 165). An octopus mother is a good mother, but also a doomed one. Octavia's slow decay, compounded by dementia-like senescence, makes her touchingly like an old lady, one who is fragile, shrunken, pale, fading. Old ladies in human thought are usually well outside models of motherhood. We don't have a word for the long period of octopus maternity which is both post-partum and pre-

Figure 20 Pacific Giant Octopus (*Enteroctopus dofleini*) female guarding her eggs, Quadra Island, British Columbia, Canada. Photo and caption by Fred Bavendam/Minden Pictures. Alamy.

birth and inexorably heads towards death. There is some consolation in its serenity: 'Octavia is the picture of peace, an octopus Madonna' (Montgomery 2015: 95).

Octavia's end-of-life introduces treasured haptic experience for Montgomery. 'Her wet grip on my skin felt gentle and familiar, the pull of her suckers tender as a kiss. ... For perhaps five minutes, Octavia stayed at the surface, holding us, tasting us, remembering us' (2015: 237). The gentleness involved – Octavia could bite, and fiercely – prompts Montgomery to offer a tender obituary summarizing a rich, full life:

> She had known the sea's wild embrace; she had mastered the art of camouflage; she had learned the taste of our skin and the shapes of our faces; she had instinctively remembered how her ancestors wove eggs into chains. She had served as an ambassador for her kind to tens of thousands of aquarium visitors, even transforming disgust into admiration. What an odyssey she had lived.
>
> (Montgomery 2015: 238)

Animalographies often end with the death of the animal subject as a natural narrative endpoint. Timothy C. Baker thinks through some. He proposes that 'it is only through humanisation, in terms of naming and attention to individual biography, that the animal can be grieved' (Baker 2019: 111). Animal death, however, rebounds on humans: it 'shows the limits not only of human supremacy but also of the ideas humans have used to consider their place in the world. It introduces a radical vulnerability that no text, no philosophy, and no work of art can encompass or explain' (Baker

2019: 131). Vulnerable species are usually vulnerable because of human activities. In animalographies, any species can be vulnerable this way. For female octopuses, nobody attacks, but death comes naturally after reproduction. In *My Octopus Teacher*, Craig Foster realizes when he sees 'his' octopus mate that her death will follow. There seems to be no word for this cross-species' melancholy in eco-lexicons (Albrecht 2019; Braidotti 2023). 'When is life grievable?' asks Judith Butler (2015), who argues 'there ought to be recognition of precariousness as a shared condition of human life (indeed, as a condition that links human and non-human animals), but we ought not to think that the recognition of precariousness masters or captures or even fully cognizes what it recognizes.' Butler is thinking about humans: 'precariousness is coextensive with birth itself (birth is, by definition, precarious) ... Precisely because a living being may die, it is necessary to care for that being so that it may live' (2015). The female octopus stays alive to give care and no care-taking will prevent her own death. Semelparity, when a species has one reproductive episode before death, as opposed to iteropathy, when a species has many (Hughes and Simon 2014), makes her life seem too short.

The period of maternal care, in which an octopus fans water over her eggs to keep them oxgyenated, may be seen as one of approaching life. The grievability, Butler's term, of the octopus mother's life is a human-projected emotion; hers might well be life satisfaction, job done and well done. Nonetheless, animalographies that feature animal death, usually at The End of a book, are sad for humans, especially when that animal's death is caused by humans. It gives empathy a space which extends beyond the ending of the text, joining two kinds of personhood – the narrative animal and the reader – in personhoods that share mortality.

The haptic makes a bridge between personhood and mortality. Interspecies life writing has many moments of significant touch. Peter Laufer goes to see a Triassic turtle in a museum. 'We hold hands a moment before we (or at least I) say goodbye; with that touch somehow I feel we are bridging her era and ours' (2018: 20). On a sport fishing expedition, Carl Safina touches a just-killed swordfish: 'when I lay four fingers on its flank, its rippling sensitivity to touch is fine and exquisite. No surface of the human body is capable of quivering so responsively. It's eerie' (2007: 142). Bagging a colossal Leatherback from aboard a research vessel, Safina confides, 'I reach down and, fully recognizing the privilege, stroke his smooth, cool, immaculate skin' (2007: 175). These examples are instances of touch at the brink of time, of death, of farewell, as if the haptic condenses a gesture of departure for which touch is more expressive than sight.

The haptic makes touch metaphysical. 'Somehow the turtles touch the souls of those they encounter. This often is not easily described ... It's somewhere between falling in love and having a religious revelation, but it's not either of these really' (Bennett and Keuper-Bennett 2008: 116). It is this erotic-sacred touch that Craig Foster celebrates in *Underwater Wild* (2021), co-authored with Ross Frylinck. Foster's preface celebrates human and oceanic bonding: 'Friendship shared with purposeless adventuring in the wild ocean is something very powerful. Every time we dived together a deep magic seemed to be unfolding, a mysterious coming together of two fractured souls.' This declaration sits opposite a photograph showing a man diving head down with outstretched arms, like an inverted crucifixion, all openness to waving kelp, a visualization of how 'wild nature is our teacher' (Foster and Frylinck 2021: xvi).

But the visual is ultimately secondary to the haptic for Foster. He shares his story of loss and healing with Frylinck, who adds his own episodes of distress and reparation through wild diving in cold water. Healing happens through touch. Both authors are transfigured by creatures who seek them out and lie relaxed and trustingly in their hands; these include pyjama catsharks, super red klingvis and a nautilus. Since wild creatures can evade touch, their voluntary touch is powerful.

Where Foster's film focused on his friendship with a female octopus, the book broadens engagement with other species. 'Knowing the inner life of a small creature is infinitely more interesting and satisfying than the outer life of a great charismatic beast' (Foster and Frylinck 2021: 28). The octopus teacher appears as a sage who is also a conduit to other species: 'she was "showing" him things he had never seen in the Great African Sea Forest, and that she was teaching him to dive in a way that created a lower "pressure signature" – meaning that he would make less disturbance in the water and thus not chase away other animals' (Foster and Frylinck 2021: 231).

Underwater Wild is heavy, even for a coffee-table book: to handle it involves haptic weightiness. (It weighed in at 3kg/7lbs on my kitchen scales.) The book's format is of roughly alternately authoring, Frylinck taking on narrative, Foster explicating photographs in lengthy captions. It works as a dialogue which – in the best Socratic tradition – enables doubts to be aired, scepticism addressed and raptures echoed. Frylinck reports Foster notices his relationships with animals shifting:

> he felt that he was being 'let into the club,' because vulnerable animals that were generally very fearful were starting to approach him. He described incredible encounters with a cuttlefish and with a pleated toadfish, telling me that both creatures had lain in his hands and even swum with him to the surface …
>
> (Foster and Frylinck 2021: 231)

In his own voice Foster tells of an encounter with an otter:

> Closer and closer it came. Then I felt it touching my fins, my legs, slowly moving up my body. The otter realized I posed no threat and eventually it was caressing my face with its extraordinary humanlike fingers. My body and my mind were on fire. The power of the experience was almost too much to bear.
>
> (2021: 282)

Both men experience trances after such encounters, with shamanic and ancestral overtones. As Frylinck puts it, 'I had swum to the wild side, where the boundary between human and animal, self and other, falls away' (2021: 288).

Science, however, keeps a boundary between human and animal, in part to assert scientific objectivity. Peter Godfrey-Smith is an Australian philosopher of science and his book *Other Minds* uses brain science, biology and underwater experiences to account for octopus otherness. Godfrey-Smith's interest is visual: he sees colour-changes akin to a language potentially readable as self-expression. I fully endorse that idea of cephalopod colour as expressive (Brant 2009). Godfrey-Smith stops short of seeing conscious subjectivity but presents cuttlefish and giant Pacific octopuses as sentient, expressive, individuals. He names some after male modernist artists like Matisse and Kandinsky. For future octopus literature, can female artists be considered? For starters there's Kahlo, O'Keefe, Dissmor, Sulter, Riley and many, many more … Eileen Agar, whose work embraced marine subjects, said in her autobiography *A Look at My Life* (1988) that as an artist 'one must have a hunger for new colour, new shapes and new possibilities of discovery' (Agar 2024: 310). It is a very octopus combination. Naming is also peculiar in Montgomery's story. Octopuses she meets in the wild are 'it', genderless. An octopus in captivity gets a name. One in the Seattle Aquarium was named Emily Dickinson because she was so shy (Montgomery 2015: 9). In the New England Aquarium, senior aquarist Bill Murphy says 'Frank, Stewy, Steve – any name for a male octopus is funny. Naming females is more challenging' (Montgomery 2015: 62). You wonder why. Classical or goddess names confer cosmic dignity – the last of Montgomery's octopus subjects is named Karma. A name is a handle – thus online usernames are termed handles; difficulty in naming indicates a failure of the haptic, unsubtly gendered.

Haptic activity is present at Godfrey-Smith's site of Octopolis, an octopus community where cameras record behaviours. Godfrey-Smith and colleagues sifted through it looking for patterns. He had thought of arm probing and lashing, common behaviour between roaming octopuses and ones in dens, as boxing. Stefan Linquist, also reviewing footage, thought instead

> of many of these interactions as 'high fives' – as arm-slaps that seemed to facilitate recognition between individuals, or at least a registration of basic roles on the site. Sometimes two octopuses would probe or whip their arms, and then settle back into a relaxed pose. Other times, the arm pokes would be followed by a fight.
>
> (Godfrey-Smith 2017: 183)

Friendly or combative, octopus arms do the talking – as the males do in mating, slipping a packet of sperm from a specialized arm, the hectocotylus, into the female's mantle. In some species it breaks off. Sometimes the males will hide in a nearby den and present only their hectocotylus arm to a reachable female.

During one long encounter, Godfrey-Smith stays close to a cuttlefish who appears to be sleeping, yet whose body ripples and fizzes with colour patterns, including an unusual shade of rust and grey-greens, and dark-yellow–pale-brown combinations, while facing out to sea.

> He pulled in his arms and exposed his beak. He tucked his arms below him in a missile-like pose, then produced a yellow flare. I kept glancing out to see if he was looking at someone – another cuttlefish or some other intruder. There was never anyone there. At one point he went into the sideways stretch that males do when they are competing with each other. Then he pulled himself into the most extraordinarily contorted shape, his skin suddenly white, with arms pulled back both above and below his head. This sequence then quieted down. I backed

off and remained higher in the water, remaining beside the den and not in front of it, and watching him calm down. And then, instantly, he seized into a wild aggressive pose, with arms straight out, sharp like thin swords, and his whole body a bright yellow-orange. It was as if the orchestra suddenly hit a wild clashing chord. The arms ended in needles, his body became covered with jagged papillae like armor. He then began roaming a little, sometimes facing me and sometimes facing out to sea. I wondered again if this was directed at me, but if it was a display, it seemed to be aimed in directions all round.

(2017: 135)

Godfrey-Smith's description shows how colourable skin and malleable arms articulate cephalopod body language. It also shows unusual decentering of the human.

Some cuttlefish behave with a level of indifference that is so intense it is hard to describe. These cuttlefish do not seem to register you as a living being at all. … Being ignored so deeply makes you wonder if you are entirely real in their watery world, as if you are one of those ghosts who does not realize they are a ghost.

(Godfrey-Smith 2017: 118)

Godfrey-Smith describes this a 'maintenance of the non-contact', surely a useful term for postcolonial theory as it hunts for terms for subaltern resistances.

In 2023 researchers analysed footage of a solitary octopus asleep who had an episode of strange behaviour – thrashing his arms about, going Nosferatu and emitting ink, all actions associated with fighting back. (In Nosferatu pose, an octopus turns dark, rises up and draws its mantle over its head to look like a stiff, vampire-like cloak.) The researchers suggested they were watching an octopus have a nightmare, possibly one reliving traumatic damage to its arms in the ocean. Rather than an unconscious language, this suggests cephalopods have an unconscious for which they have a language – as humans do, think some people, in dreams and nightmares. The researchers considered whether they were watching symptoms of dementia, but they found footage of such episodes in four octopuses. They wondered if these could potentially represent dream-enactment behaviours (Wilcox 2023). David M. Peña-Guzmán argues passionately that animals can and do dream (2022). Naturally his book has a colourful octopus on its cover, poster-species for animal consciousness.

In a 2022 article, Godfrey-Smith returns to the haptic. Again observing the gloomy octopus (*Octopus tetricus*) at Jervis Bay, Australia, he and his colleagues watched octopuses throw silt, algae and shells – with surprise, because throwing objects is uncommon behaviour in animals. They hypothesized that some throws were deliberate, one octopus taking aim at another, and distinguished between den-maintenance and interactive throws, though for some flingings it was hard to tell. 'Two females accounted for the majority (66%) of the throws, but likely half or more of individuals present threw at least occasionally, both sexes threw, and octopuses threw from locations around the site.' They report that 'a single female threw material 10 times, with 5 of these hitting a male in an adjacent den, who attempted several times to mate with her'; the male managed to duck a few times. Twelve throws were directed at a camera which had accidentally been set up too close to a den; its occupant lobbed six throws at it. Octopuses who threw were consistently dark in colour, usually a sign of octopus annoyance (Godfrey-Smith et al. 2022). Throwing shows the kinaesthetic dimension of the haptic. It also neatly fits a turn in object biography towards itineraries, or how the mobility of things brings new understandings of objects as things with stretchy stories. 'The itinerary approach also holds ideas for … a relationist ontology that involves human actors, landscapes, ecosystems, and non-human animals' (Nichols 2016). What Godfrey-Smith calls 'debris' and 'material' may have quite other terms in an octopus's haptic understanding as she flings annoyance at intrusive entities. 'There is, it seems, a kind of mental surplus in the octopus' (Godfrey-Smith 2017: 73). Expressed in body language and in dreams, it is tangibly present in their haptic abilities.

TRACKING, LOGGING, DATA DOUBLES

'It is easier to find a specific grain of sand on Waikiki Beach than a palm-sized hatchling in the central North Pacific. Baby *honu* might as well be on the moon!' (Bennett and Keuper-Bennett 2008: 60). Much scientific effort has gone into finding out where turtles go. Looking for Leatherbacks in Nova Scotia waters, Safina observes 'Leatherbacks travel inside an envelope of unknowns. How they find food in depths beyond light penetration: unknown. How well they see, smell, or hear underwater: unknown. How they sense and use currents: unknown. Life span: unknown. Habits of juveniles: unknown. Distribution and behavior of food: unknown' (Safina 2007: 154). Many underwater life writings include maps to show animal movements. Across oceans, around coasts, from breeding to feeding grounds, dotted lines mark out tracks. Such maps show creatures moving through the oceans in their own ways, different from human zones and corridors. 'The fact that West Coast-foraging Leatherbacks are born in the sands of New Guinea and the Solomon Islands was one of the most surprising discoveries in ocean ecology. … It means that the world is both bigger than anyone ever thought, and much smaller' (Safina 2007: 312). Species-focused life writing enables general readers to catch up with scientific narrative, for instance for sea turtles:

> if you know this general pattern – beach hatching followed by offshore open-ocean youth, adolescent and adult life of foraging on continental-shelf sea floors (for all species except the leatherback and Olive Ridley), then lengthy migration to a nesting beach every few years – you know what scientists spent decades unraveling.
> (Safina 2007: 29-30)

Turtle life writing used to be very beach-based, because beaches were where humans saw females coming ashore to lay eggs and hatchlings scampering to the sea. Juvenile existence is still mysterious. What sea turtles do underwater features much less in the literature than their arduous haul out, nest-digging and egg-laying; conversely, discoveries of how hatchlings develop within nests, and how they orient for their dash for the sea, provide small life storying, testimony to a new, hopeful generation. The narrative of mothers and children forms into nesting and hatching – no maternal care is identified, except in the tremendous effort she-turtles make to find a good spot to lay and fulfil each stage of laying; the newborns seem to fend for themselves, against a gamut of predators and conditions complicated by human beachfront development.

Robert Bustard was one scientist who monitored green turtles closely. Those coming ashore at Heron Island had their movements mapped in loving detail; one diagram even included the direction of the turtle's head while laying (Bustard 1972: 176, figure 7). Numbers mattered, because turtle populations depend on eggs becoming hatchlings who can return to ancestral beaches to lay again. Many turtle scientists become conservation activists because shocking declines of turtle species threaten their very subjects. Causes include egg predation, trade in turtle meat and shell, turtles drowning in fishing trawls and nets, turtles impaled on longlines, and disease. Fibropapillomatosis, a horrible condition that gives turtles tumours especially on their eyes, is for Osha Gray Davidson (2001) a sign of diseases emerging from human-polluted oceans. For Carl Safina, longlines are deadliest. He cites a study that shows longlines snare 50,000 Leatherbacks and 250,000 Loggerheads a year, besides killing many other species. 'I find it distressing, as if the ocean is a fishing-gear spiderweb' (Safina 2007: 170). Restoration of nesting beaches helps, but may not improve population numbers. Warmer temperatures in nests mean more female hatchlings, so global heating unbalances gender ratios too.

Numbers make turtle life writing into scientific decline and fall stories, with narratives of gradual recovery for some species. Turtle life writing is also eloquent about conceptual significance. For Safina, 'When a species crashes it may take down cultures grown enmeshed with it, snapping limbs off the human family tree as it falls, robbing the world of cultural complexity, leaving the human landscape simplified – leaving more of the world like all the rest of the world as the whole world grows increasingly the same' (2007: 343). Safina spends time with some Seri people in the Gulf of California, themselves an endangered group, to whom Leatherback turtles are the most sacred animal. Veneration entails a duty of stewardship, the Seri believe. Dismayed at seeing no Leatherbacks for seventeen years, in 1997 they sent a delegation. Hatchlings from a hatchery lead it, referred to not by name but by an honorific, Vulnerable One. Song, dance and vigil accompany them down the beach and seaward (Safina 2007: 343-7). For the Seri, turtles are holy beings, not data.

In the same way that Fitbit's 10,000 steps tell you nothing about the why of a person's movements, tracking data may tell you where or how deep a turtle can go, but not how she passes the time. Everyday life for green turtles off Hawai'i was studied by Peter Bennett and Ursula Keuper-Bennett simply by diving and watching. In 1993 they connected with a scientific community, via a conference.

> To our surprise, once the turtle specialists heard that we'd been observing turtles underwater for years, they began asking *us* questions: How did we tell them apart, whether they got along together, if they had favorite spots, just what is it that they did all day long – the same sort of queries that everyone had.
>
> (Bennett and Keuper-Bennett 2008: 2)

Green turtles are laidback. They eat, usually at sunset and dawn. They rest, in regular spots. They scratch against the coral, making tramples, hollows that they rest in. Foraging and rest occupy oldsters at home on their patches of reef; juveniles play tag-and-chase games which the authors suggest are also practice of escape skills. Mating is visible in mounting, though the authors observe multiple instances of all-male mounts. Although the main nesting beaches are on undisturbed islands, some *honu* nest on tourist beaches, where people are encouraged to keep their distance thanks to a 2005 campaign devised by turtle expert George Balazs, 'Show Turtles Aloha.' The *aloha* or love of the authors for their subjects extends to a degree of subjecthood: they give turtles names, though respecting their official identification via a number. 'Honu have a remarkable charisma that charms almost everyone who encounters them. People simply fall in love with the turtles' (Bennett and Keuper-Bennett 2008: 116). They propose a plausible boundary marker for devotees: 'There is a line that separates the casual observer of an animal from the truly involved. You cross it when you become interested in their waste matter' (2008: 81). Examining turtle crap is entirely compatible with the numinous, because immersion in the *honu*'s home ranges establishes benign relationships. Underwater is written as a place of beautiful companionability: 'Heaven for us happens underwater, when the late afternoon ocean shimmers electric blue and sunshine ripples gold on the backs of our *honu* friends' (Bennett and Keuper-Bennett 2008: 28).

Study of large marine animals used to depend heavily on aerial reconnaissance: connaissance came in the form of counting. Thus in 1944 Victor B. Scheffer researched sea lions. 'Our pilot swooped and spiraled [*sic*] to give us a close look at the rocks. When I wasn't face-down in a nausea bag I was counting sea lions' (Scheffer 1980: 73). Now radio and satellite tracking replace light planes, although aerial surveys are still useful. Turtle champion Sally Murphy, getting stiffly out of a plane, says, 'People think this sounds like fun, but I tell 'em four hours of plane spotting is like eight hours in a dentist's chair' (Safina 2007: 344). Surveillance from above, however, is patchily panoptic. Where Michel Foucault linked surveillance to state power, particularly the power of the state to punish, animal tracking reformulates power into the power to protect, ultimately a power also enforced by states. Gilbert Caluya thinks Foucault indicated that besides power and discipline, regimes of security were important: 'security concerns itself with neither good nor bad phenomena, but with natural occurrences and processes that become pertinent because it functions at the level of the population' (2010: 631). Scientific surveillance establishes levels of populations for species as a self-evident good. 'Finding Leatherbacks in these waters requires superior speed, persistent air support, and sophisticated daily satellite-generated sea-temperature maps', says Carl Safina (2007: 286) on board a boat in Monterey Bay. For humans, surveillance theories grapple with sinister implications like the spectres of totalitarianism. Converting them to animals requires thinking about this: if we can follow any whale to the ends of the ocean, does a purpose of notional protection for that whale or its species offset surveillance as a means of human dominance, even human totalitarianism over other species? Surveillance techniques can also create splits between scientists and diver observers. The two divers who studied Hawaiian green turtles logged 750. Their book includes a page of portraits, left and right side turtle heads to show individuality through difference of scales. They observe '*Honu* faces are delightful. Scientists aren't particularly interested in the face as a whole, but we are' (Bennett and Keuper-Bennett 2008: 32). They could read metal tags to identify a turtle, but not PIT tags, passive integrated responders – these microchips under the skin of a hind flipper require a special device to read. Surveillance technologies involve unequal access.

Nonetheless, tracking animal numbers and movements adds to information about populations. 'The more we know about animals' seasonal usage of habitats, the more we can protect the areas they need to survive', says the US National Aquarium (2022). Movebank is a database of animal tracking data, In January 2025, it included 8843 studies; 1478 taxa; 7.5 billion animal locations, and 7.4 billion other animal-borne sensor measurements (Movebank). Tools are getting smarter. In 2021 TRex arrived: 'it can track 100 animals at a time while keeping tabs on each of them, and relay information which can reconstitute each animal's visual field – what it sees, while we watch it' (Walter and Couzin 2021). Tracking is a spatial sort of life writing, following animal movements (or lack of them) to understand better what animal movements mean. Not all tracking is technological. Craig Foster learnt tracking from San masters of the !Xo people, nomadic foragers in southern Africa. 'They likened the experience to dancing and said that it brought them closer to God' (Foster and Frylinck 2021: 44). Foster teaches Frylinck the skills, starting with limpets and their algae gardens. Frylinck is fascinated:

> it was as if I had decoded a little piece of an ancient Rosetta stone, written by the limpets on the rocks. Where there had been nothing to see, suddenly a layer of meaning was revealed. ... Foraging limpets use these tracks to find their way home. I've learned to identify species by the width of the track and the pattern of movement.
>
> (Foster and Frylinck 2021: 45, 49)

This visual skillset is bodily, putting close looking and experience together. Foster proposes it harmonizes species differences. Marine tracks 'are the strings and keys that make up the musical instruments of the wild – instruments that, simply in observing them, allow us to join the symphony that is our original design' (Foster and Frylinck 2021: 65).

Technology has a different music. It mostly individuates information – a radio or satellite tag tracks one animal's movements, later collated with those of others. Individuation is not quite individuality, which raises interesting questions for life writing. Tracked animals become a numbered data stream; they may also be accorded a name and a slice of life history. Surveillance studies has a concept of the 'surveillant assemblage', 'which works by abstracting human bodies from their territorial settings into discrete flows that are later reassembled into data doubles' (Caluya 2010: 623). For humans, observes Maria Los, 'products of surveillance technologies are increasingly construed as a new form of truth ... The data double is more real than the person behind it' (2006: 86).

Marine beings have data doubles – and have done since before the digital era. Orcas, for instance, have been closely studied in North America since the 1970s:

Sometimes, studying orcas must seem rather like running a private detective agency – every animal has a personal file, containing umpteen mug-shots and an abundance of information on all the finer details of its private life. Some of these files are probably more comprehensive than their human equivalents in the vaults of the CIA, MI5 or the KGB.

(Carwardine 1994: 89-90)

Pods were originally named after orca males; it was thought they were male-led, with harems following, until it was understood they were in fact matrilines, a mother and her offspring up to the fourth generation. Writing on whale-watching in the 1990s, British conservationist Mark Carwardine amusingly explains the process by which scientists named a thousand humpback whale subjects.

There are only two rules in the humpback whale naming game. The first is that human names, like Bert or Beryl, are not allowed because they are considered too anthropomorphic. The second is that names which assume the sex of the animal, like Dr. Spock or Lady Chatterley, are also not allowed because it is usually impossible to tell the difference (unless the whale turns up with a calf, in which case it is a female.)

(1994: 102)

Every year biologists gathered for a naming party. 'The best way to tell how late in the party a whale was christened is by the length of time it takes for the biologists to explain their logic in selecting its name' (Carwardine 1994: 103). Examples – floating signifiers? – include Firefly, Bittern, Guinness, Bamboo. 'Purists might argue that the use of names encourages biologists to become too attached to their subjects', says Carwardine, who counters 'it is impossible *not* to become attached. Anyone who has had a close encounter with a humpback, just once, finds it hard to remain emotionally stable for several weeks, or even months, afterwards. So biologists who see them every day would have to be made of stone not to be affected' (1994: 103-4).

Marine animal logging and its animalography run on a mixed economy of numbers and names. Numbers have wide currency, for instance for a green turtle who began nesting in 2000. 'Although she later came to be called names such as Maui Girl, her official name is her tag number: "5690"' (Bennett and Keuper-Bennett 2008: 47). A flatback turtle (*Natator depressus*) first recorded nesting in Australia in 1977, returned often, in 2022 to a welcome of church bells. George Balazs noted 'there are pages of data on her' (1998–9; 2003:16). She, X8473, manages without a name. Colin Limpus, who tagged many turtles over five decades of research, personalizes through numbers. 'Despite tracking and monitoring thousands of animals over the years, he recognises turtles and has memorised many of their tags. "Don't you remember the names of your friends?" he asks' (Davey 2016). Googling X8473 could lead you to a Hornby

Figure 21 Whale shark (*Rhincodon typus*), twelve foot juvenile, followed by Black Jacks (*Caranx lugubris*). Baja, Mexico, Pacific Ocean. Photo and caption by Brandon Cole. Nature Picture Library.

locomotive, a Nissan car part, a Victorian portrait (AI insists on the latter); googling Colin Limpus leads to the turtle expert, though as 'Col'.

For public engagement, which is crucial in conservation science, names signify better than numbers. Loggerhead expert Hoyt Peckham dressed up in a turtle costume (a sort of double) and organized a giant turtle naming competition in Isla Magdalena, Mexico. 'It's gimmicky, sure, but it creates a friendly atmosphere for an important message' (Safina 2007: 282). An impulse to confer a name is strong. William Beebe, knowing a name, inscribed it on an otherwise mobile signifier. 'A grandfather of an Amblyrhyncus crawled out behind my seat, and I leaned back with my fountain pen and scrawled A.C., his own initials, on his greyish scales, before he shifted beyond reach' (Beebe 1924: 108). *Amblyrhyncus cristatus*, a Galápagos marine iguana, becomes the mobile text of a scientific name made personal, his own initials.

Digital nets are spreading. I have written elsewhere about shark tagging and social media (Brant 2023); I close with whale sharks, neither a whale nor a shark but the world's largest fish. First tagged in 2015, they already had a global database, *Wildbook for Whale Sharks*, created in 2003. Whale sharks have individual patterns of spots and stripes; an identifying photograph has to show this in a universal area. 'It is always the left hand side of the shark (to act as a global control variable) and must show the top and bottom of the last (5th) gill slit and where the pectoral fin meets the body' (Sharkbook). It proved easier to identify individuals than a database of eyes. 'The software that most of these photo ID projects use, including whale sharks, was originally created by NASA for identifying star systems. Therefore it's quite fitting that the Madagascan name for whale sharks, "marokintana", translates to "many stars" and the Japanese, "geger lintang", means "stars in the back"' (whalesharkdiaries 2017).

Two tagged whale sharks verged on stardom: 'Sharky McSharkface and Blue Bandit are perhaps the two tracked sharks with the most interesting stories to tell right now,' said Mark Erdmann, vice president of CI's Asia-Pacific marine programs. 'After nearly 15 months of tracking them – a record time period for whale shark satellite tagging – they've led massively different lives despite both being 4.5 meter [15-foot] males of roughly the same age' (Begen 2016).

Sharky McSharkface is a homebody who stays relatively shallow; Blue Bandit goes much farther afield and dives deep. All sixteen whale sharks tagged to date were adolescent males, raising the question of where were the others, the females, infants and adult males? (Erdmann 2017) What could you extrapolate from one cohort, juvenile males, that applies to the species, especially when two such whale sharks could be so different in habits? Tagging does tell us things we didn't know. It also tells us how little we know. Its biodata, logged, broadcast, followed, is a form of life writing – an animalography travel diary – with a tentacular digital grasp towards other bodies, other minds.

Part Three

Ocean

9

Unearthly Underwater

William Beebe was a pioneer bathyspherist as well as a helmet diver. Writing about his descent in the waters off Bermuda in 1934, he argued that 'personal exploration under the ocean really is unearthly; we are penetrating into a new world' (1934: 66). How does human exploration into the deep ocean use the figure of unearthliness? 'Unearthly' was a repurposed word. *OED*'s primary definition of it is 'Rising above what is characteristic of earth; exalted, sublime; celestial'; it was first used by Shakespeare in *The Winter's Tale* (1623, 3.1.7). A second use appeared in the early nineteenth century, to mean supernatural, ghostly, mysterious. 'Descents of any sort – personal, historic, and artistic – compel us to swerve from the literal' (Sneeden 2023: 261). If being unearthly turns on rising *above* earthly characteristics, how does sinking *down* into the ocean create distinct forms of unearthliness?

Although Planet Earth is seven-tenths water (and rising), Earth and its Oceans as a phrase has only recently appeared as a gesture to the importance of water in the composition of our world, underpinned by the 'Blue Marble' photo taken by astronauts from Apollo 17 in 1972. The BBC made the phrase Blue Planet more familiar by its ocean-themed series of 2001 and its sequels, *Blue Planet II* (2017) and *Blue Planet III* (2026). Yet the idea of a Blue Planet does not begin to encompass the vast deeps where sunlight does not penetrate and blue turns to inky black, a Black Planet. 'All of life on Earth lives in the dark at least half of the time, and much of it lives in the dark all of the time – in the depths of the sea', as Sylvia Earle puts it (1995: 110). I look first at accounts of deep dives and how a range of life writers handle their experiences of unearthliness. Technology mediates this in particular ways – and with some surprises. The second half of the chapter investigates language under pressure at depth, especially where life writers encounter other species and struggle with their strangeness. Inhabitants of this environment are often described as 'denizens of the deep' – a strange phrase in itself. It is striking how sticky the word 'weird' is: I investigate that, and a language of 'alien', to explore how life writing represents deep-sea otherness.

UNEARTHLY ENVIRONMENT – UNTETHERING THE MIND?

Oceanography is a science that has been transformed by exploration of the deep ocean. Its history accelerated when mid-nineteenth century hydrographers began in earnest to try to measure the ocean's depths by soundings (Rozwadowski 2001) and when

HMS *Challenger's* epic voyaging (1872–6) established that, contrary to earlier beliefs, there was life below 600 metres, sampled by bringing up specimens in buckets. Two interweaving histories follow: one of descents by humans, one of discoveries. Descents by humans were at first imaginary, with a long shelf life for Jules Verne's *Twenty Thousand Leagues Under the Sea*, originally serialized 1869–70, read avidly for at least a hundred years. In 1934, William Beebe went half a mile down in a bathysphere designed by its pilot, Otis Barton, also aboard. Together they made other descents, setting a record for the deepest, to 932 metres (3028 feet) on August 15. A bathysphere has a sphere shape; it dangles on a tether like a metal marble. A bathyscaph (or bathyscaphe in French spelling) has a globular cabin below an oval gasoline-filled float; it is untethered and self-propelling. In 1960, Jacques Piccard and Donald Walsh descended in their bathyscaphe *Trieste* to a new record depth, 10,911 metres, at the bottom of the Challenger Deep in the Mariana Trench. In 1979, Sylvia Earle, subsequently known as 'Her Deepness', dived off Hawai'i in *Jim*, a pressurized suit, to 1250 feet (381 metres) – still the record for an untethered human. Since the 1960s, Woods Hole Oceanographic Institute has successfully run its three-person submersible *Alvin* on several thousand dives; they include discovering hydrothermal vents. Robert Ballard devised a remotely operated vehicle, the ROV *Argo*, an unmanned deep-towed video camera sled, which helped him find the wreck of the *Titanic* in 1985, which he explored in *Alvin* in 1986. In 2012, filmmaker James Cameron went seven miles down in the Mariana Trench in *Deepsea Challenger*, a submersible of his own design with a clever stabilizing fin. Underwater drones are developing fast – in 2020, they could go down to 200 metres; in 2025, to 600 metres (Doornekamp 2020). ROVs now prevail on grounds of safety and cost, but there is a mixed economy of occasional human excursions. As James Cameron argues, 'When people hear about a robot descending it doesn't have the same value. A human pilot will come back and tell you how it felt: how cold it was and how remote it was' (Sample 2012).

Human descents need technology to protect against the cold, dark and extreme pressure of the deep sea. Ingenious devices – bathysphere, bathyscaphe, tethered submersibles, ROVs and AUVs (autonomous underwater vehicles), drones, cameras – link to surface or shore support systems, involving many people. 'One does not get to the seafloor by oneself, whether as a pilot or as a scientist', says Cindy Lee Van Dover in her memoir of being a scientist and *Alvin* pilot (1996: xiv). The history of these devices includes rivalries and collaborations between countries, disciplines, institutions and scientists; they involve money, time and fame (Casey 2023). Technological underwater history connects to space exploration in an emphatically two-way exchange: aquanautics has moments of leading astronautical directions (I can only touch on that here). Deep ocean technology puts particular emphasis on extending the functions of eyes and hands. Prosthetic vision and sampling, by cameras and manipulable arms, extend human reach. Ears too acquire prosthetics in acoustic extensions, especially sonic systems developed in and after the Cold War by military interests. Underwater life writing addresses these reconfigurations of the human body; it also attends to inner transformations. As Joe MacInnis, working closely with James Cameron, writes in an expedition blog: 'Exploration is a force that gives us meaning. It is driven by our curiosity to know what lies beyond the horizon. It is also driven by a hunger for self-discovery, an investigation of the subliminal self – something never fully realized by remotely operated vehicles' (2012). The subliminal self has a representative function: deep descenders are conscious of being human, yet in an environment so remote from human experience it can bewilder cultural identity.

Alongside the history of exploration is a history of discovery. Science is so often presented as discovery the term can get stale, but what happened in oceanography in the twentieth century was absolutely transformative for understanding Planet Earth. Discoveries were revelations. After centuries of believing the deep ocean was an inert place, featureless, empty, cold and eternally dark, oceanographers established that the deeps are active, mobile and home to much life, including unimagined habitats and organisms. 'The abyss is not a desert, it is not exclusively flat, it is not unchanging, it is not even universally cold and dark' (Van Dover 1996: 12). Geologists and biologists established that life not only began in the deep ocean but is continually remade there, as undersea volcanoes pour out magma which forms new seabed, contributes to the movement of continents and to the cycle of nutrients in seawater that sustains all life, including life on land. Around three-quarters of all volcanic activity on Planet Earth happens underwater. As Robert Ballard explained, aboard the *Alvin* submersible exploring the Galápagos Rift at 2250 metres,

> Halfway into the cruise, we realised that we had stumbled into a major scientific discovery. I saw normally staid colleagues actually skipping with pleasure down the ship's corridors to and from the lab … in effect, we had discovered what amounted to an entire separate branch of evolution down in those dark lava mounds, a virtual new planet waiting for biologists to explore.
>
> (Ballard with Hively 2000: 188–9)

It is a change so profound one can reasonably compare it to discovering the Earth is not flat.

Authors of deep dive accounts often use 'Deep' in their book titles. 'Deep' does a lot of heavy lifting: it evokes a scale of simultaneous measurability and unfathomability. Depth has relativity: over the history of diving, it becomes … deeper. A phase in which 'deep' indicates below *c*.40 metres, the limit of scuba divers using air (divers on other gas mixes can go deeper) comes to co-exist with 'deep' as a descriptor of depths beyond which no human can go without elaborate protection. The deepest point in the ocean is the Challenger Deep at the southern end of the Mariana Trench, which lies in the western Pacific Ocean between Japan and Papua New Guinea. It was identified in 1951, appropriately by HMS *Challenger II*. Since the depth was beyond the ship's echo-sounder limits, the scientists on board used old measuring tech in the form of a weighted line, which took an hour and a half to fall to the bottom (Gaskell 1960: 121). The official depth now is given variously: NOAA says 10,994 metres (36,000 feet). According to the US National Ocean Service, the average depth of the ocean is 3,682 metres (12,080 feet). Distinctions of depth are quite recent: the term 'hadal' was first proposed in 1956, by Danish oceanographer Anton Bruun, to describe the parts of the ocean deeper than 6000 metres (20,000 feet) (Blankenship-Williams and Levin 2009). Depth layers have an agreed terminology: from the surface down, you pass through the epipelagic or sunlight zone (to 200 metres); the mesopelagic or twilight zone (to 1000 metres); the bathypelagic or midnight zone (to 4000 metres); the abyssal zone (to 6000 metres) and the hadal zone (below 6000 metres).

There is now an extensive literature about the deep, positioning it as a place of exploration and encounters with strange creatures. It is also a place of poetics. James Cameron launches *Aliens of the Deep* with a conventional comparison to science fiction: 'In those worlds of imagination, I could envision myself in a spaceship landing on another planet, the first human to gaze on its wonders, the first to return to tell the tale. Now I am really doing it' (McInnis 2005: 9). Analogies between the ocean deep and outer space are a staple of deep water literature. They serve several purposes. First, they anchor otherwise overwhelmed imaginations to a discourse whose familiarity is grounding. Thus Robert Kunzig explains: 'The goals of space exploration are in a way easier to identify with; you can see them from your backyard, just by looking up, with or without a telescope' whereas paradoxically 'The deep is always hidden by water' (2000: 6). Second, the geology of the deep ocean is part of outer space, in that it belongs to a narrative of how the universe came about and how life on Earth began – and continues, thanks to underwater volcanoes. 'The mechanism that orchestrates all this activity was scarcely dreamt of 50 years ago', writes Kunzig in 2000:

> Then people regarded the ocean basins as ancient features and as unchanging ones – tedious deserts, uncharted but hardly worth charting, vacant spaces disturbed only by endless rains of sediment. If the ocean basins really were like that, it is now clear, we would not have oceans at all. There are oceans today on Earth, and there is life today on Earth, because the ocean floor itself is young and moving and constantly changing and, in that sense, alive.
>
> (Kunzig 2000: 26-7)

So Earth in the deep ocean is a complex place, old, young, part of outer space; the sea floor with its plates, ridges, magma and vents constantly reshapes Earth through the sea and makes it a living planet – processes that science journalist William Broad calls 'geopoetry' (1997: 327). Supposedly empty regions turn out to have species that challenge earthly imagination and knowledge. '"The deeper we go, the less we know," said Nick Schizas, a marine biologist at the University of Puerto Rico. "The majority of habitat of Earth is the deeper areas of the ocean. Yet we know so little about it." The reporter adds, 'The experience is much like exploring another planet in a slightly claustrophobic air bubble. And given our lack of knowledge about the deep sea, the otherworldliness felt particularly apt' (Milman 2016). Unearthliness then is both material and figurative.

The word 'strange' applies to the unknown, unfamiliar, alien – a stranger comes from another land. It gestures to what's difficult to take in, a condition of surprise or exceptionality. In Samuel Johnson's *Dictionary* (1755), 'strange' is defined as 'An expression of wonder'. In deep ocean life writings, 'strange' acts out the distancing inherent in unearthly, often through displacements of time and space. The strangest moments, strangely, occur not only in the deep but back on the surface. As Beebe puts it,

> After these dives were past, when I came again to examine the deep-sea treasures in my nets, I would feel as an astronomer might who looks through his telescope after having rocketed to Mars and back, or like a paleontologist who could suddenly annihilate time and see his fossils alive.
>
> (1934: 137)

The space-time axis normally orientates humans on Earth. Beebe's metaphors indicate estrangement from that with some violence (rocketing, annihilating): 'we seemed like unborn embryos with unnumbered geological epochs to come' (1934: 137).

Disorientation of a familiar space-time continuum appears in many accounts. In 1994 William Broad accompanied a Monterey Bay Aquarium Research Institute vessel. He watched images sent up by Ventana, a robot vessel exploring Monterey Canyon's midwater deeps down to one kilometre. 'If an alien civilisation came to look at the dominant life form on the planet, they'd be out looking at midwater creatures', said the chief scientist, Bruce H. Robison, known as Robey (Broad 1997: 216). After hours of watching numerous siphonophores, Broad took a break. Up on deck, alone, he reflected:

> Unexpectedly, the experience was a jolt that left me wobbly. My head was filled with images of unfamiliar life that had been hidden from man for millions of years. But here I was, standing on deck, gazing at the commonplace. I felt schizophrenic, torn between unrelated worlds. ... The whole experience was eerie and disorientating.
>
> (Broad 1997: 226-7)

If a shipboard spectator of ROV screens feels so dislocated from earthliness, humans descending in manned vehicles often describe strangeness in terms of estrangement from their own species. Despite being squeezed against another person, William Beebe reflected 'nowhere have I felt so completely isolated as in this bathysphere, in the blackness of ocean's depths' (1934: 174). Pondering the Challenger Deep which he visited in 2012, 'something like 50 times the size of the Grand Canyon', James Cameron commented: 'There is a vast frontier that's going to take us a while to understand. The impression to me was that it was very lunar, a very desolate place, isolated. My feeling was one of complete isolation from all of humanity' (Sample 2012).

Extreme separation, intensified by silence and darkness, removes humans from earthly and stable psychological paradigms. Auguste Piccard reported (at 13,000 feet) that 'The most frightening thing was the dreadful silence down there in our bathyscape. There is nothing but silence, darkness, and an occasional ghostly light' (Larsen 1955: 87-8). A study by psychologists in 1960 'suggested that "prolonged sensory isolation (darkness and silence) may produce intellectual-perceptual changes similar in many respects to those found in old age"' (Zubek 1960: 242). This intriguing hint of inner ageing – which can also sharpen memory – contributes to what Egon Larsen calls an uncanny world. Accompanying Beebe on one of his dives to *c*.500 metres, the ichthyologist John Tee-Van wrote 'We practically discarded all senses but sight. We became, like the bathysphere itself, two huge eyes looking out upon a world that had existed with little change for countless centuries' (Larsen 1955: 90).

Yet a new reach of memory accompanied visual concentration. For Beebe, 'From my second dive onward, submersion seemed as reasonable and my environment in general as familiar as if I could again call upon ancestral memory, this time stretching it some millions of years' (1934: 8). Comparisons with space disappear: 'when we descend beneath the surface of the waters we are most assuredly returning to an olden home, comparable in no way to aerial penetration, and infinitely more remote and fundamental than our air-breathing life today upon the dry land' (Beebe 1934: 8). Defined not by geological era but by biological form, ancestral memory extends scales of memory even to pre-human evolution. Beebe quotes a couple of lines from Langdon Smith's popular poem 'Evolution' (1895), 'When you were a tadpole/ And I was a fish', perfectly demonstrating that break with humanism which Stef Craps and other scholars see as necessary for memory studies to think ecologically (Craps 2018). The black ocean produces its own distinct deep remembering.

Besides ancestral memory, experiences of unearthliness lead to other forms of strangeness and estrangement – estrangeness, one might say, reviving a rare sixteenth-century word. In contrast to Beebe, Tjeerd van Andel, a geologist on a 1974 expedition from the Azores to the Mid-Atlantic Ridge, was insouciant about his first submersible descent to the deep. *Alvin* is snug, cosy and what falls away on descent is tension:

> Going down, the elaborate instrument checks make for a good transition. Finally the pilot gets restless, the lights go on, something shadowy is down there, and we settle like a feather on a field of snow with protruding black boulders populated with lots of stalky, feathery things. The terrain was grandiose – large lava flows with a coarse, sneaking interwoven lace of huge tubes, often with collapsed tops and caverns underneath, steep fronts up to 40 feet high.
>
> (Van Andel 1978: 153)

Van Andel keeps poetics for geology rather than organisms or atmosphere. Yet he too feels the effects of strangeness, even as dives on *Alvin* come to seem routine. 'In fact, the sense of unreality is much stronger when we are back on *Lulu*; then the strange universe so brightly lit nearby and so quickly fading into gloomy cliffs beyond is a thing that haunts me in my dreams. Perhaps it ceases to exist when we are not there' (Van Andel 1978: 155).

Returning to the surface removes him from unearthliness yet it keeps reappearing to him. As *Lulu* returns to port, he wonders if he should have steered clear of the whole expedition:

> And yet, the seafloor is so beautiful, so out-of-this-world beautiful. The misty, grandiose, mysterious landscape of craggy black and snowy, pillowy white set in the foreground with brilliantly lit small, sharp, and perfect vignettes of rock, coral,

and sponge, is unforgettable and I cannot do justice to it. I wish I could draw, it would be so superior to photography. It is an exceptional privilege to have seen this.

(Van Andel 1978: 156)

Van Andel describes himself as nostalgic to return: 'so out-of-this-world beautiful' makes unearthly here a fusion of memory, aesthetics and longing. In his first evocation of unearthliness, light and dark catalyse a ghostly aesthetic in which insubstantiality unsettles human powers. In his second unearthly moment, visuality is vivid – what people mean by etched on the memory, with etching somewhere between hand drawing and photography. It is also reattached to earthliness through the sea bed, a monochrome terrestriality whose beauty accompanies a grandiose sublime.

In a diary of 1994, James Hamilton-Paterson offers a comparable line of thinking. He was then a footloose author on the high seas with treasure-seekers, so his book, *Three Miles Down* (1998), is a romance of sorts. It is also a contribution to the footsteps genre of biography, following Beebe to the depths. In this domain '"The sea" means nothing here'. At 4938 metres, he writes 'Neither does it feel like an "abyss" or the bottom of anything; it feels like a planet taking place in the head' (1998: 210). Where Beebe and Barton dangled in a vulnerable bathysphere, Hamilton-Paterson feels so safely ensconced in a Russian *Mir* submersible that he doesn't think about death. Back on board the support ship, he writes instead of a primordial place best described in terms of time:

Where I have just returned from is wonderful beyond anything I have seen before, and partly because it is so spectacularly ungodded, too remote to be anthropomorphised. This is why I can't assign a time to it but am tempted to borrow the naturalist Philip Gosse's term *prochronic* for the 'pre-time' that existed before the Creation story in Genesis. It was so alien and peaceful as to make one profoundly calm. Untouched, unfashionable. Here were no loveable cetaceans for people to have mystical blurts over. In its salutary insistence on the primordial nothingness which is the real groundswell beneath all our lives it was notably benign and reassuring. There was nothing to fear, nothing that would not return a level gaze: something nearly indistinguishable from affection.

(Hamilton-Paterson 1998: 216)

Transfigured by the experience, 'in no describable way', Hamilton-Paterson finds in the deep ocean a psychological landscape, which becomes a psychoanalytic one. Three miles down he remembers names of people from childhood, people whom he has not thought about for years. Back in his ship bunk, he wonders why. 'I have been moving through a bath of solvent which has thinned away crusts and membranes which had built up around certain memories. I don't understand why this should have happened' (Hamilton-Paterson 1998: 217). It's a brilliant image, suggesting memories are archaeological relics. The psychologists' 1960 study of the effects of isolation reported some remarkable instances of memory-sharpening (Zubek 1960: 239), featuring clear recall of long-forgotten names and faces. In the days that follow, Hamilton-Paterson muses on the experience: 'This lost and peaceable place is not just prochronic but pro*photic*, pre-light', a darkness which was 'the heart of a slow timeless egg undergoing a Darwinian process of germination', one that can be repeated after humans have gone from the planet. But again philosophical reflections give way to a dreamscape of emotion. Deep sea creatures 'are at least open to that dissolved benignity drifting everywhere, in and out of cells, through the pores in the sediment, in brains and palps and flagellae.' Human observers are 'nobodies down there, and nothing. ... And yet they did sense the benignity of which they were a part. They did see the hidden wellspring of all planetary life' (Hamilton-Paterson 1998: 226-7).

To be benign is to be kindly, mild. To be benighted is to be overtaken by the darkness of the night. In the dark, though with strange lights, far from home, Hamilton-Paterson feels not panic or threat but secure. Benignity, 'the benignity of which they were a part', is a word that was used of things. *OED* gives an instance, planetary, quoting Alexander Pope in 1724 referring in a letter to 'A Star that ... is all Benignity, all gentle and beneficial influence.' Hamilton-Paterson's exceptional isolation from his kind appears also as distance from himself. He makes a strange switch of pronouns in his diary. His entry (23 February 1995) is sparing with first person; it ends 'It is not something they will forget' (Hamilton-Paterson 1998: 227).

Unearthliness finds a new vocabulary in the deep ocean. Writers evoke planetary space and infinite time, as you might well expect. Descent to great depth piles on a sense of time, 'years melting into centuries, and centuries into ages of geologic time', in Rachel Carson's words (1937: 324). The enormity of this time is beyond our grasp, argues Linda Williams: 'an ocean poetic of deep time suggests an evolutionary *longue durée* that, just as with cosmological time, is not only permanently beyond human control or management, but has an ontological status that cannot even be fully conceived by the human mind' (2019: 176). Yet the eternal darkness, Ballard's phrase, also evokes deep emotion and a mysterious and barely fathomable inner space, in which memory – such a crucial part of life writing! – becomes the element through which humans, species and oceans connect. Immediately after alluding to spaceship travel, James Cameron invokes metaphysics: deep ultramarine twilight is 'a hue that not only suggests the ocean's vast scale but beckons the mind to a transcendent state – a sense of cosmic unity with the ocean, with ancient time and the history of life, back to the first organisms' (McInnis 2005: 9-10). Beebe too turns to memory as a figure for 'this strange world. When once it has been seen, it will remain forever the most vivid memory in life, solely because of its cosmic chill and isolation, the eternal and absolute darkness and the indescribable beauty of its inhabitants' (1934: 175).

Ancient time is one way writers evoke profundity. They make parallels with space travel to evoke distance, mixed up with scales of time. Beebe described himself and Barton in the bathysphere 'where, sealed tight, two conscious human beings sat and peered into the abyssal darkness as we dangled in mid-water, isolated as a lost planet in outermost space' (1934: 134). Beebe often mentions the Swiss physicist, inventor and explorer Auguste Piccard: they are both explorers whose feats perversely diminish because of the cosmic scale in which they happen. 'Piccard in his aluminium car, like a mote of stardust high in air, could not have felt a smaller, less important atom in the universe than I in my tiny chamber dangling in midocean' (Beebe 1934: 161).

Piccard ascended to the stratosphere in an experimental balloon, reaching nearly ten miles high on 27 May 1931. For a while Barton's bathysphere was displayed beneath Piccard's gondola in the Hall of Science of the Century of Progress Exposition at Chicago. Piccard adapted the gondola's design into an aluminium cabin under a petroleum-filled float, becoming a bathyscaphe, FNRS 2, which made successful, untethered deep descents. In 1953, Piccard and his son Jacques took a bathyscaphe down to 3150 metres.

The early history of balloons shows that aeronauts occupied a curious position as daring heroes who pushed human achievements upwards, and mortals vulnerable to natural forces, equipment failures and fatal accidents (Brant 2017). Bathysphere and bathyscaph occupants pushed downwards with similar tenacity and risk. In 1960, Jacques Piccard and US Navy Lieutenant Don Walsh dived down the Challenger Deep in a well-tested bathyscaph, the *Trieste*. 'The bathyscaph functions like a balloon in the sea, deriving its buoyancy from lighter-than-water gasoline instead of the balloon's lighter-than-air gas', wrote Piccard, reporting he and Walsh felt increasingly slow and heavy themselves: 'I feel as if these hundreds of gallons of water are passing into my veins' (Piccard 1960). At a record-breaking depth of 10,916 metres,

> slowly, surely, in the name of science and humanity, the *Trieste* took possession of the abyss, the last extreme on our earth that remained to be conquered. And to demonstrate well all the significance of this dive, nature would have it that the *Trieste* come down on the bottom a few feet from a fish, a true fish, joined in its unknown world by this monster of steel and gasoline and a powerful beam of light. Our fish was the instantaneous reply (after years of work!) to a question that thousands of oceanographers had been asking themselves for decades.

Yet despite their historic achievement, unearthliness would prevail:

> But once the bathyscaph has departed, the searchlights have disappeared, the water stirred by our passing has subsided, and the heat brought by our presence has dissipated, the immense liquid curtain will then close over this strange interlude: the sudden arrival of man in this cold, dark, mysterious world.

Piccard's invocation of a still, black world was one of the last: a new era of exploration by manned submersibles changed how the deep is perceived. Leading the discoveries was *Alvin*, a sturdy workhorse run by Woods Hole Oceanographic Institute. WHOI had run transects in the 1960s from Martha's Vineyard to Bermuda. 'Surprisingly, they showed the biodiversity of the fauna living in the perpetual midnight of deep waters was higher than in shallower regions of the transect' (Van Dover 1996: 3–4). Cindy Lee Van Dover was unusually well-qualified to explore this midnight: she was both a marine biologist and an *Alvin* pilot.

> It is a silent world. I have set the submersible on the seabed and systematically shut down all of the systems. We call it 'going dead boat'. Silence and darkness are immediate and ultimate, all-encompassing and pervasive. I feel the silence more

than hear it; it feels cold, oppressive, alien. My voice in the silence sounds thin and
nervous, insignificant.

(1996: 50)

Van Dover was alert to the physical environment and its metaphysical effects.

The seafloor can be surprisingly rich in visual textures. Where the ocean crust
is young, lava flows dominate the landscape. The lavas pool and ripple and swirl
in frozen motion. Pillows of lava with elephant-hide skins drape the slopes of
submarine mountains like icing run down the side of a cake. Stilled lavas are torn,
ripped apart, prelude and aftermath of the violent birth of new seafloor. ... In my
audio record of the dive, I run out of adjectives to describe the subtle variations in
the lava morphologies.

(1996: 47, 96)

After two hours, they reached bottom at 3000 metres. 'Only the surface of the moon
seems as remote and desolate a destination' (1996: 94-5). Allusions to space compare
the deep's estrangeness, not its possible conquest. Van Dover observes that until the
1970s we knew almost nothing of this world:

We landed a man on the moon nearly a decade before we ever saw the heat of our
own ocean's crust exhaled through black smokers. Our forays into the deep sea
may seem Lilliputian when compared with the space exploration program, and by
NASA standards the resources of oceanographers are meagre.

(1996: 172)

The deep ocean, for Van Dover, suffered from lack of glamour. 'It has none of the
enviropolitical cachet of an Amazonian rain forest, Alaskan tundra, or Antarctic
ice shelf' (1996: 9). The discovery of epicentres of life, with startling new creatures
living in unimaginable ways, made some difference: hydrothermal vents and black
smokers made headlines and compelling footage when they started to be identified in
the 1970s. That they proved to be features which periodically collapse or die off, but
renew elsewhere, added to perception of the deep as a live place of surprises: 'in the
1990s, one group of researchers saw a chimney grow from zero to sixteen feet tall in
less than a year' (Ballard 2000: 203). Discoveries of cold seeps with chemosynthetic
organisms added to the excitement. Such habitats may not be only found on Earth: 'the
vent mania has even influenced space exploration' (Ballard 2000: 213), because places
in space, especially the moons of Jupiter and Saturn, hold similar conditions for life in
their variously frozen oceans.

In the deep, geologists could track featureless space to find these extraordinary
features, and biologists could celebrate the differences between vent communities.
Oceanography acquired an 'exclusive deep-sea submersible club that includes Russia's
Mirs, France's *Nautile*, China's *Sea Dragon*, Japan's *Shinkai*, and America's *Alvin*'
(MacInness 2012). Submersible design benefited from new materials like titanium,
fibreglass and crushed foam; there were crossovers with the space industry in terms

of ideas, people and equipment, especially low-light cameras. Yet the vulnerability of submersibles, the risk to their occupants and the expense of their support ships led to a growing view that Remote Operated Vehicles could do the job just as well. Submersibles brought up samples and pictures; ROVs could do that too, thanks to prosthetic hands and eyes, sensitive grabbers and sophisticated cameras. Why risk people's lives? Among those who had dived to the deep, some argued passionately for the value of human presence, with a spiritualist emphasis on its transfigurative effects. 'The experience of visiting these strange oases permanently changed many of us' (Ballard 2000: 185). On the other hand, new machines increased efficiency. 'Although more mobile than a bathyscaph, on a typical dive *Alvin* still travelled much farther vertically (from surface to bottom and back) than horizontally across the seafloor' (Ballard 2000: 219). ROVs extended possible time in the deeps, which was critical as funding contracted. The dream of a 'wet NASA' faded when get-rich-quick visions of exploiting oil and mineral resources were thwarted by operational difficulties. In 1984, Robert Ballard tried out *Argo*, an instrument-loaded camera sled with no passenger sphere, tethered to a winch on ship. It transmitted images in real time to the surface. 'In effect, he [the pilot] flew with a computer as co-pilot' (Ballard 2000: 222). Then came AUVs, or autonomous underwater vehicles, robots that require no human input while underwater, can be managed from ship or shore by a simple computer and can store data (rather than transmit in real time). They can stay underwater for extended periods. 'They are also scalable, or modular, meaning that scientists can choose which sensors to attach to them depending on their research objectives' (NOAA 2020). Marine geoscience finds them most useful. 'They have revolutionised our ability to image the seafloor, providing higher resolution seafloor mapping data than can be achieved from surface vessels, particularly in deep water' (Wynn 2014: abstract). They can be put to work on specific tasks. A university in Queensland developed an AUV, COTS-bot, for use on the Great Barrier Reef, tracking invasive crown-of-thorns starfish and injecting them with lethal salts. Its smaller and lighter successor, RangerBot, is 'a novel completely vision-based robotic tool that has been developed to provide coral reef managers, researchers and community groups extra "hands and eyes" in the water to help monitor and manage various threats on the Great Barrier Reef' (QUT n.d.).

Hands and eyes: by building human senses into machines, 'many researchers who could not otherwise join a deep-sea expedition can now virtually "come aboard" anytime, from almost anywhere on shore, to observe, make measurements, collect data, and conduct real-time experiments' (Ballard 2000: 309). Robert Ballard argues this expansion of constituency is democratizing. He demonstrated its potential in the *Jason Project* (1989), using *Jason* and *Hugo*, AUVs, to broadcast to a virtual community, aiming to reach 250,000 students over two weeks. The first phase went to twelve museums who built replicas of the control console so that viewers could see as if they were the operator. It was a model instance of telepresence, described enthusiastically by Ballard: 'a mind detaches itself from the body's restrictions and enters the abyss with ease, and with lightning-quick fiber optic nerves' (2000: 311). If you untether the mind, what is it free to do, and freed from? Telepresence has not persuaded everybody. Sylvia Earle argues 'there is no completely satisfactory substitute for *being* there. To really decipher the nature of this unique part of the planet, direct access, with human eyes and brains as well as instruments is essential' (1995: 49). One thing missing from telepresence is metaphysics. A robot can convey images and sounds, but it has nothing philosophical to say. It serves the sciences, with no interest in reflecting on humanity. Whereas deep-diving humans feel the power of unearthliness to untether minds, a robot has no sense of benignity, nor of coming close, even remotely, to the wellsprings of life.

WORDING THE WEIRD

The word 'strange' is deep-spread in life writings about the deep ocean. Linking environment and observer in uncertain ways, it is sometimes used of marine beings. But the word most commonly used for organisms is 'weird'. Even ichthyological expert Beebe uses it, of a female anglerfish (1934: 173). Theorizing the weird and eerie, Mark Fisher argues

> the weird is a particular kind of perturbation. It involves a sensation of *wrongness*: a weird entity or object is so strange that it makes us feel that it should not exist, or at least it should not exist here. Yet if an entity or object *is* here, then the categories which we have up until now used to make sense of the world cannot be valid. The weird thing is not wrong, after all: it is our conceptions that must be inadequate.'
>
> (Fisher 2016: 5)

Descents have mythic and literary prototypes, like going to underworlds or hell, yet the deep ocean confounded the imagination. It sharpened memory, it stretched and folded scales of time, it untethered minds. That was all strange. 'Worlds may be entirely foreign to ours, both in terms of location and even in terms of the physical laws which govern them, without being weird. It is the irruption into this world of something from outside which is the marker of the weird' (Fisher 2016: 7). What's weird about the deep ocean world is that it stays where it is, and we irrupt into it. Hence some difference between 'strange' and 'weird' in deep ocean usage: 'strange' is the effect of moving between two worlds, so far apart literally and imaginatively; 'weird' is the appearance in our world – especially a media world – of something not part of it. Fisher stresses that weird needn't be unpleasant – surrealism can make it pleasurable, for instance, in breaking up conventions. 'The form that is perhaps most appropriate to the weird is montage – the conjoining of *two or more things which do not belong together*' (Fisher 2016: 9; his italics).

Weird creatures are partly weird because they embody distortions and dislocations: gloopy-looking bodies, outsize teeth, seemingly formless shapes, departures from known and familiar shapes. Weird fish irrupt into our categories of body form and function. Weird, a handily short word for headlines, is shorthand for 'this upsets what we think we know.' A lovely instance is described by the naturalist Alfred Russel Wallace, who travelled to the Aru Islands, near what is now West Papua. He lived at Wanumbai, among the Aru people. They found him really strange. 'My very writing materials and books are to them weird things' (Wallace 1869: 2.247). He asked the

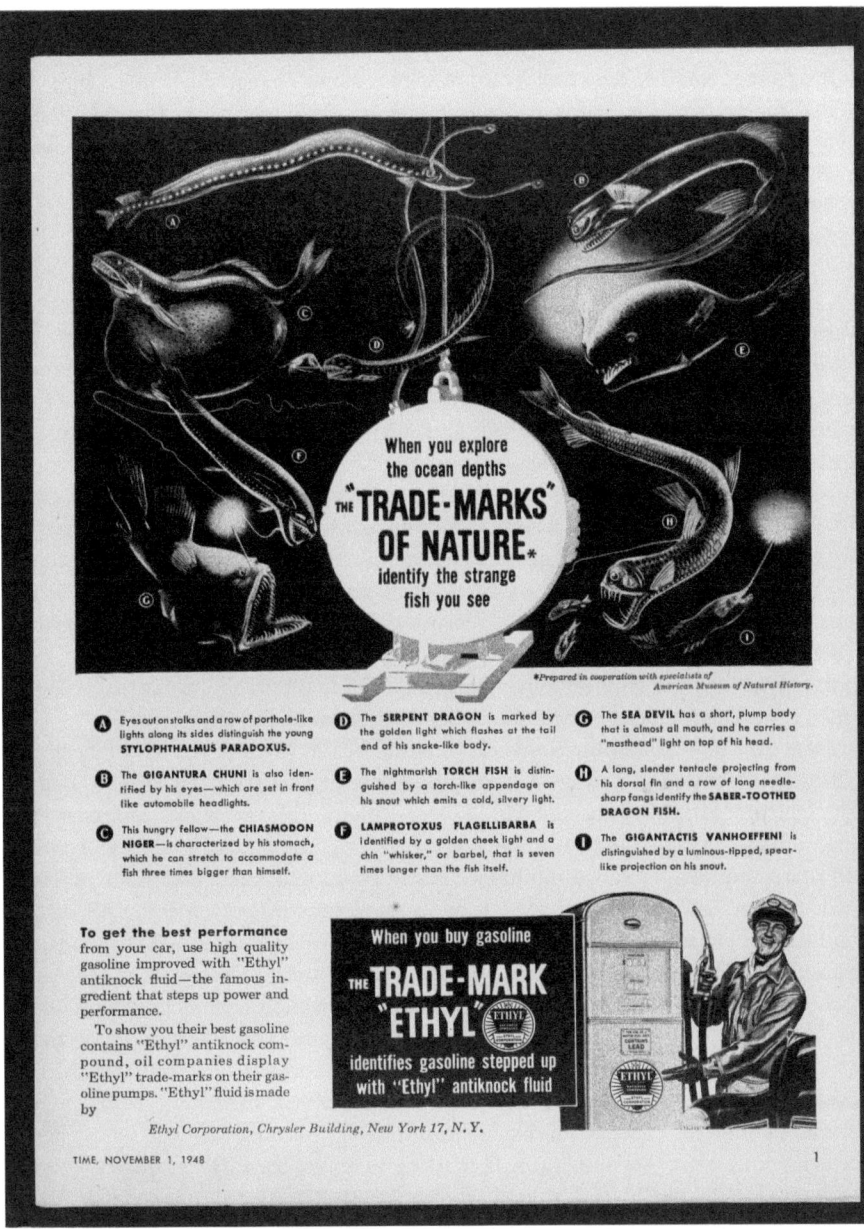

Figure 22 'Two or more things which do not belong to each other': trade marks and nature. Advertisement, *TIME* magazine, 1 November 1948. Private collection. The additive marketed here, tetraethyllead, was officially banned worldwide in 2011. It causes lead poisoning.

Aru strange questions, like where did they come from? Weirdest of all was his word 'England', which they suspected he made up. One elder was indignant:

> 'Ung-lung!' said he, 'who ever heard of such a name? – ang-lang – anger-lang – that can't be the name of your country; you are playing with us.' Then he tried to give a convincing illustration. 'My country is Wanumbai – anybody can say Wanumbai. I'm an "orang-Wanumbai;" but, N-glung! who ever heard of such a name? Do tell us the real name of your country, and then when you are gone we shall know how to talk about you.'
>
> (Wallace 1869: 2.247–8)

Weird is mutable: what was weird can become accepted as normal; conversely, a known entity can be stretched into weird in order to attract new audiences. Woods Hole Oceanographic Institute sells some deep-ocean themed merchandise with the tagline 'Keep It Weird': it begs the question why, and for whom? Fisher's discussion of weird is interested in it as a process and an effect; in the deep ocean, that process and effect apply twofold, to the environment and its inhabitants. Fisher analyses how moving between worlds, for instance in Dunsany's fiction, acquires weirdness. In modernist fiction that is frequently located in doors. The porthole of a submersible is a comparable portal. Occasionally a deep ocean diver wonders if humans look weird. Thus Sylvia Earle: 'I mused about the reception members of my species might give to a giant yellow creature of unknown origin with flashing lights whirling down from above, clutching a wiggling, crablike thing. But I left that thought for future review ...' (1995: 118). The future, it turned out, prefers weirdness to empathy.

Monterey Bay Aquarium Research Institute has a video series about deep sea marine beings, titled 'Weird and Wonderful.' It includes *Anoplogaster cornuta*, spotted just eight times in thirty years of MBARI expeditions. This episode's strapline is 'The fangtooth fish has a face only a mother could love' (MBARI 2020). Bristling with spines and sharp-toothed, the fangtooth has a beautiful lateral line, like a string of polished beads pressed into its side. Because it looks dangerous it is given some respect. In contrast, the blobfish *Psychrolutes marcidus* which lives deep around Australia elicits strange affections. It was voted the 'World's Ugliest Animal', based on photographs of decompressed specimens. The Ugly Animal Preservation Society adopted it as its mascot in 2013. It serves ugliness as an aesthetic countering cuteness, an aesthetic that awards charisma to species like pandas, whales, polar bears. The Smithsonian pointed out that in its natural habitat the blobfish is a handsome being; at the surface, its muscles collapse – it has no swimbladder to burst. They go white, hence the gelatinous mass (Schultz 2013). Discussing ugliness, Steve Heller quotes Voltaire thinking empathetically: 'Ask a toad what is beauty ... He will answer that it is a female with two great round eyes coming out of her little head, a large flat mouth, a yellow belly and a brown back' (Voltaire, *Philosophical Dictionary*, 1794; Heller 1993). But anthropomorphism prevailed: a media-promoted specimen caught in a joint Australian–New Zealand expedition became known (though its sex was never checked) as Mr. Blobby. Publicity led to soft toys, memes, smartphone games:

A photograph snapped aboard ship lit up on social media and transformed this squidgy bottom feeder into an aquatic Grumpy Cat, with devoted followers on Facebook, Instagram, Twitter and Tumblr ….To the baby boomers, a generation once young and idealistic and which felt largely unappreciated, the baby harp seal and its huge pleading eyes symbolized a certain level of ecological awareness. With the aging of those innocents, the blobfish – inert, indolent, in a state of perpetual maritime melancholy – may be the new face of our relationship with nature, the planet, the future. Mr. Blobby is a fish for a world gone soft in the head.

(Lidz 2015)

Ugly-cute splits weird into marketable gloop. Like 'weird and wonderful', these hybrid emotions combine recoil and attraction without entirely reconciling them.

Most of the features tagged as fearsome in deep-sea creatures turn out to be entirely explicable as adaptations – large fangs, for instance, stop prey escaping, which is helpful in a world of scarce opportunities. Making the most of those opportunities explains why many deep sea species have expandable jaws and stomachs to accommodate any passing meal. 'As contrasted with life at the surface, in which the primary requirements for prey capture are strength and speed, and where it helps the predator to be larger than its prey, feeding in the depths is often carried out according to a completely different set of rules' (Ellis 1996: 205). Some abilities are surprising: the gulper eel can distend its mouth membranes like an umbrella and swell its body to match; then, with a wriggle, return to its normal size, swimming along unobtrusively like a superhero in a tracksuit (BBC 2018).

One species especially upset expectations: tube worms. In 1975, diving down the Galápagos Rift in *Alvin*,

[geochemist Jack] Corliss was looking at clams – giant specimens, measuring a foot or more in length. And that was only the beginning. He and van Andel stared in amazement as shrimp, crabs, fish, and small lobster-like creatures passed their viewports. Corliss recognized a pale anemone. He could not identify the weird stuff growing on the bottom, like dandelions, or the wormy stuff attached to rocks.

(Ballard 2000: 171)

Surprised already by finding patches of warm water, the scientists moved on from weird and wormy stuff to another site, which they named the Garden of Eden. Here, clustered round boiling sulfuric vents, were thickets of white tubes with red-feathered plumes on top – tube worms.

With no eyes, no mouth or any other obvious organs for ingesting food or secreting waste, and no means of locomotion, it was no worm, snake, or eel but no plant either – the strangest creature we had ever seen …. We had discovered a new realm of life. … We felt as if we had glimpsed unknown, alien life on a new world, or at least an alternate version of life on our own.

(Ballard 2000: 173)

Van Dover echoed the otherworld trope. 'All of the ecological questions were undefined. For those of us lucky enough to be involved in this research, it is like discovering life on another planet' (1996: 82). Yet she thought beyond the idea of alien: 'giant tubeworms are 6-foot-long expletives, shouts of brilliance, startling in their vivid simplicity and exposure. Crimson plumes bloom atop long white tubes that emerge from cracks in glossy black lava.' She calls them 'a chorus of tubeworms' (1996: 76-7). The worms became poster species, *Riftia pachyptila*, heading up a new phylum, Vestimentifera, named for their collar-like arrangement at the tube's top (the phylum, along with that of pogonophores, is now known as the family Siboglinidae). The tubeworms have no gut and no anus. But, as Coleen Cavenaugh discovered, they have an organ, the trophosome. It has cells filled with bacteria that use chemosynthesis to supply the worm with nutrition. Bit by bit the weird was translated into intelligibility. Van Dover argued that despite the charisma of hydrothermal worms, bivalves and shrimps, 'the real diversity of life at vents is found among the smaller invertebrates' (1996: 62). Different species of siphonostomes, for instance, tiny parasitic copepods, infested different species. A red copepod lived among fluffy giant filamentous bacteria, 'sprinkled like paprika over the white surface of the mats' (Van Dover 1996: 63). That was woolly stuff explained. 'Dandelions' turned out to be jellyfish attached by filaments to rocks (Ballard 2000: 184; footage and more at France 2017). Gradually it was understood that there are regional differences in vent communities, and that vents themselves come and go. The weird has its own patterns.

It may be that in spite of submersible lights, we want to be afraid of the dark. Or that the glimpsing power of light in deep waters is too uncertain to banish all fears. The species described as monsters are small – most are less than a hand's length, around seven inches – yet in photographs and close-up film they fill frames, menacing with presence. Making sharp teeth seem huge gets round the challenge that in the deep, 'the scale of life can be minute, generally measured in millimetre- and centimetre-dimensioned, obscure animals that delight the scientist but do little to titillate the general public' (Van Dover 1996: 172). A confrontational aesthetic of the monstrous is a human ploy: it stages what Timothy Morton calls 'the weirdness of seeing on different scales at once' (2013: 91). Close up, vastly deep, only-just-glimpsed yet ancient life forms confuse our categories. Life writers can explain where strange species fit, taxonomically, but taxonomic placing does not easily resolve category shock.

> Almost every time a submersible or a drop-camera enters the deep-sea environment, it comes back with something new. It has left normally hard-nosed scientists lost for words. They have found mounds of 'strange little spheres', 'feathery wispy things' and 'green stringy things', as well as jelly-like blobs that could only be classified as 'animals' but little else. All these creatures were totally unknown, not only new species, but entirely new forms of life.
>
> (Honeyborne and Brownlow 2017: 272)

These scientists revert to child-like practices of descriptive naming. 'The structure of our language is relentless in forcing upon us "thing" conceptions. In English, we can transform any process or relationship into a "thing" by the simple expedient of naming "it" into a noun' (Postman and Weingartner 1975: abstract). Marine being subjects for life writers have to escape this linguistic box before their lives can be better understood.

Regular description of marine being 'things' as alien preserves their strangeness. Here 'alien' isn't so much about importing otherness of being from science fiction, which anyway often borrowed from the deep: thus H. G. Wells's Martians in *The War of the Worlds* (1898) have big eyes and a blobby mouth hung round with tentacles. Rather, 'alien' is code for recognizing another world – in this one! – with strange beings. The much-used phrase 'denizens of the deep' – denizen is rarely used in any other context – gestures to occupational rights. A denizen (the word dates from 1488, according to *OED*) is a person who dwells within a country, as opposed to foreigners. So denizens indicate life forms that inhabit the deep, as opposed to humans who can only visit. Denizen recognizes a fit between animal and place. If habitat assumes a place supportive of an animal's existence (by providing food and shelter), denizen delicately implies the animal's existence in a place is right. It stops short of the rights inherent in being a citizen, but it implies rightfulness of abode.

> As another example of the mysterious nature of the deepwater octopods, consider *Vampyroteuthis infernalis*, whose name can be translated as 'vampire squid from hell.' About eight inches long, this deepwater denizen is among the most fascinating animals on earth. It was first identified in 1903 by Carl Chun, a German teuthologist who identified it as an octopus because it had – he thought – eight arms. Then another thin pair of arms was discovered, tucked into two pockets outside the web that connects the eight arms. Taxonomically speaking, it hovers between octopus and squid in its own order, the Vampyromorpha.
>
> (Ellis 1996: 177)

The vampire squid also has bioluminescent light organs at the tip of each arm. From these it can release a sticky luminous fluid, sweeping its arms up to make a glowing cloud, confusing predators (Robison et al. 2003: 105). Despite its fearful name, it feeds on marine snow, grazing gently.

A sexed-up version of the vampire squid starred in a teasing treatise by philosophers Vilém Flusser and Louis Bec, who used it as a contorted metaphor for human constructs, particularly media culture (Flusser and Bec 2012). Reviewers saw through the human-centredness to reflect less abstrusely on species' divide. Tied to the provocation of its hellish name, exceeding even William Broad's description of anglerfish as ghoulish, demonic, nightmarish, its fanciful signifier points to human lack of understanding. In Ruth Hsu's reading,

> It is a creature of hell, a hell – Flusser shows us – of our own making: it resists our flattery; it resists our attempts to possess it through knowing it; it unapologetically lives its "primitive" and elemental everyday, unconcerned with homo sapiens' evolutionary innovations called culture and civilization; it is unconcerned with our labels and, so, is free from our attempts to colonize it in a variety of disciplinary regimes. The vampire squid from hell is our other because we have embedded our deepest fears in this figuration. Our deepest fears have to do with not being

supremely unique among animals and, in terms of western humanism, the fear is that western ontology is not the apex of homo sapiens civilizations.

(Hsu 2020: 5, 8)

But then, as Colin Dickey points out, 'the failure of [Flusser's] promise to truly understand the vampire squid's being-in-the-world', and instead to exploit it as a provocative figure, makes his treatise all about humans – and what advance is that? (Dickey 2012).

The vampire squid's problematic name is a high-end instance of language that projects human categories into the deeps. Humbler, more common words show deep ocean vocabularies getting stuck too. In 1954 Georges Houot dived with Pierre Willm in the bathscaphe FRNS III, reaching 4050 metres off Dakar. Houot grumbled that water made opaque by plankton was always described as soup: 'I'm getting sick of all this talk about soup. I admit that I once used this unfortunate metaphor. But we've had enough of it. Say plankton or whatever you like – but not "soup", and not *"bouillabaisse"* like that local journalist who wanted to go one better than his colleagues from Paris' (Houot and Willm 1955: 213). In describing the slow fall of particles of organic detritus from ocean surface to seafloor, Houot remembered Rachel Carson's phrase 'long snowfall'. The term 'marine snow', coined by Beebe, became standard. Edith Widder admired its exactness, but wished for more nuance: 'if you look closer, you notice differences – single flecks, white fluffy bits, messy clumps. The Inuit supposedly have more than fifty words to describe the various forms of snow, and marine snow may be deserving of similar linguistic largesse' (2021: 227). With media invested in the weird and exclamatory, and science invested in the biological explanatory, linguistic largesse is likeliest to be found in life writing by those who have been to the deep ocean. As James Hamilton-Paterson puts it, 'It is a magnificently alien world which cannot be comprehended by terrestrial instincts alone. It is difficult to recognise a universe from inside another' (1987: 63). Its strangeness invites something other than sensory and species chauvinism – like recognition of its unearthly magnificence.

10

Visualities

Life writing encompasses visual materials and the means to theorize them (Dow Adams 2000; Schmitt 2024). In this chapter I think about visualities – what photographer David Doubilet has called 'a visual voice' (1999: n.p.). From the first live underwater footage, shot in 1916 by John Williamson and described in his memoir *Twenty Years Under the Sea* (1935), to sharkcam livestreaming, visual depiction shares with words the challenge of representing the oceans. 'The underwater studio is a challenging environment with changing visibility, currents that can gust like underwater hurricanes, and an aquatic kingdom of shy, elusive marine life that would prefer to remain anonymous and undocumented' (Doubilet 2019). Steve Shapin reminds us that 'All pictures, photographs included, are a hybrid of the things they represent, the conventions used to represent them, the purposes for which the pictures are meant, and the schema used to interpret them. No picture maps directly onto reality' (2016: 37). What Shapin terms the 'sticky-visual', or the enduring power of some images (2016: 35) helps define the 'sticky-literary': think of the cover image of *Jaws*, which returned a language of monsters to ocean poetics. Illustrated texts draw our attention to ways of seeing: I discuss instances in black and white, and split-shot photography. Many underwater life writings have photographic inserts in which divers and marine beings acquire configurations that differ from their role in the texts. I have discussed inserts elsewhere (Brant 2024); here I explore relations between image and text via the BBC's flagship series *The Blue Planet* (2001) and *Blue Planet II* (2017), international successes in multimedia and print – the first episode of *Blue Planet II* was seen by 14.1 million people. Besides the 'book of the series', the *Blue Planet* projects saw the publication of a range of memoirs by camera operators and others involved in production. 'Image-makers' is a convenient portmanteau term. I link films and texts through the 'making-of' documentary, now a familiar finale to each episode in the television series, and explore how the written – and illustrated – accounts by image-makers present 'making-of' through life writing. Spectacle is usually invoked as the dominant televisual frame for nature documentaries but exploring how image-makers' memoirs construct 'behind-the-scenes', I propose closeness as an alternative frame for encounters.

BLACK AND WHITE: TONALITIES

Given the oceans' dazzling spectrum of colours, it may seem strange that some life-writing image-makers choose to represent marine subjects through black and white. In this section I discuss a selection of practitioners to explain the attraction. The first is wood-engraver Robert Gibbings (1889–1958; see https://www.robertgibbings.org) who was an enthusiastic helmet diver and who wrote two thoughtful and delightful accounts of life above and below water in Polynesia. The second are photographers Christian Vizl and David Doubilet (both have images viewable online). Although wood engraving and black-and-white photography are rarely considered together, both apply what Timothy Dow Adams described (2000) as 'light writing', establishing photography as a form of life writing. Since Dow Adams' now-classic book, there has been considerable analysis of the place of photography in life writing, extending to image-making in multimedia forms (Schmitt 2024).

The Blue Angels of Gibbings' *Blue Angels and Whales* (1938, 2nd edition 1946) are small reef fish. 'The blue angel can appear in any dress from pale cerulean to deep cobalt blue, accentuating or diminishing at will' (Gibbings 1946: 100). Yet Gibbings is more fascinated by light than by colour. 'Perhaps the most interesting discovery concerned a parrot fish who did not change his actual colours at all, but whose colours appeared entirely different according to the light in which he was seen' (1946: 102). 'In which he was seen': though no human is grammatically present, Gibbings' subtitle, 'A Record of Personal Experiences Below and Above Water', is carefully authenticating. Almost every page has an illustration in view: nineteen in cerulean blue (a bluey-green tone) and forty-eight in black. Reproduced from the author's original drawings, those made with pencil on xylonite drawing board have a soft tone that nonetheless allows for distinct outlines. Gibbings was an outstanding wood-engraver – he co-founded the Society of Wood Engravers in 1920 and ran the Golden Cockerell Press. A genial and humorous traveller, he was an attentive observer of the natural world including riverbanks of the Thames where he lived. Too amiable to be a rogue, he left domestic ties – a long-suffering wife and two daughters – to enjoy the open road and its freedoms. His first trip to Tahiti in 1929 came about after a complaint to his publishers: 'Next time you give me a job, for God's sake send me to the South Seas. I'm sick of English fogs' (Empson 1961: 53). He returned in 1945 to write what became *Over the Reefs* (1948), sympathetically people-focused. Patience Empson (his third and last wife) explains the attraction: 'Certainly among the Polynesian people Robert Gibbings found himself at home. Particularly in Samoa, he sensed a kinship with his own people of Ireland – the simple unhurried way of life, the gaiety and courtesy, the delight in words and story-telling' (1961: 55).

Despite the convivial appeal of island life, Gibbings spent serious time underwater, diving in a helmet. His main aim was to draw fish. 'They appeared to me more gorgeous than anything I had seen before, their shapes, their markings, and their colours seeming to vie with one another as to which could be the most bizarre' (1946: 7). He studied the changeability of colour underwater – how fish conspicuous in the shallows merged into deeper water, and how camouflage used complementarity. 'It seems, at first thought, impossible that emerald-green fish should find adequate cover among the petals of pink coral, but then emerald-green is the complementary colour of that particular shade of pink, and the fish are thereby absorbed into its shadows' (Gibbings 1946: 96). Why so much care when his output was not in colour? In Tahiti he drew fish not wanted in the kitchen:

> though in many cases I made attempts to record the colours in actual pigment, I find that more often than not my note-book has black-and-white sketches followed by notes which give but faint hints of the ever startling colouring. There were chevrons on the head, circular patches near the tail, parallel bars from head to tail, herring-bone patterns across the belly ...
>
> (1946: 8-9)

Gibbings sees through colours with a wood engraver's eye to notice shapes. His figure-ground relationships, an important principle in Gestalt art theory, take on an interplay that is more visible in contrasting black and white.

Examining live flying fish to see how their fins worked, he noted they had seemingly little up and down capacity but a curvature best for quick rise, short flight and gliding. Gibbings was not just studying a model here: he spent hours observing and drawing underwater, surrounded by unafraid fish. Their different sensorium intrigued him, differentness he images in fleeting lines, subtle positioning and complex tonalities. He did not ignore all visual conventions, sometimes showing fish with fins erect and spines ready though he recognized that was not normal fish body language (1946: 53). 'And there is always the weed, some of which covers the dead coral with the richest moss, while other forms wave in the ocean swells like banners in the wind. Drawing can but hint at the shapes. Nothing can express the movement' (1946: 59-60).

'The Lost Anchor' is a dense composition of fish movement and reef shapes. When Gibbings engraved it, he was not thinking of stories:

> My only thoughts at the time were of the contrast between the rigid metal and the free growing forms of the coral. I liked the violence of the hammered iron as opposed to the fragile composites of the reef. I saw too the helpless immobility of this dead weight while all around it played a thousand sprightly gaily coloured fish.
>
> (Gibbings 1936)

He maintained there should be no law in wood engraving about whether white on black is better than black on white – it depends on your subject, though he recommended cultivating the brilliance and spontaneity of the white line which can be seen, differently angled, in 'The Lost Anchor' (1936). That engraving has intense energy of movement – even the brain coral in the bottom left corner has lively lines. It also has – centre left – a Moorish Idol (*Zanclus cornutus*), then common in Tahiti, whose black- and- white bands 'appear as annular or semicircular patterns almost identical with the flicker of light on the surface' (Gibbings 1946: 97). Its flowing filament looks like a wavelet:

Figure 23 Robert Gibbings, 'The Lost Anchor' (1936). Wood engraving, 8 × 9½ inches. Published by the Woodcut Society, Kansas City, Missouri. Private collection.

if ever I want to re-create for myself a vision of the strange flickering light which penetrates those waters I think of the movements of this fish, just as when I want to visualize those same movements I remember the fluttering light transmitted through the scalloped surface of the lagoon.

(Gibbings 1946: 97)

Movement of light and fish represent each other in memory: both are synecdoches of underwater visuality, given form and liveliness in Gibbings' engraved life writing.

In 'The Lost Anchor', Gibbings' white lines gesture to striated or blocked space, as Deleuze and Guattari defined it (1988). But the fishes move so sinuously they evoke open space, three-dimensional freedom compared to the flatness of a two-dimensional page. The white lines – bars of light? Current? – manifest movement; the anchor, solidly occupying the central axis, does not block space but interacts with it by reflecting shiny light, while the weed makes background into jigsaw pieces. 'The Lost Anchor' suggests a story in its title – who, when, where was it lost? But story disappears in the engraving, or turns into a visually told scene of fish – I count nineteen – milling around the iron thing that has thudded into their world. Story is irrelevant compared to coexistence.

Ocean photographers are also drawn to black and white. Ernest H. Brooks II, known as Ernie Brooks, has been called the Ansel Adams of underwater photography, especially for his collection *Silver Seas* (2003). Brooks admired Hans Hass, worked with Cousteau and taught a new generation of underwater photographers, including David Doubilet and Christian Vizl, about the beauty of black and white. 'The delicate shades that gray creates have the ability to capture a sense of wonderment or freeze action in the contrasts between highlight and shadows. This grace, beauty and simplicity creates perfection and a lasting impression on the viewer' (Vizl 2020). Writing about Vizl's images, Doubilet argues that

a great underwater image is about many things. First, a photograph is always about the light – how the light falls into the sea and how the photographer uses artificial light like a paintbrush. It is about composition, tension, and placement of blocks of light and shadow, all contained within the edges of a photographic frame. A picture is also about moment, gesture, and grace.

(Doubilet 2019: 61)

Black-and-white photography stresses tonality through greys, professionally understood through a scale of light to dark, often in twenty-one increments. Writing of Figure 24, Sylvia Earle points to Vizl's 'many subtle shades of silvery grays, stark whites, and sharply defined blacks … a rare intimacy is evoked in a misty, dreamlike atmosphere'. Darkroom art is required to shade tones to make stillness and movement fuse into an image of a moment – in Earle's description, 'a moment like two enormous manta rays arching and turning in a swirling ballet of elephantine grace, then parting, pausing, and coming together to barely touch their giant fins. In Vizl's image of the touch, the electricity is palpable' (2019: 16).

The stilled movement present in a photographic 'moment' can stretch. For both Doubilet and Vizl, sea lions are subjects of pure fluidity. 'Humans swim with individual

Figure 24 'Two giant mantas showing social behavior touching each other's wing tips. Revillagigedo Islands, Mexico'. Photo and caption courtesy of Christian Vizl.

movements, as if governed by primitive clockwork mechanisms. Sea lions, however, flow and shift with weightless grace' (Doubilet 1999). Mantas and stingrays embody fluid movement too, often imaged by Doubilet in a 'half and half' image combining above and below the waves. Otherwise known as split-shots or over-under shots, this double field is technically challenging because sky and water have different light valences, and the camera dome needs to have no droplets on it. Split-shots set up a coupling in which air and underwater can rhyme, contrast or play in changeable patterns. Thus Doubilet pairs stingrays and clouds: 'I remained the whole day, watching the light change and the stingrays fly across an endless stage of clear water, sand and shifting clouds – stingrays and clouds' (1999). Time passes but the moment becomes both fixed and endless in the photograph. I am unable to reproduce Doubilet's image, but one by Alex Mustard stages similar components, linked by ripples of light.

Philippe Diolé was fascinated by the border between air and water as a veil of opacity. Doubilet too is mesmerized by the underside of the sea's surface: 'It really is a looking-glass and it is hypnotic. Light goes through it, sparkling, shafting and moving. It is emotional ...' (Gourlay 1999). Neither smooth nor striated space, possibly both, the surface as veil invites us into the sea while reminding us we live elsewhere. The surface layer links air and water through light, tonality and movement.

Among underwater photographers, a common tune is conservation. Ocean photographers invariably assert their work is meant to inspire people to understand the ocean better and therefore protect it. 'With knowing comes caring', as Sylvia Earle puts it (2019: 19). Vizl's website declares 'my main purpose as a photographer is to create poetic images showing the incredible beauty of these animals knowing they

Figure 25 Split-shot: Three Stingrays (*Dasyatis americana*) swimming over sand in shallow water, The Sandbar, Grand Cayman, Cayman Islands, Caribbean Sea. Photo and caption by Alex Mustard. Image courtesy of Alex Mustard.

carry the power of changing our perception and spark the love and empathy that we all have inside' (Vizl, Christian. n.d.). Although both Doubilet and Vizl allude to 'stories' in their images, poetry and drama provide strong alternatives. Diving off the Izu peninsula near Mount Fuji, Doubilet chooses theatre as analogy for this underwater place. 'I can never escape from its dramatic Kabuki imagery: that of a clear simple stage where actors (fish) parade in resplendent robes: tora-moray eels, cherry blossom anthias, ghost pipefish, dragonettes. All these creatures play in the deep-sea drama of Japan' (Doubilet 1999). Colour can express that drama, but black and white enhance it through contrast and shadow. As photographer Guy Gagnon says of black and white, 'Stripped of its colours, a picture becomes purer, more powerful and even poetic' (2013: 80).

BLUE PLANETS IN WRITING

'Given the large number of viewers wildlife television programmes command today, and the claims associated with them, these documentaries are a key part of the apparatus through which our increasingly urbanised societies obtain their knowledge of the natural world', says Jean-Baptiste Gouyon (2019: 2). Flagship programmes such as the *Blue Planet* series led to a substantial body of life writing that offers 'behind the scenes' knowledge, including how knowledge of the natural world was obtained by film-makers. Memoirs by image-makers foreground adventures; their moments of peril and drama often occur at the intersection of human and animal lives. The genre usually discusses technical developments in film and photography – a big topic, which Margaret Cohen has expertly addressed (2022). What's relevant to the life writing is that image-makers adopt new technologies and reflect on changes. Significant ones include the change from 16-millimetre film (*Blue Planet*) to Ultra HD digital (*Blue Planet II*); smoother aerial filming, thanks to Cineflex heligimbal, a stabilization system for a helicopter-mounted camera, set in gyroscopes which separate it from a helicopter's movements (used first in *Planet Earth*, 2006); closer aerial filming thanks to drones; new time-lapse, slow-motion and hyperlapse techniques; advances in underwater cameras, lights and diving gear. Pole-cams, which combine a camera in a waterproof housing on a light, strong stick positioned underwater, have also evolved. John Ruthven, film-maker and the only producer to work full-time on both *Blue Planet I* and *II*, explains: 'Pole-cams come in all sorts of varieties, and the more luxurious ones have video monitors and remote controls on the dry end for iris and focus. It allows you to get quick underwater shots when it might otherwise be dangerous for an underwater camera person' (2021: 77).

Camera operators are inventive with kit and its many malfunctions; they need field crafts, often in extreme conditions. As Attenborough observed of the BBC's *Frozen Planet* (2011), 'To film wildlife, particularly during the winter, required camera teams to work in the toughest conditions on Earth' (Fothergill and Berlowitz 2011: 8). Doug Allan started a mostly polar career filming Antarctica wildlife for the BBC's *Life in the Freezer* (1993). 'My perfect temperature is −18°C', he says in his photographic memoir, noting the challenges: 'Most gear will work down to −15, but as you sink towards −25 or even −35, the challenges mount. Batteries die faster, electronics become less reliable, flexible power or sound cables snap like dry spaghetti. And there's a very real danger of frost damage to the cameraperson as well as to the gear' (Allan 2012: 12). Before video, magazines of film had to be loaded and changed manually within a lightproof black bag, using only sure touch. Similarly antediluvian was diving in 10 mm wetsuits, not drysuits: 'it was like diving wearing only a layer of tissue paper' (2012: 37). Allan's attitude characterizes sang-froid: 'Tenacity is just patience showing its teeth' (2012: 16).

Besides the evolution of filming equipment, natural history film-making has a long cultural history (Cohen 2022). I pick it up here from around the 1930s to sketch in some comparative angles. Film appealed to surrealists via Jean Painlevé: his film 'The Seahorse' (1931) turned the seahorse into a spiky icon of gender equality and he made many films about small marine lives (Bellows and McDougall 2001; Cahill 2019). Small got smaller in the films of Australian Noel Monkman; he and his wife Kitty moved between coral islands, setting up makeshift studios to film. 'Strangely enough, to photograph microscopic life a great deal heavier and more elaborate equipment is needed than to photograph a herd of elephants' (Monkman 1963: 188). He started his series *The Great Barrier Reef* in 1931. 'Those five films were screened in almost every country of the world. They showed the microscopic life of the sea, the world under the sea, and the lives of sea-birds, turtles, and the coral animals that build the coral reefs' (Monkman 1963: 166).

Film had importance for modernists, as Caroline Hovanec explains: 'classical (pre-1960s) film theory considered nature films to embody the promise of cinema as a medium. … These films came closest to realizing what classical theorists considered the essential purpose of film: to let nature speak' (2019: 246). These strands of film history share a predilection for surprise – nature has much more than you know, and different visual modes can reveal nature's secrets. A series produced by British Instructional Films between 1922 and 1933, *Secrets of Nature*, made the life cycles of plants, animals and microorganisms entertaining and startling by using techniques such as time-lapse. 'Revealing secrets' is thus a well-established trope which the BBC big series refresh through new visual (and now also sonic) technologies. Revealing the secrets of filming techniques had been established as a subject, for instance by *The Making of a Natural History Film* (BBC 1972) in which clever boffins explain their methods and devices. This feature-length 'making-of' might have shrunk to a tailpiece, but David Attenborough tells a different origin story for 'making-of' segments. He says their inclusion arose from television schedulers in the United States wanting to round out the BBC's usual fifty minutes to a tidier length of an hour. 'Eventually', says Attenborough, 'we solved the problem by adding something new, something we began to call, among ourselves – clumsily but nonetheless accurately – the "Making-of".' So directors, sound-recordists, researchers and cameramen, suddenly stepped into the limelight' (Thurston 2020: Foreword). The genre had a shaky start, according to John Ruthven. 'I had started to film behind the scenes to document what we were doing. I'd tried to sell this idea of a "making-of-*Blue-Planet*" show without success at first, and was even told by a TV exec from a topical magazine show I offered it to that "underwater films are boring and only old people watch them"' (2021: 248).

The presence of humans was something that 'blue-chip' nature documentaries excluded on principle. The term reputedly came from a natural history series producer, John Sparks; Gail Davies gives his definition. '"It just means basically that kind of film, you know, which has got no people in it. Lovely, natural history. Nature in the raw. Beautifully filmed. High production values, good editing, good photography that sucks you into a place" (John Sparks, interview 13.6.95)' (Davies 1998: 16). In contrast to 'No people in it', visibly returning people to the film-making process shows that nature as spectacle is not a natural entity but a culturally constructed one. It insists on human labour, creativity and endurance as components of production. These themes are foregrounded in 'making-of' life writing. The television series' 'making-of' segments entail selection and condensation, important functions of memory work. You've just watched the episode: which sequence will be pulled out for 'making-of' re-membering? 'Making-of' memoirs double this awareness as image-makers not only write about the making of scenes, but also watching and rewatching them.

John Ruthven proposes translation as a concept that connects stages of filming; it can be expanded to include writing and reading about filming. For Ruthven, translation describes ideas becoming locations; management discussion becoming picture stories; wishlists becoming instructions to camera operators. Finally, 'a good filming team is about the things *found* in translation: what each person adds because they're tuned in and looking out for it. Success lies in the final translation, from film to viewer, when the show is broadcast and you find out if you speak the same language or not' (Ruthven 2021: 167). Translation self-awareness is well-established in life writing studies. 'The translation memoir is formed at the intersection of life writing and translation studies, in which translators interweave reflections on their practice, craft, texts they translate and positionalities they occupy. As such it is a kind of creative-critical research carried out by translators' (Grass and Robert-Foley 2024: abstract). Image-makers who work underwater have a double craft to explain – filming and diving. Where blue-chip films present 'a world of landscapes and animal behaviours that must string together in seamless unpeopled stories' (Ruthven 2021: 332), 'making-of' sequences and memoirs repopulate those worlds to expose hidden seams through narratives that combine visuality, diving and memory. Lived experience underpins their creative-critical practice. Genre boundaries, already fluid, become osmotic. Watching again a sequence he had filmed underwater, John Ruthven writes 'Now it becomes some strange dream where mutable memories and permanent video combine to form a new story different at every telling' (2021: 68).

Dreaminess in image-makers' memoirs is paradoxically compatible with professionalism, which Jean-Baptiste Gouyon proposes was established for cameramen in the 1960s–70s when they became as important as scientists in the making of natural history films (2019: 92). Memoirs show professionalism as affable and tough. Camera operators spend long hours waiting. Filming polar bears in Arctic Norway for *Blue Planet*, in a 'blind' of snow blocks to mask human scent near a den, Doug Allan highlights the importance of listening as much as motionless watching. 'I'm in touch with every shift of the wind. It's as if I'm ultra-tuned in to the nature of this wonderful place. I'm in bear world, living at bear speed, with bear senses. I feel very alive' (Allan 2012: 21). John Aitchison spent fourteen hours in a hide waiting to film eider ducklings take their first walk to the Arctic Ocean. He was so frozen he fell out of his hide like a beetle and had to be warmed up; when he returned, his subject family had already walked and he had to start again. He was further delayed by a polar bear crushing his hide (Allan 2012: 280; Aitchison 2016: 140–1). The opposite of 'no people in it', life writing places humans centrally as embodied beings with sense experiences not transmittable on film. On Bird Island in South Georgia, filming fur seals, Aitchison describes his subjects: 'The male seals arch their backs and point their muzzles at the sky, as if they are doing something difficult in yoga, but the most striking thing about them is their smell. It's pure testosterone and they reek like a room full of unwashed rugby kit' (2016: 163). Aitchison writes of encounters too bloody to broadcast, like a leopard seal feeding:

> I film her flaying a penguin; gripping its head and whipping it out of the water in a long arc. Without hands to hold it while she eats she has little choice, but in slow motion the effect is too horrible to watch and I am sure the shots will never be included in the programme. Predators must hunt but there are limits to how red in tooth and claw we want our nature films to be.
>
> (2016: 200)

Doug Anderson dives with another seal while Doug Allan and Aitchison film from above.

> When he [Anderson] climbs out he describes something extraordinary. The seal swam round him with the dead penguin in her mouth, more curious than aggressive. She came close, then dropped the penguin. It sank and Doug swam

down to retrieve it. When he held it out she took it gently from his hand and gave it back: he was being courted by a leopard seal.

(Aitchison 2016: 200)

Flayings and interspecies tenderness don't fit blue-chip templates but memoirs can describe them. Aitchison observes leopard seals catching penguins and letting them live if the penguin ejects its catch, because what the seal wants most is krill in the penguin. Camera operators add to scientific knowledge of habitats and habits: as Gavin Thurston puts it tactfully, 'sometimes our perseverance as a camera crew means we witness things that some scientists might miss' (2020: 263).

Creating a place in which to hold sequences that didn't get captured on film, life writings remind readers of the unpredictable play of chance in encounters in the natural world. This is especially true for underwater, where you can't exactly set up a hide, or wait in a tree for hours – and that has two contradictory effects. One is to present the oceans as a place of action sequences (as shown by the films) – so there is a baitball, swordfish rush in and spectacle is secured. The other is to present the oceans as a place where you have to use skills to locate wildlife – a set of hunting-related skills, often now high-tech – and luck may or may not attend you. So the oceans are potentially visually empty. 'Often you can be at sea ages and see nothing', writes Ruthven, adding 'though you might think seeing lots of whales translates into great shots, it's only one or two very close encounters, of a complete behaviour like a blow or a tail fluke plunging, that will make it to the final cut.' He kept a log 'of the number of times whales teased us with their sightings but were not close enough to film, and the final score for the whole shoot was *Blue Whales* 158, *Humans* 2' (Ruthven 2021: 259). The presentism of wildlife films, in which subjects appear in continuous procession, coexists with more ragged narrative of encounter with those subjects in the life-writing versions.

Encounters with whales have particular challenges for film-makers, and big pay-off in terms of interspecies intimacy. Whales 'now command increasing respect as fellow citizens of the planet entitled to an existence parallel and connected to our own', writes Sylvia Earle (2019: 18). Whales are exceptionally powerful signifiers because of their gigantic size; their history of near-extinctions; their vulnerability to entanglement, noise pollution and chemical contamination; their long-distance voyages; their haunting songs; their intricate social lives and group cultures. Whales also respond to whale-minded humans:

When approached in the right way, 18 metres of curious mammal will hang in the water, and a good swimmer can often ease in close. 'Good' here means having an almost indefinable affinity with the animal and the sea. It's not just how you physically move in the water, it's what's going on in your head as well. 'Good' thoughts often involve respect, fascination, a willingness to be friendly – if you can offer all these, then the whale will reciprocate, until finally you're eye to eye and do indeed have a relationship.

(Allan 2012: 39)

'The Inuit have a word, *ilira*, for the fear that accompanies awe when you are watching a polar bear', writes John Aitchison (2016: 99). He has *ilira* when meeting a pod of twenty humpback whales:

> An unearthly patch of neon green appears below our little boat. It's a whale's pectoral fin, growing larger, rising through the water. The whale surfaces beside us like a dark island. Its two nostrils open, quivering, each the size of my head. … They are the largest animals I have ever seen this close. Their tails are wider than our inflatable is long and each one weighs thirty or forty tons. … one lunges at us, open-mouthed. I film right down its throat, looking uneasily into that watery cave as its mouth wobbles and expands, filling with three tons of water.
>
> (Aitchison 2016: 150)

Staying steady enough to film is a challenge on a gyrating boat, 'so I practise as we travel, bending my knees and swaying at the hips while looking at the viewfinder, touching the tripod just enough to pan and tilt without gripping it too tightly. It feels like holding one eye to a telescope while stirring a huge pot of porridge' (Aitchison 2016: 154). Visuality can require full embodiment and body control.

Filming whales is challenging because there are laws about how close you can get. BBC natural history filming has strict ethical protocols – there must be no harm to animals, no interference with them and no faking. Unpredictable encounters, however, can up-end directives. At Fundy, Nova Scotia, Ruthven describes how a North Atlantic right whale surfaces right under the film crew's RIB, with 'a massive blow of warm air that envelops us, and a deep and resonant rumbling sound like someone blowing madly over the largest pipes in a massive church organ'. They have no licence to film at this spot and could be accused of harassment. The support ship does film, but the footage is ethically suspect. 'Typically, it was probably the most exciting never-seen footage from "behind the scenes" of the original Blue Planet series. One of the unwritten rules of documentary TV is that what is censored is almost always the most compelling' (Ruthven 2021: 72, 76). Image-makers' memoirs can restore otherwise censored material.

What defines 'compelling' in Ruthven's account is how close they are. Being atop a whale in a boat, a situation known as a whale island, was a medieval nightmare. Bestiary images show variants. One example is 'Sailors making camp on the back of a whale', BL Harley MS 4751, f. 69r. (Cockburn 2019). Open ocean camera operators feel *ilira* fear even as they desire encounter. Filming in Baja California for the BBC's series *Incredible Journeys* (1997), Gavin Thurston prepared for a grey whale heat run, which should end in mating. The money shot, rarely managed, is to film the whales' six-foot-long pink penises. He is on his own in a small kayak.

> No sooner am I in the water than the whales dive. I can see they are coming my way, so I slip on my mask, take a deep breath and dive. My heart is now pumping and the reality has sunk in. I am in 7,000 feet of water, five miles offshore, half a mile or more from the yacht in a two-metre swell. Coming towards me is

perhaps a combined 500 tonnes of testosterone-charged whales, led by a female in heat, probably desperate to get away. I have never even seen a whale before, I've certainly never dived with one. Looking straight down into the depths with visibility of at least 150 feet, I suddenly panic and get a weird sense of vertigo. I hold my breath and scan for the whales, knowing that if I see them and get my eye to the viewfinder I'll be fine. My mind will be drawn back to the job and the image and not to my irrational fear.

(Thurston 2020: 142)

The whales don't come. Next day, diving down the anchor line, both he and the producer are frightened by two huge and hostile whales swinging out of the gloom. They finally find a suitable mating pod three days later:

Now, fins, tails and penises feel 3D as they break the skyline. In between the deep resonant whale breaths and splashes, I am aware that the crew are no longer paddling. Still filming, I take my eye from the eyepiece and realise why. We are now right in the middle of the mating pod and the crew are braced for a capsize!

(Thurston 2020: 146-7)

The pod dives; he has great footage, and enough. 'It is a reminder, though, of how my perspective as a cameraman looking down a wide-angle lens can fool me into thinking I'm further away. We were lucky we didn't end up in the water' (Thurston 2020: 147). Image-makers are regularly wry about being so intent on their mechanically produced image they can miss seeing what's close to them – often close shaves with danger. Closeness is displaced from presentness into the future film, manifesting the camera operator's professionalism. Being an extension of mechanical reproduction – eye to the eyepiece – alternates with being an embodied human.

There is a third option, less usual, evident in John Ruthven's memoir: the I as camera. The word 'video' means 'I see' in Latin; video film becomes a medium of memory for the visually-minded Ruthven. Writing, for him, is translating into words the images from 'the camera of my head' (2021: 81):

Filming is an 'all-or-nothing' situation: you need pictures to show the story, and if you haven't got any it's a bit second-hand at best. But this is a book, and I can tell you what I saw as it was all recorded in my head, if not the camera. In my mind the images as I play them back are there still and real. ... An unexpected pleasure of writing this down is that I can capture a scene I thought was long lost, because the camera was never switched on or looking in the right direction. Not relying on technology, now I can replay the neural recording I have of the dive as if it were happening right in front of me ...

(Ruthven 2021: 81, 134)

His unusually full descriptions interlace film, film as metaphor and mental memory work so that dives and situations are visualized for readers too. Jean-Baptiste Gouyon thinks there is a binary for what he calls telenaturalists, as either scientific showmen or modest tellers (2019: 6, 9). In their memoirs though there is more nuance. The eye pressed to eyepiece is an informed eye, translating into an informing I on the page.

AFFECT

In image-makers' memoirs, and in 'making-of sequences', encounters with animals are the result of getting close. Theorists and critics focus on spectacle as the driver of wildlife films but in image-makers' life writing, closeness is the dominant dynamic, not spectacle. Or, more exactly, seeming physically close to animal subjects serves the films by providing footage; it serves the life writings by providing accounts of intimacy that are affect-laden. Doug Allan has fun playing with fur seals underwater, and interacting with crabeater seals: 'their gentle curiosity made me feel as if we had been accepted into their ranks for a moment. It was an intimate glimpse into their world. And the thought came to me – never to see a seal under water is like being denied the sight of a bird in the air' (Allan 2012: 96). Participation has physical risks and emotional rewards. 'Being accepted as a member of an animal group is the ultimate accolade for a wildlife photographer, though what's a mere nip to a furry is a serious puncture wound in your drysuit or even your elbow' (Allan 2012: 178). Sometimes unorthodox behaviour works: Allan sings through his snorkel as a reciprocal gesture to belugas, small white Arctic whales known as 'canaries of the sea'. '"Happy Birthday" was pretty effective, I'm sure that brought them closer' (Allan 2012: 200).

Camera operators aim to override distance by long lenses, proximity and imagination. 'It is vital to put myself in the place of the animals I'm watching, to try to see things as they see them' (Aitchison 2016: 169). Empathy tends to be easier with mammals. The book of *Blue Planet II*, authored by the executive producer and series producer, explains how a mantis shrimp has a visual system 'almost otherworldly, perhaps the most elaborate in the animal kingdom'. They have triocular vision in each eye, can see ultraviolet and can communicate with fellow shrimps through polarized light, 'a very private communication system denied to all other animals, including us' (Honeybourne and Brownlow 2017: 176). Film now tries to exceed its fashioning for human vision by using infra-red, slow-motion or critter-cams, which translate animal points of view into viewable footage. There is as yet no mantis-cam to help build empathy.

In Britain, says Caroline Hovanec, 'the *Secrets of Nature* and other natural history films do not just *reveal* the natural world via an expansion of vision; they also work to *change* viewers' affective responses to nature' (2019: 246). In particular they promoted what Hovanec calls 'secular enchantment', through life cycle stories and encounters. An enchanting sequence appears in a 2024 film featuring a robot sperm whale whose interior houses cameras and a hydrophone. It bobs along near a sperm whale pod. A female comes over, gently inquisitive: she issues greeting clicks, then, in a 'touching sign of approval', introduces her calf to the calf-size robot whale. 'An encounter, far closer than ever imagined', says John Downer in the voice-over (2024). An affectless robot can mimic enchanting behaviours, up to a point, but its purpose is to conjure enchantment around the oceanic subjects it encounters. Closeness is one way to index enchantment. In Antarctica, photographer Sue Flood woke from a nap to find an emperor penguin chick resting its wing on her gloved hand. Literally touching, affect here turns physical closeness into intimacy (Flood 2018: 121).

Closeness involves trust. Image-maker memoirs show trust in formation through spatial closeness. A striking percentage are written in the present tense, as if to shrink a time gap too. One might read closeness as a manifestation of interspecies intimacy, or even kinship, something we define in terms of our close relatives. But image-makers are well aware of intimacy as fragile and temporary; cameras orchestrate scales of distance which are marks of respect for the natural world's existence independent of humans. While some theorists critique nature as a construct, image-makers endorse it as a source of affect in search of a numinous vocabulary. Ruthven cites his father's term for dappled light on stormy days, *God light*, to describe shafts of light shining through a kelp forest. 'Dramatic on land, underwater these rays are even more amplified, and intruding into these enchanted woods, embarrassed by their beauty, religious or not, you sense something has shifted about how much you love this world' (Ruthven 2021: 135). That something is bigger than interspecies intimacy: it gestures to a beauty and benignity that folds humans into the natural world, a life-consciousness that makes you love the world more.

Reviewing a surge of animal studies in 2011, Julie Livingston and Jasbir K. Puar identify conceptual patterns:

> This growing body of literature traces the material effects of anthropocentrism (human exceptionalism), anthropomorphic projection (animals must mimic humans, are prosthetic extensions of humans), incorporation and invasion (animals can become us), transmutation (we can become animal), exotic alterity (aren't they wondrous?), and anthropogenic obliteration (animals impede human capitalist endeavors) that characterize human/nonhuman interfaces.
>
> (Livingston and Puar 2011: 3)

Livingston and Puar think 'an overly optimistic posthumanist approach can produce yet another version of humanity, resulting in bodies that are less than human (creating new "human animals")' (2011: 5). Underwater image-makers do promote their subjects as wondrous, and the aquatic bodies of divers share some of the animality of marine mammals. But there is a paradox: although promoting physical closeness, through prosthetic camera eyes, many image-maker writers locate animal difference as less relevant than equality of existence for animals and humans. What matters is that humans and animals *share* life. Like Ruthven's feeling of loving the world more, the language of closeness is bound up with recognition of unity. Visualities in underwater life writing counter spectacle by using affect to link beauty to an alchemy of love.

11

Aesthetics

This chapter explores aesthetics in relation to three paradigms. More appear in the next chapter; here I use aesthetics to reflect upon specific phenomena that feature across underwater life writing. Aesthetic theory rarely considers underwater, so I adapt various thinkers to find concepts that fit. Within this web of ideas, politics and ethics are anchor points, implicit lines in and out. Margaret Cohen and Killian Quigley propose that 'A materialist analysis of environmental aesthetics – notably one engaging such a forbidding realm as the undersea – teaches the need to take into account the specificity of the environment being represented as well as the science and technology of accessing it' (2019: 4) The specificity of bubbles, gloom and bioluminescence contributes to that project of material environmental aesthetics, though each of those hovers on the edge of immateriality too.

The first paradigm is air underwater. Marine mammals have adaptations to enable them to move between air and water; their production of bubbles has interested mathematicians and physicists. Philosophers bring other import to bubbles and aesthetics has found beauty in them. To these I add underwater authors' fascination with what I'll term the poetics of air underwater – visualizations of breath through bubbles which turn on air's visibility in the medium of water. 'Air thrusts its material status on the diver', writes Rosaleen Love (2001: 205); underwater air creates a distinct aesthetic through bubbles.

The second paradigm is that of gloom. I argue that its aesthetic effects make it a category distinct from the gothic which often accompanies hauntography. Gloom underwater occupies a larger space than its usual placing in shipwrecks, although it is in and around wrecks that critics have engaged with it. Gloom is fascinating because it produces unease, at odds with pleasures found in the beautiful; it ferments profound questions about human presence underwater.

Where bubbles invite jouissance and gloom manifests anxieties, my third category, bioluminescence, featuring glow, sparkle, shimmer and other light effects, explores how it sparks a particular dialectic of science and art, technic and magic. Life writers – and readers – see bioluminescence through a glass darkly, but mediating technology can prosthetically enable aesthetic engagements, including ones unique to the deeps.

AIR UNDERWATER: PRACTICALITIES

Fish don't breathe air: they breathe oxygen dissolved in water, which is why a fish out of water will gasp for air (with some interesting freshwater exceptions.) Even with portable air in scuba and other forms of air supply, it is challenging for humans to breathe underwater. Humans are an air-breathing species, but not at the start of their lives. Babies develop in fluid: there's a strange period, around the fourth week, when a baby acquires gill-like structures which then disappear. The standard evolutionary explanation is that a human embryo's

> 'distant ancestors were in fact aquatic, gill bearing, organisms and that the remnants of embryonic gill-like structures have been preserved in their embryological development. And though these structures in the embryos of amniotes never develop into, actual gills, they have historically been informally referred to as 'gill slits' due to their overall anatomical agreement with the corresponding structures of aquatic vertebrates which do develop into gills'.
>
> (Britain 2012)

This physiological affinity with fish, however brief, underpins a deep relationship between humans and ocean. Ninety per cent of our blood is water; between forty-five per cent (for women) and sixty (for men) of our bodies is water. Hans Hass described 'the whole succession of land animals and land plants … as marine beings in exile' (Hass 1959: 19). The idea of shared aquatic ancestors has fascinated many (Morgan 1982).

Like histories of balloons, histories of humans underwater have a standard iconography going back to antiquity. Diving histories often start with Alexander the Great using air trapped in an enclosure of some sort, which anticipates a long succession of diving bells, hose-supplied helmets and other technologies for delivering air. Two recent developments have turned to organic capacities instead: one is liquid breathing, designed by Arnold Lange (a retired heart and lung surgeon) and dramatized in the film *The Abyss* (Cameron 1989) which returns to the principle of breathing liquidly, as human foetuses do. The other approach is to train human lungs to improve capacity. Freediving has become popular, thanks to crossovers with yoga and dance (discussed in Chapter 12). In 2021 Croatian Budimir Šobat set the world record for holding a single breath underwater, lasting twenty-four minutes and thirty-seven seconds. One attraction of freediving is that it produces no bubble trail, causing less disturbance to underwater inhabitants. Freediving visuality is often uncannily still, undisturbed by bubbles whose motion, dissolution, reformation and rising remind us of our own busy and temporary sphere. The calm of their absence in freediving is almost a shock.

The human body has air spaces for which pressure has to be equalized with depth. The best known is the Eustachian tube, where relieving pressure on the ear drum, at height as well as depth, leads to the sensation of your ears popping (as in an airplane). Our sinuses are air spaces too. Our respiratory system is a network of air spaces; we want air there, but not in the bloodstream, where excess oxygen creates potentially fatal embolisms, as nitrogen does, and which divers guard against by being careful to observe decompression limits. Air-breathing mammals manage underwater thanks to various adaptations. The heartbeat of harbour seals slows from around a hundred beats per minute to ten; typically they dive for three minutes at a time, but they can stay underwater for thirty minutes and go as deep as 550 metres (1600 feet) (SeaDoc). Seals don't have air-filled ears, and like many marine mammals they have lungs that are easy to collapse and reinflate. They breathe out before diving, unlike humans. Thick fur and blubber protect against the cold of depth. 'Marine mammals also have a high concentration of hemoglobin in their blood and myoglobin in their muscles.' Both are used to store oxygen in body tissue. An extensive net of blood vessels known as the 'retia mirabilia' captures any bubbles that form in their bloodstream, protecting against the bends (Davis 2019: 133-75). In all these different ways, other species are much better adapted than humans for moving between air and water. In frozen Lake Baikal, seal mothers help pups to breathe underwater by exhaling a big bubble from which the pup can inhale (BBC *Asia* episode 3, 2024).

Knowledge of these adaptations is still emerging. Doug Allan filmed emperor penguins zooming to the surface trailing bubbles. 'The sequence we filmed for The Blue Planet raised oohs and aahs from the audience, but it was even more satisfying when it raised scientific eyebrows ten years later.' Examining single frames of the footage, scientists worked out that the bubbles acted as lubrication.

> And even more remarkable, it's the emperor itself who is controlling when to release the bubbles. The air is trapped in the thick layer of downy feathers close to the penguin's body, beneath the tough outer feathers. As it ascends, the emperor is able to relax the muscles at the base of its feathers and so release the air.
>
> (Allan 2012: 132)

Fractionally increasing speed, bubbles help an emperor exit the water higher and faster, an advantage against leopard seal predators. These are practical bubbles rather than philosophical or aesthetic ones.

BUBBLES: PHILOSOPHY, AESTHETICS AND POETICS

Water can make breath visible in aesthetic ways that involve mystery. When whales dive, a nasal plug covers the passage to their blowhole; when the whale comes up for air, muscles controlling the plug contract and allow exhalation and inhalation again. Air sacs just below the blowhole allow whales to produce sounds. The blowing whale is a staple of hunting literature because blow makes a whale visible and sometimes audible on the ocean surface. Different species have signature shapes, velocities, sounds. Melville devoted Chapter 85 of *Moby-Dick* to the workings and meanings of the sperm whale spout. Uncertain whether the whale blows water or air, he made the mystery sublime and beautiful:

> how nobly it raises our conceit of the mighty, misty monster, to behold him solemnly sailing through a calm tropical sea; his vast, mild head overhung by a

canopy of vapor, engendered by his incommunicable contemplations, and that vapor – as you will sometimes see it – glorified by a rainbow, as if Heaven itself had put its seal upon his thoughts.

(Melville 1851: 391)

Whale vapour is a figure for in-betweenness, a punctum Melville describes as 'Doubts of all things earthly, and intuitions of some things heavenly' (1851: 391). In-betweenness has also been explored in relation to bubbles. Sarah Tindal Kareem has written about the soap bubble as a trope for this in Enlightenment and Romantic poetry, seeing it as 'the iconic transparent body ... [which] exemplifies appearance itself ... with a swirl of associations' (Kareem 2015: 87). Those go back to the Greek satirist Lucian who invoked bubbles at the foot of a waterfall as an emblem of human transience. *Homo bulla*, as the trope became known, converged with bubbles as ludic, depicted especially by seventeenth-century Dutch artists who painted children playing with soap bubbles. Karel Dujardin's *Homo Bulla Est* brings together this double evocation of playful and philosophical. Spherical air bubbles image our transient world in miniature; air evokes vanitas and ephemera, yet also the human activity of making beauty, art, reflection and meaning. Dujardin made that activity explicit by the putto's gaze which is directly and delightedly fixed on the bubbles floating in air.

Dujardin's allegory is widely described as a boy blowing bubbles, but it has deeper meaning (Pointon 2009: 112). Like Botticelli's Venus, the boy has a cockleshell, but his footing – impossibly? – depends on a bubble whose pearlescence blends with that of the shell's nacre. The scallop shell holds a sprig of red coral and a string of pearls that seem to become more solid in air. A lightweight trope of value from depth, the treasures of the sea, is here given solidity, as if air underwater riffs on another old trope, that of the goddess Fortuna rolling on a rock. As Shakespeare puts it in *Henry V* (3.6.34–5), 'And her foot, look you, is fixed upon a spherical stone, which rolls, and rolls, and rolls.' Constant circulation features in Alexander Pope's philosophical poem *An Essay on Man* (1734):

Look round our world; behold the chain of love
Combining all below and all above.
See plastic Nature working to this end,
The single atoms each to other tend,
Attract, attracted to, the next in place,
Form'd and impell'd its neighbour to embrace ...
(By turns we catch the vital breath, and die)
Like bubbles on the sea of Matter born,
They rise, they break, and to that Sea return.

(Epistle III 7-12, 18-20)

Not all Renaissance, Enlightenment and Romantic bubbles are predicated on being soap bubbles. Eighteenth-century poet Mary Leapor wondered in 'The Enquiry' why 'our Eyes were made to view/ Those Orbs that glister in the fluid Blue?' She imagined a soul with microscopic eyes able to see miniature worlds in a visionary way:

Figure 26 Karel Dujardin, 'Boy Blowing Soap Bubbles. Allegory on the Transitoriness and the Brevity of Life.' 1663. Also known as *Homo Bulla Est*. Wikimedia Commons.

And Drops of Dew are mighty Oceans there:
These may have Whales that in their Waters play.

(Leapor 1748: 54-55, ll.7-8)

Bubbles encompass sliding scales of tiny and mighty, evanescent and lasting. They pack all this symbolism into a paradoxical lightness which gives them, like balloons, comic potential. Underwater bubbles are likewise ludic. Exhaling air into silvery floating rings is a scuba diver's party trick: many show-off instructors do it. (It's like blowing smoke rings.) Doing away with the instrumentality of clay pipes or soap, these bubbles take on the numinous organicism of breath made visible. One freediving website that explains how to do it also points to it as a figure of desire: 'These days, while scrolling on Instagram you probably see an epic bubble ring photo at least every second day and it is very easy to get bubble ring envy' (Kivilcim and Parsons n.d.).

The association of bubbles with jouissance is reinforced by dolphins. Dolphins like to make rings of air spin without touching them – by creating turbulence – then they swallow them. Where literary critics think the appeal of bubbles is their spherical cosmogony and how that stands in for worlds, the bubble ring is a little different. It has complicated mathematics; as it moves through the water it undulates in seemingly unpredictable ways. Paul Schröder, who has simulated them to study their geometry, comments 'There's beauty in seeing that a very simple principle all of a sudden gives rise to the complex appearance we perceive' (Perkins 2019).

Enlightenment polymath Gottfried Wilhelm Leibniz (1646–1716), who was keen on bubbles, wanted to isolate singularity from their plurality:

"Bubbles are the seed of everything," Leibniz stated in one of his early writings. Noteworthy, the obscure idea resonates with the modern inflationary universe model, in which our universe has been seen as a bubble floating in an ocean of other bubbles. In his *Monadologie* (1714) Leibniz maintained that the divine order of the universe is reflected in each of its parts, each part being called a monad, a term that means "unit" or "unity" – or a counterpart of atom.

(Liukkonen 2008)

The monad, like the soap bubble, inclines to the singular, even as other philosophers take up the stream of bubbles – a metaphor from water – to image the flow of time. Thus Robert Ginsberg, discussing ruins, proposes that

Rich moments dissolve into unenriched time. … Time fills in the gaps between moments. Against the flow of time, moments foray forth. Moments are only possible because no time exists for them. They rise, bubbles free of the stream. Inside the bubble is an interconnectedness, not ever fully dissected by our cutting probes. The moment seems seamless and endless. The monad (Gottfried Wilhelm Leibniz.) The moment to which we are moved is motionless.

(Ginsberg 2021: 161-2)

Interconnectedness appears in a particular kind of visualized breath underwater, which is also not singular. If you dive in a cave or under an overhang, you may find that if divers have been there before you, some of their bubbles lodge on the rock or coral surface. They look like little domes of mercury, silvery, reflective, quite stable. Sarah Tindal Kareem alludes to 'a mood of cognitive provisionality that enjoys the soap-bubble in full acknowledgement of its imminent bursting' (2015: 91), but these mercurial outbreaths slow down that imminence, pleasurably. Appearing severally, more fixed than provisional, these residue bubbles are unintentional organic litter, a visual trace of visitations. For theorist Peter Sloterdijk,

> Because of the constitutive primacy of relationality, we are not always aware of our relations to others. In fact, "one could say that they are as invisible as air to one another – but an air in which they lie for one another; each one inhales and exhales what the others are – the perfect conspiration" (B, 607).
>
> (Ford 2015: 262)

This gives us a new theory – conspiracy theory! – to image conspeciality between divers, and even conspeciality between divers and the ocean itself.

Underwater authors find aesthetic and poetic possibilities in bubbles which diverge from philosophical ones. Scuba divers give out trails of bubbles as they exhale. If you are above another diver, these bubbles rise into your pathway in an intimate way – you are seeing someone's breath, able to touch it. You can see your own, as William Beebe did when he donned a diving helmet: 'down below,' he wrote, 'the imprisoned air sailing upward, slips through one's fingers like balloon pearls, dry, mobile beauty, leaving only a pleasant sensation'. Reflectivity is poetic and practical for Beebe: 'I even have the sensations of a god, for in each of the spheres I have created, I see very distinctly my own image.' And he sees 'another great golden grouper just behind me, revealed by his reflected image on my ascending breath.' The image-laden bubble condenses and expands – while also acting as a rear-view mirror (Beebe 1934: 176).

Scuba enabled new pleasures from bubbles. Arthur C. Clarke loved the feel of their fizz:

> The intermittent cascades of bubbles rising from the two aqualungs below swept past me to the surface, and every one of those tiny bubbles was a beautiful, delicate shade of pink. I floated in the ascending stream, and the storm of bubbles hitting my skin as they passed produced an indescribably delightful tingling sensation which I did my best to prolong by carefully stationing myself above the divers.
>
> (Clarke 1957: 47)

Pierre de Latil wrote rapturously of the jouissance of bubbles. On only his second dive, with plenty of novel scenes and sensations, he thought 'the most marvellous thing' was his companions' bubbles. A page of description follows, in which he tracks these bursts of silver grapes, their movement, changes in shape, dilation, effervescence … completely entranced, he chases the bubbles like a child. Yet his conclusion – which is also the conclusion of the book – insists on their philosophical, aesthetic and poetic import.

Considering my words carefully, I will say that no sight anywhere in our world can give you such a feeling of being removed from your usual surroundings, and nothing can appear fresher and newer to a too-sophisticated eye. Not the mountains or the sea, not the desert or the ice, nor any terrestrial scene or the heavens themselves can provide such a dreamlike spectacle. And I hardly think that even another planet could show us anything as strange to our own world as those underwater swimmers, moving with a dreamlike quality below the surface of the sea, flying over green depths, gliding over the face of steep precipices and always leaving silver clouds behind them, bouquets of living flowers expanding as they rise, dancing and turning and finally bursting into spray on the surface.

(de Latil and Rivoire 1956: 284–5)

The detachment of bubbles, their estrangement from the body who produces them, is nonetheless compatible with joy and wonderment. Sy Montgomery compares scuba bubbles to a departing soul leaving the body, shooting stars, a song of praise (2015: 153, 142). Like de Latil, she was new to diving; both respond to bubbles as timeless, not novelties. Underwater life writers, like old painters and poets, add to the bubble as emblem, celebrating its capacities for joy, play and wonder.

GLOOM

Many authors attest to joy underwater, and the jouissance of bubbles expresses it. Some, however, counterpoint joy with gloom, a term I use to encompass a suite of uncomfortable emotions, often connected to low light. Besides Diolé's masterly exposition of metaphysical unease (discussed in Chapter 2), there are accounts that remind us of the ocean as graveyard, preserving and dissolving human bodies; as a place of colonial violence and murder, where enslaved people were forcibly drowned; as a site of wrecked ships and hopes. These histories, which are ghosts in the next chapter, mobilize force-fields other than gloom, though fear of death and alertness to spectres give gloom a distinct resonance with the drowned. Margaret Cohen and Killian Quigley argue that aesthetics provide ways into 'contingent cultural inheritances and essential psychological realities simultaneously' (Cohen and Quigley 2019: 1), and that underwater changes faculties and fantasies. 'Terrestrially-established categories shift, metamorphose, or fail altogether to apply' (2019: 1). While they stress undersea's 'ability to mobilize the uncanny', they flag up the human body and technologies as mediators of underwater impression (2019: 8). They see 'extra-physiological routes to sensation, such as memory, natural history, and repertoires of fantasy' as crucial (2019: 6). Following their lead, I explore the term 'gloom', starting from its affinity to the uncanny.

Low light and wrecks share an ambience of indistinctness, of gloom. Loom conveys enlargement too, like the outsize iceberg that loomed into view as the *Titanic* sailed towards it. Echoes between gloom and loom hint at another association, doom, as in 'doom and gloom'. Popularized by nineteenth-century newspapers, the phrase 'gloom and doom' conveys prescient pessimism. It doesn't seem to matter which term comes first, though there are more instances of doom preceding, which suggests gloom as an effect of doom. Underwater life writings show how gloom's anti-jouissance is produced by time and space.

Tim Ecott demonstrates both routes to sensations of gloom. Diving in Fiji, 'The late-afternoon light is weak underwater and there is a plankton bloom, the proliferation of microscopic life which considerably reduces the visibility.' He glimpses a hammerhead and watches batfish in the gathering dusk glinting like sequins. 'This is the time of day when the sea seems on edge' (2002: 49). He shivers, and ends the dive. Ruminating on the fondness of many British divers for their cool temperate seas, in which strong currents and poor visibility are common, he later dives in the Falmouth Estuary in Cornwall, which has no obvious attraction except that it is sheltered. He and his buddy find a big mud bank, detritus of scallop shells and 'ash-dull nothingness'. Mud, dark water and grey light coalesce into an aesthetic of gloom which induces panic at seeing nothing visibly alive: 'the sea had become an utterly hopeless and sterile environment. It was as though we were already dead things. In a wasteland. When we left the water I felt as if I had returned from Hell' (Ecott 2002: 101–2). Grey tonality has been highlighted for oceanic thinking by Þóra Pétursdóttir in 'Drift', an essay on the coastal ecologies of North Norway. She quotes J. J. Cohen, 'Grey is the fate of color at twilight', though she points out grey can be other things – the colour of sickness, of tranquillity, of toning down (Pétursdóttir 2023: 253). She ends with a redefinition for borderland archaeology: 'full of asymmetry, full of darkness, and full of regions devoid of human presence. Regions and affairs unmoved by our naming, knowledge and ignorance' (Pétursdóttir 2023: 266). Time and space refract that indifference to human presence which can deeply disturb diver writers.

Low light is not gloomy to everyone. Robert Louis Stevenson was eager to try helmet diving. In 1868, at Wick in Scotland, aged eighteen, he finally did. 'Some twenty rounds below the platform, twilight fell. Looking up, I saw a low green heaven mottled with vanishing bells of white; looking around, except for the weedy spokes and shafts of the ladder, nothing but a green gloaming, somewhat opaque but very restful and delicious' (1888: 201). Stevenson has a ladder for support; other underwater writers analyse the anxiety of descent with no reference point, 'the vertiginous panic of trying to find a horizon while you're navigating a foggy distance with no up or down', as Ralph Sneeden puts it (2023: 151). Physical and metaphysical fears merge as he gropes down an anchor line:

> being in that middle space was like what I imagine dying to be, a state where the surface loses its definition. The bottom is not yet visible, the dropping temperature begins to leech into your bones, and any promise of connection with other warm forms of life seems unlikely. Are you sinking or rising?
>
> (Sneeden 2023: 153)

Aesthetic disturbance is profound: 'meandering like some lost nonnative microbe through a closing vise of color' (2023: 154), Sneeden's uncertain descent becomes a symbol of emotional misguidedness. Midwater disorientation triggers deep anxieties. For Stephen Harrigan,

> What had scared me was all that uninhabited space between me and the bottom, the gathering gloom and density of the water, which for the first time had appeared threatening. It was a fear of falling – or not falling exactly but helplessly sliding down, without the magic power to swim or scramble back up.
>
> (1992: 235)

Harrigan then remembers his mother's great fear of water, linked to vertigo, and ends this chapter with thoughts about ravenous, witch-like mermaids. One fear leads to another, deeper. Despite critics' understandable fascination with shipwreck gloom, midwater gloom takes life writing into dark places. Nor is gothic a relevant paradigm: nothingness of water images nothingness of being, an existential horror.

Marine life can be overlooked in gloom. For all that the *Titanic* is famous as a symbol of hubris and a mass grave, footage from OceanGate's visit in 2022 shows it as a site of habitation. A fine sea pen currently resides on the bow, with a plumose anemone on the port side, waving softly white among the rusticles. When Cousteau located the wreck of the *Thistlegorm* in the Red Sea, he represented its exploration in both film and book form. Margaret Cohen reads the film sequence in *The Silent World* (1956) as full of gothic, with the uncanny evoked by a Dutch angle or canted shot, a disturbing tilt of the camera taken from German Expressionist cinema. In her fine reading, the footage has 'a tone of fascination, menace and ghostly haunting' (Cohen 2019: 159). Spectators, she argues, witness in this sequence 'a new iteration of the gothic – where the menace comes not only from the ghostly residues of the past but also … from the underwater atmosphere' (2019: 160). Cousteau's written account in *The Living Sea* (1963) has a motif of possible monstrosity, a huge fish seen by Dumas and Falco which they dub 'the Thing'. But on paper Cousteau chooses a register of abundance, not gothic. In the film, the ship's bell is rung, and the ship named by an uncanny voiceover – a female, British-accented voice in a film otherwise empty of both, as Cohen perceptively observes. In the book, 'the bronze bell hung from a standard thickly dressed with bryozoans. On the bell grew a single perfect pearl oyster. Dumas drew his knife and rapped the bell. A chime rang through the sea and a blue angelfish jumped out of the bell.' Though the monster fish gives hauntography to the wreck, 'from everything we touched there came frightened fish' and the deck is solidly paved with pearl oysters. Marine life inhabitation counters gothic with life (Cousteau with Dugan 1963: 69-70). The monster fish proves to be a huge wrasse, a Brobdignagian *Chelinus undulatus*, unthreatening. As Cohen points out, gothic – in some forms – can extend rather than undermine Enlightenment mastery through reversions to reason. Cousteau's written version shows his usual will to mastery, but his *Thistlegorm* is nonetheless recognized as a home for pearl oysters and giant wrasse. The *Calypso* crew soon leave; marine life remains, an organic force in charge of the wreck.

Others in Cousteau's circle were attentive to wrecks as oases rather than graves. Diolé praised their beauty and their calmness. 'Bearded with seaweed, home of

shellfish and octopus, quivering with fishes, they attract life and bring it to completion'
(Diolé 1954b: 54). They had particular ecological identities. Ascidians would dominate
one, Neptune's lace another (*Triphyllozoon inornatum*, a bryozoan). Yet nature-culture
entanglements invited subtle skills.

> The frontiers between wreck and marine vegetation are obliterated in the tangle
> of the seabed. You can wander a long time in the labyrinths of marine vegetation
> before finding out what is rock and what is a column overgrown with seaweed. It
> needs a skilled marine excavator to locate the most likely places and to sniff out
> valuable relics hiding under rioting sea-gardens.
>
> (Diolé 1954b: 154–5)

The sense of smell is limited underwater, so Diolé turns to photographs and marine
drawings. But he recognizes exactness is elusive. 'It takes great effort of will to get a
complete picture under water when vision is limited, shuttered by mud and seaweed'
(Diolé 1954b: 155). The autobiographical subject is figuratively here a hybrid, a camera
eye. More important than extractive cultural practices were sea-meetings, as his
chapter is titled. Here is a positive hauntography, in several senses. Though boundaries
are disturbed – wood, vegetation and sessile beings entangle – that disturbance
is productively imaginative. 'In the Mediterranean, more perhaps than anywhere
else, men, customs, climates, animals, plants and arts are interlinked. Civilisations
take shape and merge in [*sic*] one another' (Diolé 1954b: 160). This is more than an
assemblage: Diolé anticipates the need for a hydrocentric language which decentres
humans and recognizes agency in other beings. As he asks in *The Gates of the Sea*, 'why
should we not regard man as just another type of marine animal?' (Diolé 1957a: 154).

Sara A. Rich's theory of hauntology acknowledges ambivalence. 'A close encounter
with a shipwreck in its underwater realm is a brush with the eerie, horrific, and uncanny
– but also the wondrous, ecstatic, and sublime' (Rich 2021: 13). She locates those
emotions in wrecks, their dialectic tension creating attraction and disgust. Hauntology
can bridge that difference, by thinking a shipwreck is not a failure but 'a life-affirming
encounter with death' (Rich 2021: 12). It can also be a life-affirming encounter with
life. A ship may have died but, much as corpses push up daisies, its decaying body
nurtures life. It can be especially hospitable to the long-lived – thus big old lobsters live
on UK wrecks – and to the young, who hide from predators in its labyrinthine spaces.
In the Red Sea the gloomy parts of many wrecks are home to shoals of glassfish, tiny
fish who glint like fragments of light gathered from elsewhere. We miss this flourishing
of marine life if we focus only on the gloom of exclusively human-centred hauntology.

Gloom can be considered an atmosphere, something between space and bodily
sensing. Gernot Böhme theorizes atmospheres as the space of bodily presence,
which 'can then take on a mood, as a kind of tinge' (2018: 91). Böhme explores this
felt space principally in relation to architecture – that must include wrecks, which
are constructions being spatially deconstructed, and spatial constructions being
deconstructed temporally. He stresses that light and sound can generate atmosphere.
'They too, and this merits emphasis, modulate bodily felt space by creating tightness
or expansiveness, orientation, and enclosing or excluding atmospheres' (Böhme 2018:
92). Low light underwater, gloom, can create disorientation and gloominess, but that

can be lightened by sensing space differently. Böhme's aesthetics have contributed to an atmospheric turn, with critiques and developments (Griffero 2019), but prove useful for underwater life writing's evocation of gloom as a felt space in which mood, body and space coalesce in atmosphere.

SPARKS IN THE DARK: BIOLUMINESCENCE AND AESTHETICS

'The majority of our planet, it turns out, is not a *blue* planet, but a *glowing* planet' (Ruthven 2021: 220). There are possibly quadrillions of bioluminescent fish in the ocean, agrees Edith Widder, an expert on oceanic bioluminescence. 'If you measure success in terms of numbers, then bioluminescent fish are the most successful vertebrates on the planet' (Widder 2021: 146). Arguably the most numerous are bristlemouths, *Cyclothones*, who live in the twilight zone. They have light-producing organs on their bellies, producing counter-illumination to confuse predators from below. Lanternfish, possibly a greater biomass and who make up much of the deep scattering layer, also have counter-illuminating photophores, differently arranged in different species. Although these light organs are part of a fascinating array of anatomical adaptations to life in the dark, my focus here is less on marine biology and more on how bioluminescence carries illuminating aesthetics in underwater life writing. Flash, sparkle, shimmer and glow attract scientific and artistic interest, and different directions in thinking. Citing the beauty of jellyfish at 30,000 metres down, Astrida Neimanis observes that 'sensuous understandings; emotional response and imaginative projection inform oceanographic study' (2017: 57). Bioluminescence makes spectacularly visible the tensions, sometimes creative, between technic and magic, terms I take from Federico Campagna to elucidate the effects and affects of bioluminescence.

In 1934, descending in a bathysphere, William Beebe reached

> an indefinable translucent blue quite unlike anything I have seen in the upper world … the blueness of the blue, both outside and inside our sphere, seemed to pass materially through the eye into our very beings. This is all very unscientific; quite worthy of being jeered at by optician or physicist, but there it was.
>
> (Beebe 1934: 109)

Below this blue is black, a world beyond sunlight, often described as eternal darkness. Bioluminescence, however, makes black a medium for theatrical spectacles of blue. Though other colours occur – a gossamer worm produces golden sparkles when disturbed (Haddock 2022) – blue dominates: 'it was a mixture of the most brilliant blues ever to grace an artist's palette – azure, cobalt, cerulean, lapis, neon – supernatural hues', says Edith Widder (2021: xiv-v). In her book on the colour blue, Carol Mavor relates surprise to 'a bolt from the blue' (2013: 73). In the deep, blue bolts shoot through the black, startling in intensity. Bioluminescent forms are startling too: blue comes in puffs, clouds, strings, streams, pinwheels, ripples, flashes, glows, blinks and bobbing lights. Böhme describes colour as a special ecstasy, either the property of a thing or a subjective reaction to such properties. He suggests a third option: 'that one ecstasy of things might consist in being-colourful …. the colourful thing can be localized yet, in a certain way, its colourfulness is everywhere' (Böhme 2017: 50–1). Though we view footage on two-dimensional screens, the deep has three-dimensionality, and multi-directionality: bioluminescence can flash or glow from any part of this black visual field. Its colourfulness is everywhere. Except you need dark to see it, paradoxically. In an ROV Deep Rover, Widder turned off the lights and saw only dark until she tapped the thrusters, then blue lights burst out around her. 'Bioluminescence makes life that was once invisible and obscure brilliantly observable' (Widder 2021: 105).

There are various kinds of photoluminescence, or light produced from the absorption of light, including fluorescence (a property of some corals who, having absorbed ultra-violet light, glow it back in neon colours), and phosphorescence (often known as sea sparkle, triggered by movement acting on light-storing plankton). In the ocean, bioluminescence, which is chemically produced, dominates. Edith Widder dates *in situ* studies to the mid-1950s when a photomultiplier tube dipped underwater to measure sunlight picked up flashes; this led to the development of bathyphotometers to measure bioluminescence (2006: 136–7). Bioluminescence also ironically accounts for ultra-black fish, whose intense stores of melanin prevent their bodies being seen, even if they have a glowing lure (Scales 2021: 94). 'The ocean hides many secrets. But for those in the know, bioluminescence can reveal things otherwise unseen. It all boils down to being able to read the light' (Widder 2021: 119). What is this light aesthetically, and what does reading it tell us?

Widder, who specialized in bioluminescence, describes it as

> a cold chemical light, a consequence of millions of years of evolution resulting in fantastic light-emitting creatures with evocative names like crystal jelly, cockeyed squid, bearded seadevil, shining tubeshoulder, stoplight fish, and velvet belly lantern shark. Their bodies are adorned with all manner of light-emitting structures – nozzles that spew liquid blue flame, incredibly complex light organs that look like flesh-encrusting jewels but behave optically like eyes that *emit* light instead of collecting it, and absurdly glowing appendages that resemble abstract sculptures of alien life-forms from the planet Zork.
>
> (Widder 2021: xiv)

Widder's metaphors of flame, jewels and sculpture set off a collision of science, science fiction and vernacular naming. She stresses light-emitting, an agency not given to humans. Hence bioluminescence is cast as supernatural:

> Throughout history, many cultures have told stories of people and beings wreathed with halos or imbued with an irrepressible brilliance: gods, angels, fairies, saints, and jinns. To be infused with light is to be divine or supernatural, precisely because it is an impossibility for us.
>
> (Jabr 2016: n.p.)

Widder lists 'fantastic' bioluminescent marine beings, but even ones we have called 'humble', like species of sea cucumber, are able to create light. Theatrical imagery

Figure 27 Comb Jelly (*Bolinopsis mikado*) showing bioluminescence, Japan. Photo and caption by Hiroya Minakuchi. Nature Picture Library.

infuses accounts. 'I was witnessing a mysterious, sparkling pageant performed just for me', says Widder of watching comb jellies light up in figures of eight and siphonophores become glowing necklaces (2021: 111).

Woven into spectacle are the findings of science, which undo both mystery and performance-for-me with a Darwinian story of survival. Popular science dwells on lurid possibilities, an eat or be eaten plot. Bioluminescence becomes tactical, deceptive, in 'faint and furtive spikes of light that could mean anything from a fresh meal to a gruesome death' (Palumbi and Palumbi 2014: 62). This melodrama is despite the fact that of twelve functions identified by Stephen Haddock and colleagues, seven are defensive (Haddock, Moline and Case 2010). They include counter-illumination, warning off predators, using light to deceive or misdirect, using lit body parts to fool predators or deter settlers. The seventh is what's known as the burglar alarm: some think an attacked creature lights up to expose its predator, in the hope a larger predator will arrive and eat it. One such is the jellyfish *Atolla wyvillei*, nicknamed the alarm jellyfish. 'With the lights on, it looks like a scarlet sunflower with long crimson tentacles protruding out from between its translucent red petals, called lappets' (Widder 2021: 200). Touching a lappet can induce a blue light streamer; any bump to its bell produces a pulse of light; prolonged stimulus produces pinwheel displays of brilliant sapphire blue (see footage at Operation Deep Scope 2025). Widder reads that as 'a scream for help, using light instead of sound, to draw attention to an attacker' - a rape alarm rather than burglar alarm (2021: 200). Bioluminescence lights up strong, even lurid language. 'In a dark world of killers, bright signals illuminate food but also summon death' (Palumbi and Palumbi 2014: 62). Military imagery is common: thus the stoplight fish, which can emit blue light and see red light, has 'sniper-scope vision that potentially allows it to see without being seen' (Widder 2021: 198). The US Navy has been interested in bioluminescence as a phenomenon that can interfere with submarines' concealment, but territorial warfare consistently provides imagery for bioluminescent spectacle. Using ROV thrusters and a 'splat screen' that stimulates light in creatures making contact with it, Widder compares one scene to night-time news of anti-aircraft fire and bomb flashes, adding shock and awe to aesthetics (2021: 117, 109).

Stronger than militarism, stronger even than theatricality, is how bioluminescence is cast as a communicative system, a language. 'Bioluminescence is one of the oldest and most prevalent languages on Earth – and one that is largely alien to us' (Jabr 2016: n.p.). Humans do recognize one terrestrial instance, globally, in the form of blue flashing lights for emergency vehicles. But, as Widder puts it, 'a majority of the creatures on the planet are communicating using language-of-light dialects that we don't comprehend' (2021: xii). Diving in a rigid, self-contained WASP suit, she carried a blue wand 'in the hope that it would permit me to talk to the animals, Dr. Doolittle style'. It didn't, but her splat screen produced 'a library of bioluminescent signatures' (Widder 2021: 87, 117). This trope of language-writing is shared by fireworks, to which bioluminescent flarings are often compared. Widder's first experience leads her to blurt out '"It's like the Fourth of July down there!" – a highly non-scientific description' for which her colleagues teased her (2021: xiii). It is helpful to consider fireworks as analogue, as Widder does. Pyrotechnics are a form of technic in how they are made and displayed, yet to spectators they manifest as magic, an art of fountains, blooms, showers, comet streaks accompanied by bangs, whistles, screeches, which are much less discussed as an accompanying sonic aesthetic. Writing on aesthetic theory, Adorno thought 'The phenomenon of fireworks is prototypical for artworks' because fireworks, like artworks, manifest becoming actual, incandescently expressive. Fireworks and artworks deploy 'a script that flashes up, vanishes, and indeed cannot be read for its meaning' (Adorno 1984: 81). Bioluminescence has communicative meaning for marine beings who use it; like fireworks and artworks, it also has aesthetic import for humans who see it. 'Without using words, art works flash a message to the effect that "it is", against a background that says "it is not"', says Adorno (1984: 81). There are many artworks on land that use creatures who bioluminesce as a performative element – for instance, Andreas Greiner puts bacteria in containers on a piano, who light up when certain notes are struck (2014); Hunter Cole makes wedding photographs in bioluminescent light, riffing on its find-a-mate purpose (2014). Less arty but more magical was the use of rehydrated ostracods to provide covert light by which Japanese soldiers in the Pacific could read maps (Ellis 1996: 159; Jabr 2016).

Taking or making bioluminescence for land-based art points to aesthetic meaning and effect. What is at stake underwater? Scientist-memoirs like that of Edith Widder and Helen Scales aim to explain bioluminescence as communicative acts; they also want to convey its aesthetic power. 'Bioluminescence's power to captivate is evident in the descriptions of anyone so fortunate as to experience it first-hand. The adjective heard most often is *magical*' (Widder 2021: xii). I can second this: on a night dive in the Azores, my buddy and I landed below a cliff full of winking shrimps enlivened by a full moon. As we moved forward, we set off wakes of gold. The power to turn movement into moving light entranced us; like a magician, I played at sweeping light into snow angels and shazam gestures of gold. Thinking with magic helps establish aesthetics for bioluminescence.

Federico Campagna observes how magic shadows science: 'Throughout Western history, magic has acted as the silent shadow of most hegemonic cultural forms, from philosophy to theology to modern science' (2018: 113). Associated with mysterious, invisible and dark forces, magic, like the deep ocean, is 'the land of non-where ... haunted by unnameable temporality' (2018: 9-10). Campagna – who is not thinking about underwater – sees Magic as a counter to the powerful force of Technic, which 'aims not to a specific and exclusive goal, but to the limitless increase in the ability to pursue goals, which is also the limitless ability to satisfy needs' (2018: 26). Hence it is and has been a driving force behind capitalism and the Anthropocene. Working through 'scientific-technological apparatus', Technic converts people into workers, and entities into measures – so a forest becomes a stockpile of timber, or an ocean abyss becomes a suite of stealthy places for submarines. Translation of things into technical names – which depends on there still being entities surviving outside the grid of Technic's language – is accelerated by what Campagna calls 'the age of total language', driven by Big Data and obsessions that 'the language of information technology is capable of grasping the whole of the existent, and that the whole of the existent coincides with the reach of the language of information technology' (2018: 41-2). Campagna argues that language has an ontology of seriality – language is made of words that take up positions – that sustains the expandable causality which supports Technic's instrumentality. Scientific work to establish names for organisms, and explain their light-making mechanisms and functions, looks like an expression of Technic. And yet scientists reach beyond disciplinary language, even beyond the discipline of language, to convey the magic of bioluminescence.

Science has a long history of gestures towards magic, especially through wonder (Adamowsky 2015). Hunting for poetics of wonder, Glenn Willmott argues 'We need to read into wonder, to expose how we both produce it and curtail its feelings and power. Not to demystify or disenchant it, but to learn its real magic' (2018: 10). Where science is definitional, magic is O!, exclamatory. Science off the page now often adopts this mode – live commentary to deep ocean footage is heavy with exclamations of wonder. Near-inarticulacy is wonder's rhetoric. Thus scientists watched sea cucumbers unexpectedly bioluminesce: in the control room on the research ship, 'nobody could say anything except "wow"' (Hobson 2023; viewable at MBARI 2019). What was even more wow was that the sea cucumbers behaved differently in their deep home. On board ship, they glowed all over but at 1300 metres down, light rippled in waves up and down their bodies, presumably a different communicative act – and a different aesthetic import, one not quite within flash, glow, shimmer or sparkle. The nearest technical word seems elusive – this is not quite capillary wave or caustic or peristalsis; it might be hula hooping? Technic wants scientific language – *Pannychia moseleyi* is one of the sea cucumbers that glows (Bessho-Uehara, Mallefet and Haddock 2023). Artistic language has as yet no word for moving loops of light patterning.

Technology's mediation of both science and magic shapes most aesthetic experiences now, Böhme proposes, instancing 'Views through the microscope, televised images of outer space, colour and light experiences while diving or through televised underwater photography, clouds and atmospheric impressions during flight – these are fundamental viewing experiences that shape viewing habits not to mention taste' (Böhme 2018: 65). Campagna argues that Magic and Technic are not a binary, because 'Magic can be considered as a form of therapy to Technic's brutal regime' (2018: 115). In his analysis, Magic originates from a dimension which can never be reduced to any linguistic classification, nor be captured by language: the Ineffable (Campagna 2018: 115, 121). Although bioluminescence is a language, according to science, magic gives it a language with obvious aesthetics, 'spreading spheres of aquamarine sparkles and flashes', 'glorious streams of light', 'vortices of shimmering cobalt-blue' (Widder 2021: xv). Deepwater, midwater, seabed instances all add to the aesthetics of bioluminescence. Off Grand Bermuda Island in a submersible, Widder describes an instance:

> even more wonderful were the two bioluminescent anemones that we found attached to the seashell home of a hermit crab. These glowed when stroked and brought to mind wild imaginings of a deep-sea existence toting around a mobile home adorned with elaborate Victorian lamps that light up only when rubbed like Aladdin's lamp.
>
> (2021: 224)

Widder's wild imaginings instance magical thinking – here notably activated by touch.

Widder advocates being underwater as desirable for viewing. 'If we want to understand life on our planet, we need more time for watching and wondering *within its blue heart*' (2021: 96, my italics). How remote can sensing be without losing sensuousness? And can aesthetics pass through machine vision with minimal interference? How else can we see bioluminescence in the deep if not through machines? Monica Halkort argues that 'remote viewing technologies have become the primary interface for rendering the sea readable, knowable, and addressable; without them, it will be impossible to fathom much less to contain threats of extinction and death.' Halkort hopes that remote sensing and machine vision can nonetheless be folded into a materialist reading of touch promoted by feminist posthuman ethics: the tactile arms of underwater vehicles can be used for protection and care, not just Technic (Halkort 2021: 43-4). Touchingly, MBARI scientists in submersibles brush some marine beings with a paintbrush to stimulate bioluminescence. Art proves to have the best soft instrument.

There is perhaps an aesthetic medium of travel, though it goes to somewhere unwordable. Campagna gestures to a Thing-beyond-thingness.

What is the heart of a thing, of everything? Is it its name, its qualities, its physical body? Once again, if we strip a thing of all its disposable dimensions, we reach a state of ineffability. It is as if we could detect – albeit only intuitively, as words eventually fail us – at the very heart of existence, something ineffable that does the job of being that thing.

(Campagna 2018: 124)

In the deep in her submersible suit *Jim* Sylvia Earle encounters what she calls 'spark-in-the-dark creatures' (1995: 118). She responds first in scientific terms: 'bioluminescence is a widespread, fundamental phenomenon of profound importance to life in most of the biosphere' (1995: 119). But her account turns towards magic, using life writing presentness to express its dialectic with science. Having landed in a bamboo coral forest, she touches the coral spires that light up with rings of glowing blue which merge and pass through each other. It might be an instance of a burglar alarm, she thinks. (A comparable instance is viewable at MBARI 2021.) But then she thinks right outside the science box. 'Or, I ask myself, is it possible that there is no special, serious function requiring a practical explanation of the sort that will satisfy rational human enquiry? Maybe bamboo coral just is that way. Period.' (Earle 1995: 119) Intuiting the Ineffable through bioluminescence, language comes to a full stop.

12

Ocean Arts

Underwater arts span a great range of media and practices. 'Characteristics of the contemporary sense of beauty are ... indeterminacy, event, and atmosphere', says Böhme (2018: 65). This chapter discusses a selection of contemporary arts – installations, glass, ghost net art, photography, dance and sound – that engage actively with ocean and its ecological troubles via different sensory means. Several themes run through: the place of artmaking; art's atmospheres, in Böhme's sense; its relationship with technologies that extend human senses, and art's questions about agencies. Art can be made by marine beings, including art-carrying crustaceans, sessile organisms and music-making cetaceans. The flow, opacity and other properties of water itself have aesthetic effects that play into underwater arts. Analysing relations between life, water and sound, Stefan Helmreich's term 'soundings' is useful here: he uses it for exploratory thinking, specifically 'for getting at the empirical world ... for making clear the representational apparatus of the analyses ... [and] for investigating things not yet known, things whose limits are not clear or whose boundaries may be obscured' (2016: xi). I use life writing to follow the soundings of art, and art to follow the soundings of life writing.

ZOODRAMATURGIES

In 2014, visitors to the Los Angeles County Museum of Art were treated to an installation, 'Zoodram 5 (after "Sleeping Muse" by Constantin Brâncusi)' by Pierre Huyghe, in which a hermit crab clambered around an aquarium with a resin-cast copy of a Brâncusi mask, *Sleeping Muse* (1910), as its shell. In many of his works Huyghe stages encounters between human and non-human worlds; 'I choose 'Zoodram 5' (2011) because, like Huyghe's other iterations' in 'Zoodram 1' (2010) to 'Zoodram 6' (2013), its playful collisions of ideas start with an obvious contrast between art and nature, yet undo that contrast to unsettle categories, including those of art and nature.

'Huyghe's art is to be encountered by subjectively projecting oneself outside of a particular and historically contingent way of conceiving of sense, mind, and experience', says Paul Finnegan, who reads Huyghe's works through models of nature and history from Adorno and Benjamin (2020: 111). Though nature is cast as unified and history as disruptive, Adorno identifies transience as a quality that history and nature share. The relationship between nature and history can be read dialectically through the experiences of art, allegory and ruins co-created by nature and history. All are themes for Huyghe. Finnegan identifies another, abandonment. 'Architectural spaces are given over to an uncontrolled occupation of the non-human and objects from art history are left to see what other non-human agencies will do with them' (2020: 102). The hermit crab who carries a modernist mask is one instance, though 'giving over' makes light of its coercion into oceanic performance art. Finnegan reads the installation as 'a contested space of multi-species politics' in which ecological thinking denies any opposition between human order and natural order. 'As direct interventions into the bionic, Huyghe uses artifice to produce a dissonance in our perception of the unity of organisms' (Finnegan 2020: 104–5). Nature and history disintegrate as concepts: the hermit crab cracks open nature by its affixed artwork whose history is dissolved into a peripatetic and uncanny questioning of categories.

Anthropologist Mary Douglas famously defined dirt as matter out of place. Brâncuși's mask is out of place underwater, so strangely dreamy it confounds even the familiar idea of opportunism by marine creatures who use human objects for shelter. Where an octopus living in a discarded bottle presents some antithesis between use and waste, the crab's mask begs the question of what use is art? Is the mask an allegory of weighty human projections onto art? The mask puts a stylized and serene face uppermost, visible to viewers but not to the hermit crab who trundles about in a different plane. Can a hermit crab have a sleeping muse as a constituent of an interior world as well as an exterior one? If not, why not? Might all beings be unconscious of their sleeping muse?

Finnegan is one of several theoretically minded critics who see Huyghe's *Zoodram* series as a significant intervention – the 'ecologization' of contemporary art, as André Rottman puts it (2019: 84). Picking up Bruno Latour's concept of composition, putting things together, Dorothea von Hantelmann applies it to Huyghe's biological forms of creation and their undoing of Anthropocenic gaps between human and non-human.

> From the moment at which one begins to question the opposition of subjects and things, a whole series of traditional binary pairs break down. For if one no longer takes for granted the modern subject that conceives of the world as primarily a stock of resources and that – in contrast to the inorganic materials that surround it – is in exclusive possession of the freedom and agency to transform its natural environment, distinctions between organic/inorganic, human/animal, free will/ determination no longer make sense.
>
> (Von Hantelmann 2017: 91)

One can counter that the crab has very restricted agency: captive, in an artificially lit aquarium with little to do except wander and grow, it is trapped in a scopic regime for human purposes. Its agency is subject to the greater freedom of the human artist. Nonetheless, Finnegan thinks Huyghe's crab is a postnatural animal, disrupting the category of nature through animal agency.

The postnatural animal is the animal for which its body and behaviour are not its nature but its art – an art that cannot be immediately coopted into a framework of human significance. An art that embodies the animal's autonomy and agency against an identification of animality with mechanical nature. The animal as art resists being seen only as a resource.

(Finnegan 2023: 191)

Von Hantelmann notices Huyghe's resistance to narrative, a resource for art.

Huyghe often speaks of 'scenarios' in reference to his works, by which he means a set, a structure of rules and possibilities that the artist initiates but that then produce something of their own independently of the artist. A scenario without a script, in a sense. Many of his works are based on real situations, unscripted events and encounters. Contingency, chance, and inherent rules are thus always part of his works.

(Von Hantelmann 2017: 89)

What rules here? *Zoodram* imposes symbolism on a hermit crab who is allowed to write a script within the constraints of tank life, a script that may or may not share poetics with art. How are challenges to binaries exportable beyond the tank? Can postnatural animals inhabit a posthuman ocean?

Such captive crabs are a substrate for art, which they animate. Making art that marine beings repurpose more freely offers lively alternatives. Finnish artist Tuomas A. Laitinen researched octopus cognition, made glass objects, video and audio, and glyphs in graphic font and glass, to materialize knowledge as a place where language and matter co-exist (Laitinen 2019). In ten blown-glass sculptures, collectively titled 'A Proposal for an Octopus' (2016–), Laitinen constructs glass chambers, passages and bottlenecks to make an octopus playground. One octopus demonstrates exploratory curiosity and pleasure, viewable in a short video, 'Haemocyanin' (2019). Sinuous shape-making connects glass and octopus, while the transparency and glint of glass mirrors the octopus's delicate touch and default colouring. Overlaid in the video are complex effects including distorting CGI bubbles, an atonal synthesizer soundtrack and mysterious glyphs. As Louis Bury explains, the glyphs move from octopus body language to world language for humans:

In 2018, Laitinen invented an asemic typeface [one that has no semantic content], Ctongue, whose sinuous flourishes are based on the gestural movements of octopus arms. The Yeh Art Gallery show featured an expansion of the typeface, designed in collaboration with the Schick Toikka type foundry, based in Berlin and Helsinki: each line of text used a slightly different version of Ctongue, progressing from indecipherable glyphs in the top line to cursive English-language letters in the bottom line. The characters didn't become recognizably alphabetic until about line four or five, where the words BONELESS ONE became legible. This continuum of characters exemplified the way Laitinen's work uses human language to render the other-than-human world intelligible to varying degrees.

(Bury 2022: 75)

Oblique references to theorists of entanglement like Haraway and Barad are cryptically present: where Huyghe likes unscriptedness, Laitinen prefers understatement as a vehicle for enigma. He was uneasy about the ethics of conscripting an octopus; getting to know one, named Napoleon, who already lived in an aquarium tank, he took a couple of years to introduce the glass sculpture and filmed only occasionally. The artist's reticence quietly articulates the communication gap in interspecies encounters:

> Visual artworks have indeed been a popular focus for exponents of anti-anthropocentric philosophies. But the push-pull between explanation and elision, intellect and intuition in Laitinen's approach demonstrates the all-too-human linguistic binds in which these questions become entangled. His practice constitutes less a demonstration of philosophical principles than a series of stress tests of them.
>
> (Bury 2022: 77)

Yet within these stress tests Laitinen makes glass a medium of solid consideration for octopuses, inventing too a morphology of script that moves from squiggle to signs to lettering, implying communicative evolution is possible, even if its current trajectory is human-centred.

REPURPOSING: WASTE, USE, BEAUTY, CREATION

Glass, water and plastic have affinities of transparency and opacity, malleability and tonality. Glass artists' attraction to the forms and liquidities of sea life have led to representations that powerfully shape evocation of oceans and oceanic feelings. The exquisite glass models of marine invertebrates by Leopold and Rudolf Blaschka were made in the 1870s, but re-appreciated in the early twenty-first century. 'Tiny, delicate and beautiful, they capture the ethereal mystery of the deep sea … These models bring art and science together', says the Natural History Museum, London (Pavid n.d.). Sea life subjects express ideas about purity and pollution, vulnerability and timelessness for contemporary glass artists like Dale Chihuly (*Seaforms*, 2002), Asa Jungnelius ('The Seashell' 2016, Stockholm Metro), Davide Penso (Seaweeds, 2017) and Colin Reid ('Nautilus', 2018). Writing of Chihuly's *Seaforms*, and how their open, voluptuous, ribbed, organic shapes abstractly evoke ocean life, Joan Seeman Robinson argues that 'The *Seaforms* call forth associations with water, marine life and movement without depicting them and that's why they so persuasively affect us as art.' Their transparency exposes linear infrastructure like a skeletal network; their faint films of thinned colours suggest membranes and tissues – in contrast to the Blaschkas' sea life models, where intense detail excludes suggestion in favour of fact. Seeman Robinson thinks the fragility of glass adds pathos: 'loss seems integral to the material. It is the essence of glass to forecast its own disappearance and to embody its own immateriality' (Seeman Robinson 1995). In 2002 the Monterey Bay Aquarium held a big exhibition of jellyfish, 'Jellies: Living Art'; the staging included artworks in many media. Chihuly contributed a large installation of blown-glass pieces, whose undulating colours and translucence provided a visual rhyme to sea nettle jellies moving gracefully nearby. The synergy established a correspondence that stuck: two decades later, an MBARI expedition researcher looking at a midwater siphonophore compared it to 'a delicate, living Chihuly sculpture' (Simpson 2024).

Reinventing waste as art raises questions about use value, including material and aesthetic properties. Merging the shine and colours of plastic into those of glass, 'Seven Stages of Degradation' (2022, blown-glass and found plastic) by Louis Thompson and Sophie Thomas comprises seven shapes mimicking the stages of plastic bottles degrading – they twist, crumple and acquire sludge-like interiors. Waste is imaged back as corruption of the beautiful, though waste can have its own grim beauty too. Stages of degradation play across plastic-glass and art-environment boundaries, a porous border of interest to theorists who explore the art-politics border through aesthetics.

> One of the most demanding questions of our time is to consider the extent to which contemporary art is offering a critique of the order of things by creating ambient atmospheres in which the boundary between artistic production and social experience is made all too visible but the content is interchangeable.
>
> (Papastergiadis 2014: 10)

The plasticity of plastic and its malleable place in systems of both use and waste make it central to art engaging with what Papastergiadis calls 'the complex question of where the aesthetic draws its power from to produce change' (2014: 17). He explains that for influential theorist Jacques Rancière, metaphoric images that play on the ambiguity of resemblances and the instability of dissemblances create a crucial link between aesthetic experience and political engagement. Metaphors, thinks Rancière, are easily understood (Papastergiadis 2014: 11, 22).

Using a different theoretical field, Catherine Phillips takes up ocean plastic as less tractable material. Since 2004, GhostNets Australia (GNA) has worked with Indigenous communities in the Gulf of Carpentaria. 'The Gulf, in Australia's north-west, experiences high accumulations; every year up to three tonnes of ghost nets wash ashore for every kilometre of coast, and thousands of endangered sea turtles die through ghost gear entanglement' (Phillips 2017: 1149). One abandoned net removed in 2023 weighed five tonnes. The Australian Ghost Net art movement began in 2009; its collaborative work led to the Ghost Net Collective founded in 2020 by Lynnette Griffiths and Marion Gaemers. Their projects and workshops enable artworks made of rewoven ghost gear to reach museums and communities, to draw attention to how discarded industrial fishing lines, ropes and nets kill marine life and pollute the ocean. Questions of responsibility point to manufacturers and fishery workers but, as Phillips thoughtfully explores, those working with ghost nets as art material do not all agree on directions for blame or responsibility. What can be agreed on is the repurposing of deathly materials to represent Indigenous stories and marine life forms like sharks, turtles and rays who are at risk from entanglement, ingestion and habitat damage. Once sorted and cleaned, ghost gear has material properties like colour, mesh size, knot type, texture and rigidity that become aesthetic assets. Disposal of waste is difficult in remote communities, so recycling ghost gear into art returns ghosts of use to urban and global communities where awareness can be relocated and made useful to ocean campaigners. In the Indigenous gallery of the Australian Museum in Sydney, Phillips is transfixed by 'Dauma and Garom', a sculpture created by artists from Erub Erwer Meta (Darley Island Arts Centre). It tells a beautiful story of interspecies love, between a crab (Dauma) and a fish (Garom). It is made of ghost nets. Phillips wonders how to explain its effect:

> what I am meant to take away. Are these marine plastics a simple substitution – a convenient, available material? Is there a message about largely ignored burdens carried by and the resilience of indigenous communities? Is there celebration and/or a sense of loss for marine life and peoples' connections to it? Do the formed bodies project a future in which only plastic remains? Is this a prompt for a revised ethics?
>
> (Phillips 2017: 1158)

A nice instance of Rancière's interest in how art moves towards problem solving, her reflections record both affect and uncertainty about where that goes:

> I think that the bodies of the many plastic creatures carry a story about the unfair burden experienced by indigenous communities and creatures dealing with oceanic plastics, a warning about future oceanic worlds remade through plastic presence, and I can hear through them a call for social and environmental justice. But the message is not always clearly articulated.
>
> (Phillips 2017: 1159)

She quotes Lynnette Griffith's counterclaim that ghost art makes visible the issue of ocean plastic, creating affect that may develop variously: 'people are so seduced by the colour and form, and quite often the size, and it's very tactile – you want to go and touch it. So that excites people and then they want to know more ...' (Phillips 2017: 1159). Dianna Cohen and Jennifer Wagner Lawlor, who cofounded the advocacy organization Plastic Pollution Coalition in 2009, agree that art is a medium of sensual impression, useful for energizing activism. 'We want people to see the problem, but also to *feel* it. We want the visual *and* the visceral.' Discussing how plastic has got into everything, they respect its creative power. 'Today, it's almost as if plastic is itself a living artist, remaking creation down at cellular and molecular levels' (Cohen and Wagner-Lawlor 2021: 38, 28).

Ghost net creatures can also be understood as ancestral beings, not imitations of species. In Indigenous cultures, they manifest a non-human world that has agency and presence, and whose inhabitation of the sea has powerful meanings for relationships between people and other species. Part of the ancient cosmogony of water serpent beings, they bring authority to activism. In her fine study of water serpent beings throughout history and around the world, Veronica Strang explains: 'the major intention of Aboriginal art is not only to communicate cultural knowledge but also, by emanating ancestral power (via the shimmering light and colour – *bir'yan'* – of the artwork), to "act upon" the viewer' (2023: 220). Rather than rousing a response to modern pollution, this cosmogony sees ghost net art as a means of making visible the creational power of water beings.

THE QUICK, THE DEAD AND THE BEAUTIFUL

Valérie Loichot argues in *Water Graves* that 'Watery realms of unritual graves are nowhere and everywhere at once, absolutely lost and omnipresent' (2020: 139). Yet she proposes that the Caribbean is a place so associated with the specific suffering of slavery that its undersea arts are saturated by it. Discussing the work of British sculptor, environmentalist and photographer Jason deCaires Taylor, Loichot observes 'The water sites of Taylor's museums on the touristic coasts of Grenada, Aruba and Mexico unequivocally envelop the grave murmur, the smothered scream of sunken humans' (2020: 144). DeCaires Taylor made his first 'underwater museum' in 2006 at Moliniere Bay, Grenada; he now has underwater museums and sculpture parks worldwide and calculates they are visited by more than half a million visitors each year (https://underwatersculpture.com). Loichot understands his ecological intent:

> With the joint purpose of producing beauty and of providing pH-adapted supports for coral regrowth, Taylor submerges hundreds of sculpture in the coastal waters of Mexico, Antigua, the Bahamas, the Canary Islands, and the Indonesian Gili Islands, among other locations. His subaquatic work – devoted to themes as varied as slavery, migration, mythology, gardening, and mass production – welcome [*sic*] growth of new underwater life forms that become at once unrecognizable and hauntingly, dynamically beautiful.
>
> (Loichot 2020: 142)

What Katharina Fackler and Silvia Schultermandl call 'the irrecuperability of lost kin through aqueous death' (2023: 203) is gently transformed into recuperation through a spectator's kinship with the figures, and the figures' kinship with the marine life that settles on them. DeCaires Taylor's sites are both more and other than water graves.

Although deCaires Taylor's work can be read as underwater monument-making, it does other things as well. Paradoxically, his oeuvre – ongoing – can also be read as engaging with ideas of the moment – hence *The Pride of Brexit* (2019) in which three emaciated lions, recasting Landseer's patriotic lions from Trafalgar Square, crawl painfully under English chalk cliffs. Many of his works feature ecological life writing in material form. *A World Adrift* (2024), at Carriacou, near Grenada, is an underwater installation about rising sea levels, imaged through young human figures in a fragile fleet of origami-esque boats. Ironically it was delayed by Hurricane Beryl which destroyed the homes of the local children who modelled for it (Weinman 2024). So although de Caires Taylor works with ostensibly permanent material (pH-neutral marine cement), climate derangement increasingly temporizes his underwater installations.

Evoking the distinctive technique of Giuseppe Arcimboldo (1526–93) who made eye-fooling portraits using fruits, flowers, vegetables and other organic entities, deCaires Taylor's structures attract marine life who, as they colonize the installations, transform them from inert to blossoming surfaces. Mobile marine beings animate the sites. In 2021, seven nudibranchs, *Scyllaea pelagica*, crawled around the Museum of Underwater Sculpture Ayia Napa (MUSAN). They were new to the area (https://

underwatersculpture.com/art-science). The art of nature supplants the artist: the process, says deCaires Taylor, reminds us we are natural too (Taylor n.d.). Elizabeth DeLoughrey argues that 'by life casting local people for submersion, [deCaires Taylor] enables sea ontologies, rendering uninhabitable space into anthropomorphized place' (DeLoughrey 2015). But the ocean then replaces human typologies with marine ones, local in a different way. Caribbean faces and bodies bloom with pink encrusting coralline algae, sponges and corals: the installation spaces are de-anthropomorphized as local marine beings move in. Their dynamic settlement reminds us that not everything in the ocean is convertible to images of flow, fluidity and circulation. Underwater life transmogrifies in uniquely artistic ways too. Commenting on the speed of some transformations, deCaires Taylor notes they chromatically exceed human conventions. 'The colour pigmentation of some of the sponges is something I have never seen recreated by any industry or artists palette' (Preece n.d.). Where Arcimboldo's compositions play on the surprise of their composite elements, deCaires Taylor's figures become surprises through the disappearance of their original forms, recast by marine beings into organic, living, changeable collage.

Killian Quigley suggests deCaires Taylor's art catalyses a new aesthetic reading of encrustation: 'What we are learning from the sea-bottom is that concrescing things

Figure 28 Jason deCaires Taylor, 'Silent Evolution, MUSA, Mexico'. Image courtesy of the artist. The striped sergeant major (*Abudefduf saxatilis*) is a mobile visitor.

combine forms and practices of artfulness that become, as they grow together, more than the sum of their parts' (2023: 153). Quigley's model neatly defines their wavering between and dissolution of categories of artefact and ecofact. Those categories sit like theoretical encrustations over an older idea of nature as art. Reading ecofacts like artefacts, Rachel Carson described calcium ions being cycled from seawater to a mollusc's shell and, on the mollusc's death, cycled back again to be 'later incorporated into the delicate statuary of a coral reef' (1937: 325). The shell of a one-celled radiolarian was likewise a 'miracle of ephemeral beauty that might be the work of a fairy glass-blower with a snowflake as his pattern' (Carson 1937: 325). Carson's metaphors of artmaking – influenced by Beebe's fairy imaginary – make aesthetic creativity inherent in marine creatures. DeCaires Taylor gives them full and free agency.

One museum director keen on objects has argued that 'The distinction between a gallery and a museum is enormous. The gallery is about looking at a thing of beauty; the purpose of the activity is an aesthetic response. The museum is actually about the object that lets you get into somebody else's life' (Crompton 2012). Underwater art confounds that distinction, offering beauty that lets you get into other lives, human and marine. DeCaires Taylor chose the term 'museum' intentionally: 'Museums are places of conservation, education and about protecting something sacred. We need to assign those same values to the underwater world' (https://underwatersculpture. com). Museums also frame Christine and Margaret Wertheim's *Crochet Coral Reef* (2006–). Based on complex mathematical fractals, the original work has spawned satellite reefs around the world. Described by the Wertheims as an ever-evolving nature-culture hybrid, the reefs are predominantly exhibited in museums and galleries. The high culture settings confirm crotchet as art, not craft, an art here collectively made, largely by women around the world, and an art capable of expressing urgent ideas. Displayed sometimes in cases, echoing coral curiosity assemblages of the early modern period, sometimes on plinths, overspilling their stands, and sometimes in open spaces which they wildly populate, the crotchet coral reefs sling interspecies making into riotous forms. Critics use the witty term 'coralating' (Braverman 2018: 3) to describe coral's ability to inspire relational ways of thinking and being, which Marion Endt-Jones argues includes new relations between art and science, and between visitor engagement and climate politics (2020: 186). 'Interestingly, exhibition visitors instantly seem to connect with the woolly creatures through an innate sense of recognition: members of the public tend to experience the colourful crochet corals as essentially "coral-like", even if they have never seen a living reef in the flesh'. Like deCaires Taylor, the Wertheims reimagine underwater lives in multispecies terms that create new relations between art, museums and ocean habitats.

FLOATING WORLDS: UNDERWATER DANCE AND PHOTOGRAPHY

Underwater dance uses open ocean locations and enclosed tanks. Big concepts can play out in tanks which, like museum cases, frame a contained space. Böhme's theorizing of bodily space is useful here. He argues 'the simplest and most convincing way to ascertain one's bodily presence in a space is through movement. Therefore, the elements in seeing that best give us a sense of spatiality all entail movement, that is, varying perspective and changing fixation' (2017: 74). Although Böhme is thinking about a subject's perception of architectural space, his model fits the viewer of underwater dance, whose sense of bodily presence is relocated to the dancer, and whose sense of movement is also managed through camera movement. Even when space is restricted by the surrounds of a tank, dancers explore spatiality through movements not possible on land. 'The giving in to and the rebound from gravity is the source and dictator of all movement', argued Joanna Friesen, quoting dancer and choreographer Doris Humphrey; water makes that imperative clearly visible, and often an asset (Friesen 1975: 990). As Mo Tu puts it, 'The natural element of water is thus transformed from a mere background for the performance to a vehicle for discourse, creating a fluid narrative that works with the performers' (2023: 76).

Underwater dance is a growing art. Its overlap with photography was the point of Howard Schatz's photobook *Water Dance* (1995) which features naked women wreathed in soft fabrics; more recently, crisscrossing both arts are concepts of floatiness, breath, movement and speech. Both arts use ideas of beauty related to Edmund Burke's definition of beauty (1757) as a quality found in smoothness, easy gradations of line and soft colour tones, all of which he associated with femininity. Viewable online, Marianne Aventurier and Alex Voyer's *Aquaballet* (2024) uses scenes in white sand and blue midwater for oceanic beauty; Stéphane Lopez's gentle score with piano and ethereal voice themes adds to its grace. In ballet terms, Aventurier uses the splayed 'Balanchine' hand, which treats hands as expressive body parts, rather than classical ballet's tapered body extensions. Through gesture she engages with the ocean and marine beings – not through touch, because correctly she touches nothing, but through potentially connective space, the gap between bodies that gesture indicates while holding back from touch. The etymology of gesture is relevant here: it comes from the Latin *gestus*, meaning gesture, posture or carriage. Aventurier's poised body is beautifully gestural in itself, playfully orchestrating sand eels into appearance and disappearance, fluidly echoing sinuous sharks, elegantly duetting with a fin whale. Yet although Burkean beauty is present, *Aquaballet* stages beauty in Böhme's terms too, with indeterminacy, event and atmosphere informing interspecies encounters.

Humans are the focus of Emma Critchley, a British artist 'who uses a combination of photography, film, sound and installation to continually explore the human relationship with the underwater environment as a political, philosophical and environmental space' (artist website). Writing about her 'Disappearing Moon' exhibition in collaboration with Geraldine Chua (2013), Jonathan Miles responded to Critchley's untethering of signification. 'A floating chain of signifying words come to me; below, submerged, other, unconscious, before, deep, float. I need to float in these images and be with these words in order to discover their reserve without attempting to fix anything. ... Something else is in circulation; sense, gesture, affects, but in ways that are freed from inscriptive indexes' (Miles 2013).

Hair floating underwater provides sense, gesture and affect – wordless, but culturally laden: as T. S. Eliot puts it in *Ash Wednesday* (1930), 'Blown hair is sweet'. Blown hair shows movement in suspension, and hence suspension of time. Writing of Emma Critchley's portraits which reference T. S. Eliot's *Burnt Norton* (1936) in their exhibition title, one critic catches the drift. 'In water, not only are shape and form suspended, but so is time. Words, limbs and breath float in an eternal present moment, neither past nor future, neither moving nor completely still' (Wallace-Thompson 2015). Underwater art can make suspension visible through floating utterance.

> Critchley's video *There is nothing in Language, which has not come from the Senses* (2012) records a submerged man who speaks the title of the piece, masses of gorgeous bubbles flowing from his mouth. This moment of deliverance is again captured in *Figures of Speech Series 2* (2012), a photographic triptych of women underwater, expelling immense, glassy globules of undisclosed words that cover their faces.
>
> (Stock 2013)

Breath links air and water, time and language, visualized underwater in unreadable but expressive speech bubbles.

Breath is visualized a different way in *Flowers For Jeju: The Last Mermaids* (2017), photographs by Zena Holloway of the *haenyeo* or Korean Sea Women. Like the Ama in Japan, they are matrilineal sea-harvesters, an imperilled tradition. Holloway photographs them in two ways: in black and white, going about their work, and in stylized, studio portraits. Those sitters wear fewer and more showy clothes than their light and practical workdress; their poses are mostly curled with knees drawn up, strangely foetal. Using a heavy version of floatiness – fabrics are weighty, like ropes – Holloway's analogy to mermaids is given conceptual heft by the inclusion in some images of a black figure in the background, who represents a water-breath, or *mulsum*, which to the *haenyeo* embodies the temptation to stay too long underwater gathering riches, and which must be resisted (Lemmon 2018). Breath here has a visual rhyme, through black, with death.

Like hair, fabrics can manifest floatiness. Laura Trethewey quotes water-stunt coordinator Katie Rowe on abstract dreamy sequences: '"Production tends to love things that look beautiful in the water," she says, "like long flowing skirts, things that kind of swirl. Ribbons, when you're thrashing around, tend to wrap around you like a snake and try to sink you"' (Trethewey 2019: 16). Hsu-Hu Yuan's 'Underwater Dance' (2012) features a couple in light, white dress, turning and twining in a strong shaft of light. The accompanying music, Erik Satie's 'Gnossiennes N° 1, por Reinbert de Leeuw', adds to floating meaning. The gnossienne is a form devised by Satie, though known earlier to be a dance, and possibly a gnostic allusion. With no time signature or bar lines, Satie indicates slow tempos for his three gnossiennes. Formally, slowness and timelessness situate freedom through movement extended through the female dancer's hair, which floats a fraction of a moment later and farther than her body movements.

Ribbons, sashes and hair float in space aligned with the dancer, but with their own autonomous movement too. That mix makes floatiness a visualization of ambiguity. 'Water transforms women into goddesses, gravity-defying nymphs who float free from earthly restraints, but it can quickly turn on its head, showing them as dead, drowned, trapped or somehow tainted by the sea' (Trethewey 2019: 15). British artist Sue Austin recalibrates the binary. In 'Creating the Spectacle!' (2012), she performs immersive dance from a wheelchair – standard NHS issue, with propellers and aerofoils to enable turns. She wears a light summery dress and her long auburn hair floats free as she passes coral reefs; her arms make light wavy movements which offset any visual heaviness in her wheelchair. Under the title 'Finding Freedom', and to an ethereal soundtrack of 'As My Heart Sings', she tilts her head and wheelchair back to image looseness from all bodily restraints. A collective dance, 'Drops of Breath' choreographed by Sophie Bulbulyan and Apostolia Papadamaki (2015), brought together differently abled dancers and divers performing to an underwater audience at Cape Sounio, Greece; weightlessness and the soft sea floor inspire earthly-disabled movements for all bodies.

Seascapes – for which there is little language other than that borrowed from land – also have potential to universalize humans. Although Julie Gautier's powerful underwater dance *Ama* (2018) honours the famous women divers of Japan, it takes place in a tank, for purer visibility. Her collaboration with Guillaume Néry in *One Breath Around the World* (Néry 2019) leaves conceptual vessels to make ocean the surround, not a tank. Gautier is invisible, but agile camerawork turns her presence into co-production. The pair freedive in exceptional ways: as Néry explains, 'we really tried to show freediving in a new way. To explore a new way to interact with the water. Walking, running, jumping, flying. That was something that had never been done before, showing the link between humans and the water in this way' (National Geographic 2019). Oceanic space stays expansive through long perspectives of near-infinite blue, with Néry scaled small against giant rock steps and sleeping sperm whales. There is one strange narrative moment (at 6'32), when an Indigenous person with a harpoon gun stalks into sight, as if across a stage; Néry flees, as if disavowing violence. Sleek as a pale blue-clad Spiderman, he uses hands and feet for simian grasp of rocks, but the camera also follows his strong glances, as if to image human curiosity. Litheness is all: pliant and supple body-glides evoke neither exploration nor occupation but oceanic ease. Gautier and Néry filmed in locations round the world including Mauritius, Mexico and Japan, and the film ends with Néry walking out of the sea onto a touristy beach, as if to lock oceanic space into inner subjectivity. Yet the film's beauty depends on shedding above-water associations to showcase a seascape which has locality, in ice, rock, open water, but no familiar location. The film's last highlight, like Marianne Aventurier's, shows a human weaving around sperm whales whose gigantic bodies hang like sarsen stones, uprights of ancient monumentality in open, deep water. Whale mastery of vertical floating makes the beautiful into the sublime.

MUSIC, SONG AND SOUND

Spectacular nature documentaries like the *Blue Planet* series tend to use orchestral music with human choirs adding what one might call an ethereal effect. That's air-related: in underwater soundtracks, chorales side with grandeur and wonder, transposed from celestial realms to otherworldly deeps. Towards the end of their film, Gautier and Néry blend in whale tones, a gentle reminder that the deeps are worlded by other beings, ones who can voice their presence. Water itself makes sounds, not all understood by humans. In 1997, an underwater sound recorded in the Pacific mystified researchers, who called it 'The Bloop'. In 2005, it was identified as the sound of an iceberg breaking away from an Antarctic glacier (NOAA 2024). Melting glaciers also produce fizzing sounds as bubbles recover their shape; harbour seals use them as acoustic camouflage, which fades as glaciers retreat (Perkins 2015).

'To many, the ocean is "like music", a sonic conversation with the elemental' (von Hausswolf 2021: 69). Underwater soundscapes serve art and science, promoting deeper listening. 'Under Limfjord' (2020) is a hydrophone recording made by Juan Pablo Pacheco Bejarano in Limfjord, Denmark. A gentle current washes to and fro over soft-knocking stones. The soothing rhythm evokes deep time, says Bejarano, 'in sync with the sonic memory of the water in this particular place' (Bejarano 2020). Stefan Helmreich argues that hydrophone compositions promote 'the notion of water as sublimely immersive' (2016: 138) – the sublime in 'Under Limfjord' being located in immeasurable deep time. Much contemporary sound art similarly leads from the particular to the general, from a specific location to global concerns like noise pollution, evident in oceans everywhere. Norway-based artist Jana Winderen, whose recordings encompass reef chatter and melting ice, stresses the interplay of ocean sound-making by creatures and humans, including frequencies beyond human hearing. Her 2019 work, 'The Art of Listening: Under Water' is a place-based sonic collage. The colon in her title cleverly represents a transition into another medium. As her collaborator Tony Myatt puts it, listening underwater

> is something that people can't do. We don't have the physical mechanism to do it, we don't have the size of head to do it, and we don't have any way to perceive the spatial world underwater. And the oceans are the most sound-rich environments on the planet. … The surface of the water doesn't allow sound to permeate out. And so for most of us, it's invisible.
>
> (Schneider 2019)

There has, however, been considerable attention given to underwater sound by the US and Russian militaries, for whom dolphins in particular have been captive subjects, navy operatives and Advanced Biological Weapon System (ABWS), able to detect, plant and clear mines. The U.S. Navy's Marine Mammal Program, begun in the early 1960s, still uses bottlenose dolphins and California sea lions for clandestine underwater activities (Colby 2020). Science too has taken up sound studies, often to locate populations, measure distribution and behaviours. As new technologies of listening develop, what does underwater life writing contribute to understanding what we hear? In what follows I make a literary sweep through underwater soundscapes to explore communications that may be cast as language or as music. The main protagonists are whales, with other cetaceans – dolphins, orcas, porpoises – featuring as vocal species whose utterances have attracted many interpreters. Language implies sentient and sociable communication; music implies artistry. Are marine beings using language we can learn? How would understanding those languages change relationships between humans and marine beings? Machine learning is now a standard means of interpreting data sets of sounds: how does AI understand arts? Answers to such questions are changing fast. Philosophers too are turning questions inside out. Rethinking humans as animal beings, Melanie Challenger argues that 'music depends on us being animal', bypassing technology's mediation: 'responding to music … has more to do with the experience of whales deep in the Atlantic Ocean than it does with the computer through which we might be listening' (2022: 221). But since sound travels faster and farther in water than in air – almost five times faster – some resonances are lost in land listening.

Many studies show marine beings as sound-makers – drumfish, croakers, grunt(fish); the clue is often in the name. Underwater life writers frequently describe marine sound-making through imagery: a mewing cat (Ganges river dolphins); a postman rattling a gate (sea lions); an unoiled creaky door (crabeater seals); windscreen wipers (damselfish). Although culturally specific, these comparisons relate underwater sounds to terrestrial sounds we might know. Life writers shift encounters into aurality as they carefully describe sounds in sequence – for instance, hearing unseen narwhals:

> There were ratchet sounds, like fishing reels unwinding. There was a noise like the cooing of doves, which plummeted to a deep croaking roar like the call of a Micronesian pigeon – if you've ever heard one of those. Then a whistling, as if somewhere undersea a congested human, a merman, were sleeping on his back. Then the ratchet sound again. Then a groan like a tree creaking. Then an insistent noise, something like a donkey's braying. Then the trumpeting of an elephant with a very thin trunk. Then a guttural roar like a lion's.
>
> (Brower 1979: 118)

On screen, sounds of nature are often mimicked by human artifice. David Attenborough writes admiringly of Beryl Mortimer, a BBC foley artist uncannily able to create sound effects in the studio, often from the unlikeliest props. She was known affectionately as Beryl the Boot for her skill in creating footstep sounds (Attenborough 2002: 122). On paper, sound descriptions hover between noise and music:

> The song of grey seals, at least in the Western Atlantic, comprises seven different calls. They wail, moan, warble, cry, cough, snort, roar, and on Sable Island off Nova Scotia they also yodel. Underwater, they click, knock, 'trot', 'rup' and roar. The solitary bearded seal is also known to sing a complex series of trills underwater, lasting more than a minute, and these can be heard at a distance of 25km (15.5 miles).
>
> (Dickenson 2015: 44-5)

Seal song includes some sounds – snorts, roars – not thought of as music, and some that are – yodels, trills. Some of their sounds are identified as communicative – trot, rup – but need translation. Precise description can stabilize category indeterminacy, expressing what in attention studies is known as 'the Cocktail Party Problem', or receiving several messages at once and selecting one to respond to (Moray 2017: 15). Ecoacoustics listens to the party, 'the *biophony* – not a single animal noise but the interacting and overlapping sounds of an *entire living ecosystem*' (Mustill 2022: 149-50). Bioacoustics focuses more on single species, studying how animals produce, transmit and receive sound. In Baffin Island in the Arctic, Bill Curtsinger, voiced by Kenneth Brower, recalls his listening practices. He hears bioacoustically at first, then ecoacoustically. Under the ice, he dives with harp seals. They make 'a birdy *oink oink*' which compared feebly to whale song, he thought.

> But when you stopped listening to it, and began hearing instead the background it merged with – the collective babble of the species – the music was something else again. It was like ignoring the scrape of a single branch for the sound of the wind in the forest. The voices blurred with distance into a multitudinous whisper. The whisper suggested whole nations under the ice, and the vanished nations that preceded them. It might have been a song of pagophile history – the murmur of the thousands of generations that had wandered these icy seas at the top of the planet – and it was beautiful.
>
> (Brower 1979: 103)

Life writing finds common sound between species in babble, whisper and murmur, and it recognizes musical forms: voice, song. Harp seal music conjures up species' history, audible to those who listen on imaginative wavelengths.

WHALE-SPEAK, WHALE SONG

The story of whale song traditionally starts in 1967 when biologist Roger Payne was given recordings of whales by US Navy engineer Frank Watlington, who had been listening for Russian submarines off Bermuda. Working with Scott McVay, Payne realized their power to present whales as a vocal species with artistic abilities. He released a record, *Songs of the Humpback Whale*, in 1970; recordings spread around the world via a flexible disc included in the *National Geographic* magazine in 1979 – at 10.5 million copies, the largest single pressing of any record. Payne and McVay cast whale sounds emphatically as music in a scientific article. 'Humpback whales (Megaptera novaeangliae) produce a series of beautiful and varied sounds for a period of 7 to 30 minutes and then repeat the same series with considerable precision. We call such a performance "singing" and each repeated series of sounds a "song"' (Payne and McVay 1971: 597). In 1977 humpback vocalizations went into space on a golden phonograph record curated by Carl Sagan, aboard two Voyager spacecraft heading out of the solar system (Grebowicz 2017: 5). Payne was a cellist as well as a scientist; his wife Katy Payne, who had a degree in music and biology, alerted him to patterns in printouts of the sounds. (She later became a bioacoustical expert in elephant low-frequency sounds.) Payne thought whale song would catalyse conservation, and so it did: enthusiastic reception of the recordings led to new attention to whaling and protests against it. A global agreement via the International Whaling Commission (IWC) came into force in 1986 – with a few exceptions – to end commercial hunting. Payne said in 2014 he thought 'the humpback recordings would put an end to whaling because it is criminal to "make cat food out of composer-poets"' (Grebowicz 2017; 85). Artistic ability had not stopped whale slaughter earlier, despite recognition of their musicality. 'In the nineteenth century whalers were referring to "singers" in their whaling logbooks' (Janik 2009: 109). Can you interpret too musically? In her crisp account of whale song, Margret Grebowicz observes 'Performance, composition, poetry, opera, even the sea as a vaulted performance space with excellent acoustics – Payne finds all of these categories in the phenomenon of whale song without even a hint of metaphor' (2017: 86). How much metaphor should there be? Toothed cetaceans use sound to navigate and investigate: 'Each dolphin had an acoustic look at us from a slightly different angle' (Brower 1979: 128). Synaesthesia, here sound-as-vision, conveys echolocation; it is less sure about music.

What is at stake in distinctions between music and language? Language proponents can be utilitarian: for Walter Zimmer, cetacean sounds are austerely divided into 'echolocation clicks' and 'communication signals' (2011: 39). Tom Mustill observes ruefully, 'the word "language" can get you into all kinds of trouble if you combine it with the word "animal." It's something that Roger [Payne] has avoided by coining the term "whale-speak"' (2022: 89). 'Song' sticks better: science inclines to song as the output of anatomical sound production in whales. The process has been newly explained for humpbacks: each has a unique larynx which makes voiceprints individual (as in humans). 'Elemans and colleagues reveal a unique airflow pathway in the larynx of baleen whales, in which air is squeezed between a fold of tissue and a cushion of fatty material above it, causing the fold to vibrate and generate sound' (Reidenberg 2024: 40). The U-shape of this fold may explain how they can produce two sounds at once.

Whale song borrows its aesthetic partly from birdsong, and birds who sing provide analogies for functions of whale song. Hence belugas are nicknamed canaries of the sea. Their repertoire includes clicks, yelps, chirps, whistles, trills, screams, buzzsaw, pulses and, an indescribable category, 'noises'. Despite finely tuned listening, 'their complex music or language seems more inscrutable than the code of any other whale' writes philosopher and musician David Rothenberg (2008: 109). He argues that 'Music can cross cultural lines not because it is a universal language but because it is a fluid and emotional form of communication able to make use of [previously] unknown sounds' (2008: 212). Rothenberg plays his clarinet down a hydrophone in the hope that cetacean species will respond. They do, variously: his book includes a CD, featuring him improvising on clarinet and electronics, with others adding guitar, percussion, violin; whales add … whale music. Orcas (officially a species of dolphin) seem most responsive. Rothenberg had sceptical moments: 'Why would the whales want to listen to me? It's a crazy hope, to make music with animals with whom we cannot speak' (2008: 225). Calling cetacean sounds music could be as anthropocentric as giving animals intelligence tests, he suggested (79) and his faith in music as a stabilizing category wavered. 'Days alone with headphones trying to reach out to belugas and my whole notion of what can be music begins to change. I listen beyond the edge of my species, trying to find my part in the underwater soundscape' (Rothenberg 2008: 121).

Margret Grebowicz is critical of Rothenberg's approach, arguing that improvisation is not free association but has limiting codes like a language (2017: 93-7). She argues that wanting a response to music disguises investment in greeting – in other words, whether in music, language or sound, what we want is for other species to greet us. Our investment is all the stronger because whales replace aliens from outer space as the race of beings who dominate our imaginary of connection. Life writers testify to this longing for greeting. Freediving with sperm whales, James Nestor has his most powerful experience with a mother and calf; greeting is the heart of his emotional connection. Nestor writes, 'the mother and calf didn't make a U-turn to escape us. *They came back to say hello*' (2015: 188, my italics). Eye contact as usual intensifies it, adding an impression of recognition. That turns contact into connection, like the old joke of Martians meeting humans with the salutation 'Greetings, Earthling'. Could there be a marine being equivalent?

Cetacean groups clearly use communication. Part of that is functional: echolocation enables navigation and identification of things, beings, spaces. Another part is social: dolphins have signature whistles, often compared to a personal name; humpback whales have idiolects, individual sounds; orcas, sperm whales and other cetaceans have vocal clans and pods, differentiated by exclusive sounds (Mustill 2022: 69-70). As Grebowicz puts it, 'Acoustic intelligence thus ends up becoming a sort of exceptional *social* intelligence' (2017: 18). Hal Whitehead and Luke Rendell argue 'The best evidence for culture … in the cetaceans is the song of the humpback whale' (2014: 192). Heathcote Williams finds a pitch-perfect combination in *Whale Nation*: for him, whales are 'A marine intelligentsia, with a knowledge of the deep' and 'a musical society' (1988: 103).

Naming and classifying sounds becomes a taxonomic challenge for life writers. Representing the process of echolocation, Kenneth Brower turns mimetic. 'When a nearby dolphin ratchets you, you hear it less than feel it. The *tik tik tik tik tiktiktiktiktiktiktiktiktik tik tik tik tik tik tik tik tik* bounces around inside your skull and mastoid process more than in your ears. … I felt undressed' (Brower 1979: 132). Whereas whale vocalizations can be represented visually in sonograms, writers choose the visual suggestion of imagery. Listening to humpbacks off Maui, Mark Carwardine uses similes to describe sounds:

> the air was filled with a baffling medley of moans, groans, roars, snores, squeaks and whistles. Some of the sounds were like the grating of an old metal hinge, others resembled the last gurglings of a drowning man and there was one which could only be described as like the squawking of a chicken with a farmer standing on its toe.

He then uses a different cultural register, genres of music, to distinguish a particular sound sequence that he defines as music:

> In between, there was a beautiful operatic melody that reverberated around the boat and made the hairs on the back of my neck stand on end. We were listening to the plaintive song of a lone humpback whale, eerie in a way but also astonishingly soothing. It had elements of jazz, bebop, blues, heavy metal, classical and reggae all rolled into one.
>
> (Carwardine 1994: 132–3)

It is a sonic collage. David Rothenberg is geeky-precise about a different humpback: 'the range is tremendous, from the bowed bass beats of a giant sub-surface fiddle to the feedback squelches of a paraelectric guitar. Each note is solid, emphatic, determined, beaming with feeling' (2008: 3). Writing of bowhead whales, Karen Bakker upends whale music genres: 'if humpback whales are the opera stars of the oceans, bowhead whales are the jazz singers.' Why? Because 'bowheads sing multiple songs within a given year, and their songs are remarkably complex, containing simultaneous, multiple, and harmonically unrelated sounds' (Bakker 2022: 40). With comparisons to opera and jazz so various, human music provides confusing analogies.

Mediating underwater sound relies on technology. Writing in the 1990s, Carwardine reports on a piece of listening kit. 'A scientist would have called it a "directional hydrophone", which is a kind of underwater microphone used to tell where sounds are coming from. But that seemed too grand a term for what basically consisted of a ski pole, part of an old telephone, some fibreglass resin and a pair of second-hand headphones' (Carwardine 1994: 21). Thirty years on, James Nestor praises 'a subculture of do-it-yourself oceanographers who are ... cracking the secret language of cetaceans with contraptions made of pasta strainers, broomsticks, and a few off-the-shelf Go-Pro cameras' (2015: 10). Off Trincomalee in Sri Lanka, Nestor joins Fabrice Schnöller who emphatically believes sperm whale clicks are a language. Pasta strainers are part of his kit. Collected data – like orecchiette? – shows four kinds of clicks: normal clicks, for tracking down prey; creaks, for closing in on prey; codas, patterns used in social interaction, and slow clicks, which are still a mystery. Coda clicks 'sound unremarkable to the human ear – something like the *tack-tack-tack* of marbles dropped on a wood table. But when the clicks are slowed down and viewed as a sound wave on a spectrogram, each reveals an incredibly complex collection of shorter clicks inside it. Inside those shorter clicks are even shorter clicks, and so on.' Coda clicks, like Russian dolls, contain immense complexity: 'sperm whales can make elaborate revisions to their click patterns, then play them back in the space of a few thousandths of a second' (Nestor 2015: 174–5). Where Schnöller develops cheap and renegade devices, others rely on higher tech. Julie Oswald, working with fourteen captive dolphins, used AI to establish they had a repertoire of around 565 signature whistles. 'Computers had sensed, recorded, represented, organized, cleaned, complied, and analysed dolphin whistles that no human could hear, and within them discovered patterns no human could perceive' (Mustill 2022: 163). Reflecting on the difficulties of establishing the meanings of cetacean clicks and whistles, Tom Mustill concludes, borrowing another outer space trope, 'It's language, Jim, but not as we know it.' (2022: 176).

Technologies of sound capture and analysis are being transformed by machine learning. Imagine seven and a half square miles of seafloor rigged with multiple listening devices linked to the surface, aided by drones, robot fish recorders and smart tags. It exists. Project CETI (Cetacean Translation Initiative), based in Dominica, provides whale surveillance twenty-four hours a day. CETI aims 'to observe whale communication in context and to translate whale-speak' (CETI 2025). Vocalizations are linked to visual records of behaviours, providing the largest animal dataset ever compiled. 'The whales will be living in an auditory panopticon, and all of the codas and other sounds that make up their Morse code-like communications will be captured for analysis' (Mustill 2022: 185). No click can escape notice.

Craig Howes has coined the very useful term 'biobits' to describe the linguistic, biological and material traces and fragments that make up a life (2020a: 1-9). Whale databases are full of biobits; they promote connectivity through image banks that feed into biographies of whales. Writing about the management of paper and digital archives, Gunnthorunn Gudmundsdottir observes that 'the point-of-view, the attitude of the one mediating the archive, is all important' (2023: 413). Happywhale, for instance, offers visual and text biographies; its tagline is 'Your Whales as Individuals'. It plugs into a global-tracking system. Although a non-profit organization, like many, it trades on the idea of naming as ownership: 'When you name and adopt a whale, that name becomes associated with your whale forever' (Happywhale 2015–2025). 'Song' appears on its website in names given to whales, whale-watching outfits, and usernames, endorsing music as a connective term. Indigenous cultures have many practices and stories of contact in which whale communication is passed organically to humans, with specific songs embodying connections that can be resumed through whale-calling. Music here embodies what Loichot calls 'the relational sacred' (2020: 19), notionally outside organized religion but sharing with religion an idea and practice of the numinous. Whale song makes whales into artists who are the equals of human beings; it impresses the aesthetic idea that other species are as beautiful and wonderful as us.

WHALE SONG: FINALE

The history – and future history – of whale song is important because whale music is credited with sparking the conservation movement to protect whales – the first such catalyst – and because cetacean communications seem likely to be a language, which AI is speeding towards translation. When Roger Payne first listened to singing whale tapes, he was transformed, according to his friend Tom Mustill. '*If this is a humpback whale*, he thought, *this will speak to the world as no other voice has ever spoken to the world*' (Mustill 2022: 23; his italics). It did: in David Rothenberg's words, 'We would never have been inspired to try and save the whale without being touched by its song' (2008: 3). Yet the world hears patchily. In 2023 Whale and Dolphin Conservation (WDC) reported from COP28, the UN Climate Change Conference in Dubai: 'we played whale song across the conference site and throughout the city. Thousands of people heard the songs of the ocean. Some were whale song connoisseurs; others were hearing it for the first time. Everyone felt a connection. An ancient connection. They felt energised' (Goodall 2023). Apparent embedding of whale song in human culture made it post-1970s 'cultural wallpaper', as one commentator puts it (NPR 2020). But that connection to whales has to be renewed, over time. An end-game of connection begs questions, which Grebowicz puts drily. Of social media fuss around a solitary blue whale, she comments, 'many people were moved to share the whale's story, post about it, make work about it, in an effort to "connect." Ok, cupid, but connect to what, exactly? This whale? Whales in general? Other human enthusiasts of this phenomenon? People in general? Oneself?' (Grebowicz 2017: 10-11). Yet 'connect' does significant emotional work; like the sublime, it creates a relationship to something beyond the perceiving subject which then changes that subject, traditionally in enlarging ways. The immediate and communicative contact inherent in connecting is the intrinsic activity of the digital era, reinforced by social media. Disconnect gets faster in proliferating swipe-left sites. According to Google Ngrams, the word frequency of both 'connect' and 'connectivity' has risen considerably since the 1980s whereas the use of 'connection', perhaps threaded through electrical technologies now replaced by digital, has fallen by half since the early twentieth century. Whale song connects people to whales, to themselves, to other whale enthusiasts, and to an oceanic sublime. WDC's tribute to whale song makes it synonymous with 'the songs of the ocean', as if whales vocalized the ocean (rather than singing to impress potential mates). Hearing whales, people also hear the ocean, an imaginary yet real cultural object. Through song, the whales' art of music voices the ocean itself.

Along with an oceanic sublime, whale song brings out elegy. Stefan Helmreich, discussing cetology now, listens to extinctions, prefaced by 'reminders to stay tuned to the bodied, biological world of these creatures, lest we too soon hear them sing an apocalyptic swan song' (2016: 47). Apocalyptic futures arrive at deep time: you can hear both underwater.

Figure 29 Connoisseur of song: sperm whale (*Physeter macrocephalus*), female. Roseau, Dominica, Caribbean Sea, Atlantic Ocean. Photo by Tony Wu. Nature Picture Library.

Bibliography

All website references checked April 2025, and rechecked November 2025. Websites not functioning when rechecked are marked with an asterisk *.

Abram, David. 1996. *The Spell of the Sensuous: Perception and Language in a More-than-Human World*. New York: Knopf Doubleday.

Adamowsky, Natascha. 2015. *The Mysterious Science of the Sea, 1775-1943*. London: Routledge.

Adler, Antony. 2019. *Neptune's Laboratory: Fantasy, Fear, and Science at Sea*. Boston, MA: Harvard University Press.

Adorno, T. W. 1984. *Aesthetic Theory*, eds. Gretel Adorno and Rolf Tiedemann, trans. C. Lenhardt. London: Routledge and Kegan Paul.

Ads of Brands. 2021. 'Ad of the Day'. 6 May. https://adsofbrands.net/en/news/ad-of-the-day-sheba-announces-world-s-largest-coral-restoration-program/2056.

Agar, Eileen. 2024. *A Look at My Life*. London: Thames & Hudson.

Agassiz, Elizabeth Cary and Alexander Agassiz. 1865. *Seaside Studies in Natural History: Marine Animals of Massachusetts Bay. Radiates*. Boston, MA: Ticknor and Fields.

Aitchison, John. 2016. *The Shark and the Albatross: Adventures of a wildlife film maker*. London: Profile Books.

Alaimo, Stacey. 2013. 'Feminist Science Studies and Ecocriticism: Aesthetics and Entanglement in the Deep Sea', in Greg Garrard (ed.), *The Oxford Handbook of Ecocriticism*, 188-204. Oxford: Oxford University Press.

Albrecht, Glenn. 2019. *Earth Emotions: New Words for a New World*. Ithaca, NY: Cornell University Press.

Alcock, Alfred. 1902. *A Naturalist in Indian Seas, or, Four Years with the Royal Indian Marine Survey Ship 'Investigator'*. London: John Murray.

Allamand, Carole. 2018. 'Autobiographical pact, forty-five years later'. *The European Journal of Life Writing*, VII: 51-6.

Allan, Doug. 2012. *Freeze Frame: A Wildlife Cameraman's Adventures on Ice*. N.P.: Tartan Dragon.

Allmark-Kent, Candice. 2021. 'How to read fishes: science, empathy, and *Salar the salmon*.' *Society & Animals*, 30 (2): 170-87. https://doi.org/10.1163/15685306-12341569.

Arthur, Paul Longley. 2014. 'Biographical Dictionaries in the Digital Era', in Paul Longley Arthur and Katherine Bode (eds), *Advancing Digital Humanities: Research, Methods, Theories*, 83-92. Basingstoke: Palgrave Macmillan.

Asbjørnsen, Peter Christen and Jørgen Engebretsen Moe. 1914. *East of the Sun and West of the Moon*. London: Hodder & Stoughton.

Attenborough, David. 2002. *Life on Air: Memoirs of a Broadcaster*. London: BBC Books.

Austin, Hayley. 2022. [Film] *The Body of the Snake; fighting to save Snake River salmon*. https://hayleyaustin.com/project/snake-river-salmon.

Austin, Sue. 2012. [Dance] 'Creating the Spectacle!' Part 1: Finding Freedom. https://www.youtube.com/watch?v=IPh533ht5AU.

Aventurier, Marianne and Alex Voyer. 2024. [Dance] *Aquaballet*. https://www.youtube.com/watch?v=Wz5gzFvzHT4.

Bacchilega, Cristina. 2013. *Fairy Tales Transformed? Twenty-First-Century Adaptations and the Politics of Wonder*. Detroit, MI: Wayne State University Press.

Bachelard, Gaston. 1994. *The Poetics of Space* (1958), trans. Maria Jolas. Boston, MA: Beacon Press.

Bachelard, Gaston. 1999. *Water and Dreams: An Essay on the Imagination of Matter* (1942), trans. Edith R. Farrell. Dallas, TX: Dallas Institute Publications.

Bailey-Charteris, Bronwyn. 2024. *The Hydrocene: Eco-Aesthetics in the Age of Water*. Abingdon, Oxon: Routledge.

Baker, Timothy C. 2019. *Writing Animals: Language, Suffering, and Animality in Twenty-First-Century Fiction*. Cham: Springer.

Bakker, Karen. 2022. *The Sounds of Life: How Digital Technology Is Bringing Us Closer to the Worlds of Animals and Plants*. Princeton, NJ: Princeton University Press.

Balazs, George. 1998–1999, 2003. Field Notebooks Australia. https://georgehbalazs.com/honulani-the-turtle-beach-of-laniakea/field-notebooks-of-george-h-balazs/australia.

Balcombe, Jonathan. 2017. *What a Fish Knows: The Inner Lives of Our Underwater Cousins*. London: Oneworld Publications.

Ballard, Robert D. with Will Hively. 2000. *The Eternal Darkness: a personal history of a deep sea exploration*. Princeton, NJ: Princeton University Press.

Balon, Eugene K. 1994. 'Interview with Eugenie Clark'. *Environmental Biology of Fishes*, 41 (1-4): 121-5.

Bass, George. 1964. Review of Honor Frost, *Under the Mediterranean* (1963). *Antiquity*, 38 (149): 70-2.

Bearzi, Giovanni. 2020. 'Marine Biology on a Violated Planet: From Science to Conscience'. *Ethics in Science and Environmental Politics*, 20: 1–13. https://doi.10.3354/esep00189.

Beck, Alice. 2021. 'Microbiomes as companion species: an exploration of dis- and re-entanglements with the microbial self'. *Social and Cultural Geography*, 22 (3): 357–75. https://www.tandfonline.com/doi/abs/10.1080/14649365.2019.1593490.

Beebe, William. 1906. *The Log of the Sun: A Chronicle of Nature's Year*. New York: Garden City Publishing.

Beebe, William. 1919. *Jungle Peace*. New York: Henry Holt.

Beebe, William. 1924. *Galápagos: World's End*. New York: G.P. Putnam's Sons.

Beebe, William. 1926. *The Arcturus Adventure: An Account of the New York Zoological Society's First Oceanographic Expedition*. New York: G.P. Putnam's Sons.

Beebe, William. 1928. *Beneath Tropic Seas: A Record of Diving Among the Coral Reefs of Haiti*. New York: Halcyon House.

Beebe, William. 1932. *Nonsuch: Land of Water*. New York: Brewer, Warren & Putnam.

Beebe, William. 1934. *Half Mile Down*. Chicago, IL: Cadmus Books, E. M. Hale.

Beebe, William. 1938. *Zaca Venture*. New York: Harcourt, Brace.

Beebe, William. 1942. *Book of Bays*. New York: Harcourt, Brace.

Begen, Molly. 2016. 'On the Trail of "Sharky McSharkface"'. 30 August https://www.conservation.org/blog/on-the-trail-of-sharky-mcsharkface*

Bejarano, Juan Pablo Pacheco. 2020. [Sound] 'Under Limfjord'. https://ocean-archive.org/view/2739.

Bellows, Andy Masaki and Marina McDougall with Brigitte Berg (eds). 2001. *Science Is Fiction: The Films of Jean Painlevé*. Cambridge, MA: MIT Press.

Beng K. C. and Corlett R. T. 2020. 'Applications of environmental DNA (eDNA) in
    ecology and conservation: opportunities, challenges and prospects'. *Biodiversity and
    Conservation*, 29 (7): 2089–121.
Bennett, Peter and Ursula Keuper-Bennett. 2008. *The Book of Honu: Enjoying and
    Learning about Hawai'i's Sea Turtles*. Honolulu: University of Hawai'i Press.
Beolens, Bo, Michael Grayson and Michael Watkins. 2023. *Eponym Dictionary of Fishes*.
    Caithness: Whittles Publishing.
Berwald, Juli. 2022. *Life on the Rocks: Building a Future for Coral Reefs*. New York:
    Riverhead Books.
Bessa, Filipa, Norman Ratcliffe, Vanessa Otero, Paula Sobral, João C. Marques, Claire M.
    Waluda, Phil N. Trathan and José C. Xavier. 2019. 'Microplastics in gentoo penguins
    from the Antarctic region'. *Scientific Reports*, 9 (1): 14191. https://doi.org/10.1038/
    s41598-019-50621-2.
Bessho-Uehara, Manabu, Jérôme Mallefet and Steven H. D. Haddock. 2023. 'Glowing sea
    cucumbers: Bioluminescence in the Holothuroidea', in Annie Mercier, Jean-Francois
    Hamel, Andrew Suhrbier and Christopher Pearce (eds), *The World of Sea Cucumbers:
    Challenges, Advances, and Innovations*, 361–75. Cambridge, MA: Academic Press.
Beyer, Hawthorne L., Emma V. Kennedy, Maria Beger, Chaolun Allen Chen, Joshua
    E. Cinner, Emily S. Darling, C. Mark Eakin, Ruth D. Gates, Scott F. Heron, Nancy
    Knowlton, David O. Obura, Stephen R. Palumbi, Hugh P. Possingham, Marji Puotinen,
    Rebecca K. Runting, William J. Skirving, Mark Spalding, Kerrie A. Wilson, Sally
    Wood, John E. Veron and Ove Hoegh-Guldberg 2018. 'Risk-sensitive planning for
    conserving coral reefs under rapid climate chnage'. *Conservation Letters*, 11 (6). https://
    doi.org/10.1111/conl.12587.
Blankenship-Williams, Lesley E. and Lisa Levin. 2009. 'Living deep: a synopsis of hadal
    trench ecology'. *Marine Technology Society Journal*, 43 (5): 137–43.
Böhme, Gernot. 2017. *Atmospheric Architectures: The Aesthetics of Felt Spaces*, trans. and
    ed. Anna-Christina Engels-Schwarzpaul. London: Bloomsbury.
Bouchet, Philippe, Wim Decock, Britt Lonneville, Bart Vanhoorne and Leen Vandepitte.
    2023. 'Marine biodiversity discovery: the metrics of new species descriptions', *Frontiers
    in Marine Science*, 10:929989: 1–14.
Bradbury, Roger. 2012. 'A World Without Coral Reefs'. *New York Times*, 13 July.
Braidotti, Rosa, Emily Jones and Gonda Klumbytė (eds). 2023. *More Posthuman Glossary*.
    London: Bloomsbury.
Brant, Clare. 2009. 'Translating Cuttlefish: Underwater Lifewritings'. *Biography*, 32 (1): 114–27.
Brant, Clare. 2017. *Balloon Madness: Flights of Imagination in Britain, 1783–1786*.
    Woodbridge, Suffolk: Boydell.
Brant, Clare. 2021. 'The Sentience of Sea Squirts', in Ina Batztke, Lea Espinoza Garrida and
    Linda M. Hess (eds), *Life Writing and the Posthuman Anthropocene*, 123–56. Cham:
    Palgrave.
Brant, Clare. 2023. 'Here for 450 Million Years, Going Now: Ocean Timelines, Climate
    Crisis, and Life Writing'. *Biography*, 46 (4): 753–74.
Brant, Clare. 2024a. 'Sharks and Lords of the Sharks' in Eike-Christian Heine (ed.), special
    issue, 'Submerged: Diving and the Undersea in Environmental History', *Journal of
    Environmental Humanities* 9: 47–70.
Brant, Clare. 2024b. 'Inserting the Manfish: Hybridity in Underwater Memoir Illustrations'
    in Arnaud Schmitt (ed.), *Hybridity in Life Writing: Combining Text and Images*, 67–85.
    Cham: Palgrave.

Bratton, Susan. 2004. 'Thinking like a Mackerel: Rachel Carson's *Under the Sea-Wind* as a Source for a Trans-Ecotonal Sea Ethic'. *Ethics & the Environment*, 9 (1): 1-22.

Braudel, Fernand. 1976. *The Mediterranean and the Mediterranean World in the Age of Philip II*, trans. Siân Reynolds. Second edition, 2 vols. New York: Harper and Rowe.

Braverman, Irus. 2018. *Coral Whisperers: Scientists on the Brink*. Oakland, CA: University of California Press.

Breuggeman, Peter. 2003. 'Diving under Antarctic ice: A history, 1902 – 1964'. http://www.peterbrueggeman.com/uw/DivingUnderAntarcticIceHistory.pdf.

Bright, Damien A. and Roy Kimmey. 2021. 'Does anything dive? Diving beyond the metaphor'. *Techniques & Culture*, 75: 1-21. https://doi.org/10.4000/tc.15034.

Britain, Troy. 2012. 'Gill Slits by Any Other Name … ' Playing Chess with Pigeons, 12 May. https://pigeonchess.com/2012/05/31/gill-slits-by-any-other-name.

British Broadcasting Corporation (BBC). 1972. [Film] The Making of a Natural History Film. (Horizon). 23 November. https://archive.org/details/TheMakingofaNaturalHistoryFilm.

British Broadcasting Corporation (BBC). 2018. 'Gulper eel caught on camera in Hawaii'. 21 September. https://www.bbc.co.uk/news/av/science-environment-45600523.

British Sub-Aqua Club (BSAC). [Film, c.1960] Club diving in Weymouth. https://www.youtube.com/watch?v=ZuK0LD85WBI.

Broad, William J. 1997. *The Universe Below: Discovering the Secrets of the Deep Sea*. New York: Touchstone.

Brooks, Ernest H. II. 2003. *Silver Seas: A Retrospective*. Santa Barbara, CA: Media 27.

Brower, Kenneth, with photographs by William R. Curtsinger. 1979. *Wake of the Whale*. London: Hutchinson/Friends of the Earth.

Brown, Culum, Kevin Laland and Jens Krause (eds). 2011. *Fish Cognition and Behavior*. Second edition. Oxford: Blackwell.

Bryant, Miranda. 2025. 'Seafood firm offers bounty to catch 27,000 escaped salmon off Norway'. *The Guardian*, 11 February.

Bucklin, Ann, Dirk Steinke, Leocadio Blanco-Bercial. 2011. 'DNA barcoding of marine metazoa'. *Annual Review of Marine Science*, 3 (1): 471-508. https://doi.org/10.1146/annurev-marine-120308-080950.

Bulbulyan, Sophie and Apostolia Papadamaki. 2015. [Dance] 'Drops of Breath'. https://dropsofbreath.com/the-actions/drops-of-breath-underwater-performance.

Buntin, Simmons B. 2002. 'The Language of the Reef: An Interview with Rosaleen Love'. *Interviews*, Issue 12, *Terrain.org*. https://www.terrain.org/2002/interviews/rosaleen-love.

Burke, Edmund. 1998 (1st edn 1757). *A Philosophical Enquiry into the Origin of our Ideas of the Sublime and Beautiful*, ed. Adam Phillips. Oxford: Oxford University Press.

Burrows, William. 1955. 'Palolo'. *Journal of the Polynesian Society*, 54 (1): 137-54.

Burton, Maurice. 1960. *Under the Sea*. New York: Franklin Watts, Inc.

Bury, Louis. 2022. 'Reaching beyond the human'. *Art in America*, March, 74-9.

Bustard, Robert. 1972. *Sea Turtles: Their Natural History and Conservation*. London: Collins.

Butcher, Melissa. 2010. 'From "fish out of water" to "fitting in": The challenge of re-placing home in a mobile world'. *Population, Space and Place*, 16 (1): 23-36.

Butler, Judith. 2015. 'When is life grievable?' Blogpost, *Verso*, 16 November. https://www.versobooks.com/en-gb/blogs/news/2339-judith-butler-precariousness-and-grievability.

Cahill, James Leo. 2019. *Zoological Surrealism: The Nonhuman Cinema of Jean Painlevé*. Minneapolis, MN: University of Minnesota Press.

Caluya, Gilbert. 2010. 'The post-panoptic society? Reassessing Foucault in surveillance studies'. *Social Identities*, 16 (5): 621–33.

Cameron, James. 1989. [Film] dir. *The Abyss*.

Campagna, Federico. 2018. *Technic and Magic: The Reconstruction of Reality*. London: Bloomsbury Academic.

Carrington, Richard. 1960. *A Biography of the Sea. The Story of the World Ocean, Its Animal and Plant Populations, and Its Influence on Human History*. London: Chatto and Windus.

Carson, Rachel. 1937. 'Undersea'. *The Atlantic Monthly*, September, 322–5.

Carson, Rachel. 1951. *The Sea Around Us*. New York: Oxford University Press.

Carson, Rachel. 1965a. *Under The Sea-Wind. A Naturalist's Picture of Ocean Life* (1941). London: Panther Books.

Carson, Rachel. 1965b. *The Sense of Wonder. A Celebration of Nature for Parents and Children*. New York: Harper & Row.

Carwardine, Mark. 1994. *On the Trail of the Whale*. Guildford: Thunder Bay Publishing.

Casey, Susan. 2010. *The Devil's Teeth: A True Story of Obsession and Survival Among America's Great White Sharks*. London: Vintage Books.

Casey, Susan. 2015. *Voices in the Ocean: A Journey into the Wild and Haunting World of Dolphins*. New York: Doubleday Books.

Casey, Susan. 2023. *The Underworld: Journeys to the Depths of the Ocean*. New York: Doubleday Books.

Cavarero, Adriana. 2008. *Horrorism: Naming Contemporary Violence*, trans. William McCuaig. New York: Columbia University Press.

Centeno, Miguel and Peter Callahan, Paul Larcey, Thayer Patterson (eds). 2023. *How Worlds Collapse: What History, Systems, and Complexity Can Teach Us About Our Modern World and Fragile Future*. London: Routledge.

CETI (Cetacean Translation Initiative). 2025. https://www.projectceti.org.

Challenger, Melanie. 2022. *How to Be Animal: What It Means to Be Human*. Edinburgh: Canongate Books.

Chamel, Jean and Yael Dansac. 2022. 'Relating with more-than-Humans: Interbeing Rituality and Spiritual Practices in a Living World', in Jean Chamel and Yael Dansac (eds), *Relating with More-than-Humans*, 1–17. Cham: Palgrave. https://doi.org/10.1007/978-3-031-10294-3_1.

Charbonneau, Rebecca. 2021. 'The Cosmic Mirror'. *Galactic Gazette*, 29 March. https://wolba.ch/gazette/cultural-astronomy-series-the-cosmic-mirror*.

Chassagnol, Anne. 2010. 'Darwin in Wonderland: Evolution, Involution and Natural Selection in *The Water Babies* (1863)'. *Miranda*, Issue 1. https://journals.openedition.org/miranda/321.

Chen, Cecilia, Janine MacLeod and Astrida Neimanis (eds). 2013. *Thinking with Water*. Montreal: McGill-Queen's University Press.

Chico, Tita. 2018. *The Experimental Imagination: Literary Knowledge and Science in the British Enlightenment*. Stanford, CA: Stanford University Press.

Clark, Eugenie. 1953. *Lady With a Spear*. New York: Harper Brothers.

Clark, Eugenie. 1969. *The Lady and the Sharks*. New York: Harper & Row.

Clarke, Arthur C. 1956. *The Coast of Coral*. London: Frederick Muller.

Clarke, Arthur C. 1957. *The Reefs of Taprobane: Underwater Adventures Around Ceylon*. London: Frederick Muller.

Clover, Charles. 2004. *The End of the Line: How Over-fishing Is Changing the World and What We Eat*. London: Ebury Press.

Cockburn, Calum. 2019. 'Whale of a Time', British Library blogpost, 2 May, featuring Harley MS 4751, f.69r. https://blogs.bl.uk/digitisedmanuscripts/2019/05/whale-of-a-time.html*

Cohen, Dianna and Jennifer Wagner-Lawlor. 2021. 'Downhill from Everywhere: Plastic Pollution Coalition and the Force of Art', in Ingeborg Reichle (ed.), *Plastic Ocean: Art and Science Responses to Marine Pollution*, 19–45. Berlin: De Gruyter.

Cohen, Margaret. 2014. 'Denotation in alien environments'. *Representations*, 25 (1): 103–26.

Cohen, Margaret. 2019. 'The shipwreck as undersea gothic', in Margaret Cohen and Killian Quigley (eds), *The Aesthetics of the Undersea*, 155–66. Abingdon, Oxon: Routledge.

Cohen, Margaret. 2022. *The Underwater Eye: How the Movie Camera Opened the Depths and Unleashed New Realms of Fantasy*. Princeton, NJ: Princeton University Press.

Cohen, Margaret and Killian Quigley (eds). 2019. *The Aesthetics of the Undersea*. London: Routledge.

Colby, Jason M. 2020. 'Conscripting Leviathan: Science, cetaceans, and the Cold War'. *Diplomatic History*, 44 (3): 466–78. https://doi.org/10.1093/dh/dhaa011.

Cole, Hunter. 2014–17. *Living Light: Photographs by the Light of Bioluminescent Bacteria*. https://www.huntercole.org/artwork/living-light/bioluminescent-weddings*.

Colebrook, Claire. 2009. 'Derrida, Deleuze and haptic aesthetics'. *Derrida Today*, 2 (1): 22–43. https://www.euppublishing.com/doi/10.3366/E1754850009000360.

Collins, Martin A. 2003. 'The genus *Grimpoteuthis* (Octopoda: Grimpoteuthidae) in the north-east Atlantic, with descriptions of three new species'. *Zoological Journal of the Linnean Society*, 139: 93–127.

Colombi, Benedict J. 2012. 'Salmon and the adaptive capacity of Nimiipuu (Nez Perce) culture to cope with change'. *American Indian Quarterly*, 36 (1): 75–97.

Conti, Anita. 1955. *Deep Sea Saga* (*Racleurs d'océans*, 1952). London: William Kimber. https://agencevu.com/en/photographer/anita-conti.

Conti, Anita. 1957. *Géants des mers chaudes*. Paris: André Bonne.

Cook, Mercer. 1953. 'Clement Richer: Novelist from Martinique'. *The French Review*, 27 (1): 36–40.

Coral Reef Rescue Initiative. 2020. 'Modern Portfolio Theory'. https://coralreefrescueinitiative.org/modern-portfolio-theory.

Corona. 2021. 'Help Us Restore the Ocean'. https://coralvita.co/corona.

Cousteau, Jacques-Yves with Frédéric Dumas. 1953. *The Silent World*. London: Hamish Hamilton.

Cousteau, Jacques-Yves with James Dugan. 1963. *The Living Sea*. London: Hamish Hamilton.

Cousteau, Jacques-Yves and Philippe Cousteau. 1970. *The Shark: Splendid Savage of the Sea*, trans. Francis Price. London: Cassell.

Cousteau, Jacques-Yves with Philippe Diolé. 1971. *Life and Death in a Coral Sea*, trans. J. F. Bernard. London: Cassell.

Cousteau, Jacques-Yves with Philippe Diolé. 1973. *Octopus and Squid: The Soft Intelligence*, trans. J. F. Bernard. London: Cassell.

Cox, Claire. 2026. *The Poetry of Disaster: Chernobyl, Katrina, and the Anthropocene*. Cham: Palgrave.

Craps, Stef. 2018. 'Introduction', in Stef Craps, Rick Crownshaw, Jennifer Wenzel, Rosanne Kennedy, Claire Colebrook and Vin NardizziRosanne Kennedy, 'Memory studies

and the Anthropocene: A roundtable'. *Memory Studies*, 11 (4): 498–515. https://doi.
org/10.1177/1750698017731068.

Crawford, Dean. 2008. *Shark*. London: Reaktion Books.

Creed, Barbara. 1993. *The Monstrous Feminine: Film, Feminism, Psychoanalysis*. London:
Routledge.

Critchley, Emma. 2012. [Photographs] 'A shift in sight, sound, movement & touch'. https://
emmacritchley.com/photographs/a-shift.

Critchley, Emma. 2015. [Photographs] 'At the Still Point of the Turning World', *Cabin
Gallery*, London. https://www.emmacritchley.com.

Crompton, Sarah. 2012. 'Neil MacGregor interview: Shakespeare's Restless World: A
history in objects'. *The Telegraph*, 13 April.

Cropp, Ben. 1965. *Shark Hunters*. London: Angus and Robertson.

Cropp, Ben. 1993. [Film] dir. *The Coral Reefs Are Dying*.

Crowder, William. 1935. *Dwellers of the Sea and Shore*. London: Macmillan.

Culbert, John. 2018. 'Theory and the limits of travel'. *Studies in Travel Writing*, 22 (4):
343–52. https://doi.org/10.1080/13645145.2019.1624072.

Curtis, Brian. 1949. *The Life Story of the Fish: His Morals and Manners*. London: The
Scientific Book Club.

Dadoun, Roger. 1989. 'Fetishism in the Horror Film', in James Donald (ed.), *Fantasy and
the Cinema*, 38-61. London: BFI Publishing.

Dalla Costa, Mariarosa and Monica Chilese. 2014. *Our Mother Ocean: Enclosure,
Commons, and the Global Fishermen's Movement*, trans. Silvia Federici. New York:
Common Notions.

Davey, Melissa. 2016. 'Saving loggerhead turtles: the annual sacrifice to preserve an
ancient journey'. *The Guardian*, 31 December. https://www.theguardian.com/
environment/2016/dec/31/saving-loggerhead-turtles-the-annual-sacrifice-to-preserve-
an-ancient-journey.

Davidson, Osha Gray. 1998. *The Enchanted Braid: Coming to Terms with Nature on the
Coral Reef*. New York: John Wiley & Sons.

Davidson, Osha Gray. 2001. *Fire in the Turtle House: The Green Sea Turtle and the Fate of
the Ocean*. New York: Public Affairs.

Davies, Gail. 1998. 'Networks of Nature: Stories of Natural History Film-Making from the
BBC'. DPhil thesis, University College London.

Davis, Randall W. 2019. *Marine Mammals: Adaptations for an Aquatic Life*. Cham:
Springer.

Day, Trevor. 2018. *Sardine*. London: Reaktion Books.

De Latil, Pierre. 1954. *The Underwater Naturalist* (*L'homme chez les poisons*, 1951), trans.
Edward Fitzgerald. London: Jarrolds.

De Latil, Pierre and Jean Rivoire. 1956. *Man and the Underwater World* (*À la Recherche du
Monde Marin*, 1954), trans. Edward Fitzgerald. London: Jarrolds.

Deleuze, Gilles and Félix Guattari. 1988. *A Thousand Plateaus: Capitalism and
Schizophrenia*, trans. Brian Massumi. London: Athlone.

DeLoughrey, Elizabeth. 2015. '"Moments in Passing;" Maritime Futures of the
Anthropocene', 1-16, www.underwatersculpture.com.

DeLoughrey, Elizabeth. 2021. 'Toward a Critical Ocean Studies for the Anthropocene', in
Daniela Zyman (ed.), *Oceans Rising*, 112-18. London: Sternberg Press.

Derrida, Jacques. 2006. *Specters of Marx: The State of the Debt, the Work of Mourning and
the New International*. London: Routledge.

Devine, David. 1955. *Boy on a Dolphin*. London: John Murray.

Dickenson, Victoria. 2015. *Seal*. London: Reaktion Books.

Dickey, Colin. 2012. 'On the trail of the vampire squid from hell'. *Los Angeles Review of Books*, 12 October. https://lareviewofbooks.org/article/on-the-trail-of-the-elusive-vampire-squid-from-hell.

Diolé, Philippe. 1954a. *Au Bord de la Terre: Fragments de la Vie d'un Plongeur*. Paris: Editions Albin Michel.

Diolé, Philippe. 1954b. *The Undersea Adventure* (*L'Aventure Sous-Marin*, 1951), trans. Alan Ross. London: Sidgwick and Jackson.

Diolé, Philippe. 1957a. *The Gates of the Sea* (*Les Portes de la Mer*, 1953), trans. Alan Ross. New York: Julian Messner.

Diolé, Philippe. 1957b. *4000 Years Under the Sea: Excursions in Underwater Archaeology* (*Promenades d'Archéologie Sous-Marines* 1954), trans. Gerard Hopkins. London: Pan Books.

Diolé, Philippe. 1959. *L'Eau Profonde*. Paris: Gaillard.

Dobrin, Sidney I. 2021. *Blue Ecocriticism and the Oceanic Imperative*. Abingdon, Oxon: Routledge.

Donahue, Jasmine. 2023. *Birdsplaining: A Natural History*. Aberystwyth: New Welsh Review.

Doornekamp, Rachel. 2020. 'Underwater Drone 101 – All you need to know'. *Deep Trekker*, 3 March. https://www.deeptrekker.com/news/underwater-drone-101.

Doubilet, David. 1999. *Water Light Time*. New York: Phaidon Press.

Doubilet, David. 2003. *Fish Face: Portraits*. London: Phaidon Press.

Doubilet, David. 2019. 'Dreaming in the Sea', in Christian Vizl, *Silent Kingdom: A World Beneath the Waves*, 61-2. San Rafael, CA: Earth Aware Editions, MandalaEarth.

Doukan, Gilbert. 1957. *The World Beneath the Waves*, trans. A. and R. M. Case. New York: John de Graff.

Dow Adams, Timothy. 2000. *Light Writing and Life Writing: Photography in Autobiography*. Chapel Hill, NC: University of North Carolina Press.

Downer, John. 2024. [Film] *Spy in the Ocean*. Episode 1, 'Deep Thinkers', John Downer Productions. https://www.youtube.com/watch?v=M8iFyKGUASA.

Driscoll, Kári and Eva Hoffman (eds). 2018. *What Is Zoopoetics? Texts, Bodies, Entanglement*. Cham: Palgrave.

Drucker, Philip. 1965. *Cultures of the North Pacific Coast*. San Francisco, CA: Chandler Publishing.

Duby, Georges. 1953. *La Société aux XIe et XIIe siècles dans la région mâconnaise*. Paris: Armand Colin.

Dugan, James. 1948. 'The First of the Menfish', repr. *Historical Diver*, 2004, 12 (4): 16-21.

Dugan, James. 1960. *Man Explores the Sea*. London: Penguin Books.

Dumas, Frédéric. 1976. *30 Centuries Under the Sea*, trans. Philip A. Facey. New York: Crown Publishers.

Dunaway, Finis. 2005. *Natural Visions: The Power of Images in American Environmental Reform*. Chicago, IL: University of Chicago Press.

Dunn, Lucy. 2024. 'Fabien Cousteau, proteus and the race to live under the sea'. *Boat International*, 28 October. https://www.boatinternational.com/yachts/editorial-features/fabien-cousteau-proteus-underwater-habitat.

Dunsany, Lord [Edward J. M. D. Plunkett, Lord]. 1905. *The Gods of Pegana*. With Illustrations in photogravure by S. H. Sime. London: Elkin Matthews.

Dunsany, Lord [Edward J. M. D. Plunkett, Lord]. 1912. *The Book of Wonder*. Illustrated by Sidney H. Sime. London: William Heinemann.

Duong, Tiffany. 2021. 'What's a Siphonophore and Why Is There One on the UN This Week?' *Ecowatch*, 24 April. https://www.ecowatch.com/siphonophore-un-building-2655086999.html.

Duthuit, Claude. 1962. [Film] dir. *Nautical Archaeology/ Beginnings: 1960–1962*. www.youtube.com/watch?v=wfTNndbjVk0.

Dutton, Peter, Scott Benson and Creusa 'Tetha' Hitipeuw. 2008. 'Pacific Leatherback Sets Long-Distance Record.' *The State of the World's Sea Turtles*, SWOT Report III.

Earle, Sylvia A. 1995. *Sea Change: A Message of the Oceans*. New York: G. Putnam's Sons.

Earle, Sylvia A. 2009. 'A Blueprint for Restoring the World's Oceans.' *Yale Environment 360*, 12 October.

Earle, Sylvia A. 2019. 'Introduction', in Christian Vizl, *Silent Kingdom: A World Beneath the Waves*, 16–19. San Rafael, CA: Earth Aware Editions, MandalaEarth.

Ecott, Tim. 2002. *Neutral Buoyancy: Adventures in a Liquid World*. London: Penguin Books.

Edgar, Graham. 2023. 'The Great Southern Reef is in More Trouble than the Great Barrier Reef.' *The Conversation*, 22 March. https://theconversation.com/the-great-southern-reef-is-in-more-trouble-than-the-great-barrier-reef-201235.

Elias, Ann. 2019. *Coral Empire: Underwater Oceans, Colonial Tropics, Visual Modernity*. Durham, NC: Duke University Press.

Ellis, Richard. 1996. *Deep Atlantic: Life, Death and Exploration in the Abyss*. New York: Alfred A. Knopf.

Ellis, Richard. 2013. *Swordfish: A Biography of the Ocean Gladiator*. Chicago, IL: Chicago University Press.

ELOKA (Exchange for Local Observations and Knowledge of the Arctic) n.d. https://eloka.nsidc.org/narwhal-research.

Ely, Steve. 2021a. *The European Eel*. Sheffield: Longbarrow Press, 2021.

Ely, Steve. 2021b. 'Body of Dark: On writing 'The European Eel'. Blogpost, 2 July. https://longbarrowblog.wordpress.com/2021/07/02/body-of-dark-steve-ely.

Empson, Patience. 1961. 'Robert Gibbings and the South Seas.' *Journal de la Société des Océanistes*, 17: 52–5. https://doi.org/10.3406/jso.1961.1883.

Endt-Jones, Marion. 2020. 'Cultivating "Response-ability": Curating Coral in Recent Exhibitions.' *Journal of Curatorial Studies*, 9 (2): 182–205.

Environment Agency (UK). 2023. 'Warning of invasive pink salmon threat to UK fisheries.' 26 June. https://www.gov.uk/government/news/environment-agency-warns-of-invasive-pink-salmon-threat-to-uk-fisheries.

Environmental Defense Fund. 2021. 'How can digital technologies support climate-resilient oceans and communities?' 27 September. https://www.edf.org/sustainable-fishing/technology-solutions.

Erdmann, Mark. 2017. 'Update: What we're learning about the world's largest fish.' Conservation International, 1 August. https://www.conservation.org/blog/update-what-were-learning-about-the-worlds-largest-fish.

Fackler, Katharina and Silvia Schultermandl. 2023. 'Kinship as critical idiom as oceanic studies.' *Atlantic Studies*, 20 (2): 195–225. https://www.tandfonline.com/doi/full/10.1080/14788810.2022.2079900.

Falco, Albert and Philippe Diolé. 1977. *The Memoirs of Falco Chief Diver of the Calypso*, trans. Joseph Harriss. London: Cassell.

Farchi, Gai. 2020. 'Literature Underwater: The Oceanic Becomings of Nothomb and Darrieussecq.' *French Forum*, 45 (2): 189–204. https://doi.org/10.1353/frf.2020.0015.

Farrier, David. 2019. *Anthropocene Poetics: Deep Time, Sacrifice Zones, and Extinction.* Minneapolis, MN: University of Minnesota Press.

Feder, Helena (ed.). 2021. *Close Reading the Anthropocene.* Abingdon, Oxon: Routledge.

Finnegan, Paul. 2020. 'The Idea of Natural History in the Word of Pierre Huyghe'. *Antennae: The Journal of Nature in Visual Culture*, 50 'Remaking Nature': 95-117.

Finnegan, Paul. 2023. 'The Postnatural Animal in Contemporary Art', PhD thesis, University of Plymouth.

Fisher Mark. 2016. *The Weird and the Eerie.* London: Repeater Books.

Flood, Sue. 2018. *Emperor: The Perfect Penguin.* Woodbridge, Suffolk: ACC Art Books.

Florko, Katie R. N., Cody G. Carlyle, Brent G. Young, David J. Yurkowski, Christine Michel and Steven H. Ferguson. 2021. 'Narwhal (*Monodon monoceros*) detection by infrared flukeprints from aerial survey imagery'. *Ecosphere*, 12 (8): e03698. https://doi.org/10.1002/ecs2.3698.

Flusser, Vélim and Louis Bec. 2012. *Vampyroteuthis Infernalis: A treatise: With a report by the Institut scientifique de recherche paranaturaliste*, trans. Valentine A. Pakis. Minneapolis, MN: University of Minnesota Press.

Ford, Brian J. 1999. *The Secret Language of Life: How Animals and Plants Feel and Communicate.* New York: Fromm International.

Ford, Derek R. 2015. 'The Air Conditions of Philosophy of Education: Toward a Microsphereology of the Classroom', in Eduard Duarte (ed.), *Philosophy of Education*, 261-68. Urbana, IL: University of Illinois.

Fortescue, Hon. J. W. 1897. *The Story of a Red Deer.* London: Macmillan.

Foster Craig. 2020. [Film] dir. *My Octopus Teacher*, Netflix.

Foster, Craig and Ross Frylinck. 2021. *Underwater Wild.* Boston, MA: Houghton Mifflin Harcourt.

Fothergill, Alastair and Vanessa Berlowitz. 2011. *Frozen Planet: A World Beyond Imagination.* London: BBC Books.

Fotiade, Ramona. 2013. *A Bout de Souffle: French Film Guide.* London: I.B. Tauris.

Foucault, Michel. 1998. 'What Is an Author?' in James D. Faubion (ed.), *Essential Works of Foucault 1954-1984*, trans. Robert Hurley and others, vol. 2, Aesthetics, Method, and Epistemology, 205-22. New York: The New Press.

France, Scott C. 2017. 'Enigmatic Invertebrates: The Dandelion Animal'. https://archive. oceanexplorer.noaa.gov/okeanos/explorations/ex1706/logs/july30/welcome.html

Franklin, H. Bruce. 2008. *The Most Important Fish in the Sea: Menhaden and America.* Washington, DC: Island Press.

Freud, Sigmund, 2005 (1st edn 1930). *Civilisation and Its Discontents*, ed. and trans. James Strachey. New York: W. W. Norton.

Frey, Rodney. 2000. *Salmon Always Goes Up River An American Indian Epic Retold by Rodney Frey*, 28 September. https://www.lib.uidaho.edu/digital/turning/PDF/Salmon. pdf.

Fricke, H. and S. Fricke. 1977. 'Monogamy and sex change by aggressive dominance in coral reef fish'. *Nature*, 266 (5605): 830-2. https://doi.org/10.1038/266830a0.

Friesen, Joanna. 1975. 'Perceiving Dance'. *The Journal of Aesthetic Education*, 9: 97-108. https://doi.org/10.2307/3331982.

Gagnon, Guy. 2013. Interview, *Black and White Photography* (UK), 151: 80-1.

Gaskell, Thomas F. 1960. *Under the Deep Oceans: Twentieth Century Voyages of Discovery.* London: Eyre & Spottiswoode.

Gibbings, Robert. 1936. *The Lost Anchor A Wood Engraving by Robert Gibbings with A Foreword by the Artist.* Kansas City, MO: The Woodcut Society.

Gibbings, Robert. 1946 (1st edn 1938). *Blue Angels and Whales: A Record of Personal Experiences Below and Above Water*. London: J. M. Dent and Sons.

Gibbings, Robert. 1949 (1st edn 1948). *Over the Reefs*. London: Readers Union with J. M. Dent & Sons.

Gibbings, Robert. Website: https://www.robertgibbings.org.

Gillman Len Norman and Shane Donald Wright. 2020. 'Restoring indigenous names in taxonomy'. *Communications Biology*, 3: 609. https://doi.org/10.1038/s42003-020-01344-y.

Gilmore, Leigh. 2017. *Tainted Witness: Why We Doubt What Women Say About Their Lives*. Columbia: Columbia University Press.

Gilpatric, Guy. 1938. *The Compleat Goggler, Being the First and Only Exhaustive Treatise on the Art of Goggle Fishing …* New York: Dodd Mead.

Ginsberg, Robert. 2021. *The Aesthetics of Ruins*. Amsterdam: Rodopi Press.

Giraud, Eva Haifa. 2019. *What Comes After Entanglement? Activism, Anthropocentrism, and an Ethics of Exclusion*. Durham, NC: Duke University Press.

Glissant, Édouard. 1997. *Poetics of Relation*, trans. Betsy Wing. Ann Arbor, MI: University of Michigan Press.

Godfrey-Smith, Peter. 2017. *Other Minds: The Octopus and the Evolution of Intelligent Life*. London: William Collins.

Godfrey-Smith, Peter, David Scheel, Stephanie Chancellor, Stefan Linquist and Matthew Lawrence. 2022. 'In the line of fire: Debris throwing by wild octopuses'. *PLOS One*, 9 November. https://doi.org/10.1371/journal.pone.0276482.

Goggin, John M. 1960. 'Underwater archaeology: Its nature and limitations'. *American Antiquity*, 25 (3): 348–54.

Goodall, Ed. 2023. 'Outcomes for whales and dolphins from COP28'. Whale and Dolphin Conservation Society, 21 December. https://uk.whales.org/2023/12/21/outcomes-for-whales-and-dolphins-from-cop28.

Gordon, Dennis. 2016. 'Corals, anemones and jellyfish – Cnidaria – the nettle animals'. *Te Ara - the Encyclopedia of New Zealand*. http://www.TeAra.govt.nz/en/corals-anemones-and-jellyfish/page-1.

Gorsky, Bernard. 1956. *Moana (Vastness of the Waters)*, trans. Alec Brown. London: Elek Books.

Gould, Carol Grant. 2006. *The Remarkable Life of William Beebe, Explorer and Naturalist*. Washington, DC: Island Press.

Gourlay, Graeme. 1999. 'Beneath the surface', in David Doubilet, *Water Light Time*. New York: Phaidon Press.

Gouyon, Jean-Baptiste. 2019. *BBC Wildlife Documentaries in the Age of Attenborough*. Cham: Palgrave.

Grass, Delphine and Lily Robert-Foley. 2024. 'The Translation Memoir: An Introduction'. *Life Writing*, 21 (1): 1–9. https://doi.org/10.1080/14484528.2023.2281044.

Great Barrier Reef Foundation. 2025. 'The Value'. https://www.barrierreef.org/the-reef/the-value.

Grebowicz, Margret. 2017. *Whale Song*. London: Bloomsbury, Object Lessons.

Green, Jeremy. 2016. Review of *Archaeology Beneath the Sea* [by George F. Bass (1975)] in *The International Journal of Nautical Archaeology*, 45 (2): 469–81.

Greiner, Andreas. 2014. 'Toccata for Pyrocystis Fusiformis'. https://www.andreasgreiner.com/works/toccata-for-pyrocystis-fusiformis.

Griffero, Tonino. 2019. 'Is There Such a Thing as an "Atmospheric Turn"? Instead of an Introduction', in T. Griffero and M. Tedeschini (eds), *Atmosphere and Aesthetics*, 11–62. Cham: Palgrave Macmillan. https://doi.org/10.1007/978-3-030-24942-7_2.

Griffiths, Jay. 2006. *Wild: An Elemental Journey*. London: Penguin Random House.

Grimble, Arthur. 1952. *A Pattern of Islands*. London: John Murray.

Grosz, Elizabeth. 2011. *Becoming Undone: Darwinian Reflections on Life, Politics, and Art*. Durham, NC: Duke University Press.

Gudmundsdottir, Gunnthorunn. 2023. 'Emptying the attic: The family archive in transition'. *Life Writing*, 20 (2): 409–20. https://doi.org/10.1080/14484528.2022.2048776.

Guedes, Patrícia, Fernanda Alves-Martins, Javier Martínez Arribas, Sumita Chatterjee, Ana M. C. Santos, Amir Lewin, Longji Bako, Paul W. Webala, Ricardo A. Correia, Ricardo Rocha and Richard J. Ladle. 2023. 'Eponyms have no place in 21st-century biological nomenclature'. *Nature Ecology Evolution*: n.p. https://doi.org/10.1038/s41559-023-02022-y.

Gunn, Rachel, Cassandra E. Benkwitt, Nicholas A. J. Graham, Ian R. Hartley, Adam C. Algar and Sally A. Keith. 2023. 'Terrestrial invasive species alter marine vertebrate behaviour'. *Nature Ecology and Evolution*, 7: 82–91. https://doi.org/10.1038/s41559-022-01931-8.

Haddock, Steven. 2022. 'Bioluminescence in the deep sea: How and why do animals create their own light?' *MBARI*, 18 May. https://www.youtube.com/watch?v=aPUF40j47-o.

Haddock, Steven, Mark Moline and James Case. 2010. 'Bioluminescence in the sea.' *Annual Review of Marine Science*, 2: 443–93. https://doi.org/10.1146/annurev-marine-120308-081028.

Haig-Brown, Roderick L. 1947 (1st edn 1931). *Silver: The Life Story of an Atlantic Salmon*. London: A & C Black.

Half Hours in the Deep: The Nature and Wealth of the Sea. 1898. London: James Nisbet.

Halkort, Monika. 2021. 'Post-Human Tactility: Sensing Death in the Mediterranean Sea', in Daniela Zyman (ed.), *Oceans Rising*, 42–5. London: Sternberg Press.

Hamblyn, Richard. 2021. *The Sea*. London: Reaktion Books.

Hamilton, Healy, Norah Saarman, Graham Short and Anna B. Sellas. 2017. 'Molecular phylogeny and patterns of diversification in syngnathid fishes.' *Molecular Phylogenetics and Evolution*, 107: 388–403. https://doi.org/10.1016/j.ympev.2016.10.003.

Hamilton-Paterson, James. 1987. *Playing with Water*. New York: New Amsterdam Books.

Hamilton-Paterson, James. 1998. *Three Miles Down: A Hunt for Sunken Treasure*. London: Jonathan Cape.

Happywhale. 2015–2025. https://happywhale.com/home;https://happywhale.com/adoptawhale.

Haraway, Donna. 2008. *When Species Meet*. Minneapolis, MN: University of Minnesota Press.

Haraway, Donna. 2016a. *Staying with the Trouble: Making Kin in the Chthulucene*. Durham, NC: Duke University Press.

Haraway, Donna. 2016b. 'Tentacular Thinking: Anthropocene, Capitalocene, Chthulucene.' *e-flux* 75.

Harrigan, Stephen. 1992. *Water and Light: A Diver's Journey to a Coral Reef*. Boston, MA: Houghton Mifflin.

Harvell, Drew. 2025. *The Ocean's Menagerie: How Earth's Strangest Creatures Reshape the Rules of Life*. London: The Bodley Head.

Hass, Hans. 1952. *Diving to Adventure: Harpoon and Camera Under the Sea*, trans. Barrows Mussey. London: Jarrolds.

Hass, Hans. 1954. *Men and Sharks*, trans. Barrows Mussey. London: Jarrolds.

Hass, Hans. 1956. *I Photographed Under the Seven Seas*, trans. James Cleugh. London: Jarrolds.

Hass, Hans. 1959. *We Came from the Sea: Adventure Under the Water and Science in the Sun*, trans. Alan Houghton Broderick. New York: Doubleday.

Hass, Lotte. 1972. *Girl on the Ocean Floor*, trans. Eva and Robin Sawyers. London: George G. Harrap.

Hassler, Stefanie. (ed.) 2018. *Tidalectics: Imagining an Oceanic Worldview Through Art and Science*. Cambridge, MA: MIT Press.

Hedgpeth, Joel W. 1956. Review of Pierre de Latil, *The Underwater Naturalist* (1954), *Scientific Monthly*, 82 (3): 143.

Heller, Steve. 1993. 'Cult of the ugly', *Eye* 9 (3). https://www.eyemagazine.com/feature/article/cult-of-the-ugly.

Helmreich, Stefan. 2009. *Alien Ocean: Anthropological Voyages in Microbial Seas*. Oakland, CA: University of California Press.

Helmreich, Stefan. 2016. *Sounding the Limits of Life: Essays in the Anthropology of Biology and Beyond*. Princeton, NJ: Princeton University Press.

Herman, David. 2016. 'Animal Autobiography; Or, Narration Beyond the Human', special issue Animal Narratology, *Humanities*, 5 (4): 82. https://doi.org/10.3390/h5040082.

Hill, Tessa and Eric Simon. 2024. *At Every Depth: Our Growing Knowledge of the Changing Oceans*. Columbia: Columbia University Press.

Hines, Sarah Marie. 2013. '"Taste of the world": A re-evaluation of the publication history and reception context of Andrew Lang's Fairy Book series, 1889-1910,' PhD thesis, Edinburgh. https://www.era.lib.ed.ac.uk/handle/1842/7792.

Ho, Jonathan K. I., Jayanthi Punimoorthy, Amrita Srivathsan and Rudolf Meier. 2020. 'MinION sequencing of seafood in Singapore reveals creatively labelled flatfishes, confused roe, pig DNA in squid balls, and phantom crustaceans'. *Food Control*, 112 (12): 107144. https://doi.org/10.1016/j.foodcont.2020.107144.

Hobson, Melissa. 2023. 'Sea cucumbers surprise scientists with spectacular light show'. *New Scientist*, 10 November, article 2397168.

Hoegh-Guldberg, Ove, Emma V. Kennedy, Hawthorne L. Beyer, Caleb McClennen and Hugh P. Possingham. 2018. 'Securing a long-term future for coral reefs'. *Trends in Ecology and Evolution*, 33 (12): 936-44.

Hollis, Tim. 2006. *Glass Bottom Boats and Mermaid Tails: Florida's Tourist Springs*. Mechanicsburg, PA: Stackpole Books.

Holloway, Zena. 2017. 'Flowers for Jeju: The Last Mermaids'. https://zenaholloway.com/portfolio/seawomen.

Honeybourne, James and Mark Brownlow. 2017. *Blue Planet II: A New World of Hidden Depths*. London: BBC Books.

Horden, Peregrine and Nicholas Purcell. 2006. 'The Mediterranean and "the New Thalassology"'. *The American Historical Review*, 111 (3): 722-40.

Houot, Georges and Pierre Willm. 1955. *Two Thousand Fathoms Down*, trans. Michael Bullock. London: Hamish Hamilton and Rupert Hart-Davis.

Hovanec, Caroline. 2019. 'Another Nature Speaks to the Camera: Natural history and Film Theory'. *Modernism/Modernity*, 26 (2): 243-65.

Howes, Craig. 2020a. 'Biobits and the Life Writing Environment – From Micro to Macro.' *Journal of Modern Life Writing Studies*, 14: 1-9.

Howes, Craig. 2020b. 'Life Writing'. *Oxford Research Encyclopedia of Literature*. Oxford: Oxford University Press. https://oxfordre.com/literature/view/10.1093/acrefore/9780190201098.001.0001/acrefore-9780190201098-e-1146.

Hsu, Ruth Y. 2020. 'Flusser's Vampyroteuthis Infernalis: Homo Sapiens' Posthuman Future?' *Flusser Studies*, 30: 1-10. https://www.flusserstudies.net/archive/flusser-studies-30-november-2020.

Huff, Cynthia. 2017. 'After Auto, After Bio: Posthumanism and Life Writing'. *Auto/biography Studies*, 32 (2): 279–82.

Huff, Cynthia. 2019. 'Situating Donna Haraway in the Life-Narrative Web'. *Auto/biography Studies*, 34 (3): 375–84.

Hughes, William and Andrew M. Simons. 2014. 'The continuum between semelparity and iteroparity: Plastic expression of parity in response to season length manipulation in *Lobelia inflata*'. *BMC Evolutionary Biology*, 14: 90.

Hunt, Leigh. 1836. 'The Fish, the Man, and the Spirit'. As 'Man and Fish', in *Birds, Beasts and Fishes*, compiled by Ruth Manning-Sanders, 184-5. London: Oxford University Press, 1962.

Hunter, I. Q. and Matthew Melia (eds). 2022. *The Jaws Book: New Perspectives on the Classic Summer Blockbuster*. London: Bloomsbury Academic.

Hutchins, Rob. 2025a. 'Mexico: "Goals met" to protect last eight vaquita from extinction', *Oceanographic Magazine*, 16 January. https://oceanographicmagazine.com/news/mexico-goals-met-to-protect-last-eight-vaquita-from-extinction.

Hutchins, Rob. 2025b. 'Scientists hail third manta ray species "evolution in action"'. *Oceanographic Magazine*, 28 July. https://oceanographicmagazine.com/news/scientists-hail-third-manta-ray-species-evolution-in-action.

International Fund for Animal Welfare (IFAW). 2001. Veterinary Report, Canadian Commercial Seal Hunt, Prince Edward Island. https://www.harpseals.org/about_the_hunt/ifaw_vet_report_2001.pdf*;https://harpseals.org

International Society for Phylogenetic Nomenclature (PhyloCode). 2020. http://phylonames.org/code/chapters/1.

Jabr, Ferris. 2016. 'The Secret History of Bioluminescence', *Haika Magazine*, 20 May. https://hakaimagazine.com/features/secret-history-bioluminescence.

Jacobsen, Rowan. 2016. 'Obituary: Great Barrier Reef (25 Million BC- ...)' *Outside*, 11 October. https://www.outsideonline.com/outdoor-adventure/environment/obituary-great-barrier-reef-25-million-bc-2016.

Jamie, Kathleen. 2005. *Findings*. London: Sort of Books.

Janik, Vincent M. 2009. 'Whale song'. *Current Biology*, 19 (3): 109-11. https://doi.org/10.1016/j.cub.2008.11.026.

Järviluoma, Helmi and Lesley Murray (eds). 2023. *Sensory Transformations: Environments, Technologies, Sensobiographies*. London: Taylor & Francis.

Jasper, David and Olivier Salazar-Ferrer. 2016. *Embodiment: Phenomenological, Religious and Deconstructive Views on Living and Dying*. London: Routledge.

Johannes, R. E. 1981. *Words of the Lagoon: Fishing and Marine Lore in the Palau District of Micronesia*. Berkeley, CA: University of California Press.

Johnson, Matthew. 2004. 'What Would the Salmon Say? An Argument for Supplementation to Help Rebuild Naturally Reproducing Salmon Populations in the Columbia Basin'. *Public Land & Resources Law Review*, 24: 46-73.

Johnson, Rachel. 2006. 'The Past and Future Hero: The Henty Boy in the Twenty-First Century?' *The Henty Society Bulletin*, 1-14.

Johnson, Samuel. 1755. *A Dictionary of the English Language*. 2 vols. London: J. and P. Knapton.

Jones, Steve. 2007. *Coral: A Pessimist in Paradise*. London: Little, Brown.

Jost, L., Mario Humberto Yanez-Muñoz, Jorge Brito, Carolina Reyes-Puig, Juan Pablo Reyes-Puig, Juan M. Guayasamín, Santiago R. Ron, Catalina Quintana, Gabriel Iturralde, Luis Baquero, Marco Monteros, Alina Freire-Fierro, Diana Fernández, Glenda Mendieta-Leiva, J. Francisco Morales, Adam P. Karremans, J. Antonio Vázquez-García, Gerardo A. Salazar, Eric Hágsater, Rodolfo Solano, Germán Carnevali Fernández-Concha and Marcelo Arana. 2023. 'Eponyms are important tools for biologists in the Global South'. *Nature Ecology Evolution*, 7: 1164–57. https://doi.org/10.1038/s41559-023-02102-z.

Jue, Melody. 2020. *Wild Blue Media: Thinking Through Seawater*. Durham, NC: Duke University Press.

Kanngieser, Anja and Zoe Todd. 2020. 'Kincentric: From Environmental Case Study to Environmental Kin Study'. *History and Theory*, 59 (3): 385–93. https://doi.org/10.1111/hith.12166.

Kareem, Sarah Tindal. 2015. 'Enlightenment Bubbles, Romantic Worlds'. *The Eighteenth Century*, 56 (1): 85–104.

Keartes, Sarah. 2015. 'Great white sharks flail while they poop (yes, we have video)'. *Earth Touch News Network*, 1 December. https://www.earthtouchnews.com/oceans/sharks/great-white-sharks-flail-while-they-poop-yes-we-have-video.

Kelly, Stephen. 2022. 'How underwater cities could solve Earth's overpopulation problem'. *BBC Science Focus Magazine*, 16 December. https://www.sciencefocus.com/planet-earth/underwater-cities-overpopulation.

Kenyon, Ley. 1961. *Discovering the Undersea World*. London: University of London Press.

Kim, Bo-Mi, Angel Amores, Seunghan Kang, Do-Hwan Ahn, Jin-Hyoung Kim, Il-Chan Kim, Jun Hyuck Lee, Sung Gu Lee, Hyoungseok Lee, Jungeun Lee, Han-Woo Kim, Thomas Desvignes, Peter Batzel, Jason Sydes, Tom Titus, Catherine A. Wilson, Julian M. Catchen, Wesley C. Warren, Manfred Schartl, H. William Detrich III, John H. Postlethwait and Hyun Park. 2019. 'Antarctic blackfin icefish genome reveals adaptations to extreme environments'. *Nature Ecology and Evolution*, 3: 469–78. https://doi.org/10.1038/s41559-019-0812-7.

Kimmerer, Robin Wall. 2021. *The Democracy of Species*. New York: Penguin.

Kirksey, S. Eben and Stefan Helmreich, 2010. 'The Emergence of Multispecies Ethnography'. *Cultural Anthropology*, 25 (4): 545–76.

Kivilcim, Emily and Dan Parsons. n.d. 'How to Blow the Best Underwater Bubble Ring', Blog, *Freediving Central*. https://freedivingcentral.com/blog/how-to-blow-the-best-underwater-bubble-ring.

Klingel, Gilbert C. 1942. *Inagua: which is the name of a very lonely and nearly forgotten island*. London: Robert Hale.

Kolbert, Elizabeth. 2021. *Under a White Sky: The Nature of the Future*. London: The Bodley Head.

Kooser, Amanda. 2020. 'See a giant siphonophore, a bizarre ocean creature that looks like silly string'. *CNet*, 6 April. https://www.cnet.com/science/see-a-giant-siphonophore-a-bizarre-ocean-creature-that-looks-like-silly-string.

Kosmalska, Joanna. 2022. 'Defining Migration Writing'. *Journal of Literary Theory*, 16 (2): 331–50. https://doi.org/10.1515/jlt-2022-2028.

Koumoundouros, Tessa. 2020. 'What the Heck Is This Long, Hypnotic Stringy Thing Floating in the Ocean?' *ScienceAlert*, 8 April. https://www.sciencealert.com/researchers-filmed-the-longest-known-stringy-stingy-thingy-floating-in-the-ocean.

Kunzig, Robert. 2000. *Mapping the Deep: The Extraordinary Story of Ocean Science*. London: Sort of Books.

Kurlansky, Mark. 1999. *Cod: A Biography of the Fish That Changed the World*. London: Vintage.

Kurlansky, Mark. 2008. *The Last Fish Tale: The Fate of the Atlantic and Our Disappearing Fisheries* London: Jonathan Cape.

Laitinen, Tuomas A. 2016. [Installation] 'Haemocyanin (A Proposal for an Octopus)'. https://ocean-archive.org/collection/16.

Laitinen, Tuomas A. 2019. http://www.tuomasalaitinen.com.

Landeen, Dan and Allen Pinkham. 1999. *Salmon and His People: Fish and Fishing in Nez Perce Culture*. Lewiston, ID: Confluence Press.

Lang, Heather. 2016. *Swimming with Sharks: The Daring Discoveries of Eugenie Clark*. Park Ridge, IL: Albert Whitman.

Larsen, Egon. 1955. *Men Under the Sea*. London: Phoenix House.

Latour, Bruno. 1993. *We Have Never Been Modern*, trans. Catherine Porter. Cambridge, MA: Harvard University Press.

Latour, Bruno. 2017. 'Anti-Zoom', in Michael Tavel Clarke and David Wittenberg (eds), *Scale in Literature and Culture*, 93-101. Cham: Palgrave Macmillan.

Latour, Bruno. 2018. *Down to Earth: Politics in the New Climatic Regime*. Cambridge: Polity Books.

Laufer, Peter. 2018. *Dreaming in Turtle: A Journey Through the Passion, Profit, and Peril of Our Most Coveted Prehistoric Creatures*. New York: St. Martin's Press.

Leapor, Mary. 1748. *Poems upon Several Occasions*. London: J. Roberts.

Lefebure, Nadine. 1995. *Femmes Océanes: les Grandes Pionnières Maritimes*. Grenoble, France: Glénat.

Lejeune, Philippe. 1971. *L'Autobiographie en France*. Paris: Armand Colin.

Lemmon, Jackie. 2018. 'Flowers for Jeju: The Last Mermaids: An Interview with Zena Holloway'. *Beautiful Bizarre*, 12 March. https://beautifulbizarre.net/flowers-for-jeju-the-last-mermaids-an-interview-with-zena-holloway.

Lichatowich, Jim, Rick Williams, Bill Bakke, Jim Myron, David Bella, Bill McMillan, Jack Stanford, David Montgomery, Kurt Beardslee and Nick Gayeski. 2018. *Wild Pacific Salmon: A Threatened Legacy*. St Helen's, OR: Bemis Printing.

Lidz, Franz. 2015. 'Behold the blobfish: How a creature from the deep taught the world a lesson about the importance of being ugly'. *Smithsonian Magazine*, November. https://www.smithsonianmag.com/science-nature/behold-the-blobfish-180956967.

Liukkonen, Petri. 2008. 'Baron Gottfried Wilhelm von Leibniz (1646–1716)'. https://greencardamom.github.io/BooksAndWriters/leibnitz.htm.

Livingston, Julie and Jasbir K. Puar. 2011. 'Interspecies'. *Social Text*, 106, 29 (1): 3-14. https://doi.org/10.1215/01642472-1210237.

Lloyd, Andrea. 2012. 'Dickens Grows a Beard', British Library blogpost, 9 February. https://blogs.bl.uk/untoldlives/2012/02/dickens-grows-a-beard*;https://www.bl.uk/stories/blogs.

Lockwood, Devi. 2020. 'This Might Be the Longest Creature Ever Seen in the Ocean'. *New York Times*, 14 April. https://www.nytimes.com/2020/04/14/science/longest-animal-ocean.html.

Loichot, Valérie. 2020. *Water Graves: The Art of Unritual in the Greater Caribbean*. Charlottesville, VA: University of Virginia Press.

Lopez, Barry. 1986. *Arctic Dreams: Imagination and Desire in a Northern Landscape*. London: Picador.

Lophelia. 2025. https://www.lophelia.org.

Los, Maria. 2006. 'Looking into the future: surveillance, globalization and the totalitarian potential', in David Lyon (ed.), *Theorizing Surveillance: The Panopticon and Beyond*, 69–94. London: Routledge.

Lourie, Sara. 2016. *Seahorses: A Life-Sized Guide to Every Species*. Lewes, East Sussex: Ivy Press.

Love, Rosaleen. 2001. *Reefscape: Reflections on the Great Barrier Reef*. Washington, DC: Joseph Henry Press.

Lu, Donna. 2020. 'Deep-sea anglerfish fuse bodies to mate thanks to an odd immune system'. *New Scientist*, 30 July. https://doi.org/https10.1126/science.aaz9445.

Lubin, Joan. 2017. 'The Stature of Man: Population Bomb on Spaceship Earth', in Michael Tavel Clarke and David Wittenberg (eds), *Scale in Literature and Culture*, 143–75. Cham: Palgrave Macmillan.

Lysen, Flora and Patricia Pisters. 2012. 'Introduction: The smooth and the striated'. *Deleuze Studies*, 6 (1), 1–5. https://doi.org/10.3366/dls.2012.0042.

Macfarlane Kitty. 2019. [Song] 'Glass Eel'. https://www.youtube.com/watch?v=LvN1aRc-uFo.

MacInnis, Joseph. 2012. 'Believing in Exploration'. Expedition Journal, James Cameron's Deepsea Challenge, 4 April. https://deepseachallenge.com/milestones/expedition-journal.

MacMahon, A. F. Magri. 1946. *Fishlore: British Freshwater Fishes*. London: Pelican Books.

Maddock, Ant (ed.). 2008. 'Cold-water Coral Reefs', UK Biodiversity Action Plan; Priority Habitat Descriptions. *BRIG*. http://jncc.defra.gov.uk/page-5706.

Mahadevan, Kumar. 2010. 'Mote Marine Laboratory: Exploring the Secrets of the Sea Since 1955'. 19 November. https://mote.org/about-us/history.

Manta Trust, The. 2025. https://www.mantatrust.org/idthemanta.

Margulis, Lynn. 1988. *The Symbiotic Planet: A New Look at Evolution*. New York: Basic Books.

Mariani, Stefano, Charles Baillie, Guiliano Colosimo and Ana Riesgo. 2019. 'Sponges as natural environmental DNA samplers'. *Current Biology*, 29 (11): R401–2. https://doi.org/10.1016/j.cub.2019.04.031.

Marino, John A. 2004. 'The Exile and His Kingdom: The Reception of Braudel's Mediterranean'. *The Journal of Modern History*, 76 (3): 622–52.

Marzouk, Zach. 2022. 'Huawei AI tech used to filter out invasive salmon species in Norway river trial'. *ITpro*, 25 August. https://www.itpro.com/technology/artificial-intelligence-ai/368884/huawei-ai-filter-invasive-salmon-norway-rivers.

Masschelein, Anneleen and Rebecca Roach. 2018. 'Putting Things Together: Interviewing as Creative Practice'. *Biography*, 41 (2): 169–78. https://doi.org/10.1353/bio.2018.0018.

Mavor, Carol. 2013. *Blue Mythologies: Reflections on a Colour*. London: Reaktion Books.

MBARI (Monterey Bay Aquarium Research Institute). 2019. 'Bioluminescence: Behavior, biochemistry, and genomics', in *Annual Report*. https://annualreport.mbari.org/2019/story/bioluminescence-behavior-biochemistry-and-genomics.

MBARI (Monterey Bay Aquarium Research Institute). 2020. 'Weird and Wonderful: The fangtooth fish has a face only a mother could love'. https://www.youtube.com/watch?v=zkBJ-IMtWh8).

MBARI (Monterey Bay Aquarium Research Institute). 2021. 'Bioluminescence in the deep sea: Glow-in-the-dark corals light up the deep ocean'. https://www.youtube.com/watch?v=GD7g1c5-CJU.

McCann, Paul. 2008. 'Lord Dunsany in the Context of Fantasy and Fairy Tale'. *The Victorian Web*. https://victorianweb.org/authors/dunsany/polm3.html.

McCoy, J. J. 1975. *A Sea of Troubles*. New York: Seabury Press.

McGlynn, Terry. 2013. 'It's taxonomist appreciation day!' *Small Pond Science*, 19 March. https://smallpondscience.com/2013/03/19/its-taxonomist-appreciation-day.

McGovern, Ann. 1987. *Shark Lady: True Adventures of Eugenie Clark*. New York: Scholastic Inc.

McInnis, Joseph. 2005. *James Cameron's Aliens of the Deep: Voyages to the Strange World of the Deep Ocean*. Washington, DC: National Geographic Books.

McInnis, Joseph. 2012. James Cameron's Deep Sea Challenge, Expedition Journal, 4 April. https://deepseachallenge.com/milestones/expedition-journal.

McKee, Alexander. 1967. *Framing the Sea: First Steps into Inner Space*. London: Souvenir Press.

McKillop, Niall. 2000. *Rondo One-Eye: A Seal's Story*. Inverness-shire: Crowhill Books.

McKnight, J. Chris and Ian L. Boyd. 2018. 'Pinniped Life History', in Bernd Würsig, J. G. M. Thewissen and Kit M. Kovacs (eds), *Encyclopedia of Marine Mammals*. Third edition, 722–6. Cambridge, MA: Elsevier.

Melville, Herman. 1851. *Moby-Dick; Or, The Whale*. New York: Harper and Brothers.

Mentz, Steve. 2020. *Ocean*. New York: Bloomsbury, Object Lessons.

Mentz, Steve. 2024. *An Introduction to Blue Humanities*. Abingdon, Oxon: Routledge.

Meretoja, Hanna. 2022. 'Life and Narrative', in Paul Dawson and Maria Mäkelä (eds), *The Routledge Companion to Narrative Theory*, 273–85. Abingdon, Oxon: Routledge.

Meyer, Josh. 2023. 'Under the sea and ready for war? US wants to spend billions on spy submarine to fend off ocean-deep China, Russia advances'. *USA Today*, 29 May.

Michael, Chris. 2020. 'What lies beneath: Our love affair with living underwater'. *The Guardian*, 8 June. https://www.theguardian.com/environment/2020/jun/08/what-lies-beneath-our-love-affair-with-living-underwater.

Michel, Ellinor. 2016. 'Anchoring Biodiversity Information: From Sherborn to the 21st century and Beyond'. *Zookeys*, 550: 1–11. https://doi.org/10.3897/zookeys.550.7460.

Michelet, Jules. 1861. *The Sea (La Mer)*. New York: Rudd and Carleton.

Middleton, Guy. 2017. *Understanding Collapse: Ancient History and Modern Myths*. Cambridge: Cambridge University Press.

Miles, Jonathan. 2013. 'Drawn into the Deep', Disappearing Moon Exhibition Catalogue. Singapore: Singapore International Foundation and British Council.

Miller, Lulu. 2020. *Why Fish Don't Exist: A Story of Loss, Love and the Hidden Order of Life*, New York: Simon and Schuster.

Miller, Simon III. 2020. 'Dive Log History'. https://scubaboard.com/community/threads/dive-logs-history.599427.

Milman, Oliver. 2016. 'The deep ocean: plunging to new depths to discover the largest migration on Earth.' *The Guardian*, 17 August. https://www.theguardian.com/environment/2016/aug/17/ocean-research-marine-life-bermuda-coral-reefs-nekton-triton-vessel.

Milman, Oliver, Christian Bennett and Mike Bowers. 2014. 'The Great Barrier Reef: An obituary.' *The Guardian*, 26 March. https://www.theguardian.com/environment/ng-interactive/2014/mar/great-barrier-reef-obituary.

Mitman, Gregg. 2009. *Reel Nature: America's Romance with Wildlife on Film*. Seattle, WA: University of Washington Press.

Mogdans, Joachim. 2019. 'Sensory ecology of the fish lateral line system: Morphological and physiological adaptations for the perception of hydrodynamic stimuli'. *Fish Biology*, Special Issue: The Sensory Ecology of Fishes, 95 (1): 53–72. https://doi.org/10.1111/jfb.13966.

Monkman, Noel. 1956. *Escape to Adventure*. Sydney: Angus and Robertson.

Monkman, Noel. 1963. *Quest of the Curly-Tailed Horses: An Autobiography*. London: Angus and Robertson.

Montgomery, Sy. 2015. *The Soul of an Octopus: A Surprising Exploration into the Wonder of Consciousness*. London: Simon & Schuster.

Moray, Neville. 2017. *Attention: Selective Processes in Vision and Hearing*. London: Routledge.

Morgan, Elaine. 1982. *The Aquatic Ape. A Theory of Human Evolution*. London: Souvenir Press.

Morton, Michael Quentin. 2015. 'Calypso in the Arabian Gulf: Jacques Cousteau's Undersea Survey of 1954'. *Liwa*, 7 (13): 3-28.

Morton, Timothy. 2010. 'Queer Ecology'. *PMLA*, 125 (2): 273-82.

Morton, Timothy. 2013a. *Hyperobjects: Philosophy and Ecology After the End of the World*. Minneapolis: University of Minnesota Press.

Morton, Timothy. 2013b. 'She Stood in Tears Amid the Alien Corn: Thinking Through Agrilogistics'. *Diacritics*, 41 (3): 90-113.

Movebank 2025. https://www.movebank.org/cms/movebank-content/about-movebank.

Mukundarajan V. N. 2022. 'How a Diver Developed a 20-Year Old Friendship with a Tiger Shark.' *Medium*, 3 February. https://mukundarajanvn.medium.com/how-a-diver-developed-a-20-year-old-friendship-with-a-tiger-shark-ad9b439d40af.

Muñoz Morcillo, Jesús and Caroline Y. Robertson-von Trotha (eds). 2020. *Genealogy of Popular Science: From Ancient Ecphrasis to Virtual Reality*. Bielefeld: transcript Publishing.

Mustill, Tom. 2022. *How to Speak Whale: A Voyage into the Future of Animal Communication*. London: William Collins.

National Aquarium [anon]. 2022. 'Connecting Dots: The Science of Tracking Wildlife.' 5 December. https://aqua.org/stories/2022-12-05-connecting-dots-the-science-of-tracking-wildlife.

National Geographic [anon]. 2019. 'This freediving couple reveals the world underwater live never before.' 25 April. https://www.nationalgeographic.com/adventure/article/freedivers-guillaume-nery-julie-gautier-one-breath-around-world.

National Oceanic and Atmospheric Administration (NOAA). 2020. 'What Is an AUV?' https://oceanexplorer.noaa.gov/facts/auv.html.

National Oceanic and Atmospheric Administration (NOAA). 2024a. 'What Is the Bloop?' National Ocean Service, 16 June. https://oceanservice.noaa.gov/facts/bloop.html.

National Oceanic and Atmospheric Administration (NOAA). 2024b. 'How deep is the ocean?' https://oceanexplorer.noaa.gov/facts/ocean-depth.html.

National Public Radio (NPR). 2020. 'Two Heartbeats a Minute'. April 10. https://www.npr.org/transcripts/809336135.

Navakas, Michele Currie. 2023. *Coral Lives: Literature, Labor, and the Making of America*. Princeton, NJ: Princeton University Press.

Nedeau, Ethan. 2005. 'Where have all the eels gone?' *Gulf of Maine Times*, 9 (2), Summer: n.p.

Neimanis, Astrida. 2017. *Bodies of Water: Posthuman Feminist Phenomenology*. London: Bloomsbury Academic.

Néry, Guillaume and Julie Gautier. 2019. [Film/dance] *One Breath Around the World*. https://www.youtube.com/watch?v=OnvQggy3Ezw.

Nestor, James. 2015. *The Deep: Freediving, Renegade Science and What the Ocean Tells Us About Ourselves*. London: Profile Books.

Netboy, Anthony. 1980. *Salmon: The World's Most Harassed Fish*. London: André Deutsch.

Newcastle, University of. 2020. 'The new face of the plastics crisis'. 5 March. https://www.ncl.ac.uk/press/articles/archive/2020/03/eurythenesplasticus.

Nichols, Catherine A. 2016. Review of *Things in Motion: Object Itineraries in Anthropological Practice*. Eds. Rosemary A. Joyce and Susan D. Gillespie. Santa Fe: SAR Press, 2015. *Museum Anthropology Review*, 10 (2): 161–162. http://dx.doi.org/10.14434/mar.v10i2.22520.

Nichols, Wallace J. 2009. *HuffPost*: 'Oceanophilia: The Neuroscience of Emotion and the Ocean'. 8 November. https://www.wallacejnichols.org/126/491/huffpost-oceanophilia.html.

Nora, Pierre de. 1989. 'Between Memory and History: *Les Lieux de Memoire*'. *Representations*, 26, Special Issue: Memory and Counter-Memory, Spring: 7-24.

Normark, John. 2023. 'Water as a Hyperfact', in Sara A. Rich and Peter B. Campbell (eds), *Flat Ontologies: Oceanic Thought and the Anthropocene*, Contemporary Philosophy for Maritime Archaeology, 231-49. Leiden: Sidestone Press.

Norwood, Daniel. 2021. 'Interview with the Pros: Christian Vizl'. *Dive Photo Guide*, 17 April. https://www.divephotoguide.com/underwater-photography-special-features/article/interview-pros-christian-vizl.

Nweeia, Martin T. 2024. 'Biology and cultural importance of the narwhal'. *Annual Review, of Animal Biosciences*, 12: 187–208.

Nweeia, Martin T., Frederick C. Eichmiller, Peter V. Hauschka, Gretchen A. Donahue, Jack R. Orr, Steven H. Ferguson, Cortney A. Watt, James G. Mead, Charles W. Potter, Rune Dietz, Anthony A. Giuseppetti, Sandie R. Black, Alexander J. Trachtenberg and Winston P. Kuo. 2014. 'Sensory ability in the narwhal tooth organ system'. *The Anatomical Record*, 297: 599-617. https://doi.org/10.1002/ar.22886.

Ocean Census. 2023. https://oceancensus.org/mission.

Ocean Exploration Trust. 2025. 'Ihikūholu: Hawaiian Name Granted to Majestic Sea Pen'. https://nautiluslive.org/blog/2025/01/03/ihikuholu-hawaiian-name-granted-majestic-sea-pen.

Oceanographic Magazine. 2021. 'Ocean art meets photography: Interview with Francesca Page'. https://oceanographicmagazine.com/features/ocean-art-francesca-page.

Oceans North Conservation Society, World Wildlife Fund Canada, and Ducks Unlimited Canada. 2018. *Canada's Arctic Marine Atlas*. Ottawa: Ontario: Oceans North Conservation Society.

Oldstone-Moore, Christopher. 2005. 'The Beard Movement in Victorian Britain'. *Victorian Studies*, 48 (1): 7-34.

Operation Deep Scope. 2005. 'Eye-in-the-Sea Bioluminescence'. https://www.youtube.com/watch?v=xjaNzZt2olk.

Oppermann, Serpil. 2023. *Blue Humanities: Storied Waterscapes in the Anthropocene*. Cambridge: Cambridge University Press.

Oreskes, Naomi. 2021. *Science on a Mission: How Military Funding Shaped What We Do and Don't Know About the Ocean*. Chicago, IL: University of Chicago Press.

Paddon, Bert. 1917. 'Autobiography of a Fish'. *Richmond River Herald and Northern Districts Advertiser*, Tuesday 16 October. The Richmond River Herald and Northern Districts Advertiser (NSW : 1886–1942). https://trove.nla.gov.au/newspaper/article/125931801.

Palumbi, Stephen R. and Anthony R. Palumbi. 2014. *The Extreme Life of the Sea*. Princeton, NJ: Princeton University Press.

Papastergiadis, Nikos. 2014. 'A Breathing Space for Aesthetics and Politics: An Introduction to Jacques Rancière'. *Theory, Culture & Society*, 31 (7/8): 5–26.

Pare, Sascha. 2023. 'Barreleye fish: The deep-sea weirdo with rotating eyes and a see-through head'. *LiveScience*, 15 August. https://www.livescience.com/animals/fish/barreleye-fish-the-deep-sea-weirdo-with-rotating-eyes-and-a-see-through-head.

Pavid, Katie. n.d. 'Colour in the Collections: Blaschka glass models'. National History Museum. https://www.nhm.ac.uk/discover/colour-in-collection-blaschka-glass-models.html.

Payne, Roger S. and Scott McVay. 1971. 'Songs of Humpback Whales: Humpbacks Emit Sounds in Long, Predictable Patterns Ranging over Frequencies Audible to Humans'. *Science*, 173 (3997): 585–97. https://doi.org/10.1126/science/173.3997.585.

Peat, Neville. 2010. *The Tasman: Biography of an Ocean*. London: Penguin.

Peña-Guzmán, David M. 2022. *When Animals Dream: The Hidden World of Animal Consciousness*. Princeton, NJ: Princeton University Press.

Perez, Craig Santos. 2020. '"The Ocean in Us": Navigating the Blue Humanities and Diasporic Chamoru Poetry'. *Humanities*, 9 (66): 1–11.

Perkins, Robert. 2019. 'Solar Flares, Bubble Rings, and Ink Chandeliers'. *Caltech News*, 26 July. https://www.caltech.edu/about/news/solar-flares-bubble-rings-and-ink-chandeliers.

Perkins, Sid. 2015. 'Melting glaciers' fizzing bubbles lead to noisy seas'. *Science*, 6 March. https://www.science.org/content/article/melting-glaciers-fizzing-bubbles-lead-noisy-seas.

Pestelli, Leo. 1962. 'Sullo schermo "Ti-Koyo e il suo pescecane" : la straordinaria amicizia tra un indigeno e uno squalo'. *La Stampa*, 23 November.

Petrossian, Gohar A. 2019. *The Last Fish Swimming: The Global Crime of Illegal Fishing*. Santa Barbara, CA: Praeger Publishing.

Pétursdóttir, Þóra. 2023. 'Drift', in Sara A. Rich and Peter B. Campbell (eds), *Flat Ontologies, Oceanic Thought and the Anthropocene*, 251–68. Leiden: Sidestone Press.

Pew Trust 1993. 'Robert E. Johannes'. https://www.pewtrusts.org/en/projects/marine-fellows/fellows-directory/1993/robert-johannes.

Phillips, Catherine. 2017. 'Discerning ocean plastics: Activist, scientific, and artistic practices'. *Environment and Planning A*, 49 (5): 1146–62. https://doi.org/10.1177/0308518X16687.

Piccard, Jacques. 1960. 'Man's Deepest Dive' (*National Geographic* August 1960), in 'James Cameron's Deepsea Challenge'. https://deepseachallenge.com/the-team/1960-dive.

Pietsch, Theodore W. 2009. *Oceanic Anglerfishes: Extraordinary Diversity in the Deep Sea*. Berkeley, CA: University of California Press, 2009.

Pilcher, Jane. 2016. 'Names, Bodies and Identities'. *Sociology*, 50 (4): 764–79.

Pittwater Online News. 2016. 'Early Pittwater Paddlers, Oarsmen, Rowers and Scullers: The Paddon Family of Clareville (or Clairville)'. 14-21 February, Issue 251. https://www.pittwateronlinenews.com/early-pittwater-rowers-the-paddon-family-history.php.

Pointon, Marcia. 2009. *Brilliant Effects: A Cultural History of Gem Stones and Jewellery*. New Haven, CT: Yale University Press.

Pope, Alexander. 1734. *An Essay on Man*. London: John Wright.

Postman, N. and C. Weingartner. 1975. 'THINGNESS'. *Pediatrics* 56 (2): 172. https://doi.org/10.1542/peds.56.2.172.

Preece, Robert. N.d. 'Sculpture Magazine Interview [with Jason deCaires Taylor]'. https://underwatersculpture.com/about/essays.

Price, Catherine and Sophie Chao. 2023. 'Multispecies, More-Than-Human, Non-Human, Other-Than-Human: Reimagining idioms of animacy in an age of planetary unmaking'. *Exchanges: The Interdisciplinary Research Journal*, 10 (2): 177–93. https://exchanges.warwick.ac.uk/index.php/exchanges/article/view/1166/1049.

Priestley, J. B. 1957. 'They Come from Inner Space' (1953), in *Thoughts in the Wilderness*, 20–6. London: William Heinemann.

Priestley, Joseph. 1996. *The History and Present State of Electricity, Vols. I and II*. New York: Johnson.

Pringle, Patrick. 1959. *Modern Adventures Under the Sea*. London: George G. Harrap.

Probyn, Elspeth. 2016. *Eating the Ocean*. Durham, NC: Duke University Press.

Prosperi, Franco. 1955. *Lord of the Sharks*, trans. Camilla and Guido Roatta. London: Hutchinson.

Prosperi, Franco. 1959. *Vanished Continent: An Expedition to the Comoro Islands*, trans. David Moore. London: Hutchinson.

Prozek, James. 2010. *Eels: An Exploration, from New Zealand to the Sargasso, of the World's Most Mysterious Fish*. London: Harper.

Pyle, Richard L. 2008. 'Names, Concepts, Codes and Lots of Confusion'. Bishop Museum, Honolulu, 19 October. https://www.youtube.com/watch?v=vPVm5S0qIcs.

Pyle, Richard L. 2016. 'Towards a Global Names Architecture: The future of indexing scientific names'. *ZooKeys*, 550: 261–81.

Quaratiello, Arlena Rodda. 2004. *Rachel Carson: A Biography*. London: Bloomsbury Press.

Quigley, Killian. 2022. 'Reading the Anthropocene Ocean', in C. Rosol and G. Rispoli (eds), *Anthropogenic Markers: Stratigraphy and Context, Anthropocene Curriculum*. Berlin: Max Planck Institute for the History of Science. https://doi.org/10.58049/ppqy-vd84.

Quigley, Killian. 2023. *Reading Underwater Wreckage: An Encrusting Ocean*. London: Bloomsbury Academic.

QUT [Queensland University of Technology]. n.d. *Science: Reef Research*. 'Eliminating invasive reef species – COTSbot and RangerBot'. https://research.qut.edu.au/reefresearch/our-research/eliminating-invasive-reef-species-cotsbot-rangerbot.

Ravenscroft, Tom. 2022. 'Adidas and Parley for the Oceans launch floating tennis court in Great Barrier Reef'. *Dezeen*, 21 January. https://www.dezeen.com/2022/01/21/adidas-parley-for-the-oceans-floating-tennis-court-great-barrier-reef.

Readfern, Graham. 2025. 'Catastrophic': Great Barrier Reef hit by its most widespread coral bleaching, study finds'. *The Guardian*, 21 January.

Rees, Amanda and Charlotte Sleigh. 2020. *Human*. London: Reaktion Books.

Reidenberg, Joy S. 2024. 'An Innovative Way for Whales to Sing'. *Nature*, 627 (7), 40–2.

Remsen, David. 2016. 'The uses and limits of scientific names in biological informatics'. *Zookeys*, 550: 207–23. https://doi.org/10.3897/zookeys.550.9546.

Rich, Sara A. 2016. https://shipwreckhauntography.wordpress.com.

Rich, Sara A. 2021. *Shipwreck Hauntography: Underwater Ruins and the Uncanny*. Amsterdam: Rodopi.

Rich, Sara A. and Peter B. Campbell (eds). 2023. *Flat Ontologies, Oceanic Thought and the Anthropocene*. Leiden: Sidestone Press.

Richardson, Susan. 2022. *Where the Seals Sing: Exploring the Hidden Lives of Britain's Grey Seals*. London: William Collins.

Richeri, Clément. 1951. *Ti-Coyo and His Shark*, trans. Gerard Hopkins. London: Rupert Hart-Davis.

Ricoeur, Paul. 1992. *Oneself as Another*, trans. Kathleen Blamey. Chicago, IL: Chicago University Press.

Roach, John. 2005. 'Great White Breaks Distance, Speed Records for Sharks'. *National Geographic*, 6 October. www.nationalgeographic.com/animals/article/great-white-breaks-distance-speed-records-for-sharks.

Roach, Mary. 2016. 'What I Left Out: Sharkpedo?' *Undark*, 8 November. https://undark.org/2016/08/11/sharks-explosives-world-war-ii-mary-roach-what-i-left-out.

Roberts, Callum. 2012. *The Ocean of Life: The Fate of Man and the Sea*. New York: Penguin.

Roberts, Callum. 2019. *Reef Life: An Underwater Memoir*. London: Profile Books.

Robison, Bruce H., Kim R. Reisenbichler, James C. Hunt and Steven H. D. Haddock. 2003. 'Light Production by the Arm Tips of the Deep-Sea Cephalopod *Vampyroteuthis infernalis*'. *The Biological Bulletin*, 205 (2): 102-9.

Roksandic, Mirjana, Charles Musiba, Predrag Radović, Joshua Lindal, Xiu-Jie Wu, Estrela Figueiredo, Gideon F. Smith, Ivan Roksandic and Christopher J. Bae. 2023. 'Change in biological nomenclature is overdue and possible'. *Nature Ecology & Evolution*, August, 7 (8): 1116–67. https://doi.org/10.1038/s41559-023-02104-x.

Rooper, George. 1886. *The Autobiography of a Salmon (Salmo Salar)*. Second edition. London: J.S. Virtue.

Rothenberg, David. 2008. *Thousand Mile Song: Whale Music in a Sea of Sound*. London: Basic Books. Audio sample at https://www.youtube.com/watch?v=807LSbW28Po.

Rottman, André. 2019. '"The Medium is Leaking": Notes on the Work of Pierre Huyghe and the "Ecologization" of Contemporary Art'. *Grey Room*, 77: 84–97. https://doi.org/10.1162/grey_a_00281.

Roughley, T. C. 1941. *Wonders of the Great Barrier Reef*. London: Angus & Robertson Limited.

Roy, Eleanor Ainge. 2020. 'Intelligent drones': albatross fitted with radar detectors to spot illegal fishing'. *The Guardian*, 31 January. https://www.theguardian.com/world/2020/jan/31/intelligent-drones-albatross-fitted-with-radar-detectors-to-spot-illegal-fishing.

Rozwadowski, Helen M. 2001. 'Technology and ocean-scape: Defining the deep sea in the mid-nineteenth century'. *History and Technology*, 17 (3): 217-47. https://doi.org/10.1080/07341510108581993.

Rozwadowski, Helen M. 2005. *Fathoming the Ocean: The Discovery and Exploration of the Deep Sea*. Cambridge, MA: Harvard University Press.

Rozwadowski, Helen M. 2012. 'Arthur C. Clarke and the Limitations of the Ocean as a Frontier'. *Environmental History*, 17 (3): 578-602.

Rozwadowski, Helen M. 2013. 'From Danger Zone to World of Wonder: The 1950s Transformations of the Ocean's Depths'. *CORIOLIS: The Interdisciplinary Journal of Maritime Studies*, 4 (1): 1-20.

Rozwadowski, Helen M. 2018. *Vast Expanses: A History of the Oceans*. London: Reaktion Books.

Russell, F. S. and C. M. Yonge. 1949. *The Seas: Our Knowledge of Life in the Sea and How It Is Gained*. London: Frederick Warne.

Ruthven, John. 2021. *The Whale in the Living Room: A Wildlife Documentary Maker's Unique View of the Sea*. London: Robinson.

Safina, Carl. 2007. *Voyage of the Turtle: In Pursuit of the Earth's Last Dinosaur*. New York: Henry Holt.

Safina, Carl. 2010. *The View from Lazy Point: A Natural Year in an Unnatural World*. New York: Henry Holt.

Sale, Peter F. 2021. *Coral Reefs: Majestic Realms Under the Sea*. New Haven, CT: Yale University Press.

Salmon Enhancement Group. 2013. 'Meet the 7 Species of Pacific Salmon.' 17 April. https://spsseg.org/meet-the-7-species-of-pacific-salmon.

Sample, Ian. 2012. 'James Cameron's historic solo dive'. *The Guardian*, 26 March. https://www.theguardian.com/environment/2012/mar/26/james-cameron-historic-solo-drive

Sands, Danielle. 2023. 'Empathy Beyond the Human', in Rosa Braidotti, Emily Jones and Goda Klumbyte (eds), *More Posthuman Glossary*, 43–5. London: Bloomsbury.

Saunders, Max. 2010. *Self Impression: Life-Writing, Autobiografiction, and the Forms of Modern Literature*. Oxford: Oxford University Press.

Scales, Helen. 2018. *Eye of the Shoal: A Fishwatcher's Guide to Life, The Ocean and Everything*. London: Bloomsbury Sigma.

Scales, Helen. 2021. *The Brilliant Abyss: True Tales of Exploring the Deep Sea, Discovering Hidden Life and Selling the Seabed*. London: Bloomsbury Sigma.

Schaberg, Christopher. 2023. *Adventure: An Argument for Limits*. London: Bloomsbury.

Scharpf, Christopher. 2014. *The ETYFish Project*: Fish Name Etymology Database. https://etyfish.org.

Scharpf, Christopher. 2023. 'ETYFish_Fish-centric Guide to Zoological Nomenclature' (rev). Etyfish.org, 1-13.

Schatz, Howard. 1995. *WaterDance*. New York: Graphis Inc. https://howardschatz.com/books/waterdance.

Scheffer, Victor B. 1969. *The Year of the Whale*. New York: Charles Scribner's Sons.

Scheffer, Victor B. 1970. *The Year of the Seal*. New York: Charles Scribner's Sons.

Scheffer, Victor B. 1980. *Adventures of a Zoologist*. New York: Charles Scribner's Sons.

Schmidt Ocean Institute. 2023. 'Scientists Discover New Deep-Sea Octopus Nursery in Costa Rica'. Press release, 28 June. https://schmidtocean.org/scientists-discover-new-deep-sea-octopus-nurseries-in-costa-rica.

Schmitt, Arnaud (ed.). 2024. *Hybridity in Life Writing: Combining Text and Images*. Cham: Palgrave.

Schneider, Tim. 2019. 'Why an Artist and a Scientist Teamed Up to Bring the Sounds of the Undersea World into the Heart of Miami's Art Fair Week'. *ArtNet*, 5 December. https://news.artnet.com/art-world/jana-winderen-tony-myatt-the-art-of-listening-1723458.

Schrope, Mark. 2009. 'Corals, Earth's Canary in Coal Mines, Facing "Calamitous" Global Declines'. *Yale Climate Connections*, 1 September. https://yaleclimateconnections.org/2009/09/corals-earths-canary-in-coal-minesfacing-calamitous-global-declines.

Schultz, Colin. 2013. 'In Defense of the Blobfish: The "World's Ugliest Animal" Is Our Fault'. *Smithsonian Magazine*, 13 September. https://www.smithsonianmag.com/smart-news/worlds-ugliest-animal-blobfish-6676336.

SeaDoc Society, The. n.d. 'Harbor seal facts'. https://www.seadocsociety.org/harbor-seal-facts.

Seeman Robinson, Joan. 1995. 'Chihuly Seaforms'. https://www.chihuly.com/life/writings/chihuly-seaforms.

Seibel, Svetlana. 2022. '"Fleshy stories": Towards Restorative Narrative Practices in Salmon Literature'. *Transmotion*, 8 (1): 39–73.

Serventy, Vincent. 1955. *Australia's Great Barrier Reef*. London: Phoenix House Limited.

Seuss, Dr. 1960. *One Fish Two Fish Red Fish Blue Fish*. New York: Beginner Books, Inc.

Shapin, Steven. 2016. 'What do you mean by a lie?' *London Review of Books*, 38 (9): 35-7.

Sharkbook. n.d. https://www.sharkbook.ai.

Sheldrake, Merlin. 2020. *Entangled Life: How Fungi Make Our Worlds, Change Our Minds, and Shape Our Futures*. London: Vintage.

Shelton, Richard. 2009. *To Sea and Back: The Heroic Life of the Atlantic Salmon*. London: Atlantic Books.

Sheppard, Charles. 2014. *Coral Reefs: A Very Short Introduction*. Oxford: Oxford University Press.

Shick, J. Malcolm. 2018. *Where Corals Lie: A Natural and Cultural History*. London: Reaktion Books.

Shore, Randy. 2017. 'Millions of Atlantic salmon introduced to B.C. streams since 1905'. *Vancouver Sun*, 25 September.

Simpson, Emily. 2024. 'Gaming for the good of our ocean'. 1 May. https://www.montereybayaquarium.org/stories/into-the-fathomverse.

Smith, Sidonie and Julia Watson. 2010. *Reading Autobiography: A Guide for Interpreting Life Narratives*. Second edition. Minneapolis, MN: University of Minnesota Press.

Sneeden, Ralph. 2023. *The Legible Element: Essays*. Rochester, MA: Eastover Press.

Snow, C. P. 1961. *Two Cultures and the Scientific Revolution*, the Rede Lecture 1959. New York: Cambridge University Press.

Somerset Eel Recovery Project. 2025. https://www.somerseteels.com.

SpongeBob. N.d. *SpongeBob & Friends Adventures Wiki*, 'Shark Lord'.

Spotila, James R. 2004. *Sea Turtles: A Complete Guide to Their Biology, Behavior, and Conservation*. Baltimore, MD: The Johns Hopkins University Press.

Stafford-Deitsch, Jeremy. 1991. *Reef: A Safari Through the Coral World*. London: Headline Book Publishing.

Stankowski, Sean and Mark Ravinet. 2021. 'Quantifying the use of species concepts' *Current Biology*, 31 (9): R428-9.

Starck, Walter. 1979. *The Blue Reef: A Report from Beneath the Sea*. Told to Alan Anderson, Jr. New York: Alfred A. Knopf.

Steene, Roger. 1990. *Coral Reefs: Nature's Richest Realm*. Bathurst: Crawford House Press.

Stevenson, Robert Louis. 1892. 'The Education of an Engineer' (1888), in *Across the Plains with Other Memories and Essays*, 192-206. London: Chatto & Windus.

Stillman, Barry C. 2002. 'Making Sense of Proprioception: The meaning of proprioception, kinaesthesia and related terms'. *Physiotherapy*, 88 (11): 667-76.

Stock, Marybeth. 2013. 'Genevieve Chua and Emma Critchley's "Disappearing Moon"'. 27 March. https://artasiapacific.com/shows/genevieve-chua-and-emma-critchley-s-disappearing-moon..

Strang, Veronica. 2023. *Water Beings: From Nature Worship to the Environmental Crisis*. London: Reaktion Books.

Straughan, E. R. 2012. 'Touched by Water: The Body in Scuba Diving'. *Emotion, Space and Society*, 5 (1): 19-26.

SUPERFLEX. 2021. 'Vertical Migration'. https://superflex.net/works/vertical_migration.

Svensson, Patrik. 2020. *The Gospel of the Eels: A Father, a Son and the World's Most Enigmatic Fish*, trans. Agnes Broomé. London: Picador.

Taçon, Paul S. C., Meredith Wilson and Christopher Chippendale. 1996. 'Birth of the Rainbow Serpent in Arnhem Land rock art and oral history'. *Archaeology in Oceania*, 31 (3): 103-24.

Tailliez, Philippe. 1954. *To Hidden Depths*. New York: E.P. Dutton.

Tailliez, Philippe. 1964. *Aquarius* (1961), trans. Dennis George. London: George G. Harrap.

Talairach-Vielmas, Laurence (ed.). 2011. *Science in the Nursery: The Popularisation of Science in Britain and France, 1761-1901*. Newcastle: Cambridge Scholars Publishing.

Talbot, Frank. 2012. '60 Years Ago on East Africa's Coral Reefs', in Peter F. Sale and Alina M. Szmant (eds), *Reef Reminiscences: Ratcheting back the shifted baselines concerning what reefs used to be*. Hamilton, Ontario: United Nations University Institute for Water, Environment and Health.

Tambets, Meelis Tambets, Einar Kärgenberg, Ain Järvalt, Finn Økland, Martin Lykke Kristensen, Anders Koed and Priit Bernotas. 2021. 'Migrating silver eels return from the sea to the river of origin after a false start'. *Biology Letters*, 17 (9): 1-8. https://doi.org/10.1098/rsbl.2021.0346.

Tarter, Jill. 2010. 'What if there's somebody else out there?' *CNN*, 20 April.

Taylor, Jason deCaires. n.d. Artist website. https://underwatersculpture.com.

Tazieff, Haroun. n.d. *South from the Red Sea*, trans. Naomi Lewis. London: The Travel Book Club.

Telesca, Jennifer E. 2020. *Red Gold: The Managed Extinction of the Giant Bluefin Tuna*. Minneapolis, MN: University of Minnesota Press.

Tepper, Joseph. 2013. 'Master of Monochrome'. *Scuba Diver* Through the Lens No. 6.

Thaman, Konai Helu. 2003. 'Decolonizing Pacific Studies: Indigenous Perspectives, Knowledge, and Wisdom in Higher Education'. *The Contemporary Pacific*, 15 (1): 1–17.

Thewissen, J. G. M. 2018. 'Highlights of Cetacean Embryology'. *Aquatic Mammals*, 44 (6): 591-602. https://doi.org/10.1578/AM.44.6.2018.

Thompson, E. P. 1966. 'History from Below'. *Times Literary Supplement*, 7 April, 279–80.

Thomson, Basil. 1968. *The Fijians: A Study of the Decay of Custom*. London: Dawsons of Pall Mall.

Thurston, Gavin. 2020. *Journeys in the Wild: The Secret Life of a Cameraman*. London: Seven Dials.

Thyssen-Bornemisza, Francesca. 2021. 'Sounds Too Many', in Daniela Zyman (ed.), *Oceans Rising*, 64-8. London: Sternberg Press.

Tieu, Lyn, Cory Bill, Jacopo Romoli and Stephen Crain. 2020. 'Testing theories of plural meanings'. *Cognition*, 205, December: 104307. https://doi.org/10.1016/j.cognition.2020.104307.

Tillman, Albert and Zale Perry. 2001. *Scuba America: The Human History of the Sport of Diving*. Orcas Island USA: Whalestooth Publishing.

Torre, Stephen. 2008. 'Literary Representations of the Great Barrier Reef', *Etropic: Electronic Journal of Studies in the Tropics*, 7: n.p. https://doi.org/10.25120/etropic.7.0.2008.3433.

Treadwell, James. 2005. *Autobiographical Writing and British Literature, 1783-1834*. Oxford: Oxford University Press.

Trethewey, Laura. 2019. *The Imperiled Ocean: Human Stories from a Changing Sea*. New York: Pegasus Books.

Trexler, Adam. 2015. *Anthropocenic Fictions: The Novel in a Time of Climate Change*. Charlottesville, VA: University of Virginia Press.

Tsing, Anna. 2015. *The Mushroom at the End of the World: On the Possibility of Life in Capitalist Ruins*. Princeton, NJ: Princeton University Press.

Tsing, Anna Lowenhaupt and Jennifer Deger, Alder Keleman Saxena and Feifei Zhou. 2024. *Field Guide to the Patchy Anthropocene: The New Nature*. Stanford, CA: Stanford University Press.

Tu, Mo. 2023. 'Go Beneath the Surface: A Study on Underwater Dancing'. *Art and Design Review*, 11: 73-9. https://doi.org/10.4236/adr.2023.112006.

Turner, G. L'e. 1984. 'Obituary Derek John de Solla Price 1922–1983'. *Annals of Science*, 41 (2): 105-7.

UNESCO/ Intergovernmental Oceanographic Commission. 2018. *Ocean Literacy for All: A toolkit*. IOC Manual and guides, 80. https://unesdoc.unesco.org/ark:/48223/pf0000260721.

United Nations (UN). N.d. 'Definitions of Genocide and Related Crimes'. https://www.un.org/en/genocide-prevention/definition.

United Nations (UN). N.d. https://www.un.org/en/observances/oceans-day.

United Nations (UN). 2021. https://oceandecade.org/who-we-are.

Urry, Amelia. 2016. 'Satirist writes obituary for the Great Barrier Reef'. *Grist*, 14 October. https://grist.org/climate-energy/satirist-writes-obituary-for-the-great-barrier-reef-internet-takes-him-all-too-seriously.

Van Andel, Tjeerd. 1978. *Tales from an Old Ocean*. London: Norton.

Van den Hengel, Louis. 2012. 'Zoegraphy: Per/forming Posthuman Lives'. *Biography*, 35 (1): 1–20.

Van der Meij, Sancia ET. 2014. 'Host species, range extensions, and an observation of the mating system of Atlantic shallow-water gall crabs (decapoda: cryptochiridae)'. *Bulletin of Marine Science*, 90 (4): 1001–10. https://doi.org/10.5343/bms.2014.1017.

Van Dover, Cindy Lee. 1996. *The Octopus's Garden: Hydrothermal Vents and Other Mysteries of the Deep Sea*. Boston, MA: Addison-Wesley.

Van Neste, Aaron. 2022. 'Alien Oceans as Climate Salvation: Finding Hope in Kinship with the Deep Blue Unknown', in Sune Borkfelt and Stephan Matthias (eds), *Literary Animal Studies and the Climate Crisis*, 245–66. Cham: Palgrave.

Veron, J. E. N. [Charlie]. 1996. Silver Jubilee Award, Australian Marine Sciences Association Inc. https://www.amsa.asn.au/wp-content/uploads/2014/10/charlie_vernon_1996.pdf.

Veron, J. E. N. [Charlie]. 2017. *A Life Underwater*. Docklands, Australia: Penguin Random.

Vine, Peter. 2019. 'Red Sea Research: A Personal Perspective', in Najeeb Rasul and Ian Stewart (eds), *Oceanographic and Biological Aspects of the Red Sea*, 215–37. Cham: Springer International Publishing. https://doi.org/10.1007/978-3-319-99417-8_13.

Vizl, Christian. 2019. *Silent Kingdom: A World Beneath the Waves*. San Rafael, CA: Earth Aware Editions, MandalaEarth.

Vizl, Christian. 2020. 'In Memoriam: Ernest H. Brooks II'. 26 November. Dive Photo Guide. https://www.divephotoguide.com/underwater-photography-special-features/article/memoriam-tribute-ernie-brooks.

Vizl, Christian. n.d. Artist website: 'Artist's Statement'. https://www.christianvizl.com/about.

Von Hantelmann, Dorothea. 2017. 'Thinking the Arrival: Pierre Huyghe's Untilled and the Ontology of the Exhibition', in Nanne Buurman and Dorothee Richter (eds), *Documenta: Curating the History of the Present*, 33, June: 89–96. https://www.on-curating.org/issue-33.html.

Von Hausswolf, Carl Michael. 2021. 'freq_wave: 7 Seas', in Daniela Zyman (ed.), *Oceans Rising*, 69–77. London: Sternberg Press.

Waldie Peter A., Simon P. Blomberg, Karen L. Cheney, Anne W. Goldizen and Alexandra S. Grutter. 2011. 'Long-Term Effects of the Cleaner Fish *Labroides dimidiatus* on Coral Reef Fish Communities'. *PLoS ONE* 6 (6): e21201. https://doi.org/10.1371/journal.pone.0021201.

Wallace, Alfred Russel. 1869. *The Malay Archipelago: The Land of the Orang-utan, and the Bird of Paradise*. 2 vols. London: Macmillan.

Wallace-Thompson, Anna. 2015. 'At the Still Point of the Turning World'. https://www.emmacritchley.com/writing/at-the-still-point-of-the-turning-world.

Walsh, Linda S. 2017. 'Water and Dreams: Exploring Bachelard's concepts through new audiovisual works for the oboe', DPhil. thesis, University of Technology, Sydney.

Walter, Tristan and Iain D. Couzin. 2021. 'TRex, a fast multi-animal tracking system with markerless identification, and 2D estimation of posture and visual fields.' *eLife*, 10: e64000. https://doi.org/10.7554/eLife.64000.

Ward, Francis. 1911. *Marvels of Fish Life as Revealed by the Camera*. London: Cassell.

Ward-Perkins, Bryan. 2005. *The Fall of Rome and the End of Civilization*. Oxford: Oxford University Press.

Warde, Paul, Libby Robin and Sverker Sörlin. 2018. *The Environment: A History of the Idea*. Baltimore, MD: Johns Hopkins University Press.

Watt, Robert A. 1989. *A Glossary of Scottish Dialect Fish and Trade Names*. Aberdeen: Scottish Fisheries Information Pamphlet Number 17.

Weinman, Steve. 2024. 'Hurricane delayed diver's climatic artificial reef.' *Divernet*, 28 October. https://divernet.com/world-dives/north-central-america/hurricane-delayed-divers-climatic-artificial-reef.

Werner, Abraham Gottlob. 2018. *Werner's Nomenclature of Colours Adapted to Zoology, Botany, Chemistry, Mineralogy, Anatomy and the Arts* (1814). Bristol: Read. https://mymodernmet.com/werner-nomenclature-of-colours.

Weston, Phoebe. 2021. 'Jellied, smoked, baked in pies – but can the UK stop eels sliding into extinction?' *The Guardian*, 16 June. https://www.theguardian.com/environment/2021/jun/16/a-rewilding-project-on-uk-rivers-aims-to-stop-eels-sliding-to-extinction-aoe.

Whalesharkdiaries. 2017. 'Photo Identification: How Star System Algorithms Have Lead [*sic*] to Identifying Whale Sharks.' 7 November. http://www.whalesharkdiaries.com/did-you-know/photo-identification-star-system-algorithms-lead-identifying-whale-sharks.

White, Jessica. 2020. 'From the Miniature to the Momentous: Writing Lives through Ecobiography', a/b *Auto/Biography Studies*, 35 (1): 13–33. https://doi.org/10.1080/0898 9575.2020.1713587.

Whitehead, Hal and Luke Rendell. 2014. *The Cultural Lives of Whales and Dolphins*. Chicago, IL: Chicago University Press.

Whittaker, Geraint Rhys. 2023. 'Creatively connecting science, society and the sea: a mini-review of academic literature focusing on art-science collaborations and the ocean'. *Frontiers in Marine Science*, 10. https://doi.org/10.3389/fmars.2023.1234776.

Widder, Edith. 2006. 'A Look Back at Quantifying Oceanic Bioluminescence: Seeing the Light, Flashes of Insight and Other Bad Puns'. *Marine Technology Society Journal*, 40 (2): 136–7. https://doi.org/10.4031/002533206787353321.

Widder, Edith. 2021. *Below the Edge of Darkness: Exploring Light and Life in the Deep Sea*. London: Virago Press.

Wilcox, Christie. 2023. 'Octopuses may have nightmares'. *Science*, 19 May. https://www.science.org/content/article/octopuses-may-have-nightmares.

Williams, Heathcote. 1988. *Whale Nation*. London: Jonathan Cape.

Williams, Linda. 2019. 'Deep time and myriad ecosystems', in Margaret Cohen and Killian Quigley (eds), *The Aesthetics of the Undersea*, 167–79. Abingdon, Oxon: Routledge.

Williamson, Henry. 1927. *Tarka the Otter: His Joyful Water-Life and Death in the Country of the Two Rivers*. New York: G.P. Putnam's Sons.

Williamson, Henry. 1944. *Salar the Salmon*. London: Faber and Faber.

Williamson, Henry. n.d. The Henry Williamson Society. '*Salar the Salmon*': Critical reception. https://www.henrywilliamson.co.uk/bibliography/a-lifes-work/salar-the-salmon.

Willmott, Glenn. 2018. *Reading for Wonder: Ecology, Ethics, Enchantment*. Cham: Palgrave Macmillan.

Wilson, David. 2021. 'Great underwater lives: The Pulvénis brothers'. *ScubaBoard.com*, post 30 December. https://scubaboard.com/community/threads/great-underwater-lives-the-pulvenis-brothers.615865/#post-9611237.

Wilson, David. 2022. 'Rowena Kerr: A long forgotten British (female) diving pioneer'. ScubaBoard.com, post 21 July. https://scubaboard.com/community/threads/rowena-kerr-a-long-forgotten-british-female-diving-pioneer.623234.

Winderen, Jana. 2019. [Sound] 'The Art of Listening: Under Water'. https://www.janawinderen.com/;https://tba21.org/silencing_of_the_reefs.

Woods Hole Oceanographic Institute (WHOI). 2021. 'WHOI collaborates to bring video installation to United Nation Headquarters'. Press release, 15 September. https://www.whoi.edu/press-room/news-release/whoi-collaborates-to-bring-video-installation-to-united-nation-headquarters.

Wynn, Russell B., Veerle A. I. Huvenne, Timothy P. Le Bas, Bramley J. Murton, Douglas P. Connelly, Brian J. Bett, Henry A. Ruhl, Kirsty J. Morris, Jeffrey Peakall, Daniel R. Parsons, Esther J. Sumner, Stephen E. Darby, Robert M. Dorrell and James E. Hunt. 2014. 'Autonomous Underwater Vehicles (AUVs): Their past, present and future contributions to the advancement of marine geoscience'. *Marine Geology*, 352: 451-68. https://doi.org/10.1016/j.margeo.2014.03.012.

Yong, Ed. 2023. *An Immense World: How Animal Senses Reveal the Hidden Realms Around Us*. London: Vintage.

Yuan, Hsuhu. 2012. [Dance] 'Underwater Dance'. https://www.youtube.com/watch?v=PbNpauLjiK0.

Zerarki, Ayad. 2023. *Scuffle in Coral Reefs* (Moral Tales: Lessons from the Animal Kingdom). Independently published.

Zhivkoplias, Erik, Jean-Baptiste Jouffray, Paul Dunshirn, Agnes Pranindita and Robert Blasiak. 2024. 'Growing prominence of deep sea life in marine bioprospecting'. *Nature Sustainability*, 7: 1027–37. https://doi.org/10.1038/s41893-024-01392-w.

Zimmer Walter M. X. 2011. 'Cetacean sounds', in *Passive Acoustic Monitoring of Cetaceans*, 39-95. Cambridge: Cambridge University Press. https://doi.org/10.1017/CBO9780511977107.

Zubek, J. P., W. Sansom and A. Prysiaznuik. 1960. 'Intellectual changes during prolonged perceptual isolation (darkness and silence)'. *Canadian Journal of Psychology/Revue canadienne de psychologie*, 14 (4): 233–43. https://doi.org/10.1037/h0083186.

Zuern, John David. 2024. 'Life Writing at the Terminus: Glacier Memoirs and Planetary Relationality'. *European Journal of Life Writing*, XIII: 1-27. https://doi.org/10.21827/ejlw.13.41115.

Zyman, Daniela (ed.). 2021. *Oceans Rising*. London: Sternberg Press.

Index